D1134723

AREA HANDBOOK
for
URUGUAY

Co-Authors

Thomas E. Weil

Jan Knippers Black
Kenneth W. Martindale
David S. McMorris
Sally Engle Merry
Frederick P. Munson

Research and writing were completed on
August 21, 1970

Published 1971

Library of Congress Catalog Card Number: 75-609527

For sale by the Superintendent of Documents, U.S. Government Printing Office
Washington, D.C. 20402–Price $3.25

FOREWORD

This volume is one of a series of handbooks prepared by Foreign Area Studies (FAS) of The American University, designed to be useful to military and other personnel who need a convenient compilation of basic facts about the social, economic, political, and military institutions and practices of various countries. The emphasis is on objective description of the nation's present society and the kinds of possible or probable changes that might be expected in the future. The handbook seeks to present as full and as balanced an integrated exposition as limitations on space and research time permit. It was compiled from information available in openly published material. An extensive bibliography is provided to permit recourse to other published sources for more detailed information. There has been no attempt to express any specific point of view or to make policy recommendations. The contents of the handbook represent the work of the authors and FAS and do not represent the official view of the United States government.

An effort has been made to make the handbook as comprehensive as possible. It can be expected, however, that the material, interpretations, and conclusions are subject to modifications in the light of new information and developments. Such corrections, additions, and suggestions for factual, interpretive, or other change as readers may have will be welcomed for use in future revisions. Comments may be addressed to:

The Director
Foreign Area Studies
The American University
5010 Wisconsin Avenue, N.W.
Washington, D.C. 20016

PREFACE

In 1970 the Oriental (Eastern) Republic of Uruguay, noted for its dedication to democratic and orderly political processes, its high standard of living, and its comprehensive social welfare system, faced challenging problems involving economic conditions and maintenance of internal security. The government, with the adoption of extraordinary powers, was endeavoring to eliminate threats to the economy and to suppress political enemies who resorted to criminal acts to advance their cause.

This book represents an effort to provide a compact and objective exposition and analysis of the dominant social, political, and economic characteristics of Uruguayan society. It is designed to give readers both within and outside the government an understanding of the dynamics of the component elements of Uruguayan society and an insight into the needs, goals, and achievements of the people. A number of consultants, many of them with firsthand knowledge of the country, have provided data not available in printed sources. The authors alone are responsible for the final draft.

English usage follows *Webster's Third New International Dictionary* (unabridged). Spanish words and phrases, which have been used only when adequate English equivalents were lacking, are defined at first appearance. If they are employed frequently they are listed in the Glossary. Spanish is based on *Appleton's Revised Cuyas Dictionary*.

COUNTRY SUMMARY

1. COUNTRY: Oriental (Eastern) Republic of Uruguay (República Oriental del Uruguay).

2. GOVERNMENT: Democratic, republican government divided into executive, legislative, and judicial branches. Constitution of 1967 vests executive power in president; legislative power in the General Assembly, divided into the Senate and Chamber of Representatives; and judicial power in Supreme Court of Justice. Constitution also provides for establishment of industrial and cultural organizations under state ownership. Suffrage granted to citizens eighteen years of age or over.

3. POPULATION: About 3 million. In 1970 almost half of total lived in Montevideo. Over 90 percent of population of European descent, principally Spanish and Italian origin. Small number of *mestizos* (see Glossary) and Negroes. During nineteenth and twentieth centuries, population augmented by waves of immigration, primarily from Europe.

4. SIZE: Slightly over 72,000 square miles. Greatest north-south extent, about 350 miles; east-west, about 240 miles. Smallest country in South America.

5. TOPOGRAPHY: Bordered on east by Atlantic Ocean; on south by Río de la Plata estuary; on west by Río Uruguay, which serves as border with Argentina; and on north with streams and relief features separating it from Brazil. Geographical regions consist of fertile agricultural coastal lowlands and pastoral plateau interior, a gently rolling grassland with numerous low hill systems. No deserts or high mountains. Many rivers and streams, and swamps and lagoons near eastern coast. Excellent drainage system throughout country.

6. LANGUAGES: Spanish, the official language, spoken almost universally. Dialect in common use influenced by Italian vocabulary and pronounciation. Knowledge of English increasing among educated groups.

7. RELIGION: Roman Catholicism, the professed religion of most of the people. Church and state officially separate, and religious freedom guaranteed. About 4 percent of population, Protestant or Jewish.

8. EDUCATION: In 1968 about 600,000 students enrolled in schools at all levels, a large majority in free public system. In late 1960's average amount of schooling for those over age fifteen was

five years, and literacy rate for those over fifteen estimated as high as 97 percent. Overall rate in excess of 90 percent.

9. HEALTH: Generally excellent. Low death rate, and high and increasing rate of longevity. Medical payments provided under wide variety of public, mutual, and commercial programs. Most of hospital facilities, government operated. Number and quality of medical personnel and facilities generally satisfactory but concentrated in Montevideo and some departmental capitals. Principal causes of death: circulatory diseases and cancer. Few endemic diseases or epidemics, and good public preventive medicine program. Extensive environmental sanitation program and good diet and nutrition contribute to general health of population.

10. CLIMATE: Temperate, with moderate seasonal changes and little regional variation. Generally adequate rainfall well-distributed regionally and seasonally. Cool, damp, and windy springs; warm summers; mild autumns; chilly winters, but frost and freezing temperatures virtually unknown. Seasonal high winds and occasional extreme droughts and floods lend variety and unpredictability to climate.

11. JUSTICE: At apex of judicial system is Supreme Court of Justice created in 1907, followed by four appellate courts and a number of lawyer courts and justices of the peace. Death penalty abolished in 1909. Contentious-Administrative Tribunal, a special legal body to ensure that governmental acts do not violate Constitution. Tribunal of Accounts appointed by General Assembly to supervise execution of federal budget.

12. ADMINISTRATIVE DIVISIONS: In 1970 there were nineteen political divisions known as departments, each with at least two members in the Chamber of Representatives. Country divided into four military regions.

13. ECONOMY: Mixed economy in which both public and private enterprise participate. Most sectors of economy effectively controlled by state, either directly or through public agencies. State also engaged in industrial and commercial activities, in some cases as monopoly and in others in partnership with private companies.

14. INDUSTRY: Light industry predominant; processing of agricultural and animal products accounts for about half of manufacturing output. Industrial plants small, and operating costs relatively high. Biggest industry, raising of livestock; more than 80 percent of land area used for this purpose. Most important manufactures: foodstuffs and beverages, textiles, construction and building materials, chemicals, metallurgical and mechanical products, and petroleum and coal derivatives. Domestic industry provides 80 percent of consumer goods.

15. LABOR: Labor force estimated at slightly over 1 million in late 1960's; about one-fourth female. Substantial increase in union

membership since mid-1960's, but no reliable statistics available. In mid-1960's estimates varied from 150,000 to 350,000. In 1970 many conditions of employment were fixed by legislation, and wage-price controls had been in effect since 1968, leaving labor a limited role as collective bargaining agent.

16. EXPORTS: Equivalent of US$199 million in 1970. Traditional products—wool, meat, and leather—accounted for 80 to 90 percent of total value of exports. Share of livestock products growing, wool exports becoming relatively less important. Rise in exportable surplus of meat expected from continuation of pasture improvement program and reduced domestic consumption because of higher prices.

17. IMPORTS: Equivalent of US$171 million in 1970. Raw materials, capital goods, and fuels and lubricants, principal import categories. Nonessential imports discouraged; imports deterred by high customs duties, prior deposits, and surcharges, plus policy of protecting local industries as aid to industrialization and economic diversification.

18. FINANCE: Inflation remained a problem in 1970, although restrained by firm governmental measures in late 1960's. Recurring annual budgetary deficits of public sector had led to accelerating increases in prices. Dual problem of inflexible tax structure and rigid requirements for current expenditures.

19. COMMUNICATIONS: Telephone-telegraph system owned and operated by government. Telephone system heavily overburdened, and new installations difficult to obtain. In 1970 about 195,000 telephones in operation, or approximately 65 telephones for each 1,000 inhabitants. International radio-telephone and radio-telegraph connect country with all parts of the world.

20. RAILROADS: State-owned railroads consist of four principal systems. 1,870 miles of standard guage (4 feet, 8½ inches), 260 locomotives, 200 passenger cars, and 3,500 freight cars. Montevideo, hub of railway system with four main lines to Brazilian and Argentine borders.

21. ROADS: Highways radiate fanlike from Montevideo and connect all important areas; highway traffic principal carrier of passengers and freight. Intercity bus service frequent to most parts of country, most popular means of transport. Most of country's roads unpaved; major highways being improved in 1970.

22. RIVER TRANSPORTATION: In 1970 about 700 miles of inland waterways reportedly navigable; Río Uruguay by far most important. Oceangoing vessels could travel 140 miles up this river to Paysandú, and lighter draft ships could proceed 60 miles farther to Salto.

23. PORTS AND PORT FACILITIES: Ports on estuary of Río de la Plata and Atlantic coast include country's most important port—

Montevideo— and Colonia, Punta del Este, and La Paloma. Several commercial ports on Río Uruguay. National Port Administration in 1970 engaged in programs to reconstruct present harbor and port facilities, and long-range plan to transform Montevideo into leading port of Río de la Plata basin.

24. AIRFIELDS: Principal airfield at Montevideo. Other urban centers have small landing strips.

25. PRINCIPAL AIRLINES: State-owned airline serves interior of country and provides service to Brazil, Paraguay, Bolivia, and Argentina. Private airline operates between Uruguay and Argentina. Foreign airlines furnish service to United States and Europe; several airlines connect Montevideo daily with most important cities in South America.

26. MERCHANT MARINE: Coastal navigation fleet has total cargo capacity of 29,200 tons; ocean transport fleet has total cargo capacity of 131,000 tons.

27. INTERNATIONAL AGREEMENTS AND TREATIES: Party to Inter-American Treaty of Reciprocal Assistance, General Agreement on Tariffs and Trade, Latin American Free Trade Association, Latin American Nuclear Free Zone Treaty, and River Plate Basin Treaty.

28. AID PROGRAMS: Through mid-1969 World Bank and allied agencies lent country equivalent of US102 million. Inter-American Development Bank loans equivalent to slightly over US$61 million. Technical assistance from United Nations Development Program equivalent to almost US$8 million. Total economic assistance from United States through mid-1970 almost US$124 million, including loans, grants, and sales and donations of agricultural commodities. Receives assistance from the United States Military Assistance Program.

29. INTERNATIONAL OBLIGATIONS AND MEMBERSHIPS: Member of United Nations and many of its affiliates and specialized agencies, International Court of Justice, Organization of American States, Pact of Bogotá, Inter-American Development Bank, and Charter of Punta del Este (Alliance for Progress).

30. ARMED FORCES STRENGTH: Compulsory military service not required. Total armed forces about 17,000. Army about 12,000, with infantry, artillery, cavalry, and engineer units. Navy about 1,800, with two destroyers, one subchaser, four patrol, and other vessels. Air force around 1,600, with about sixty aircraft—jet fighters and transport and training aircraft. No paramilitary forces, but about 120,000 trained reserves.

URUGUAY

TABLE OF CONTENTS

LIST OF ILLUSTRATIONS

LIST OF TABLES

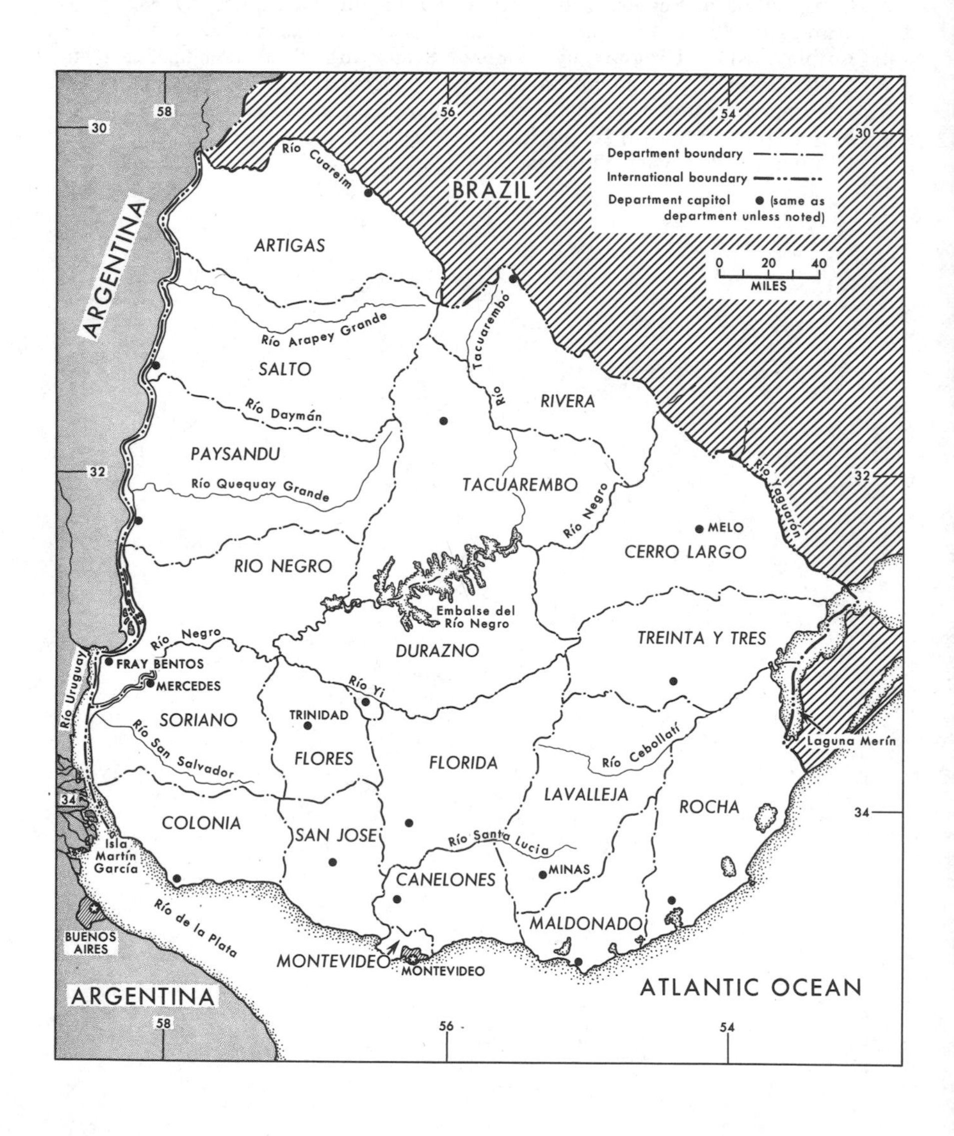

Figure 1. Uruguay.

SECTION I. SOCIAL

CHAPTER 1

GENERAL CHARACTER OF THE SOCIETY

The Oriental (Eastern) Republic of Uruguay, situated on the east coast of South America between Argentina and Brazil, is a land of low hills and rolling grassy plains with abundant pastureland, a temperate climate, and an adequate water supply—all of which combine to make stockraising the basic element in the economy. The designation "Oriental Republic of Uruguay" derives from the location of the wedge-shaped country on the east bank of the Río Uruguay, which forms the country's frontier with Argentina and flows into the great estuary of the Río de la Plata, on the shores of which both Montevideo, the capital of Uruguay, and Buenos Aires, the capital of Argentina, are located. The undulating grasslands slope gently upward from the 120-mile Atlantic coastline to the boundary with Brazil in the northeast. With an area of approximately 72,000 square miles, Uruguay is the smallest country in South America.

The country is the only one in South America with no extensive uninhabited areas, but population distribution is characterized by a heavy concentration in and around Montevideo, where almost half the people live. There are no other cities of comparable size.

The population, approximately 3 million in 1970, is almost entirely of European descent. Many of the people are of Italian origin, but Spanish is the national language, and the cultural background is predominantly Spanish.

In 1970 the character of the society directly mirrored the history of the country. Along with the language, Roman Catholicism, the prevailing religion, was a legacy of the Spanish colonial period. Since the Spanish settlers had not superimposed their rule on an existing Indian civilization and since most of the Indians who roamed the territory had been eliminated in the early days of the colony, the population as a whole was homogeneous.

A spirit of independence and devotion to democratic ideals reflects to some extent the traditional life of the wide-ranging *gauchos* (cowboys) who had opened up the country. The territory, neglected by the conquistadors in their search for precious metals, was first exploited by hardy pioneers who gained a livelihood by killing cattle and horses for their hides and who were largely a law unto themselves.

The people's love of independence also reflects their experience as citizens of a buffer state. During colonial times Portugal and Spain were rivals for control of the territory and, subsequently, Argentina and Brazil made it an object of contention. A national hero is José Gervasio Artigas, who led an unsuccessful attempt to achieve autonomy for the country within a regional federation. Independence was gained in 1828 at the end of a war between Brazil and Uruguayan patriots who were supported by Argentina. Civil wars, invasions, and foreign intervention, however, harassed the country until the end of the nineteenth century.

The pattern for the country's future political development was set in 1903, when José Batlle y Ordóñez was elected president. Batlle advocated political and social reforms that were very much in evidence in 1970—extensive welfare measures and government participation in many sectors of the economy. A system of government by a presidential board or council advocated by Batlle was in effect from 1919 to 1933 and again from 1952 to 1966. The Colorado Party, which had controlled the government since 1865, lost the election of 1958 to the Blanco Party but returned to power after the elections in 1966. At this time the voters approved a constitutional amendment that reestablished a one-man presidency.

In 1970 the growth of the urban population and a decline in the rural population represented a trend that had started in the colonial era. *Criollos* (descendants of Europeans who settled in the New World during the Spanish colonial period) were the dominant element in the interior; immigrants and first- and second-generation citizens were in the majority in the coastal areas.

The people are proud of the country's outstanding educational system. There is, however, an oversupply of professional people in most fields and a limited number of persons with vocational skills. In spite of overcrowding in professional fields, most students prefer academic courses to technical training.

In the late 1960's the central government expended more than twice the Latin American average on education, which was free for primary and secondary students and virtually free at the university level. The overall literacy rate was the highest in Hispanic America —over 90 percent.

The society is noted for its tolerant attitudes, and European immigrants arriving in the nineteenth and twentieth centuries have easily assimilated. Most immigrants came from Spain and Italy and became the backbone of the urban middle class, whose standards have tended to dominate the social and cultural life of the country. Characteristic of these attitudes are respect for social mobility, trade unionism, and education.

Although the society as a whole is homogeneous, differences between immigrant groups and *criollos*—in traditions, occupations, and historical background—tend to create misunderstandings. These differing approaches are partially reflected in the two traditional political groupings: the Colorados, traditionally supporting the cause of middle and lower class citizens; and the Blanco Party, traditionally representing large landowners, the church hierarchy, and big business. *Mestizos* (persons of mixed European and American Indian ancestry), Negroes, and mulattoes are so limited in numbers that they do not form distinct ethnic groups, nor do they play any significant role in the society. The standard of living is higher than the levels found in most parts of the world. For all but the small number of people with the lowest incomes the food supply is varied and ample, and the average daily per capita intake of calories and protein is rated as among the world's highest.

The people enjoy the use of extensive medical facilities, particularly in Montevideo, along with ample retail outlets and recreational opportunities. Good medical care and sanitation, combined with ample diet, have contributed to one of the world's highest longevity rates. Even in rural slum conglomerates and on small farms in the interior, living conditions are generally better than those in similar areas in many other countries.

Most of the people have considerable time for recreation because of the short working hours in offices, banks, and stores and a remarkable number of national holidays. Among the many sports soccer is the most popular. Other recreational opportunities are found in the form of extensive beaches such as those on the Río de la Plata estuary, sports and social clubs, theater and ballet, and almost universal gregariousness—in cafes, in homes, at carnivals, and in the exchange of visits in rural areas.

The society is noted for its advanced welfare system, which provides retirement and pension benefits for virtually everyone and is so all-embracing that private welfare activities play a relatively small part in the lives of the people. Criticisms of the welfare structure include the contention that the large number of family allowance and retirement plans, conducted under separate legislative authorizations, have led to high costs and to abuses and confusion. Also, the government employs a remarkably large number of people—in excess of 20 percent of the labor force. In 1970 the government, realizing that demands of the welfare system had exceeded the country's ability to support it, was examining means of restructuring the system.

In 1970 the society was composed of large middle and lower classes and a small upper class in urban areas and in southern rural areas and large lower and small upper classes in the northern regions. The middle class embraced a larger proportion of the population than in most Latin American countries, and acceptance of its ideals and values was widespread. The ideology of the Colorado Party was strongly influenced by middle class concepts.

Another feature of the social structure was the high degree of urbanization, resulting from the location of some three-fourths of the people in towns and cities, with almost half the total population concentrated in Montevideo. Although social mobility existed, the society was less fluid than it had been in the past. Nevertheless, most upper class individuals—landowners and business and financial leaders—had not acquired the sense of exclusiveness found in many other countries, and they continued to believe in the personal dignity of people of all classes.

In the rural regions of the north there was an upper class of landholders and a lower class of paid laborers. Along the eastern and southern coasts and in adjoining areas there were many small family farms, whose owners were generally of the middle class, which supplied produce to the city.

Most of the people favored the small nuclear family. This was particularly true of the urban dweller who wished to limit his family to the number of children for whom he could provide. Middle and upper class families regarded relatives as important—for social and economic reasons. Although most women remained in the home, they enjoyed more independence than women in many other Latin American countries, and substantial numbers were attending the university and preparing for careers.

Most Uruguayans respect individualism, regard the family as important, disdain manual labor, and tend to adopt fatalistic attitudes. These values, derived largely from the Hispanic tradition, have been supplemented by the concepts of nineteenth-century European immigrants who placed emphasis on more rationalistic and secular views on social justice, security, and the enjoyment of life. Nevertheless, traditional values were still important in 1970—particularly in the interior, where the rural upper class tended to maintain a paternalistic role.

The Constitution of 1830 granted freedom of worship for all faiths, and the Constitution of 1919 provided for separation of church and state. Although Roman Catholicism is the dominant religion, the church has not achieved the position of power that it has enjoyed in many Latin American countries. The ideas of English and French secular philosophers and the lack of sympathy for the church shown by many nineteenth-century immigrants have had their effect. In 1970 the greatest regard for the church was found among the urban upper classes and in the poorer rural areas. At the same time the majority of the clergy and laymen favored alleviation of the problems of the poor; some were devoted to reforming the political system and to the redistribution of wealth.

In 1970 the broadly based cultural life of the people reflected the

Spanish heritage, the aspirations of the revolutionary movement against Spain that had culminated in independence, the influence of nineteenth-century European writers and artists, and the impact of contemporary social changes. In the field of creative writing there was a tendency to superimpose metaphysical contemplation and fantasy on the older styles. At the same time the folklore of the *gaucho* continued to enjoy popularity.

Traditionally, the people have accorded great respect to writers, artists, and scholars, and the government has sponsored a national symphony orchestra, schools of drama and ballet, and a national theatrical company.

Uruguayan cultural development received its first notable impetus during the early years of the nineteenth century, when the revolt against Spain inspired patriotic drama and poetry. After independence romantic forms tended to replace classic styles in literature. In the late nineteenth and early twentieth centuries philosophers with an empirical approach to the analysis of human problems won acceptance over those who persisted in a metaphysical approach. This development was regarded by José Enrique Rodó (1871–1917), the noted lyricist and essayist, as an alarming trend toward materialism, and in his writings he urged the people to uphold the spiritual elements of their Spanish heritage.

In the early twentieth century, largely as a result of Rodó's influence, there appeared a new literary movement, known as modernism, which was characterized by simplicity of style. Also in the early twentieth century, novelists, dramatists, and short story writers began to examine and portray conflicts between the cultures of the immigrant and the *gaucho* and the more challenging problems of urban existence.

Mass media play a vital part in the lives of the people. The great majority read daily newspapers, most of which are published in Montevideo and are speedily distributed to all parts of the nation. Virtually every home has a radio receiver, and telecasts reach an estimated one-third of the population.

Freedom of speech and freedom of the press are guaranteed by the Constitution, and the country has been noted for the extent to which these rights have been honored. In 1968, however, in the face of subversive activities, the government declared a limited state of siege, and in 1969 a law was decreed placing restrictions on publications of reports that were considered to affect national security. Under these regulations a number of publications were closed for limited periods.

The people have taken pride in their adherence to ideals of stable democratic government. Except for a coup in 1933, after which the president exercised one-man rule until 1938, politics have been practiced within a constitutional framework since the beginning of the century. Elections have been orderly, and transfers of power have been peaceful.

The parties in the two-party system—Colorados and Blancos—are divided into a number of factions, a condition that makes it difficult for the chief executive to maintain party unity or to exercise his authority.

In 1970 two minor political parties were: the Leftist Liberty Front (Frente Izquierda de Libertad—FIdel), a Communist front organization including a pro-Cuban group; and the Christian Democratic Party (Partido Democrático Cristiano—PDC), a leftist, democratically oriented group favoring radical reform.

An illegal organization, calling itself the National Liberation Movement (Movimiento de Liberación Nacional—MLN) or the Tupamaros, was a clandestine urban guerrilla group of extreme leftists whose campaign against the government included robberies, kidnappings, and murder. The Tupamaros, taking their name from Tupac Amaru, the Inca rebel who led the uprising against the Spanish in 1780, commenced operations in the early 1960's. In 1970 their membership included students, members of the clergy, government workers, professionals, and intellectuals. In 1970 the government was adopting strong measures to counteract the criminal activities of the Tupamaros. These measures were creating a polarization in attitudes toward the government, with antigovernment elements claiming that established political processes and civil liberties were being undermined.

The country's foreign relations have reflected the efforts of a small nation to advocate self-determination, respect for human rights, the pacific settlement of disputes, and economic cooperation. The country has depended principally on regional and world organizations and on the rivalries of its neighbors for the maintenance of its independence. In 1970 the government was endeavoring to expand its foreign trade and to cooperate with its neighbors in developing the industrial power resources of the Río de la Plata basin.

In 1970 the government was endeavoring to carry out a stabilization program to counteract inflation, along with the effects of declining productivity and export earnings, and mounting welfare payments. In the late 1960's the government's efforts had been hindered by the resistance of those who characterized extraordinary measures as a threat to the country's democratic customs and traditional internal stability. Widespread unrest and violence by striking students and workers had led to the imposition of emergency controls.

The labor force in 1970 was more than 80 percent urban, despite the fact that the bulk of the country's wealth was derived from pastoral and agricultural pursuits. A continuing growth of the services sector, including a remarkably large proportion of government employees, had led to a considerable amount of underemployment, which also posed a problem.

During the twentieth century the society's democratic tradition, its extensive social services, and an absence of dire poverty have combined to minimize conditions that usually generate common crime. In 1970, however, the police and the armed forces were fully occupied with the task of suppressing the activities of the Tupamaros, whose crimes were allegedly committed for political reasons.

The armed forces, since the beginning of the century, have been noted for their aloofness from politics. Between 1904 and 1970, with the exception of the mid-1930's, the country was administered by civilian governments. In 1970 the army appeared to be extending tacit support to the president, who was under attack by the opposition in the General Assembly for retaining emergency security measures. The president had told the people that they must be prepared for a period of austerity and sacrifice, and in mid-1970 there were indications that economic conditions were improving.

CHAPTER 2

PHYSICAL ENVIRONMENT

With an area of 72,172 square miles, the country is the smallest in South America. With the exception of Canada, it is the only country in the Western Hemisphere located entirely outside the tropics. Excluding Newfoundland, all of its land surface lies to the east of the North American continent, and the capital city of Montevideo is about 600 miles east of Bermuda. Its time zone is two hours earlier than Eastern Standard Time.

The perimeter of the wedge-shaped country, often described as compact and homogeneous, is devoid of pronounced extrusions or intrusions (see fig. 1). The low plateau of the interior is marked by gentle up-and-down features except in the northeast, where the eroded hill ranges have sharp edges. The coastal lowlands have gently uneven characteristics featured by rivers and streams, sand dunes, small hill systems, and isolated knolls.

Compactness of the country and the lack of high relief features have combined to make easier the construction of a good transportation network, in which all major roads and railroads originate along the frontiers and converge on Montevideo. This convergence is at once a cause and a consequence of the development of a settlement pattern that has resulted in the accumulation of almost half the population in the capital city, a concentration unrivaled in the Western Hemisphere. In addition, population density decreases in proportion to the distance from Montevideo, and the principal cities of the interior center are located along access routes leading to Montevideo.

A transitional geological buffer between the landmasses of Argentina and Brazil, abundantly watered Uruguay is in a technical sense almost an island. Nearly all of its eastern perimeter is marked by a large tidal lagoon on the north and by the Atlantic Ocean. The southern coast is bordered by the great Río de la Plata estuary, and on the west the country is separated from the northern part of Argentina by the Río Uruguay. About two-thirds of the northern border corresponds to the course of major and minor rivers. Some border questions between Uruguay and its two contiguous neighbors, Argentina and Brazil, remain unsettled. None, however, represents serious problems, and irredentism is not an issue.

About 70 percent of the country lies in the La Plata drainage basin, an enormous area drained by the Uruguay and Paraná river systems. Development of the waterpower resources of this region is an important projected program in which Uruguay, Brazil, Argentina, Paraguay, and Bolivia are to participate.

Most of the countryside is made up of wide expanses of undulating prairie, an extension of the humid pampa of Argentina, broken in places by low ranges of hills pointing southwestward from the highlands of southern Brazil. Narrow lowlands of the Río de la Plata littoral and the Río Uruguay flood plain are devoted primarily to farming. The remainder of the country is a low, broken plateau divided into cattle and sheep ranches. About 90 percent of the territory is devoted to agricultural and pastoral undertakings. The topsoil is generally thin, but 70 percent of the land is considered tillable. There is little known mineral wealth except for iron deposits discovered in the 1960's, which have not yet been developed (see ch. 19, Industry).

The relatively rugged northwest is the only subtropical part of the country. The remainder enjoys a moderate and pleasant temperate-zone climate marred only by winter fogs and occasional high winds. It is, however, an uncertain climate marked from time to time by droughts and floods.

Because plateau and plain are broken up by barbed-wired fences dividing them into ranches and farms, it is only in the northwest that a few of the larger indigenous animal species survive. Wildfowl are numerous in the lagoons and marshes of the Atlantic coast, however, and game and other bird species abound on the plateaus and along the southern coast. The generally excellent deep-sea and surf fishing are at their best in the vicinity of Punta del Este.

The rural settlement pattern corresponds to regional differences; farms occupy the coastal lowland, and cattle and sheep ranches are found on the interior plateau. In general, population density is the greatest near Montevideo, the one great urban center, and least in parts of the country remote from the capital.

NATURAL FEATURES

Topography

The country represents a transition from the pampas of Argentina to the hilly uplands and valley intersections of southern Brazil's Paraná plateau. In general, it is a country of gentle hills and hollows.

This rolling characteristic is general but less evident close to the eastern, southern, and western borders. In the northeast corner, adjacent to Laguna Merín, is a low plain area where rice is grown under irrigation. Directly southward, a narrow alluvial Atlantic coastal plain is broken by sand dunes, marshes, and coastal lagoons.

Infertile stretches of sandy soil extend inland for distances of up to five miles. At Punta del Este, the coastline leaves the Atlantic to veer westward sharply for more than 200 miles along the Río de la Plata estuary to the mouth of the Río Uruguay, the estuary's westernmost extremity. The littoral is somewhat broader here and merges almost imperceptibly with the grasslands and hills of the interior.

Soils consist of sands, clays, loess, and alluvium deposited by the numerous streams. The black soil is rich in potassium and enriched by decay of the lush cover of vegetation. Soils of similar composition are found on the flood plain of the Río Uruguay, which forms the country's western frontier. Along this flood plain, however, in the portion to the north of the mouth of the Río Negro there are extensions of the interior hill ranges that encroach on the flood plain.

The remaining three-fourths or more of the country consists of a rolling plateau, featured by ranges of low hills that become more prominent in the north as they merge into the highlands of southern Brazil. The geological foundation of most of the region is made up of gneiss, red sandstone, and granite, and an extension of the basaltic plateau of Brazil reaches southward in a broad band west of the Río Negro. Corridors between the hill ranges are floored with clay and sedimentary deposits.

Legend holds that when the ship of the discoverer Magellan first made landfall in the Río de la Plata, on sighting the conical hill west of the site of what was to become Montevideo, his lookout called out in Portuguese "Monte vide eu" (I see a mountain). This quite possibly is how the capital city acquired its name, but the country as a whole is so lacking in lofty relief features that its highest peak is Cerro Mirador in Maldonado Department near the southern coast. Its height is 1,644 feet.

The most important of the *cuchillas* (hill ranges) are the Cuchilla Grande and the Cuchilla de Haedo. Only in these and in the Cuchilla Santa Ana along the Brazilian frontier do altitudes with any frequency exceed 600 feet. Both of the two major ranges extend southwestward from Brazil, one on the eastern flank and one on the western, in directions roughly defining the course of the country's principal river, the Río Negro. To the east, the Cuchilla Grande and its several spur ranges form the country's most extensive hill system and its most important drainage divide. Here, ridges are frequently 1,000 feet or more in elevation. West of the river in the northern portion of the Cuchilla de Haedo, near the Brazilian border, is the site of the Uruguayan countryside's most nearly rugged terrain. Elevations are low, but eroded layers of sandstone and laval deposits sometimes overlaid by basalt give sharp outlines to the topography.

The rolling character of the land surface derives from the presence of dozens of these *cuchilla* ranges. Insignificant as relief features, they have been important factors in the development of the country. In many instances the ridges serve as administrative boundaries and as the routes followed by the roads and railroads, which frequently tend to avoid the underbrush-clogged lowlands along the rivers and streams. In addition, they contribute to a drainage system much more effective than that of the Argentine pampas, where the uncompromising flatness of the land prevents much runoff after rains and causes surface water to accumulate.

Hydrography

The name of Uruguay, first applied to the Río Uruguay, may have been taken from the Guaraní Indian word *uruguä*, meaning a kind of mussel. Another explanation is that it derives from Guaraní word-components meaning birds that come from the water. Both are indicative of a well-watered land. Most of the country's frontiers are riverine; rivers, streams, and occasional watercourses form an elaborate tracery over the entire country; lakes and lagoons are numerous; and a generally high water table makes well-digging easy.

The largest of the rivers is the Río Uruguay, but the country can claim only partial title to it. The river marks the entire western boundary with Argentina and extends farther to the north as a portion of the Argentina-Brazil frontier. It is flanked by low banks, and disastrous floods sometimes inundate large areas. The Río de la Plata, marking the entire southern boundary, is actually an estuary of the Atlantic Ocean and is saline except at its western extremity, where the Paraná and the Uruguay spew enormous quantities of fresh water into it.

There are three systems of internal rivers and streams: those flowing westward into the Río Uruguay, those flowing eastward either into the Atlantic Ocean or into tidal lagoons, and those flowing southward into the Río de la Plata.

Most of the rivers draining westward originate in the inland hills and descend through narrow valleys to join the Río Uruguay. The longest and most important, however, is the Río Negro, which rises in southern Brazil. It bisects the country as it flows southwestward over a distance of some 500 miles to join the Río Uruguay south of the town of Fray Bentos. Its principal tributary, and the country's second most important river, is the Río Yi, which flows a distance of 140 miles from its source in the Cuchilla Grande. Other major western rivers originate in the Cuchilla de Haedo and join the Río Uruguay north of Paysandú.

The rivers flowing eastward originate in the Cuchilla Grande and are shallower and more variable in flow. They empty into lagoons, located behind the coastal dunes, or directly into the Atlantic through small estuaries. The largest of these, the Río Cebollatí, flows into Laguna Merín. The irregularity of the country's drainage pattern is illustrated by the fact that the headwaters of this eastward-draining river lie some fifty miles to the west of that of the westward-draining Río Yi.

In 1937 work began on a Río Negro dam at a site a short distance upstream from the town of Paso de los Toros in the central part of the country. The resulting reservoir, called the Embalse del Río Negro, with a length of 87 miles and a surface area of over 4,000 square miles, is the largest manmade lake in South America. At a later date a second dam was constructed on the river a few miles downstream from the first. The two dams are sites of major hydroelectric power installations.

The largest of the eastern coastal lagoons is the Laguna Merín. Serving as a part of the northeastern frontier with Brazil and with its northern extremity located entirely in Brazil, it discharges its waters through that country's São Gonçalo Canal. Strung along the coast between the Brazilian border of Punta del Este are a half-dozen other lagoons with surface areas of fifteen to seventy square miles as well as numerous smaller ones. Some are fresh water, while others have direct tidal connection with the Atlantic and as a consequence are brackish.

Some 775 miles of the country's rivers are reported to be navigable. This figure, however, apparently includes 235 miles along the Río de la Plata estuary. On the Río Uruguay oceangoing vessels of up to fourteen feet in draft can ascend 140 miles to Paysandú, and vessels with drafts of up to nine feet can continue 60 miles farther to Salto, where passage is blocked by falls. Much of the Río Negro is obstructed by sandbanks and shallows, but it is navigable by coastal vessels for about 45 miles upstream from its mouth. Rivers navigable for some distance by shallow-draft small craft include the Yi and Quequay Grande in the west, the Cebollatí in the east, and the Santa Lucia in the south.

Geographical Regions

The land is homogeneous, and changes in topography, climate, and vegetation are limited in character and moderate in degree. The two principal regions of the country are the Agricultural Lowland and the Pastoral Plateau Interior.

The agricultural Lowland starts in Maldonado Department and follows the littoral of the Río de la Plata westward for the full extent of the estuary in a band averaging about fifty miles in depth. It is sometimes regarded as continuing northward along the Río Uruguay in a narrowing band as far as the river town of Salto.

Rarely, the sand dunes and swamps of the Atlantic plain are also included. Soil, relief, and vegetation vary considerably within the Agricultural Lowland, which merges gradually with the rolling grasslands of the interior, but it is an area of varied and intensive agriculture in which most of the population lives. The Pastoral Plateau Interior makes up the remaining three-fourths or more of the country. In general, sheep ranches occupy the territory to the north of the Río Negro, and cattle ranches prevail to the river's south.

Mineral Resources

The country's deficiency in minerals has limited the development of industry. With the exception of a fairly large deposit of 40 percent iron ore that has been located in the central part of the country, the search for metallic minerals has been generally unavailing. In early 1970, however, plans were reported for development of ilmenitic beach sands along the coast between Montevideo and Aguas Dulces on the Atlantic as a source of rutile, zircon, and monazite. Manganese, copper, lead, and gold discoveries do not appear to be in commercially useful concentrations, and initial offers of offshore leases for petroleum prospecting have failed to arouse much interest.

Building materials located in the south-central part of the country make up most of the nonmetallic minerals production. Good quality marble, granite, talc, limestone, building stone, and sand are produced for domestic use and sometimes for export. Semiprecious stones, such as opal, agate and onyx, are found in limited quantities in Salto and Artigas departments. Under Uruguayan law all products of the subsoil are the product of the state.

Vegetation

Most of the country is grassland, some of the native prairie grasses similar to those of the Argentine pampas having been replaced by planted varieties with higher yields value. In the spring these grasslands are interlaced with wildflowers, including the verbena, which is said to have caused the Anglo-Argentine writer W. H. Hudson to give the title *The Purple Land* to a nineteenth-century book. Vegetation in general is temperate except in the northwest, where forests are thick, trees are dressed with creepers, and orchids grow.

Less than 3 percent of the country is forested. Most of the native forest occurs in bottom lands of watercourses, particularly in the northeast, where stretches of mixed forest and woodland in the valleys link the region to corresponding natural features in southern Brazil. Among the hardwoods are algarrobo, quebracho, urunday, and guayabo. Other forest species include the scarlet-flowered ceiba, acacia, alder, willow, myrtle, mimosa, rosemary, and aloe.

Vines and underbrush are sometimes heavy, and medicinal herbs native to these woodlands include sarsaparilla, camomile, and quinine. The rocky slopes of the low hills are frequently covered with bracken.

The only trees indigenous to the grassy plateaus are the palm and the *ombú*, a long-lived growth that is more herb than tree. The pulpy wood of the *ombú* does not have much use, even as fuel, but the growth achieves considerable height and interrupts the monotony of the wide stretches of grassland while providing welcome shade to cowboys and cattle. Planted stands of palm are found along the Atlantic coastline where, together with plantations of maritime pine and eucalyptus, they were set out to half the inward drift of the beach dunes. These trees and poplars are often found along roads and surrounding houses in all parts of the country.

Wildlife

The larger indigenous animals have virtually disappeared, except in the broken terrain of the semitropical northwest. Among the species still sometimes seen are the rhea (or American ostrich), nutria, small deer, puma, jaguar, wildcat, fox, anteater, and several kinds of small rodent. Seals swarm over the rocky Lobos Island at the mouth of the Río de la Plata near Punta del Este. In 1970, however, more than 90 percent of the national territory was being used economically, and barbed-wire fences striated the rangeland. There was little remaining room in which wild animals could roam.

Salt-water fish abound in three fishing zones. These are the low zone, which extends from Colonia, across the Río de la Plata from Buenos Aires, eastward to Piriápolis; the middle zone, one of the world's finest game-fishing sectors and a prime locality for commercial fishing, from Piriápolis to Punta del Este, some twenty-five miles to the east; and the high zone, from Punta del Este along the Atlantic coastline to the Brazilian border.

Among the principal species are the *corvina negra* (black bass), mackerel, tuna, *merluza* (hake), mullet, sole, whiting, and anchovy. Weakfish, drumfish, and bluefish are the most sought-after surf-casting catch off Punta del Este. The best known of the fresh-water species is the golden-yellow dorado, a kind of salmon or trout.

The Atlantic coastal swamps and lagoons teem with waterfowl, including the flamingo, swan, crane, and white heron. On the plateau and along the Río de la Plata littoral are found the partridge, quail, native crow, vulture, lapwing, hummingbird, cardinal, and a tiny burrowing owl. The *hornero* (oven-bird) builds its oven-shaped nest on fenceposts and telegraph poles in all parts of the country, and parakeets and other tropical birds are sometimes encountered in the semitropical northwestern uplands.

The reptiles include a dangerous viper called the *víbora de la cruz*, rattlesnakes, lizards, and tortoises. An occasional alligator is seen along the shores of the Río Uruguay. Venomous spiders are fairly common, and locust swarms appear periodically in portions of the interior plateau.

Climate

The small size and even physical characteristics of the country limit the extent of regional variations in climate, although the generally temperate weather conditions are replaced by the almost tropical in the northwest, where they are similar to those prevailing in northern Argentina and Paraguay. The absence of high relief features to act as weather barriers makes it especially susceptible to climatic variations caused by external influences, particularly in coastal lowlands. These variations are caused by the downward movement of air masses from the Brazilian highlands; anticyclones originating in the south Atlantic; and, periodically, winds blowing northward from the Argentine pampas.

In all parts of Uruguay except the northwest, spring is usually damp, cool, and windy; summers are warm; autumns are mild; and winter cold is made uncomfortable by dampness, although frost and freezing temperatures are virtually unknown. About half of the days of the year are usually sunny, but fogs are common from May to October, especially near the coasts. It is also during this part of the year that drops in temperature between midday and the hours of darkness are most pronounced.

As reported by six widely scattered meteorological stations over a thirteen-year period, mean annual temperatures ranged from 61.4°F. at Punta del Este on the southern coasts to 67.7°F. at Artigas in the northwest. Seasonal variations were limited. The lowest average during a month in Punta del Este was 51.6°F. in July, and the highest was 70.5°F. in January. In Artigas the lowest was 55.8°F. in July, and the highest was 79.7°F. in January.

The mean annual rainfall is about 42 inches, rainfall decreasing in direct proportion to distance from the coasts. Winter rains are the most frequent, but autumn rains are the heaviest. There is no definite dry season. Rainfall tends to be lowest in summer, but summer thunderstorms are frequent. Regionally, rainfall during the thirteen-year period ranged from an average of 35.35 inches in Punta del Este to 49.25 inches in Artigas.

High winds are a disagreeable characteristic of the weather, particularly during the winter and spring, and wind shifts are pronounced. The hot *zonda*, blowing out of the north, may be replaced by an occasional violent and chilly *pampero* during the winter months. Resulting from the meeting of cool winds blowing northward over Argentina with warm air masses moving southward, the *pampero* causes massive backing up of waters of the Río de la Plata and rains accompanied by sudden drops in temperature over Uruguay. A localized windy phenomenon is the *tormenta*, a sudden convectional activity accompanied by thundershowers. The various winter and spring winds have the salutory effect of keeping the atmosphere fresh despite the prevailing humidity, and the easterly maritime winds of the summer season temper the hot temperatures of midday.

Despite the absence of extreme seasonal changes in weather conditions, day-to-day changes are considerable. In the coastal lowlands these are moderated somewhat by proximity to the Atlantic or the Río de la Plata. On the interior plateau, however, they can reach uncomfortable extremes such as those that occurred during 1967. The year was marked by a lengthy drought resulting in the drying up of waterholes and streams, which occasioned the loss of a considerable number of livestock. The ending of the drought was accompanied by unusually cold weather and torrential rains, particularly in the north, where the drought had been at its worst. Swollen streams overflowed their banks and spread over the pastures to cause the death by starvation or drowning of many more cattle or sheep. It was the worst year in terms of weather since 1959, and the arbitrary measure of eight good years between two bad ones is as good as any for measuring the irregularity of the generally pleasant but unpredictable climate.

BOUNDARIES AND POLITICAL SUBDIVISIONS

The country is bounded on the north and northeast by Brazil and on the south and west by Argentina. The southeast portion of the perimeter is on the Atlantic Ocean. Boundaries correspond generally with natural features, a majority of them riverine and other water features.

From a point on the Atlantic seaboard just above the 34th parallel, the Brazilian frontier extends northward along the course of minor streams and the principal channel of the Laguna Merín to about the 33d parallel, where it continues northwestward to the tripoint with Brazil and Argentina on the Río Uruguay. Rivers mark most of this section of boundary, although its middle one-third follows the ridges of a range of hills and an arbitrary straight line. Although the full extent of the Brazilian boundary has been demarcated, in 1970 there was still some question about the true source of one of the boundary rivers and about sovereignty over a small river island.

From the tripoint on the Río Uruguay, the boundary with Argentina extends directly southward along the course of that river and is delineated for its full extent of about 340 miles to the Río de la Plata. With ratification in 1965 of a 1961 treaty, title to most of the numerous islets dotting the river was agreed upon. In 1970, however, both countries continued to claim certain islands in the Río de la Plata near the river's mouth below the town of Punta Gorda. The most important was Martín García, administered by Argentina and the traditional detention place for its political prisoners.

In 1961 the governments of Uruguay and Argentina issued a joint declaration defining the outer limits of the Río de la Plata estuary as a line running southwestward from Punta del Este in Uruguay to Cabo San Antonio in Argentina. For most of its length, however, the Río de la Plata is more than thirty miles in width, a principally salt-water estuary of the Atlantic Ocean. Although Uruguay has stated that it is a true river, certain other nations have held that it is an international waterway.

The 1961 compact did not include agreement as to where in the estuary the border between the two countries should be drawn. Uruguay has generally held that the border should be the median line between the two coasts, whereas Argentina has claimed that it should follow the deepest channel, a course that for the most part lies relatively close to the Uruguayan shoreline. In addition, there has been some disagreement over the location of the median line itself. In 1969 conversations aimed at reaching agreement with respect to the location of the boundary in the estuary were initiated.

Another significant event of late 1969 relating to sovereignty over the waters of the estuary was the Uruguayan government's issuance of a decree proclaiming sovereignty over all territorial waters to a distance of 200 nautical miles from the shoreline for purposes of fishing and exploitation of the resources of the ocean floor. Earlier in the same year, the distance had been extended from 6 to 12 nautical miles. The decree extending the claim to 200 miles included the statement that there would be no interference with the innocent passage of air and surface craft over the water at distances between 12 and 200 miles, but that fishing in this zone by foreign flag vessels would require prior authorization by the executive branch.

The principal political subdivisions of the country are its departments. With the exception of the department of Montevideo, which occupies only 0.3 percent of the national territory, they range in size from Canelones, with 2.6 percent, to Tacuarembó, with 9.0 percent. Departmental boundaries for the most part correspond to natural features. The courses of rivers and streams are the most frequently used, the Río Negro alone bordering on seven departments. The ridges of the innumerable *cuchillas* are also frequently used, and in some instances borders correspond to old property lines. There are no important straight-line sections of internal borders. The country as a whole is so compact, however, that political subdivisions cannot be said to correspond to geographical regions or ethnic settlement patterns.

The nine blue and white horizontal stripes of the national flag represent the number of departments in existence in 1830, the time at which the flag was adopted. By 1970 the number had increased to nineteen by means of an evolutionary process in which towns grew in size and importance and extended their influence into the surrounding countryside. The capital is invariably the most important urban center in the department, and in thirteen instances departments bear the name of their capitals. They do not significantly affect political and socioeconomic patterns. There are some differences within the country, but these tend to be regional or urban-rural rather than departmental (see ch. 4, Population and Labor Force; ch. 5, Ethnic Groups and Languages; ch. 16, Political Values and Attitudes).

SETTLEMENT PATTERNS

Although no city in Uruguay other than Montevideo has a population much in excess of 60,000, the country is the most urbanized in South America, for about half of the country's people live in the capital city. The continuing nature of the shift in concentration of population is suggested by the circumstances that the 1963 census found 46.3 percent of the people living there and that a 1967 estimate raised the proportion to 49 percent. For 1970 an estimate of 50 percent seems moderate. In no country of the world is population so concentrated in a capital city except in city states such as Luxembourg and Singapore (see ch. 4, Population and Labor Force).

The importance of Montevideo as a settlement lodestone is further emphasized by a glance at the density of population in the rest of the country. In the capital city and in the remainder of the department of Montevideo and the neighboring department of Canelones, the population density in 1963 averaged 980 per square mile. In the remainder of the southern lowlands it was 22 per square mile, and in the interior plateau region it was 13. Within the plateau interior itself, that part south of the Río Negro was more heavily populated than that to the river's north. The only exception to the general pattern of settlement growing progressively sparser in direct proportion to the linear distance from Montevideo occurs in the Río Uruguay flood plain, where intensive agricultural and pastoral activities are practiced and the largest individual urban concentrations outside of the capital city are found.

The other major urban centers are the department capitals and these, without exception, are located on major transportation routes converging from the frontiers toward Montevideo. To the west and south, the Río Uruguay and the Río de la Plata estuary connect Montevideo with the waterside departmental capitals of Salto, Paysandú, Fray Bentos, Mercedes (via the navigable lower reaches of the Río Negro), and Colonia. Each of these centers also has direct highway access to the national capital. The north-south highway route from Rivera on the Brazilian frontier passes through the capitals of Tacuarembó, Durazno, Florida, and Canelones. Farther eastward, the Pan American Highway system links Melo, Treinta y Tres, and Minas. The remaining five departmental capitals also lie on highways linking Montevideo and the frontier (see ch. 21, Trade).

Smaller towns of the interior also have tended to develop along access routes to Montevideo. Lateral routes crossing the country from east to west are remarkably few, but as a general rule market towns are found at crossroads.

Farm villages are not characteristic of the countryside, and small individual farms are numerous in the south. During the late 1960's, however, over half the national territory was in pastoral or agricultural estates of more than 2,000 acres, and about seventy of the estates had more than 25,000 acres. In some of the large properties, workers lived in large clusters having the characteristics of towns, but a more frequent pattern was the scattering of a few dwellings in the immediate work areas. In addition, there were the *rancheríos* (collections of up to 200 rural slum shanties strung out along watercourses or roads) housing itinerant workers during off seasons and the families of regular ranch or farm hands who were not ordinarily permitted to live with their family heads on the worksite. Estimates with respect to number of people living in *rancheríos* varied considerably, but the total may have been as much as one-fifth of the rural population (see ch. 7, Living Conditions).

CHAPTER 3

HISTORICAL SETTING

In 1970 the early history of the country was clearly reflected in the characteristics of the people and their culture. Spanish, the national language, and Roman Catholicism, the prevailing religion, were legacies of the colonial period. The virtual absence of *mestizos* (people of mixed European and American Indian ancestry) was traceable to the fact that the Spanish settlers did not superimpose the colony on an existing Indian civilization, as was the case in some other parts of Latin America, and the indigenous tribes in the territory were eliminated at an early date. The people's spirit of independence and freedom of action may mirror the life of the wide-ranging *gauchos* (cowboys) who opened up the country in colonial times, as well as the nation's experience in contriving to survive, during its early history, as a buffer state.

The struggle between Spain and Portugal and, later, between Brazil and Argentina for control of Uruguay loomed large in the early history of the country. Lacking precious metals, the territory was not exploited by the Spaniards until settlers moved in to gain a livelihood by slaughtering horses and cattle for their hides.

The people honor their national hero José Gervasio Artigas, who in 1820 launched an unsuccessful attempt to gain autonomy for the country within the boundaries of a regional federation. In 1828 independence was finally and formally gained after a war fought by Argentina and the Uruguayan patriots against Brazil. Civil wars, foreign intervention, and invasions harassed the country until the beginning of the twentieth century.

A leader known as the Father of Modern Uruguay was José Batlle y Ordóñez, who served as president in the early twentieth century and established the pattern for the future political development of the country. Batlle initiated social and political reforms that were still in evidence in 1970—extensive welfare programs and widespread government control and operation of enterprises.

The early history of political rivalry is preserved in the names of the two political parties. Colors worn for identification by the troops of the two Uruguayan leaders who opposed each other at the battle of Carpintería in 1836 were red (*colorado*) and white (*blanco*). The Colorado party, whose most prominent leader in the late nineteenth and early twentieth centuries was Batlle y Ordóñez, took up the cause of the urban middle and lower class citizens, whereas the National Party (Partido Nacional), commonly known as the Blanco party, represented the large landowners, the Church hierarchy, and persons in big business. The Colorados, who controlled the government from 1865 to 1958, were defeated by the Blancos in the elections of 1958 and 1962 but returned to power after the 1966 election. Except for a period of rule by decree between 1933 and 1938, politics in the twentieth century have been conducted within a constitutional framework, and transfers of power from one party to the other have been orderly.

Throughout the history of the Republic, the economy has been based primarily on pastoral and agricultural production and the export trade. Thus the lives of the people have been directly affected by world conditions determining the prices paid for their exports. In this connection the growth of industry, commerce, and banking and the appearance of a middle class and an articulate laboring class have tended to perpetuate the traditional rivalry between the city and the countryside.

In the mid-twentieth century the country faced serious economic difficulties. Agricultural producers had not taken full advantage of modern methods, exports failed to earn as much foreign exchange as was needed, and industry was disrupted by strikes and demands for higher wages. Inflation ate up the benefits originally intended for a vast number of recipients in one of the most far-reaching social welfare structures in the world. In the face of widespread dissatisfaction, governments in the mid-twentieth century were making determined efforts to put stabilization programs into effect, but the distribution of wealth had been so generous that it threatened to outrun the productivity of the country's economy.

Having been the target of numerous foreign interventions in the nineteenth century, the country has had a foreign policy of nonintervention in the affairs of other nations. It has played an active role, however, in international organizations.

History shows that a country originally peopled by frontiersmen who were a law unto themselves became a laboratory of political and social experimentation that has produced a society notably dependent on its government for social services and everyday needs.

THE COLONIAL PERIOD

In 1493 and 1494 papal bulls were issued dividing the New World between Portugal and Spain, and the Treaty of Tordesillas (1494) provided that the line of demarcation should be drawn 370 leagues west of the Cape Verde Islands. This line, which crossed the continent of South America near the mouth of the Amazon, secured for Portugal the title to Brazil. All territories to the west were to belong to Spain.

Early in the sixteenth century Juan Diaz de Solís, sailing for Spain and searching for a strait leading to the Pacific Ocean, landed with some of his followers on the shores of the estuary of the Río de la Plata. De Solís and his companions were killed by Charrúan Indians, and the remaining members of the expedition loaded their ships with brazilwood and returned to Spain.

The rivers emptying into the estuary were explored by Sebastian Cabot, sailing for Spain, who named one of them the Río de la Plata because of a mistaken notion that silver deposits existed in the area. Another explorer, who founded the settlement of Buenos Aires, was a Spanish knight named Pedro de Mendoza, who led an expedition seeking a route from the estuary to the Pacific. The settlement was attacked by Indians, and Mendoza returned to Spain.

During the sixteenth century most of the Spaniards who landed on the eastern shores of the estuary were driven off by the warlike Charrúas, who fought with clubs, bows and arrows, and *bolas* (stones fastened to thongs). Lacking precious metals, the land did not attract colonists to the extent that other areas of the New World did, and it was the last region to be claimed for Spain.

Jesuit and Franciscan missionaries came to Uruguay in 1624 and, gathering Indians in mission villages, spread Spanish influence. They played an important role in holding Uruguay against the Portuguese, who founded Nova Colonia de Sacramento on the Río de la Plata opposite Buenos Aires in 1680. In 1767, however, Jesuits were banned from Spanish territories in the New World, and their settlements were gradually broken up. It was not until 1726 that the Spaniards established Montevideo as a stronghold against the Portuguese in Brazil to the north (see ch. 10, Religion).

In 1776 the lands of the Río de la Plata region were separated from the control of the viceroy in Lima, Peru, and the Viceroyalty of La Plata was established with Buenos Aires as the viceregal seat. In the same year the Spaniards seized Nova Colonia de Sacramento, which was formally ceded to them by Brazil in 1777. This cession consolidated Spanish control over the Banda Oriental, or eastern bank of the estuary, for the time being.

In 1796 Spain was at war with England, and Spanish power was declining. A series of British naval and military expeditions against the Viceroyalty of La Plata revealed Spain's weakness to the *criollos* (see Glossary) of Buenos Aires and Montevideo, and dissatisfaction with Spanish rule increased as the people learned more about English government and the possible benefits of trading with England. During a seven-month occupation of Montevideo in 1807, the British published a newspaper that praised the liberties enjoyed by the English and pointed up the repressive government of the Spaniards. Thus were sown seeds of rebellion. In 1808 Spanish prestige was further weakened by the news that Napoleon had placed a Bonaparte on the Spanish throne.

The Uruguayans' revolt against Spain was initiated in 1811 by José Gervasio Artigas (1764—1850), a *gaucho* who became the hero of the independence movement. Artigas, scion of a family that had settled in Montevideo in 1726 and known to Uruguayans as the Father of Uruguayan Independence, had been dissatisfied with the administration of the viceregal government in Buenos Aires, particularly with its discrimination against Montevideo in commercial affairs. He was influenced by federal ideas, and he issued to delegates sent to a constituent assembly at Buenos Aires in 1813 a set of instructions destined to become famous in South American history—*The Instructions of the Year Thirteen.* The delegates were to urge adoption of a declaration of independence and to propose the formation of a confederation of the provinces in the former Viceroyalty of La Plata. The assembly, however, refused to seat the delegates from Banda Oriental.

In 1814 Artigas took command of Uruguay's army. Argentine rebel forces captured Montevideo but were driven out by General Artigas. In 1815 Artigas declared Uruguay independent, and the revolutionary government of Argentina was compelled to recognize the independence of Uruguay.

After fighting the revolutionary government at Buenos Aires, the Spanish forces, and Brazilian troops, Artigas managed to dominate the city of Montevideo. In 1816 Brazilian forces attacked Montevideo from the north, but Artigas led his troops against them. Artiga's struggle against attackers continued until 1820, when the Portuguese captured Montevideo and Artigas fled to Paraguay.

In 1821 Uruguay was annexed to Brazil and known as the Cisplatine Province until 1825, when Uruguayan refugees from Buenos Aires, reinforced by Argentine troops, crossed the Río de la Plata and started a land and sea war between Argentina and Brazil. The "Thirty-three Immortals," led by Juan Antonio Lavalleja, issued a declaration of independence from Portuguese rule in August 1825. In February 1827 the Brazilian forces were defeated by Argentine and Uruguayan troops at Ituzaingo, and in May of the same year a preliminary convention of peace was signed between Brazil and Argentina, containing a provision that Uruguay should be independent and free. This conflict between Brazil and Argentina over Uruguay came to an end when, with English mediation, a treaty creating La República Oriental de Uruguay (The Eastern Republic of Uruguay) was signed on August 27, 1828.

INDEPENDENCE

A constituent assembly convened in November 1828 at San José and appointed a provisional governor, after which Argentine and Brazilian troops left the country. The name of the new nation, La República Oriental del Uruguay, was formally adopted and the constitution approved in 1830. The following year Uruguayan representatives returned from Brazil and Argentina to report that the governments of these countries had recognized the new nation and accepted the constitution. In keeping with a proclamation of the constituent assembly issued in July 1830, military and civil authorities swore to defend and support the constitution, which was adopted on July 18, 1830. José Fructuoso Rivera was elected the first president.

The constitution provided for a centralized form of government. Executive authority was vested in a president, a cabinet, and a permanent committee of the congress empowered, during the recess of congress, to keep a watch on the execution of the laws and the constitution. The president, who was given important powers, was elected by the congress for four years. The cabinet was composed of as many officers as might be necessary and the congress consisted of a senate and a house. The units of local government were designated departments; and in the chief town of each department there was a *jefe politico*, or executive magistrate, appointed by the president (see ch. 12, The Governmental System).

In the summer of 1832 Juan A. Lavalleja, who had led the "Thirty-three Immortals" in 1825, launched a revolt against the president. Two months later the rebels were defeated at Tupambay and Lavalleja fled to Brazil. Two years later he attempted another uprising, which was also put down.

After the election to the presidency of Manuel Oribe, a general who had figured prominently in the war for independence, the Republic appeared to be entering on an era of peace and prosperity. President Oribe permitted Lavalleja and his followers to return from Brazil. Juan Manuel de Rosas, dictator in Argentina, sent soldiers to aid President Oribe against the ex-president, Rivera, who had led a revolt, and in September 1836 President Oribe defeated Rivera's forces at Carpintería. It was in this battle that Oribe's soldiers wore white hatbands and Rivera's troops, red hatbands or badges. These colors became the symbols of the Blancos and the Colorados, the two parties that continued to divide the sympathies of the people in 1970.

In 1838 the Colorados, led by Rivera, defeated the forces of President Oribe, who fled to Buenos Aires, and Rivera was again elected to the presidency. In the following year President Rivera, with the support of the French and of Argentine emigrés, issued a declaration of war against Rosas. With the aid of Rosas's troops, Oribe, who had joined Rosas in a plan for uniting Argentina and Uruguay, then laid siege to the Colorado forces at Montevideo.

LA GUERRA GRANDE

Oribe's siege of Montevideo marked the beginning of La Guerra Grande (The Great War), which lasted from 1843 to 1852. The struggle took on an international character when England and France, with a view to protecting their nationals and to preserving Uruguay as a buffer state, blockaded the Río de la Plata estuary in 1845 and sent troops to Uruguay. Likewise, the Italian patriot Giuseppe Garibaldi and his "red shirts" joined the Colorados in the fight against Rosas's forces. When Justo José de Urquiza, the Argentine *caudillo* (political strongman) who unseated Rosas, lifted the siege of Montevideo, the Colorados were left in power.

YEARS OF RIVALRY, 1852–1903

After the termination of La Guerra Grande the country experienced a half century of almost unrelieved turbulence. Most of the population were frontiersmen with little regard for law and order, and Argentina and Brazil continued to intervene in Uruguay's affairs. The political lines drawn in the 1830's evolved into two rival parties: the Colorados, supported originally by followers of Artigas, who identified themselves as defenders of Uruguayan sovereignty and as champions of the common man and liberalism; and the Blancos, who stood for order and conservatism and declared themselves protectors of the faith.

General Venancio Flores, the Colorado who became president in 1854, endeavored to maintain order by requesting Brazil to intervene. As a result Brazilian troops were stationed in Uruguay for three years. In 1857 a Uruguayan politician formed a plan for annexation of Uruguay to the province of Buenos Aires, and invaders from Argentina bent on carrying out this scheme were captured and shot.

Certain administrative reforms were made in the late 1850's and early 1860's, but in 1865 the Brazilians helped Venancio Flores to overthrow his Blanco rival. When the Paraguayan dictator Francisco Solano Lopéz came to the assistance of the Blancos, Argentina, Brazil, and Uruguay formed a tripartite alliance against Paraguay and waged a five-year war in which Paraguay was decisively defeated. Thus the Colorados were left in power in Uruguay and maintained control of the government until 1958.

At the end of the Paraguayan War in 1870 a considerable number of Uruguayans thought in national terms. The influence of the older type of *caudillo* had declined. Fencing of lands had ended the free ranging of the *gauchos*; railways had begun to unite the country; and a new middle class of doctors, lawyers, and traders had appeared in the cities, where Spanish, Italian, and other immigrants had settled.

The Colorados put down an insurrection started by a Blanco in 1870. In 1872, through the mediation of the Argentine consul, an agreement was reached that made concessions to the insurrectionary leaders and gave the Blancos a share in the emoluments and functions of government.

During the last three decades of the nineteenth century, there were frequent confrontations and clashes between the Colorados and the Blancos and among competing rival factions of the Colorados. A growing gulf between the capital city and the interior contributed to a solidification of the previously somewhat amorphous ideologies of the two parties as the Colorados recruited the urban immigrant groups, especially the laborers, and the Blancos represented the more conservative rural elements. Between 1875 and 1890 three Colorado presidents administered authoritarian governments.

The first of a succession of professional military men to dominate Uruguay for some twenty years was Colonel Lorenzo Latorre, who came into power in 1875. During a period of more than three years opponents of his rule were assassinated or, in some cases, disappeared. At the same time suppression of political expression appeared to divert energies into other fields, and José Pedro Varela, influenced by educators in the United States and by Domingo Faustino Sarmiento in Argentina, brought to fruition his remarkable work in the educational field: in 1877 a public school system was established with facilities for technical, as well as general, training. The University of Montevideo, founded in 1849, was expanded and improved (see ch. 8, Education).

Growth of commerce and industry in the early 1870's was only temporary, and the year 1875, when public credit collapsed, was known as "The Terrible Year." In 1880 President Latorre resigned in the face of opposition, and his successor resigned two years later. In 1882 General Máximo Santos was elected president for four years, and in the same year Uruguay concluded a treaty with Spain acknowledging Uruguay's independence.

President Santos was succeeded in 1886 by General Máximo Tajes, who moved to the presidency from the Ministry of War. He placated some of the dissident elements among the Colorados and Blancos—something that neither Latorre nor Santos had done—and disbanded army units that he regarded as unreliable. A prominent lawyer, Julio Herrera y Obes, who succeeded President Tajes, administered the government with a firm hand and gained the distinction of being the first president of Uruguay to serve out his constitutional term without the necessity of fighting armed insurrectionists.

A civil war started by the Blancos in 1897 under the leadership of Aparicio Saravia was settled by an arrangement whereby the Blancos, who now called themselves nationalists, were granted control of six of the nineteen departments and given minority representation in the Chamber of Representatives. This was the first time in Uruguayan history that foreign mediation had not been utilized in the settlement of a major dispute (see ch. 14, Foreign Relations).

In 1899 Juan L. Cuestas, who had served as provisional president after the assassination of President Juan I. Borda, was elected constitutional president. During his term of office a French company began operations to improve the harbor of Montevideo. President Cuestas placed restrictions upon the exercise of Roman Catholicism and tried to prevent admission to the country of friars and priests (see ch. 10, Religion).

By 1900 political instability and foreign intervention had interfered with the orderly development of natural resources, had discouraged investment by Uruguayans and of foreign capital, and had hindered immigration. Between 1830 and 1900 approximately forty armed revolts had taken place. With the help of some 400,000 immigrants, however, the population had increased from about 60,000 in 1830 to more than 900,000 at the beginning of the twentieth century.

In 1900 almost 50 percent of the citizens remained illiterate, and only a small percentage of the national budget was allotted to education. During the 1880's and 1890's the armed forces in the process of keeping one regime or another in power, used from one-third to one-fifth of the budget, and the foreign debt, principally to England, had burgeoned. In 1901 some 40 percent of the budget went into service on foreign debts (see ch. 8, Education; ch. 22, Finance).

Such measures as improved seed selection, introduction of better stock, and increased attention to soils had been retarded by recurring political warfare. During the last quarter of the nineteenth century some progress had been made in the production of processed foods, clothing, shoes, and textiles, but the first packinghouse was not built until 1904 (see ch. 18, Agriculture; ch. 19, Industry; ch. 4, Population and Labor Force).

JOSÉ BATLLE Y ORDÓÑEZ AND HIS TIMES

The course of events beteen 1903 and 1929 was profoundly affected by José Batlle y Ordóñez, president from 1903 to 1907 and from 1911 to 1915. He dominated the Colorado party until his death in 1929, and his influence was still felt in 1970.

Batlle founded the newspaper *El Dia* (The Day) in 1886 and carried on a crusade for "a moral force for the regeneration of the country." He believed in a democratic form of government and in constitutional procedures and promoted measures designed to protect the country against the emergence of dictatorships. In his editorials he attacked leaders of both parties, running the risk of severe reprisals, and created a body of liberal sentiment within the Colorado party. He has been called the founder of modern Uruguay.

When Batlle was inaugurated early in 1903 the Blancos, or nationalists, controlled six departments that were virtually autonomous. Aparacio Saravia, the *gaucho* leader of the Blanco revolt in 1897, commanded the Blanco guerrilla bands in the north. In January 1904 war broke out. After almost nine months of fierce fighting the rebel leader was killed and peace was signed at Acequá in September 1904. The agreement provided for general amnesty, for recognition of the government by the rebels, and for supervision of elections by party committees. The rebels were to lay down their arms and surrender their fortified towns, and funds were to be distributed among civil and military leaders of the rebellion. These peace terms reflected President Batlle's determination to unify the country and to proceed with social and economic reforms.

In 1907 President Batlle turned the office over to his political ally Claudio Williman and sailed to Europe, where he spent four years studying governmental systems. He was particularly impressed by the government of Switzerland, with its executive responsibility vested in the Federal Council, its national monopolies of public utilities, and its social legislation.

Under President Williman a number of significant reforms were put into effect. He reorganized the cabinet. Additional executive offices were created to facilitate administration of the departments, capital punishment was abolished, an organic law for the University of Montevideo was approved, and another law set up a national institute for the deaf. The nation's revenues were handled so carefully that President Williman completed his term with an unprecedented surplus in the treasury.

Batlle y Ordóñez was elected president for the second time on March 1, 1911, sixteen days after he had returned from Europe. He immediately announced proposed economic and political measures so novel and sweeping that many members of his party were disturbed, and violent opposition was aroused among the Blancos. Nevertheless, political persecutions ceased, and freedom of the press was respected. The government initiated a study of the social welfare of its people. The secretary of finance undertook to collect statistics on living conditions and supply and demand in the labor sector. Agricultural machinery and seeds were exempted from import duties, and a luxury tax was levied on jewelry.

President Batlle had the support of the workers, who recognized him as a champion of social legislation; and as an effective foe of waste and corruption, he won the admiration of many outside of his own party. After leave the presidency in 1915 he continued his campaign for reform, urging in his editorials that Uruguay abolish the office of president and substitute a *colegiado* (national council or "collegiate executive") in which virtually all elements of public opinion would be represented. When a constitutional convention was convened in 1917 the drafters agreed on a compromise—to retain the presidency but limit its powers to administration, national defense, and foreign relations, and to establish a nine-member *colegiado* whose jurisdiction would extend to education, health, commerce, public works, industry, and finance. The budget, however, was to be a responsibility of the president. The new constitution, which replaced that of 1830, also provided for election of the president by direct popular vote and for complete separation of church and state (see ch. 10, Religion).

Other reforms advocated by Batlle y Ordóñez, many of which were adopted during his lifetime, were full freedom of speech and press, free and effective suffrage, university education for women, free primary and secondary rural schools, the eight-hour day for workers, the right to strike, regulation of working conditions, minimum wages, and old-age pensions. With a view to protecting domestic industry, he secured the adoption of high tariffs.

Not all the innovations proposed by Batlle met with great success or universal popularity. Among these projects were the State Insurance Bank, a government monopoly of the light and power business, a government-owned railway system, government management of the port of Montevideo, and a government-owned packinghouse (see ch. 19, Industry; ch. 21, Trade; ch. 22, Finance).

During World War I the Uruguayan vessel *Rosario* was sunk by a German torpedo, and the government, in October 1917, broke off diplomatic and commercial relations with Germany. In 1919 Uruguay signed the Treaty of Versailles and joined the League of Nations (see ch. 14, Foreign Relations).

After World War I the state monopoly companies enjoyed moderate success during the prosperous period of the 1920's but, like the rest of the economy, they were adversely affected by the drop in prices for meat, hides, and wool resulting from the world depression of 1929. During the 1920's presidents and councils could volley problems back and forth but, when the economic depression set in, differences between the two led to a political crisis of grave proportions. After a split between socialist and conservative elements in the Colorado party, the conservative leader Gabriel Terra was elected president.

President Terra believed the Constitution of 1919 prevented him from carrying out much-needed economic measures. Unemployment was increasing, meat exports had dropped, various autonomous state operations were on the verge of bankruptcy, and government deficits had burgeoned. In the face of these developments and the ineffectiveness of a bickering council, President Terra in 1933 dissolved the council and the congress and governed by decree (see ch. 13, Political Dynamics; ch. 16, Political Values and Attitudes).

In 1934 a new constitution, adopted after a plebiscite, abolished the council and transferred its principal powers to the president. In 1934 President Terra was reelected and governed by decree until the end of his term in 1938. He was succeeded by his brother-in-law, General Alfredo Baldomir.

By 1938 employment had risen, and the economic situation had improved. During President Baldomir's term of office the Batlle tradition was revived. President Baldomir, under pressure from organized labor and the Blanco party, reestablished the council and insisted on free elections and freedom of the press.

The Blancos persistently attempted to obstruct legislation introduced under President Baldomir and, during World War II, criticized the Colorados' policy of cooperation with the United States in hemispheric defense. They also opposed the government's severance of relations with the Axis powers in January 1942. In the face of threatened disorder President Baldomir postponed elections scheduled for February 1942 until the following November when constitutional amendments were submitted to the electorate.

The main goal of the constitutional amendments approved by the electorate in November 1942 was to keep the minority opposition from blocking action by the government. The revised constitution reflected the influence of the late Batlle y Ordóñez.

When President Baldomir's successor declared war on the Axis powers in 1945, the Blancos, who had opposed President Baldomir when he broke relations with the Axis in January 1942, were again antagonized. The country's principal concern on the international front during the 1944—55 period was the threat to Uruguay posed by the Argentinian leader Juan Domingo Perón who, like Juan Manuel de Rosas, wanted to reunite the territories of the former Viceroyalty of La Plata under Argentine leadership. When Perón penalized Uruguay for refusing to move into an Argentine sphere of influence—by instituting economic sanctions—the United States helped counteract these actions by shipping wheat and extending loans (see ch. 14, Foreign Relations).

In 1951 President Martinez Trueba advocated revival of the *colegiado*, and in a national plebiscite his proposal was adopted by a slim margin. Subsequently a new constitution, promulgated in 1952, abolished the presidency and vested executive power in a nine-man council. The late Batlle y Ordóñez's goal was thus achieved, but deadlocks often developed in council proceedings when Blanco conservatives, who held a minority position in the council, undertook to block legislation introduced by the Colorados.

After the downfall of Perón in 1955 the people of Uruguay became keenly aware of the fact that their basic problems were economic. Soaring prices stimulated strikes for ever-increasing wages. The whole economy was affected by the low price of wool, which had declined steadily after World War II. The value of the peso (see Glossary) had dropped sharply, with a crippling effect on the country's extensive social security system. The meatpacking industry suffered severely. Communist groups increased their activity and student unrest spread. In the election of November 1958 the Colorados, who had controlled the government for ninety-three years, were overwhelmingly defeated by the Blancos, who won majorities in both houses of Congress and six of the nine seats in the council.

THE BLANCOS, 1958—67

The Colorados were defeated in an election in which the Blancos leveled charges of wastefulness, padding of government payrolls with redundant employees, failure to introduce austerity measures, and corruption and inefficiency in the operation of government agencies. They also charged that the Colorados had coddled the unions which made extravagant demands, that they subsidized industries and imports which encouraged consumption habits the people could ill afford, and that they expanded the social security system so extensively that thousands of people in their fifties were able to stop working and draw pensions.

Led by eighty-five-year-old Luis Alberto de Herrera, the Blancos—traditionally the champions of the bankers, conservative landholders, businessmen, and high clergy—promised to restore the value of the peso and to stimulate livestock and agricultural production. The pledge to restore the value of the peso appealed particularly to people receiving pensions worth only a fraction of their original value. When Herrera died in April 1959, a month after the Blancos had taken office, Benito Nardone assumed party leadership and promised to carry out the Blancos' election pledges.

In 1959 inflation continued, strikes erupted, the worst floods in the country's history wiped out crops and livestock and further reduced export earnings, and the trade deficit reached an alltime high. The efforts of the government to carry out promises made during the election were, for the most part, ineffectual. After the election of 1962, in which the Blancos were victorious but with a reduced majority in Congress, the government experienced increasing difficulty in funding its social services. Efforts to prop up the peso were abandoned, and the peso was further devalued (see ch. 22, Finance).

In 1965 the government faced new financial and monetary crises. Washington Beltrán, president of the council, announced a new ten-year economic program which aroused widespread opposition.

Strikes protesting the emergency measures made it necessary to use troops to operate public services. Many union leaders and demonstrators were arrested and the council declared a state of siege.

In 1966 economic conditions showed some improvement. Wool and meat exports increased to some extent, the tourist trade increased, and foreign money once more flowed into the country's banks (see ch. 22, Finance; ch. 21, Trade).

During his term of office Washington Beltrán announced his intention to abolish the council. In the national election held in November 1966 the people, after a fifteen-year trial, voted to abandon the *colégiado* and to choose a president for a five-year term. The Colorados won a decisive victory and a retired air force general, Oscar Gestido, was inaugurated president in March 1967.

CHAPTER 4

POPULATION AND LABOR FORCE

In 1970 the population was 3 million or a little less. Males and females were almost equal in number, although women slightly outnumbered men in urban areas and males predominated in the countryside. Although only one city, Montevideo, had a population much in excess of 60,000, over 80 percent of the population was urban, for half of the people lived in Montevideo. The increasing concentration of people in the capital city had been in process since the colonial era, and in 1970 the relative growth of the urban population and relative depopulation of the countryside showed no signs of abating.

Uruguayans are primarily of European origin, Spanish and Italian predominating. Immigrants and first- and second-generation Uruguayans predominate in most of the agricultural coastal lowlands. *Criollos* (descendants of Europeans who settled in the New World during the colonial period) are in a majority on the pastoral plateau interior. In Montevideo the population is mixed.

Despite excellent health conditions that have rewarded the people with the greatest longevity in Latin America, an extremely low birth rate and extensive emigration result in a rate of population expansion so low that it is generally regarded as the country's principal population problem. The limited size of the domestic market inhibits the development of an extensive industrial establishment and of markets overseas. In addition, the rapid aging of the population as a whole, coupled with the unusually early retirement made possible by a liberal welfare system, places a progressively heavy burden on those in their productive years.

Although most of the country's wealth derives directly or indirectly from agricultural and pastoral activities, the labor force—like the population as a whole—is more than 80 percent urban, despite the fact that families on farms and ranches tend to be somewhat larger than those in cities and towns. This trend toward urbanization, unrivaled in South America except possibly in Argentina, derives from the fact that the country has not fully exploited its comparative advantage in agriculture and is the principal factor underlying its slow rate of economic growth during recent years.

The large size and continuing growth of the services sector, overburdened with a high proportion of government employees, reflect a substantial amount of underemployment. The overt unemployment, however, is also high.

Despite an excellent educational system and a high rate of school enrollment, the general preference of all levels of society for academic over vocational training limits the acquisition of vocational skills. In 1970, there was an abundance of highly trained professional people in most fields, although serious shortages continued to exist in some areas. Many professionals are believed to have emigrated, but the supply is so great that their loss is not seriously felt. In many fields, in fact, university graduates are often unable to find work in their chosen professions.

Although Uruguay has a population based largely on immigration, during most of the present century its immigration policy has been a somewhat restrictive one. This was eased to some extent in 1965, but many feel that the impediments to economic growth imposed by a scanty population, low growth rate, and extensive emigration make it imperative that the government take positive steps to encourage a selective increase in immigration in order to facilitate economic growth.

POPULATION STRUCTURE AND DYNAMICS

The national census of 1963 found 2,592,600 people to be living in the country, a figure that has been adjusted upward to 2,649,000 to compensate for underenumeration. Population growth rates are dependent on estimates, since before 1963 the country had not conducted a census since 1908. At that time there had been 1,043,000 residents.

Estimates for other years are numerous, but all indicate a rate of growth much slower than that in most Latin American countries. An official estimate of the population in 1950 was 2,193,000. A research organization estimate of 2,868,000, made in 1968, forecast 3,777,000 by 1983. These estimates are fairly consistent with those of the Inter-American Development Bank, which in 1969 estimated a current population of 2,852,000 and projected a figure of 3,251,000 for 1980.

The average annual rate of population growth during the 1960's is most frequently estimated to be 1.3 percent. The highest rate, reported for the year 1969, is 1.4 percent. In general, however, observers accept 1.3 percent as an average for the decade. The International Planned Parenthood Federation (IPPF) estimated a percentage of 1.2 for 1969, the lowest according to its calculations for any country in the Western Hemisphere.

An authoritative series of estimates indicated a decline in the average rate of population increase from 1.55 percent for the years 1950—55 to 1.46 for 1955—60 and 1.41 for 1960—65. The same series showed a percentage of 1.25 in 1966 and in 1967 before a slight rise to 1.26 in 1968.

Uruguay was secularized early in the present century, and the traditional pontifical ban on birth control has been frequently ignored (see ch. 10, Religion). The association for Family Planning and Research on Reproduction, founded in 1962 and associated with the IPPF, is a major Uruguayan family planning organization to which the government has made available equipment and facilities in public hospitals and public health centers. In 1969 it operated nine clinics that provided sex education, treatment for sterility, family planning services, and treatment of genital diseases. The campaign has been concentrated in the lower income residential areas of Montevideo. In 1969 the association, which has received external assistance from the Church World Service and other international sources, organized the first Latin American training course on sex education and family planning. It was attended by forty-one representatives from twenty countries.

Uruguayans live longer than any other people on the continent. They also produce fewer children per capita. Although most countries need to stem the growth of their populations, many Uruguayans hope that an increase of the birth rate can be achieved through an extension of their already extensive welfare system to include family subsidies as its central feature.

The birth rate in 1963 was reported at 24 per 1,000 population, and the total death rate was 9 per 1,000. The birth rate was among the lowest in the world, but the death rate was correspondingly low. Rural birth and death rates were both slightly higher than urban. Statistics are lacking with respect to this phenomenon, but the underlying cause is clear: rural families were larger, but it was the young people—girls in particular—who found themselves redundant on the farms and moved to the town and cities.

Infant deaths under the age of one year were at the outstandingly low rate of 43 per 1,000 in 1966. The subtraction of the number of deaths from the number of births would indicate a population increase for the year of 1.3 percent. Since this is only slightly above the generally estimated growth for 1968, it would appear that there was virtually no net loss of population through emigration. A United Nations estimate, however, indicates that 1966 reports of death were virtually complete but that between 12 and 17 percent of the births went unrecorded. The clear implication is that the number of unreported births is sufficient to reflect a considerable net population exodus during recent years.

Data from various sources on life expectancy at birth are not entirely consistent, but the variations are small. The Social Progress Trust Fund of the Inter-American Development Bank reported an average expectancy of 69.2 years for the period 1965—70, with women outliving men by an average of three years. More detailed United Nations figures reported for the early 1960's indicate an even longer lifespan. The average longevity was listed at seventy-one years, with sixty-eight years for men and seventy-three for women.

The 1963 census showed nearly equal numbers of males and females, as did a projection for 1970 made in 1968 (see table 1). In 1963, 49.8 percent were male and 50.2 percent were female. Projections calculated for 1965, 1970, and 1980 indicated little anticipated change in this proportion, the 1980 projection showing the female majority rising to about 51 percent. The 1963 census figures, however, revealed that males predominated in the country and females in the towns. Only 43 percent of the rural population in 1963 was female. Although comparative figures are not available, in 1970 this figure had probably dropped still lower. This relatively faster urbanization of females is a worldwide phenomenon that is particularly conspicuous in Latin America. Girls are less useful in the fields than boys and, with the mechanization of agricultural and pastoral activities, the young females are the first to become surplus. Conversely, with the relative increase in the education of women and the increase of urban clerical and other service jobs, female job opportunities in cities and towns register relative increases.

By Latin American standards the population is extraordinarily mature in years. It was estimated in 1968 that a little more than 36 percent of the population was under the age of twenty. In fast-growing Latin America, a population half of which is under twenty is not uncommon. The aging of the population—a combined consequence of a low and decreasing birth rate, greater longevity, and an increasing rate of emigration—is expected to continue. It appears to be a trend that commenced about 1960. An international economic consulting organization reported in 1969 that 26.2 percent of the working force in 1950 had been under the age of fifteen and that, while the percentage had risen to 27.9 in 1963, it was expected to decline to 24.3 in 1975. For the group fifteen to sixty-four years of age the corresponding percentages for 1950, 1963, and 1975, respectively, were 65.9, 64.2, and 64.7. The proportion of the working force aged sixty-five and over was unchanged at 7.9 percent between 1950 and 1963 but was expected to rise sharply to 11.0 by 1975.

The increasing average age of the economically active Uruguayan has had a remarkable side effect. Although the size of its labor force in relation to the population as a whole is among the highest in the Western Hemisphere, sources of the nation's livelihood are increasingly concentrated in fewer and fewer hands. The availability of

*Table 1. Age-Sex Distribution of Uruguayan Population for 1970**
(in thousands)

Age	Male	Female	Total
0—4	145	139	284
5—9	139	134	273
10—14	131	127	258
15—19	119	117	236
20—24	108	108	216
25—29	101	101	202
30—34	97	99	196
35—39	100	101	201
40—44	99	99	198
45—49	87	88	175
50—54	76	78	154
55—59	69	69	138
60—64	58	58	116
65—69	46	48	94
70 and over	63	82	145
Total	1,438	1,448	2,886

*As projected in 1968.

Source: Adapted from Centro Latino de Americano Demográfica, *Boletín Demográfico*, I, No. 1, January 1968, p. 6.

early retirement for the older age group that is enjoying increasing longevity, the increasing availability of education for young people, and a decreasing birth rate are compelling mature people in their productive years to support increasing proportions of both the young and the old.

The fact that in 1963 there were a few more males than females at birth, in early childhood, and through adolescence is characteristic of the worldwide biological process. It is similarly characteristic that nearly 57 percent of the people over the age of seventy were women. Between the ages of twenty and seventy, however, the numbers of males and females remained virtually equal. This phenomenon is related to the fact that during recent years emigration appears to have been substantially greater than immigration, but the country's excellent system of medical care, the absence of wars, and the lack of civil disorder severe enough to lead to the death of a statistically significant number of men have undoubtedly been contributing factors. Another feature of the age-sex statistical data is the failure of the proportion of female deaths to show any relative increase during the main childbearing years. This is directly attributable to the country's generally good diet, satisfactory sanitary conditions, and fine medical care (see ch. 7, Living Conditions).

MIGRATORY MOVEMENTS

Immigration

During most of the colonial era the country was a sparsely populated outpost of the Spanish viceroyalty that was to become Argentina. As late as 1830 it had a predominantly rural and masculine population consisting principally of landowners and their *gauchos* (see Glossary) and numbering no more than 60,000. By the end of the century immigration had increased the number to about 915,000, and a large middle class, primarily urban and located in or near Montevideo, had developed. Most were from Europe, but a substantial number came from Argentina and Brazil (see ch. 5, Ethnic Groups and Languages).

During the nineteenth century a variety of inducements to immigration was offered, but after about 1850 many of the newcomers moved on to Argentina, where soils were richer and land was more readily available. Between 1879 and 1903 there was an average net annual immigration of about 4,000. At the turn of the century, however, civil strife abated and immigration increased. Between 1880 and 1935 the net annual gain from newcomers ranged from 3,000 to 20,000; from 1900 to 1930 the average was about 15,000.

The last of the laws encouraging immigration was enacted in 1890, and the first of the actions to control the flow was taken in 1911 under President José Batlle y Ordóñez. As of 1970 there had been no significant change in the immigration policy, and the general rule was to give preference to skilled persons. This preference became intensified after the onset in 1929 of the worldwide depression when, in 1932, immigrants were largely limited to farmers and skilled workers entering with employment contracts and to certain persons with special qualifications. Immigration data covering the years of World War II are incomplete, although the movement appears to have turned downward after 1938. Again on the basis of incomplete data, between 1948 and 1955 there appear to have been about 50,000 new arrivals, the number rising irregularly from 3,900 in 1948 to a peak of nearly 9,400 in 1955.

Of the 50,000 arriving between 1948 and 1955, some 16,000 were minors or persons without specific occupations (not including the wives of working men). Of the 16,000 listed as economically active, almost 50 percent reported agriculture as their occupation, but only a small minority could report themselves as trained agronomists. The high percentage listed as occupied in agriculture may be explained by the fact that it has been traditional practice for prospective urban merchants emigrating to Latin America to list themselves as farmers in order to facilitate their entry.

During recent years a large proportion of the newcomers has entered under sponsorship of the International Committee for

European Migration (ICEM), originally a cooperative organization for resettlement of stateless people and refugees. Between 1952 and 1966 ICEM resettled more than 13,000 immigrants in Uruguay. After the mid-1950's, however, the flow abated with the remarkable European economic recovery. During the late 1950's and early 1960's one source estimated the number at about 6,000 annually. An isolated figure for 1959, however, listed a total of 2,189.

Immigrants have tended to congregate in Montevideo, and the children of those who have settled in rural areas are far more likely to move to the capital city or other urban centers than the children of *criollos*. There is also a considerable immigrant and second-generation concentration in the cities and towns along the eastern bank of the Río Uruguay. The rural immigrant and second-generation population tends to concentrate in the agricultural lowlands, leaving the pastoral interior plateau to the *criollos*.

Emigration

It was hoped that Uruguay might benefit substantially from a selective immigration program sponsored by the government and ICEM in the early 1960's. By the late 1960's, however, there was increasing demand for more positive action by Uruguay itself. Extensive emigration of longtime foreign residents, as well as natives, had occurred. Specific data available are fragmentary and imprecise. In 1969 a spokesman for the University of the Republic stated that the university itself had no means of counting the exodus of its former students and that even the Ministry of Foreign Relations was unable to report on the number of emigrants since so many people were leaving the country with tourist visas in their passports, never to return. In addition, there is no satisfactory statistical system for adding to the population those citizens who have returned for permanent residence after having emigrated.

The statistical count of emigration is further complicated by indications that an undetermined, but allegedly large, portion is clandestine. One newspaper in 1968 estimated that nearly 500,000 Uruguayans were living in Buenos Aires alone and that an even larger number lived in southern Brazil. It added that 8,000 Uruguayans had gathered for August 25 festivities in New York City and that the Uruguayan diaspora might amount to as many as 2 million.

The same newspaper noted that only guesses were possible because, in particular, those emigrating to Buenos Aires were accustomed to simply "cross the river" without the benefit of a passport. In some unexplained manner they then established their Argentine resident status and gradually transferred their families and possessions. It concluded by asserting that this movement had been initiated by skilled workers but that these had later been followed by the unskilled.

An impartial commercially sponsored opinion poll in 1968 concluded that emigrants substantially outnumbered immigrants and that the typical emigré was a young unmarried male from the upper strata of society. This description, however, was probably also applicable to the typical immigrant. Anticipation of better work opportunities abroad was the most frequently cited incentive for emigration.

A majority of those polled stated that they were satisfied with life in Uruguay, but nearly one-third expressed some degree of interest in emigrating, and approximately the same proportion of parents queried saw no objection to the emigration of their children. The same poll showed the principal countries of destination in order of preference to be the United States, Argentina, West Germany, Spain, Brazil and Venezuela, Canada, Italy, and France. This poll was based on only a limited sampling. Another newspaper survey reported that emigrés preferred Argentina to the United States because of the absence of a language problem and because of the diminished danger of the shock attached to cultural change.

The University of the Republic has complained of a serious loss of teachers and researchers, but the information available in 1970 did not support the contention that the exodus had constituted a "brain drain" at the professional level. In the late 1960's only a fraction of the lawyers were practicing law, doctors were competing for patients, and there were virtually no openings for young graduating architects. There was a serious shortage of agronomists, veterinary surgeons, and some kinds of engineers. There was no evidence, however, of excessive emigration of professionals in these categories (see ch. 8, Education).

The International Bank for Reconstruction and Development, (also known as the World Bank) in 1968 noted that 14,000 skilled and professional people were being added to the labor force annually, and it was estimated that several thousand were emigrating. It appears, however, that skilled workers below the professional level were the ones who represented the real loss to the economy. Professionals were probably leaving the country because of an inability to find adequate employment at home. Moreover, the indications that the bulk of those leaving the country were going to nearby parts of Argentina and Brazil suggest that a high proportion of the emigrant wave was made up of working-class people.

In 1970 a number of professional and skilled people were going abroad, but they did not leave serious vacancies behind them. A United Nations study covering the years 1962—66 on the number of Uruguayan immigrants admitted to the United States and Canada did not include complete statistics for the United States. The breakdown of the 258 admitted to Canada, however, suggested a kind of pattern. Of those admitted, 102 had occupations. There was 1 engineer (a figure for the United States was available in this category; there were 25), 3 natural scientists (3 also to the United States), 2 physicians (13 to the United States), and 1 professional nurse (13 to the United States). During the period 1 social scientist was admitted as an immigrant to the United States and none to Canada.

Internal Migration

Probably the most significant of the migratory movements affecting Uruguay has been within the country itself—its internal migration. It has not been the progressive urbanization that has affected all Latin American states during the twentieth century but, rather, a concentration of population in one urban area. Since colonial times the capital has been the chief urban center, but its 30 percent of the population at the time of the census of 1908 increased to 45 percent as registered in the census of 1963 and to an estimated figure of at least 50 percent in 1970.

In 1970 there were no real cities except Montevideo. Paysandú and Salto on the Río Uruguay were the next urban centers in size, each with not much more than 60,000 in population. Some of the more important departmental capitals, such as Fray Bentos, Colonia, and Durazno, had populations in the 15,000 to 20,000 range. Most of the remainder of the population was clustered in small crossroads or riverbank towns (see ch. 2, Physical Environment).

Young rural people tend to go first to a nearby town, where employment opportunities are found to be inadequate. They go next to the departmental capital, where there may be a corresponding lack of employment opportunity. Sometimes this migration takes several generations. Eventually, however, it reaches its goal in Montevideo. It has been estimated that in the 1960's this out-migration from the farms to the towns averaged about 11,000 persons each year. They came primarily from the livestock-producing area, particularly from the sheep country north of the Río Negro.

In particular, rural girls tend to leave home at an early age. An agricultural and stockraising census conducted during 1966 found that more than 6,000 of some 177,000 females under the age of fourteen were not living in a family group. This was more than twice the rate for males in the same age group.

There are many reasons for the progressive movement away from the farms and ranches. In most rural localities the nearest school offers only four years of primary schooling. In almost none are there any secondary schools. Employment opportunities are limited, and health conditions and the amenities of life compare unfavorably with those in other parts of the country. In addition, there is not much chance for the landless farmers to get land. In 1970 there were many large estates, and tax policies had not yet provided a compelling disincentive to the continued holding of large tracts of underutilized land. It was primarily this circumstance that prompted the several protest marches to Montevideo during the 1960's of the sugar workers from Artigas Department.

A study of the prospects for Uruguay written in 1945 noted, perhaps prophetically, that so long as the national life remained concentrated in the capital city, that city would function as a magnet, with what might be a frequent disrupting effect on the balance of the economy as a whole. Although Montevideo is by no means the largest city in South America, in relation to the size of the country for which it serves as the capital, it can best be defined among the cities of Latin America as a megalopolis.

Montevideo exercises a unique attraction for migrants from the interior. Montevideo is where the banks and the money are. It is the only important port, the chief commercial center, and the industrial capital. During recent years relatively more new industries and more new industrial employment opportunities have appeared in the capital city than anywhere else in the country. Though data are incomplete, business costs may have risen more sharply in the countryside than in the town. For example, in terms of comparison with the meat prices that the rancher could demand, the cost of forty- to forty-five-horsepower tractors increased by approximately 50 percent between 1960 and 1966. Similarly, one statistical series shows the price to farmers and ranchers of wheat dropping in real value by 37 percent and that of milk by 29 percent between 1960 and 1968 (see ch. 18, Agriculture).

There are other reasons for migrating from the countryside or from the crossroads village. Montevideo has an average standard of living higher than that elsewhere in the country, although village and rural workers tend to overestimate the extent of this difference and are often unaware of the greater hazard of unemployment. Cultural elements play their part. In rural areas primary schools usually do not offer the full primary schedule customary in urban institutions, and secondary and vocation schools are close to nonexistent. It is only in Montevideo that it is possible to obtain a university degree (see ch. 8, Education). Social stratification in rural localities makes it extremely difficult for the worker to rise above the level into which he was born. Upward mobility is much easier in the capital city, where the extensive social legislation is best enforced, with a consequent leveling effect on society.

Probably an important reason for the low level of internal migration from one rural area to another is the virtual absence of homesteading opportunity. As early as 1961 an agricultural census found only 1.4 percent of the land to be in the public domain. The National Land Settlement Institute (Instituto Nacional de Colonización), was formed in 1948 and has been assigned to promote equitable land distribution and exploitation. The absence of public lands, however, has hindered its ability to move people, and during the years 1962 through 1969 it was able to relocate only about 850 families.

A remaining form of internal migration is seasonal. One group in this category is composed of sugar-field workers employed during the cutting season. The center of the sugarcane industry is in Artigas Department. The cutters work in beet sugar fields along the Río Uruguay, however, and cross the borders with Argentina and Brazil regulary to join cane cutters from those countries. When the cane-cutting season ends, they often remain to seek employment in the rice fields. Whole families move with their few belongings; women work with their men in the fields, and children help with the loading. In this mixed sector of society, a kind of Portuguese appears to be the lingua franca.

The sugar workers begin work during the sugarcane harvest season (*zafra*) of four months duration around the urban center of Bella Unión in the northwestern corner of Artigas Department. From there, they move southward along the course of the Río Uruguay to the department of Paysandú for sugar beets. Later they fan out over the country to gather potatoes, citrus fruits, grapes, or other harvest items. In March some move northward across the Brazilian border to gather rice.

POPULATION PROBLEMS

In 1968 an independent Montevideo newspaper set forth briefly a listing of the country's major demographic problems. Among these it mentioned a sparse population with a low and declining birth rate, sagging immigration, and a wave of emigration of young people since World War II. It also observed that in this highly urbanized country there were too few people to provide a market large enough to support a healthy and diversified industrial establishment. The highest longevity rate in Latin America, coupled with the early retirement made possible by the generous public welfare system and the increasing proportion of young people remaining longer in the educational system, leave relatively few adults in the productive age brackets to support the remainder of the population.

STRUCTURE AND DYNAMICS OF THE LABOR FORCE

Age and Sex Composition

A sampling from the 1963 population census resulted in the conclusion that the economically active population included about

39.2 percent of the total. Some 58.9 percent of the males and 19.6 percent of the females were either employed or seeking employment (see table 2). Because there has never been a comprehensive labor force census and the 1963 population census was the first since 1908, data showing age and sex dynamics of the labor force are not available.

The percentage of Uruguay's population included in its labor force in 1963 was fifth highest among the twenty-two independent nations of the Western Hemisphere. Some qualifying statements, however, are in order. During the late 1960's the labor force included a minimum of 12 percent unemployed and a considerable number of underemployed. It also included many government employees with work weeks of thirty hours or less and seasonal and migratory workers employed during half a year or less. Overall, the reported employment rate represented an increase from an estimated 34 percent in 1940.

The country's low birth rate, high rate of retention of young people in schools, and provision for early retirement combined to maximize the proportion of the labor force in the middle years of life. In 1963 nearly half (448,220 out of a total of 1,015,500) were between the ages of thirty and forty-nine. Employment of juveniles and adolescents was at about the average for Latin America. It should be noted, however, that some secondary school and most university students held part-time jobs while continuing their educations. Early retirement is reflected in the 1963 figures by the drop from the 54.6 percent of those fifty to fifty-four years old who were in the labor force to the 30.3 percent of those sixty to sixty-four, in a country with an average longevity of about seventy-one years.

Table 2. Composition of Economically Active Uruguayan Population, by Sex and Age Group, 1963
(in percent)

Age	Male	Female	Total
Under 15	3.5	1.5	2.6
15—19	69.2	29.7	49.3
20—24	93.4	40.2	66.9
25—29	96.8	37.2	66.3
30—49	96.6	30.8	63.4
50—54	86.9	20.4	54.6
55—59	72.8	16.5	45.8
60—64	52.3	9.0	30.3
65 and over	22.5	3.5	12.1
Unknown	77.2	32.4	49.7
All Ages	58.9	19.6	39.2

Source: Adapted from *Yearbook of Labour Statistics, 1969*, Geneva, n.d., p. 23.

The highest rate of employment of women in 1963 was for those between the ages of twenty and twenty-four, but it remained high for those between twenty-five and twenty-nine years. Since women most commonly abandon their jobs because of marriage and the bearing of children, these figures suggest that Uruguayan women do not marry young, a conclusion consistent with the fact that most of them are well-educated urban dwellers. In most societies, it is young women in this category who are most likely to continue working and to defer marriage until they reach full maturity.

Because the comparative data from the 1961 and 1966 agricultural censuses are relatively recent, they are useful, although they represent samplings of an economic sector constituting less than 18 percent of the total labor force. Between the two recent agricultural census counts, employment on farms and ranches of more than about 2.5 acres (1 hectare) declined about 9.1 percent. The 146,147 males employed in 1966 were 91.4 percent of the number who had been working in 1961. The 45,417 females were 89.3 percent. Both men and women were migrating from country to town, but it was the women who were moving faster.

Composition by Economic Sector and Occupational Category

The most recently available firm data on composition of the labor force by economic sector, based on a 5-percent sample of the 1963 population census, as analyzed by the International Labor Office, give a total of 957,100 (see table 3). Data by sex for economic sectors were not available. By type of employment, however, females made up 22.3 percent of the employers and self-employed, 25.7 percent of the salaried employees and wage earners, and 13.9 percent of the family workers. This count shows 235,800 females, or nearly 25 percent of the total, as members of the 1963 labor force.

These figures, the most complete ones available with respect to employment by economic sector, are deficient in the sense that they do not include those individuals seeking employment for the first time and members of the armed forces. Such persons are included in other International Labor Office data based also on the 1963 census, which report a 1963 working force of 1,015,500 (see table 4).

A characteristic of the economically active population in 1963 was the small size, relatively the smallest in South America, of the unpaid-family-worker category, a reflection of the high degree of urbanization of the country. Since rural boys are permitted to work in the fields at the age of twelve and Latin American child labor is primarily a rural and male phenomenon, most of this relatively small group were probably teenage boys.

Because there was no census between 1908 and 1963, there is a

Table 3. Employment in Uruguay, by Economic Sector and Type, 1963

Economic sector	Employers and self-employed	Salaried employees and wage earners	Family workers
Agriculture, forestry, hunting, and fishing	69,100	97,500	13,500
Mining and quarrying	400	1,700	.....
Manufacturing	52,100	156,400	900
Construction	9,500	39,100	100
Electricity, gas, water, and sanitary services	200	17,300	.....
Commerce	45,500	83,900	1,500
Transport, storage, and communication	10,800	50,300	.....
Services	40,700	233,600	400
Activities not adequately described	6,100	25,400	900
Total	234,400	705,200	17,300

Source: Adapted from *Yearbook of Labour Statistics, 1969,* Geneva, n.d., p. 86.

shortage of material on the extent of the growth of the labor force. One series of statistical estimates, expressed in percentages for the years 1955, 1961, and 1965, reported those engaged in agricultural, pastoral, and related pursuits in the three years to have been 26.5, 22.4, and 18.8 percent of the total respectively, with the pastoral representing an average of three-fifths of employment in the sector. Industry employed 20.4, 22.7, and 23.1 percent, respectively. Construction accounted for 5.0, 4.2, and 3.7 percent. Trade, service, and the unemployed included the remaining 48.0, 50.9, and 54.3 percent of the labor force. These data are estimates only and inconsistent in minor detail with some other figures quoted.

Occupational Skills

The quality of occupational skills appears to bear a direct relation to the degree of education achieved by the personnel in the economic sector involved. Output in terms of the per capita portion of the gross domestic output at current factor costs by economic sector was lowest in agriculture and highest in services. There were a great many of the poorest people engaged in the services sector, but it was also in the services sector that most of the highest incomes were found.

In 1969 it was estimated that rural productivity averaged about 20 percent below that of the economy as a whole, although productivity on large pastoral operations was reported high in relation to that on farms and ranches below about 125 acres (50 hectares) in

Table 4. Distribution of Uruguayan Labor Force by Occupation, 1963

Occupation	Male	Female	Total	Percent
Professional, technical, and related	25,400	35,100	60,500	5.9
Administrative, executive, and managerial	13,400	1,100	14,500	1.4
Clerical	90,300	33,600	123,900	12.2
Sales	77,900	20,100	98,000	9.7
Farmers, fishermen, hunters, loggers, and related	174,900	3,500	178,400	17.6
Miners, quarrymen, and related	1,800	....	1,800	0.2
Workers in transport and communication occupations	35,200	200	35,400	3.5
Craftsmen, prod.-process workers, and laborers not elsewhere classified	226,200	52,800	279,000	27.5
Service, sport, and recreation	50,400	86,900	137,300	13.5
Workers not classifiable by occupation	39,100	14,800	53,900	5.3
Members of the armed forces	12,700	100	12,800	1.3
Persons seeking work for the first time	13,300	6,700	20,000	1.9
Total	760,600	254,900	1,015,500	100.0

Source: Adapted from *Yearbook of Labour Statistics, 1969,* Geneva, n.d., pp. 192—193.

size. Skills are relatively the lowest in the sheep country north of the Río Negro where the population is sparse and there is relatively the highest concentration of Negro and Indian mixtures. This is the least developed part of the country and, because the population is so scattered, schools are few and education relatively limited. Children twelve to fifteen years of age, too young to have acquired significant skills, are more likely to be employed in the fields than in the schoolroom.

South of the Río Negro, in the cattle country, there is a heavy concentration of descendants of the earlier settlers. In this area, and along the bank of the Río Uruguay, a greater frequency of towns and the greater density of the rural population permit a readier access to schools and acquisition of skills. This is true to a still greater degree in the agricultural lowlands, where second- and third-generation descendants of immigrants are found.

Productivity and the level of skills are relatively low in the industrial sector of Montevideo and the few other localities that support industrial establishments. Most of the plants in the 1960's were reported to be using outmoded equipment and layouts, and the pronounced preference of primary school graduates for academic rather than technical or vocational secondary educations made employers place considerable reliance on on-the-job training. In addition, the dropout rate was significantly higher in technical and vocational than in agricultural schools (see ch. 8, Education).

The proportion of workers in the services sector was much too high for the welfare of the economy, but the level of skills was also high. Office workers were well trained. Physicians, lawyers, bankers, and economists were highly competent. Because of the excessive number of public servants, their productivity was low, but their level of capability was generally high. In the 1960's the chief dilemma of the country's economy was that the level of skills among manual workers was relatively low but that at the same time the number of skilled white-collar and professional people exceeded the ability of the economy to absorb them. As early as 1961 it had been remarked that the college-graduate market was supersaturated.

Unemployment

There appears to have been a sharp rise in unemployment in the early 1960's. No official figures were available, but in 1961 an estimated 8.6 percent were unemployed, and this percentage was reported to have increased to 12.3 in 1963. Organized labor claimed that the 1963 figure, derived from a sampling of the 1963 population census, was much too low with respect to the industrial sector.

The actual number of people out of work is largely a guessing game. One 1963 evaluation from a private source reported the total at anywhere from 12.5 percent to 25 percent of the labor force. In 1964 a United States agency suggested a range of from 12 to 20 percent. During the mid-1960's the figure of 12 percent was most frequently quoted for the nation as a whole. That figure did not, however, include the redundant public employment, which an austerity government was attempting to reduce. The partial price-wage freeze instituted by the government in 1968, coupled with its efforts to reduce the number of public employees, in 1970 had presumably increased the proportion of the labor force drawing unemployment compensation. The unemployment rate was believed to be much lower in the countryside, where rates as low as 4 percent were mentioned. In that sector, however, underemployment was prevalent, and the unemployed frequently left for the cities and towns, with the effect of easing the lack of work opportunity in the countryside and worsening it in the more heavily populated areas.

With the institution of the austerity program that followed the abandonment of the *colegiado* (collegiate executive—see Glossary) in 1967, unemployment apparently moved sharply upward. In late 1968 it was reported that 31.4 percent of the textile workers were unemployed and that this level was being approached in other industrial sectors.

The government, however, was acutely aware of its unemployment problem and attempted to deal with it in a variety of ways.

There was a liberal unemployment compensation program, and provisions for early retirement were in part designed to make jobs available for younger workers (see ch. 7, Living Conditions; ch. 20, Labor Relations and Organization). Many white- and blue-collar workers, particularly government servants, had short workweeks. This was presumably with the intent of making more jobs available, but the intent was frustrated to the extent that many people with relatively few work hours held second, and even third, jobs. Since 1967, however the government had instituted a variety of measures to reduce redundant public employment, both in the civil service and in unprofitable government-operated business enterprises (see ch. 13, Political Dynamics).

The construction industry was in a virtual stagnation and its personnel were out of work from the mid-1960's to late in the 1960's when a substantial public housing program was initiated. On farms where the head of the family was the owner or operator of the property, outright unemployment was as low as 4 percent. There was, however, considerable labor redundance in the sense that four members of a family might till fields that could be worked as effectively by two. Landless farmworkers who made up at least half of all farmworkers may work only half of the year, and it is estimated that some 4 percent of the migrant hands are surplus even in the busy months of March, April, and May. In the eyes of this group, the solution of their problem is acquisition of land. It has become a *cause célèbre*. This has been particularly evident in the case of the sugar workers of Artigas Department who have three times, most recently in 1968, engaged in protest marches to Montevideo demanding distribution to them of about 74,000 acres (30,000 hectares) of sugar land that they claim to be lying idle (see ch. 20, Labor Relations and Organization).

In 1970 it was impossible to find an exact unemployment figure. Outright unemployment in rural areas probably was only about 4 percent, but this included employment through parts of the year so brief as to encourage a flight to Montevideo. One analyst speculated that the wave of strikes in 1968 was motivated principally by fear of income loss through inflation, whereas the strikes of 1969 tended to reflect a fear of higher unemployment.

Overall, in the late 1960's, 12 percent had become a kind of universally accepted figure for Uruguayans out of work. It was a speculative figure, however, because of the incompleteness of census data and because so many people, agricultural and construction workers for the most part, worked only a few months during the year. Uruguay is one of the few countries of the world for which the 1969 *Yearbook of Labor Statistics*, issued by the International Labor Office, was unable to furnish data.

It has been argued that the early retirement encouraged by the country's advanced welfare legislation reduces unemployment by making more employment available to young people. This philosophy has considerable acceptance within the country but seems vulnerable to the opposite position that jobs create jobs in a kind of multiplier process.

The progressive mechanization of agricultural processes on the larger commercial farms and the slow growth of the urban industrial sector of the economy have contributed to the growth of unemployment. Young unemployed people leaving the land have found no job offerings in urban areas. The trouble, during postwar years, is that the industrial sector has not been growing at a rate sufficient to absorb the influx of workers from the countryside made surplus by mechanization and other improvements in agricultural and pastoral productive practices.

Advanced labor legislation, including such incentives as minimum industrial wages and guarantees of early retirement on substantial pensions, and a high level of employment in the public sector, coupled with a generous unemployment compensation program, have been palliatives inherited from the Batlle political regime. Unemployment compensation is available to all able-bodied persons over the age of fifteen who have lived two or more years in the country and who participate in the state pension fund for industry and commerce. They are not eligible, however, if the unemployment is the consequence of strikes, misdemeanors, voluntary separation from employment, or certain other causes.

Compensation is limited to 180 days in the calendar year, but the pension fund board may extend the limit by a further 60 days if the conditions of a particular occupation require it. The program is funded from state pension fund contributions.

CHAPTER 5

ETHNIC GROUPS AND LANGUAGES

In 1970 the population was almost entirely of European descent. It could be divided roughly into two groups: the *criollos*, or descendants of the Europeans who settled in the New World during the colonial period, and the immigrants of the nineteenth and twentieth centuries. The former group was generally found in the northern interior; the latter, in Montevideo and the southern agricultural lowlands. In 1970, however, many rural landowners of *criollo* origin had taken up residence in the city, and there was some migration of the *criollo* ranch workers to the capital city.

The earliest white inhabitants of the country came from Argentina and Paraguay in the seventeenth and eighteenth centuries. They thus established the dominance of Spanish language and culture in the colony. They were attracted by the rich herds of cattle and horses that had proliferated on the rolling Uruguayan grasslands since their introduction early in the seventeenth century. At first the main attraction was the hides, which could be easily obtained; later, meat and wool became important both for domestic consumption and for export. The country was gradually divided into large cattle and sheep ranches, called *estancias* (see Glossary), owned and operated by the *criollos*. The *gaucho*, or cowboy, who roamed free across the plains or worked as a ranch hand, always inseparable from his horse, is typical of this period. In 1970 the *criollo* population was still primarily engaged in cattle and sheep ranching.

During the nineteenth and early twentieth centuries, immigrants arrived, primarily from Europe. Most took up residence in the cities, Montevideo in particular, or in the surrounding agricultural areas, where they entered commerce, industry, government, and farming. Spain and Italy contributed the largest number; smaller groups came from France, England, Germany, Eastern Europe, and Russia. In 1970 the immigrants and their descendants formed the backbone of the urban middle class, which dominated social and cultural life. The high value placed on education, social mobility, and trade unionism in the country is largely the result of the immigrants' influence.

The *criollo* and immigrant groups are racially and linguistically almost identical but differ in outlook, traditions, historical origins, and means of livelihood. In 1970 the urbanized immigrant element dominated national culture, although the rural landowning *criollos* exerted a strong conservative influence on the government.

Most immigrants assimilate quickly into the predominantly immigrant society of the coast, particularly those who already possess a Latin culture and language and are of the Roman Catholic religion, such as the Spaniards and Italians. A few ethnic communities exist in the cities, but they are not major factors in the structure of society or in political life. There are few foreign-language newspapers, and the tendency is for all immigrant groups to learn Spanish rapidly. There is no official government policy encouraging assimilation, but the generally tolerant attitude of the citizens eases the adjustment.

The small Indian population of nomadic hunters and subsistence farmers inhabiting the country when the Spaniards arrived led a simple, family-oriented way of life. By the mid-nineteenth century, as a result of wars and intermarriage with the growing white population, the last of the pureblooded Indians had vanished. A *mestizo* (person of mixed European and American Indian ancestry) group can still be found in the northern departments, but it represents only a small percentage of the nation's inhabitants. There is an even smaller number of Negroes and mulattoes, predominantly in the northern section. These are remnants of an active slave-trading era. Neither group forms a distinct ethnic community (see ch. 3, Historical Setting).

Spanish is the official and almost universally spoken language. The dialect in common use is the *porteño*, (people of the port) type found in Buenos Aires. Italian has been the major foreign influence on the language, changing pronunciation and introducing new vocabulary. French and English have added many loanwords, particularly in the realms of food, sports, modern technology, and commerce. There are many bilingual Portuguese-Spanish speakers in the border provinces of the north, and some Portuguese influence is discernible in the speech of most northern residents. The elite tend to learn English as their second language.

THE WHITE POPULATION

Criollos

In 1970 the country's population was over 90 percent white. The ethnic composition was largely the product of the influx of European immigrants throughout the nineteenth and early twentieth centuries. A smaller number of whites were the descendants of Spaniards who settled in the interior during the colonial period. The term *criollo* was historically used to refer to those born in the New World of Spanish parents, but it has been broadened to refer to anything traditionally Uruguayan, in contrast to things European or modern.

Spanish settlers were first attracted to Uruguay from the Argentine provinces of Entre Ríos and Santa Fé and from Paraguay in the mid-seventeenth century by the herds of cattle and horses descended from the stock introduced into the country at the beginning of the seventeenth century.Their primary interest was hides. Dealers in hides began to set up trading posts and, by the end of the century, the business was flourishing (see ch. 3, Historical Setting).

One of the most colorful figures of the colonial period was the *gaucho*. He lived a completely free and independent life, subsisting almost entirely from the cattle that were available to anyone who could slaughter them. His diet was almost exclusively meat, preferably roasted on a spit; his house was a tent of oxhides stretched across sticks, his chairs were horse and cattle skulls, and his clothes were generally patched with leather when cloth was unavailable or too expensive. Boots were sometimes made by pulling the unbroken hide of horses' legs over the feet while they were still warm, molding them to fit. The character of the cowboy has been idealized; he is described as grim, taciturn, shadowy, violent, and unfettered. Many cowboys had a somewhat Indian appearance. Since the early hunters and traders almost never brought women with them, mingling with the Indian women was commonplace. Thus, the ancestors of the cowboys include the warlike Charrúas and the powerful Guaraní.

North of the Río Negro many cowboys became outlaws, working singly or in groups to smuggle cattle and horses across the border to Brazil. Burglary was another popular activity; ranchhouses of this period were built to be defended like fortresses. South of the Río Negro, however, a more stable laboring population began to emerge. People worked on the ranches as cowhands and in the meat-cutting establishments. During the eighteenth century the land was gradually carved up into *estancias*. By the 1880's a method of refrigerating and shipping meat had been developed, adding greatly to the profitability of sheep and cattle ranching.

Barbed wire was invented at about the same time, enabling the fencing of the open pastures. The loss of the open prairies heralded the end of the cowboy way of life. Although there are no longer cowboys in the old form, they have been idealized, appearing often in literature, art, statuary, and entertainment. The Semana Criolla, or Week of the Creole, is devoted to the reenactment of the cowboy era. People attend by the thousands, many wearing cowboy dress, eating the traditional barbecue, and watching the performance of bronco busting and other traditional cowboy skills (see ch. 3, Historical Setting; ch. 7, Living Conditions).

The population of the entire country at the time of independence in 1828 was no more than 100,000. The majority were cowboys, shepherds, and *estancia* owners scattered across the rolling grasslands, with only a small educated elite in Montevideo.

The *criollos* have generally remained on the land, either as ranch hands or *estancia* managers or owners. They constitute one of the two major ethnic groupings of the white Uruguayans: the *criollos* and the immigrants. There is no sharp line between these two groups; they are racially almost identical, speak the same language, and move freely from one group to the other. The significant differences lie in outlook, traditions, means of livelihood, and regional concentration. Many of the wealthy *estancia* owners live part of the time in the cities, principally Montevideo, leaving the ranch to be administered by a farm manager. These people participate in the life of both groups but usually maintain their primary loyalty to the rural society.

Immigrants

In 1970 the large majority of the population was descended from the immigrants from Europe during the nineteenth and early twentieth centuries. Compared to many other countries in Latin America, the number of immigrants was small but, because of the small population at the time of independence, the effect on the nation has been notable. No exact statistics are available, but probably 700,000 people entered the country between 1836 and 1926; some sources estimate the total number of immigrants at 1 million. In 1829, one year after independence, Montevideo had a population of about 9,000, 12 percent of the total. Since most immigrants settled in Montevideo or in the agricultural areas surrounding the city, the immediate effect on urban growth was remarkable. As early as 1840 there were more foreign-born than native residents living in the capital city, and in 1889, 114,000 nationals and 100,000 foreigners lived in Montevideo. In 1872 one-fourth of the national population was foreign born; and by 1900, one-third, with first-generation Uruguayans representing a substantial part of the rest (see ch. 4, Population and Labor Force).

The preponderance of immigrants arriving during the nineteenth and early twentieth centuries came from Spain and Italy, with smaller numbers from other European countries and the Middle East. Many others came from Europe indirectly, migrating from Brazil or Argentina. Many came in hope of a better life, others because of domestic crises or persecution, and others as political refugees. Some of the earliest immigrants were French and Spanish Basques who, driven by political and religious conflicts and overpopulation, began to arrive soon after independence. Portuguese, French, and German immigrants were also numerous in the early years of independence. By 1840 the French constituted a substantial part of the population of Montevideo, but the subsequent immigration from France was relatively small. In 1940 the German community was estimated to be around 8,000, or about 0.4 percent of the total population, and in 1970 continued to make up only a small part of Uruguay's population.

During the same period many British citizens came to Uruguay, at first to work on the ranches, often as owners of their own *estancias*, and later as administrators and technicians employed by the railroads, gasworks, and other utilities built by British firms and capital. In *The Purple Land*, his semiautobiographical novel about Uruguay in the 1870's, W. H. Hudson describes his encounters with British ranchers scattered across the remote parts of the interior. The British residents made major contributions in stockbreeding techniques and later in meatpacking. In the mid-twentieth century the influence of the small permanent British population remained strong. A few Irish, Scotch, and Welsh also immigrated during the nineteenth century.

The Jewish population includes Russian, German, and Eastern European Jews, as well as Sephardic Jews, who originally came from the Iberian peninsula. Before independence Jews were generally not permitted in the colonies, although a few entered covertly. Most of the present population came in three waves, starting in the 1890's, when pogroms in Russia drove large numbers to seek refuge in other countries. During the 1920's another wave of Jewish immigrants chose to live in Uruguay in hopes of a better life. The Nazi persecution of the 1930's drove many more German Jews to Uruguay, where traditions of political and religious liberty offered hope of freedom from persecution. The first group was generally of lower class origin; the later waves of immigrants were mostly middle class and contributed their skills and training to the country.

A small number of Lebanese and Syrians moved to the country in the late nineteenth and early twentieth centuries, taking up their traditional occupation of trade and marketing, most often becoming textile merchants. Small numbers of Portuguese, Armenians, Russians, and Poles entered toward the close of the nineteenth century.

By far the greatest contribution came from Italy and Spain. Immigration from these countries continued throughout the nineteenth and twentieth centuries, although by 1970 it had slowed to a trickle. The relative proportions of the two countries varied, depending on political events and internal crises but, on the whole, Spain contributed the largest share. Between 1948 and 1955, 50,000 Europeans immigrated, of whom 58 percent were Spanish and 37 percent Italian. In 1968, 54 percent of European immigrants were Spanish, and 22 percent Italian.

Most immigrants settled in the cities, particularly Montevideo, or took up farming in the adjacent agricultural lowlands. As recently as 1968, 94 percent of all immigrants remained in Montevideo, and almost all of the rest stayed in Canelones or Colonia, close to the urban centers of the south. The *criollos* have traditionally scorned the menial labor of agriculture and, as a result, the initiation of cultivation in the southern part of the country was primarily the product of the immigrants' efforts.

German, British, French, and other northern Europeans tended to come from middle class backgrounds, while the Spaniards and Italians were more often of working class origin. The Spaniards became laborers, servants, and small businessmen, often working as grocery clerks, bartenders, waiters, taxidrivers, and doormen. The Italians were more versatile in their choice of occupations. Northern Italians often went into the agricultural regions, becoming tenant farmers or occasionally farmhands on the cattle estates; southern Italians were more likely to become urban factory workers, masons, skilled artisans, and small businessmen. Although many of the immigrants from both countries were of rural origin, most preferred the excitement and opportunity offered by urban life.

Exact statistics on the present ethnic composition of the country are unavailable. In 1970 an estimated 14 percent of the population was foreign born, while up to 75 percent were second- or third-generation immigrants. Spanish and Portuguese surnames predominate, and almost one-fourth are either Italian or Hispanicized from Italian. In 1963 the Italian government reported 39,000 Italians living in Montevideo and about 250,000 Uruguayans of Italian descent living in the country, or 10 percent of the nation as a whole. Most reside in Montevideo or Salto, the second largest city. Other sources claim that Italians make up 15 percent of the total and Spaniards 45 percent. A colony of about 25,000 Slavs lives in Montevideo, constituting 1 percent of the population. The Jewish population is approximately 40,000, or 1.6 percent, of whom 26,000 are of Eastern European origin, 8,000 are Sephardim of Iberian descent, and 7,000 are German and West European Jews.

The effect of the European immigration on the country has been profound. It has produced an urban society that is largely middle class. The immigrants have contributed European liberal ideas, including a firm belief in the value of education, social welfare programs, and trade unionism. When most of the population came from Europe, there was little free land left. As a result, they tended to remain in the city or become small farmers rather than *estancia* owners. The secular ideals of nineteenth- and twentieth-century Europe eroded the power of the Roman Catholic Church, preventing it from achieving the influence and prestige it has typically had in Latin America. The country has been a melting pot (see ch. 6, Social Structure; ch. 10, Religion).

THE INDIGENOUS INDIAN POPULATION

In 1970 the *mestizo* population was estimated to represent between 5 and 10 percent of the total and was concentrated in the northern interior. The *mestizos* are the descendants of the nomadic Charrúa and Chana Indian tribes, which had been pushed into the area from Paraguay by the more highly developed Guaraní Indians sometime before the Spanish Conquest. They became subsistence farmers and hunters; the women grew corn, beans, and melons, while the men hunted game and fished. Their way of life was simple; clans formed the highest level of social organization.

The Guaraní empire that stretched from Paraguay east of the Chaco to northern Argentina and southern Brazil embraced some of northern Uruguay. The Guaraní Indians had a settled, organized way of life, centered around large communal houses made of tree trunks and leaf thatch, in which whole family groups were housed and subsisted on simple agriculture.

Members of the first Spanish expedition to land in the Río de la Plata region in 1516, were killed by Charrúa Indians. Their continued fierce resistance to Spanish conquest served to discourage settlement in this region during the sixteenth and early seventeenth centuries. During this period the Charrúas learned the art of horsemanship from the Spaniards in adjacent areas, strengthening their ability to resist subjugation (see ch. 3, Historical Setting).

The Indians were eventually subdued by the large influx of Argentines and Brazilians pursuing the herds of cattle and horses. Through intermarriage and some deliberate extermination, the number of Indians rapidly diminished, and by 1850 the pureblooded Indian had virtually ceased to exist. Traces of Indian ancestry are apparent, however, in many residents of the northern departments.

NEGROES AND MULATTOES

In 1970 there were between 40,000 and 60,000 people of African descent in the country, or only about 1 to 2 percent of the total, of whom perhaps less than 1 percent could be classified as Negro rather than mulatto.

From 1756 until the early nineteenth century, thousands of Africans from the West Coast of Africa and Mozambique were brought to Montevideo. The number remaining in the country probably totaled a few thousand. During the late eighteenth and early nineteenth centuries, however, Negroes constituted about 20 percent of the total population. In 1843, of about 31,000 residents of the capital city, some 6,000 were Negroes. During this period, the Negro population contributed significantly to the economic development of the country.

The sharp drop in percentage since that period is largely the result of the influx of European immigrants during the nineteenth and twentieth centuries. Perhaps 4,000 Negro slaves were sold across the border to Brazil between 1832 and 1841, when it became clear that slavery would soon be abolished in Uruguay but not in Brazil. Many slaves were used in the army, and later many emancipated Negroes enlisted.

In 1970 most of the Negro and mulatto population lived in the northern part of the country and worked as farm or ranch hands. Many were the descendants of Brazilian slaves who escaped across the border before the abolition of slavery in Brazil in 1888. Even fewer Negroes and mulattoes reside in Montevideo. In the city most of them live in tenements and hold such jobs as clerk, bellboy, busdriver, janitor, soldier, and newspaper seller. Although there is no closely knit ethnic community, many Negroes live together in tenements where some remnants of the African traditions, such as music and dance, are passed down from generation to generation. Increasing numbers of whites, however, are taking up residence in slum areas, diluting the Negro community and mixing the remaining elements of African culture with the dominant European patterns.

In contrast to the tremendous influence of African music and dance apparent in the festivals of Carnival in Brazil, only a few blacks appear among the whites for Montevideo's festivities, and their music and dance do not differ greatly from that of the whites. African religions have been so submerged in Catholicism that the saints now take the places of the old gods, and even the names and number of the gods in the African pantheon are forgotten.

Not all urban Negroes are poor tenement dwellers. A group exists that is slightly better off, dresses better, and concerns itself with the arts. They frequent cultural centers, form social clubs, and often engage in writing and painting. Many feel responsible for maintaining African culture and defending Negro rights. The arts attract a substantial portion of the Negro community.

ASSIMILATION AND INTERGROUP ATTITUDES

Uruguayans are tolerant of foreigners, and assimilation is in almost all cases accomplished quickly and easily. There is no particular government policy encouraging immigrants to learn the history and character of the country in order to develop patriotism, but the adaptation is usually rapid. For Spaniards, the culture and language are very similar and, even for Italians, the differences in language, religion, temperament, and culture are not great enough to erect major barriers. Italian immigrants assimilate remarkably fast, and by the third generation they are usually fully Hispanicized. Rarely do they remain a separate ethnic group.

Other nationalities tend to assimilate almost as quickly, although a few vestiges of ethnic communities remain. The Jewish group maintains its own school system, a community press in Yiddish, as well as Spanish, and three radio programs that provide both daily news from Israel and local reports. The Jews are divided into four communal organizations in Montevideo: the East European Ashkenazic, Sephardic, German, and Hungarian, each with its own rabbi and communal building and some with their own clubs, schools, welfare agencies, publications, and cultural activities. A total of six synagogues serve the community. *Unzer Fraint*, a Jewish daily newspaper with leftist leanings, and *Das Geméinde Blatt*, the publication of the German Jews, inform the community. Only about 15 percent of all Jewish children attend Jewish schools, however, and about 3 percent reach the secondary level. Jewish youth organizations carry on their activities in Spanish and there is in general a tendency for many in the community to replace Yiddish with Spanish (see ch. 15, Public Information).

A small English-speaking community exists, served by a daily and a twice weekly newspaper, which carry information about social club, school, and church affairs in the Anglo-American community, as well as some brief foreign and national news stories. There are American and British schools in the city and an Anglican and several Protestant churches. An Italian-language newspaper, *L'Ora D'Italia*, comes out every other week, and in the past there was a German daily newspaper. The combined circulation of all foreign-language newspapers, however, is very small. The number of people living in distinctly ethnic communities is minimal and has little influence on political or social life.

The prevailing attitude toward the small Negro population is one of acceptance of their position as members of a low stratum of society. There is no official policy of discrimination and, in most cases, Negroes may use any café, bar, cinema, or beach; vote in any election; send their children to any school; or attend any church they choose. In 1937 the Partido Autoctono Negro (Autochthonous Negro Party), for the assertion of Negro rights, was founded. Its existence was brief, however, because the Negroes preferred to vote for the traditional parties rather than give their votes to a protest party. The attitude toward Negroes is in most cases based on class rather than race, since the poorer classes of all colors find it difficult to enter middle and upper class society.

To the extent that any ethnic division can be said to exist in the country, it is between the residents of the *campo*, or the interior plateau, and those of the capital. To citizens of Montevideo, even Canelones, the department directly north of the city, is sometimes considered the *campo*. The distinction is neither racial nor religious but economic and historical. Individuals may easily move from one group to the other, but the two differ in outlook and way of life. The residents of the first region, the *campo*, are *criollos*, generally ranchers or ranch hands who live on scattered *estancias* or small settlements and, occasionally, in the smaller northern cities. The living standard is generally much lower than that of Montevideo.

The residents of the second region are largely of recent immigrant stock. It consists of the capital, with almost 50 percent of the people, and the agricultural lowlands surrounding and serving the urban centers of the south. This area dominates national culture, forms national policy, runs the government, and benefits from the generous welfare programs. Most urbanites work in the civil service, business, industry, commerce, services, or on the farms in the surrounding countryside. They idealize the cowboy, forming cowboy clubs and holding annual cowboy festivals, but they tend to ignore the inequities between capital and *campo*. In general, the *criollos* are more sympathetic to the Catholic church than the immigrant population, which is often either Protestant or secular in its values. Traditionally, the *criollos* belonged to the conservative Blanco party, and immigrants to the progressive Colorado party; membership in both was a family matter. To change sides was a serious matter. Even in 1970 party membership tended to follow the *criollo*-immigrant dichotomy (see ch. 13, Political Dynamics; ch. 7, Living Conditions).

LANGUAGE

Spanish, the official language, is spoken by almost all Uruguayans. The particular type of Spanish in common parlance, almost identical to the dialect of Buenos Aires, is less conservative than that of the interior of Argentina. The *porteño* or Rio Platense accent, as it is popularly called, reflects the influence of immigrants, principally in the realm of vocabulary and pronunciation. Vowels are thickened, and the soft Spanish pronunciation of *ll* and *y* is hardened to approximate an English *j*. This linguistic trait, *yeismo*, is considered uncultured by recent immigrants from Spain and from other parts of Latin America.

Italian has had the greatest impact of any immigrant language on the *porteño* dialect, changing pronunciation and adding words. Instead of the Spanish *adios*, most people use the Italian *chau* or *addio* to say goodbye. *Morgar* (to eat) is another Italian contribution. English has provided many words and phrases for modern technology and commerce, sports, food, and social life. One has *five o'clock tea* at any time and travels on the *omnibus*. Popular sports are *basquetbol* (basketball), *fútbol* (soccer), and *beisbol* (baseball); one may drink a *jaibol* (highball) or a *coctel* (cocktail) or perhaps even eat a sandwich at a *bar*. In the area of business, one can go to a *mitin* (meeting) with an *agenda*. English advertising, academic, and technical phrases may be translated literally, including expressions, such as "round trip," "to play a role," or "to kick the bucket."

French influence has been less important, restricted to a few words, such as *boite* (nightclub), *chalet*, and *boutique*, and to foods. Africans have contributed a few words as well, mostly terms for dances or musical instruments.

The language of the country reflects its ranching origins. It is rich in the vocabulary of the *estancia* and horses, often drawing its metaphors from this sphere. Cowboy influence is apparent in the replacement of the Spanish verb *cabalgar* (to ride a horse) with *jinetear*, meaning either "to tame wild horses by riding them" or "to ride a horse publicly, with ostentation." The language spoken in the north of Uruguay has some idiomatic expressions and vocabulary of Indian origin, principally from Quechua, the tongue of the Incas, and from Guaraní.

In northern departments near the Brazilian border, some Portuguese-Spanish bilingualism and language-mixing exist. The northern area had a substantial Brazilian settlement in the past, over which Spanish language and culture have been imposed. There are several places where a pure Portuguese is spoken; others where a *dialecto fronterizo* (border dialect), a combination of Spanish and Portuguese, exists; and still others where only a slight Portuguese influence on the Spanish is apparent. The latter region extends across much of the northern part of the country. In the largest border town, Rivera, over 70 percent of the inhabitants are bilingual, and a few speak exclusively Portuguese. The languages are mutually intelligible to most residents of the city, and it is possible for an Uruguayan and a Brazilian to communicate, each speaking his national language. In discussions between nationals of the two countries, however, it is more common for both to use Portuguese. Most of the teachers in Rivera feel that the common use of Portuguese makes learning correct Spanish most difficult and influences the pronunciation and grammar of the Spanish-speaking children. Some teenagers even develop an exaggerated use of Portuguese loanwords and grammatical constructions.

The urban educated elite commonly know some English, since they are required to have a reading knowledge of it for graduation from academic secondary school. The United States and British cultural institutes offering language training are well attended, and knowledge of English is increasing. French was the traditional language of the elite, but its use has declined since World War II. Some recent immigrants maintain their native language, but the tendency is to learn Spanish and drop the foreign tongue in order to become assimilated.

CHAPTER 6

SOCIAL STRUCTURE

In 1970 the social structure consisted of large middle and lower classes and a small upper class in the urban and southern rural areas and small upper and large lower classes in the northern rural regions. Although the majority of the population in the nation as a whole was of the lower class, the middle class was larger than in most Latin American countries and exercised a powerful influence on much of the society. The values and ideals of the middle class were accepted by a large part of the country, and the political ideology of the dominant Colorado Party has been extensively influenced by middle class ideas.

A second major characteristic of the social structure, in addition to the importance of the middle class, was the high degree of urbanization. About three-fourths of all Uruguayans live in towns or cities, and almost one-half live in the capital city itself. The population is ethnically, linguistically, and racially homogeneous. The secondary and tertiary sectors of the economy are well developed, and large numbers of persons are employed in the civil service, private enterprise, personal services, and the nationalized industries; in contrast, the primary sector employs a relatively small part of the population. The long life expectancy means that there are many older people, and a significant part of the population is composed of retired and pensioned individuals.

Social mobility is possible, but the society is less fluid than it has been in the past. Education is the primary avenue for social advancement. Most of the population is literate. The large middle class generally has at least some secondary education. Most people are well informed about national events and are avid consumers of the mass media. The great majority participate in national life, including political affairs, cultural endeavors, and social events. The entire population, including the rural lower class of the smallest landowners, tenant farmers, and wage laborers, is fully incorporated into the monetary economy.

The middle class is especially influential because of the character of the upper and lower classes. The upper social group of landowners and business and financial leaders, although wealthy, never developed the strong aristocratic tradition and sense of exclusiveness typical of many neighboring Latin American countries. Most upper class individuals continue to believe in the equal personal dignity of all human beings. Most of the lower class is assisted by the generous government welfare programs. The few who are not are found almost exclusively in the rural north and in shantytowns on the outskirts of Montevideo and some interior towns. Consequently, the society is fairly homogeneous, and the poles of wealth and poverty are not so apparent as in most other Latin American countries.

Rural social structure in the livestock regions of the north is divided into a landholding upper class and a lower class engaged in paid farm labor. The typical form of landownership is the *estancia* (large ranch or country estate), which employs a few rangers and workers to tend the livestock and repair the fences. Along the southern and western coasts and around the interior towns of the coastal region, however, fairly prosperous small family farms are the rule. They generally produce for city consumption and have a psychological and ideological orientation toward the urban areas.

The small nuclear family prevails in much of the country. The urbanite who believes in the importance of education for his children chooses to limit his family to the number of children he can afford. Consequently, small families are the norm for the urban middle class and increasingly for the rest of the country as well. Relatives outside the nuclear family are of great social and economic importance to the upper and upper middle classes but play a declining role farther down the social ladder. Women enjoy a more independent and emancipated position than in most other Latin American countries. The majority remain in the home, but it is not unusual for a woman to gain an education and pursue a career.

Divorce was legalized early in the twentieth century, and one procedure provides that a divorce can be obtained simply at a wife's request. Although divorce rates have been increasing, they are still low. Most marriages are stable, and the family is typically a cohesive, harmonious unit. In the lowest levels of society, many do not contract a formal marriage, and male-female relationships are often short lived. The mother-centered family, in which a woman is the fulcrum of a large group of children and lives with a succession of men to whom she is not married, is typical of poorer families in the stockraising north. The declining demand for agricultural labor in 1970 forced many young people from this area to migrate, splitting up the family and severing ties with more distant relatives.

DEVELOPMENT OF THE CLASS SYSTEM

For the first 100 years of the country's history the inhabitants were almost exclusively *gauchos* (cowboys) and hide dealers, scattered across the grasslands and making their livelihood from the abundant herds of sheep and cattle. When Montevideo was established in 1726, it was intended to be a frontier fort; 100 years later, at the time of independence, it was still small, with only 6,000 inhabitants and a very small educated elite (see ch. 3, Historical Setting).

During the early nineteenth century the land was gradually carved into large *estancias*, but in many cases the life style of the *estancia* owner was not significantly different from that of his ranch workers or the *gauchos*. On the *estancias* and in the small interior towns there was considerable contact between the classes, and life was generally simple for all levels of society. An energetic and fortunate *gaucho* with no prestigious family background or education might acquire a large tract of land and stock. Consequently, although the large landowners came to hold substantial power and influence in the country, they were slower to develop an aristocratic tradition based on the prestige of landholding and the family pedigree than many other Latin American countries; and many retained an egalitarian outlook.

The country also lacked any large racial or ethnic minority group that could serve as an inexpensive labor force for the enrichment of the landowners. Slaves were imported in the late eighteenth and early nineteenth centuries, but the total number was always small. They were principally owned by urban residents and usually worked as domestic servants, urban construction workers, and field hands on truck farms or were hired out as artisans or laborers by their owners. Few families owned more than five; the average slaveowner possessed two or three. The army provided a ready avenue for slaves to win freedom before the abolition of slavery and a means of achieving social prestige and standing afterward. The Indian population was always small and by 1832 had been virtually eliminated (see ch. 5, Ethnic Groups and Languages).

During the nineteenth century the social structure of the majority of the country was gradually transformed from a semifeudal system based on the ownership of land to a class society with a growing middle class and an expanding industrial and commercial lower class. Trade with foreign countries became increasingly important, necessitating the emergence of a prosperous group of middlemen based in the city. A center of economic power was thus established that was often in conflict with that of the rural landowners and contributed to the internal dissensions that inspired the wars of the nineteenth century.

This long succession of civil and international wars was disruptive to the colonial social fabric. Much of the population was actively involved in the fighting, and the armies tended to live off the land, seizing the crops and animals of the peasants and occasionally resorting to scorched earth tactics. When José Gervasio Artigas left the country in 1812 with his 12,000 followers, he took with him a substantial portion of the rural population and one-quarter of the population of the entire country. The Great War (La Guerra Grande) of the 1840's and the Paraguayan War of 1865—70 had similarly unsettling effects on the country (see ch. 3, Historical Setting).

Another source of change was the tide of European immigration. The immigrants generally assumed urban occupations in government and industry or initiated commercial farming along the southern coast and the Rio de la Plata estuary. They were often of lower class background and usually remained in the lower ranks of society, but they were aware of the importance of educating their children. Many second- and later-generation immigrants became important commercial and industrial leaders, professionals, or civil servants (see ch. 5, Ethnic Groups and Languages).

After the introduction of barbed wire for fencing the ranges in the 1870's, the *gaucho* was gradually reduced to the status of a wage-earning worker. As the export of raw and processed agricultural products gained in importance, the new industrial and commercial leaders of both *criollo* (see Glossary) and immigrant descent rose in power and influence. The emergence of a significant domestic market increased the demand for commercial middlemen to handle the mushrooming trade.

The middle class of the late nineteenth and early twentieth centuries was a relatively thin layer between the landowning and commercial elites and the large mass of *gauchos*, agricultural workers, and industrial laborers. The middle class was an amalgam of professionals, such as lawyers, doctors, writers, publishers, artists, and teachers in secondary schools and the university, government officials, members of the secular clergy, and lower and middle sectors of the officer corps.

Society experienced a rapid transformation during the first three decades of the twentieth century. The center of political power shifted decisively to the capital city. As early as 1900 Montevideo had 30 percent of the population and was attracting ranch owners to establish part-time residence in the city. By the mid-1920's, 50 percent of the gross national product was produced by the manufacturing and processing sectors of the economy, which also provided the majority of the new jobs for the rapidly growing urban population. In the same period the government greatly expanded its industrial and administrative functions, requiring an ever-expanding corps of government employees. The working classes grew in size and influence, organizing into unions early in the twentieth century (see ch. 20, Labor Relations and Organization).

The middle class expanded rapidly, drawing upon the immigrant population, and emerged as a powerful political force under the aegis of the Colorado Party. The urban middle and lower classes profited most from the social reforms and welfare programs of José Batlle y Ordóñez, although he was careful not to antagonize the landowning elites.

Since 1930 the trend toward the increasing dominance of Montevideo and of the urban middle class has continued. The rural population has declined since 1951 as the result of migration to the cities, reflecting not only the common belief that opportunity lies in the city but also the stagnation of the rural economy. Shantytowns have appeared on the outskirts of Montevideo and the towns in the livestock region, which are inhabited primarily by ranch workers driven out of the countryside by mechanization and a lack of work. In the same period there has been an increase in the proportion of the society than can be classified as middle class.

SOCIAL STRATIFICATION

The society is homogeneous and unstratified in comparison with those of many other Latin American countries, leading some scholars to claim that the country has no social classes. The society, however, can be divided into upper, middle, and lower classes, based on the criteria of occupation, wealth, education, life style, and family prestige. The social distinction between manual and non-manual labor is of particular symbolic importance; most people prefer low-level white-collar work to skilled manual labor, even when earnings for manual work are higher. Although educational and occupational achievements are important to an individual's status, family and personal connections are also of great significance.

Although the middle class is usually estimated to be slightly under one-third of the total population, the norms and values of this group exert a disproportionately large influence on society. Furthermore, the economic circumstances of those in the highest and lowest income brackets contrast less than in many other Latin American countries because of the historical underdevelopment of the landowning aristocracy and the government welfare measures, which ameliorate the poverty of most of the lowest levels of society. In 1970 about 2 to 5 percent of the society could be classified as upper class and approximately two-thirds as lower class.

The Upper Class

The small upper class is composed of the wealthiest and most influential landowners, businessmen, and financiers as well as political, ecclesiastical, administrative, and military leaders and the most successful professionals.

Upper class status is largely a function of wealth and occupation, but family background is important. The upper stratum is composed of families descended from the colonial *criollos*, in addition to some families who trace their origins to the more recent immigrants but combine the qualities of wealth, education, and prestige necessary for high status. University education is a usual concomitant of upper class position, although a few commercial and industrial leaders have less education, and not all with a university education achieve upper class status. A particular mark of prestige is teaching a few courses at the university as an avocation rather than a full-time occupation (see ch. 8, Education). The upper class group has traditionally had a cosmopolitan outlook, generally oriented toward Europe, although the United States has assumed increasing importance in recent years.

Family position and wealth influence an individual's ability to afford a higher education; inherited family wealth or land enable an individual to maintain a high social position; and family connections are often decisive in obtaining prestigious jobs. The top political posts are often held by members of a few large families, and the family firm continues to be an important form of private enterprise.

The great majority of the productive land in the country is held in large estates of over 2,500 acres, whose owners form the rural upper class. About one-fifth of this land is concentrated in the hands of a small number of families in estates over 12,500 acres, and an estimated 600 families control, directly or indirectly, one-third to one-half of the fertile land in the country. A dozen or so families have holdings of more than 100,000 acres. About 5 percent of all landowners are of the upper class.

In 1970 there were indications that the size of landholdings was increasing as smaller landowners were forced to migrate in search of better opportunities. The tendency for family properties to be broken up by inheritance is counteracted by the formation of family corporations to hold the land over several generations. This practice, although prohibited in the mid-1960's, had already proceeded far enough to ensure the continuance of large landholdings (see ch. 18, Agriculture).

The magnates of industry, commerce, and finance form the core of the urban upper class. A leading Uruguayan sociologist includes the following categories in the upper class of the cities: industrial proprietors with fifty or more employees, commercial proprietors with nine or more employees, owners of banks and financial institutions, large stockholders, managers of large corporations, managers of foreign enterprises and capital, administrators of the large public corporations, and owners of large tracts of real estate in urban areas. Professionals in the highest ranks, such as successful doctors, dentists, lawyers, writers, engineers, and architects, are accorded upper class status, as are military officers of the grade of colonel and above, prelates of the Roman Catholic Church, educational leaders, top-level bureaucrats, and the most important political leaders at the national and municipal levels. A few foreign lawyers, bankers, and technicians representing foreign investments and capital can also be included in the top stratum.

The relations between various segments of the upper class are close, particularly at the highest levels. Many of the landowning elites are also active in commercial and industrial ventures in Montevideo or have family ties to the business and financial leaders. Much of the urban upper class is actually composed of members of the powerful landowning families. A large landowner, or *estanciero*, may own a large share of a food-processing industry, a commercial television station, or an important newspaper. Powerful industrial firms often have close ties with foreign capital, domestic and foreign middlemen, and bank directorates. Appointment or election to top political posts is usually dependent on the ability to deliver the vote, a function often related to wealth and influence (see ch. 13, Political Dynamics).

The Middle Class

Uruguay's middle class is generally considered to be quite large, ranging from low-level white-collar workers, such as clerks, to moderately wealthy industrialists or government employees. The middle class is not a uniform or cohesive group. It includes people of both old *criollo* and recent immigrant descent; those who have attended only primary school as well as those who are university graduates; property owners and those who possess no real estate; and some who feel secure in their status and others who fear falling back to their working-class origins. The typical middle class individual, however, is the descendant of a European immigrant of the nineteenth or twentieth century, lives in Montevideo or an interior town, and works as a civil servant, small businessman, moderately successful professional, or salaried bank or business employee at the white-collar level.

A belief in education is one of the most significant attributes of the middle class. The hallmark of the traditional middle class of the nineteenth century was education, and it was schooling that enabled the sons of immigrants to achieve positions of responsibility in society. Education has always served as the principal avenue of social mobility for the middle class. Some academic secondary schooling is almost essential for middle class status and is far preferable to technical or vocational training, which prepares an individual for the lower status manual occupations. A middle class child who fails in academic secondary school may be sent to a business training course, which prepares him for a low-level white-collar occupation and consequently enables him to maintain his class position (see ch. 8, Education).

The improvement of public services is of paramount importance to the middle class, which is often dependent on city transportation, communications, roads, water, and power. The group tends to support industrialization, which opens up new middle-status job opportunities. Involvement of the state in economic affairs is encouraged as a means of preserving stability and counteracting the demands of the masses and the ruling elites. Furthermore, the middle class tends to be nationalistic, seeking to preserve uniquely Uruguayan characteristics from foreign influence and disruption.

The middle class group can be subdivided into three levels, depending on occupation, education, wealth, family origin, and life style. The upper middle class includes university professors, high public officials, private business executives, owners of small firms, middle-level military and police officials, medium-sized landowners, managers of moderately sized farms, commercial and financial employees, and owners of significant amounts of urban real estate. They emulate the values and life style of the upper class and, in some cases, strive to move into the higher group. Many are members of established families of the old middle class in existence before the social transformations of the early twentieth century; others are formerly upper class persons who could not maintain their family position.

The lower segments of the middle class are typically somewhat smaller landowners, low-level government employees, office clerks, minor functionaries in business and industry, primary school teachers, lower echelon military and police officials, minor technicians, overseers of farm and industrial workers, and middle class pensioners. Many members of this group have working-class origins and are anxious to identify themselves solidly with the middle class. Their middle class status is often insecure. In many cases their educational attainments are limited to the primary- or business-school level.

The middle section of the class conforms most closely to the middle class pattern typical of the country. It is found both in Montevideo and in the interior towns.

The effects of middle class values and norms are apparent in the development of mass public education, public services in the urban areas, and a comprehensive social welfare system. The middle group is literate and politically aware; the country has developed an extensive mass media of newspapers, radio, television, and publications to satisfy its demands. The rest of the society follows the middle class lead in widespread political participation and extensive perusal of the mass media (see ch. 15, Public Information).

The middle class tends to engage in conspicuous consumption. In a family with a modest income, the wife may work as well as the husband to enable the family to purchase appliances, such as a refrigerator, a washing machine, or a television set, housing in a fashionable area, or elegant clothes.

Moderation and security are key middle class principles. Although the group may be progressive in times of general social improvement, when society is undergoing a crisis it is likely to obstruct change, seeing security in the maintenance of even a precarious status quo. Middle class individuals favor stabilization by state action, although they are careful to defend their civil rights. During the economic crisis of the late 1950's and 1960's, the middle class experienced increasing pressure from inflation, which reduced the real incomes of many on fairly fixed salaries. Consequently, most accepted in principle the government stabilization measures put into effect in 1968, although the measures were firmly resisted by those groups whose interests were directly harmed (see ch. 22, Finance).

The Lower Class

The urban lower class includes skilled and unskilled industrial workers, domestic servants, soldiers, and manual workers employed by the government. In the rural areas very small landowners, tenant farmers, tractor drivers, horse tamers, and salaried ranch and farm hands are regarded as lower class. Most members of this group perform manual labor and have only attained the primary level of education. The feeling of insecurity typical of the lower middle class is generally absent in the lower class, since there is little anxiety over a decline in social status and the government welfare system provides a cushion of security. At the same time, the lower class worker profits from gradual economic progress and the trend toward a leveling of social differences. The union movement, active since the early twentieth century, has succeeded in raising the wages of some skilled blue-collar workers above the level of lower white-collar workers.

Most of the rural lower class are agricultural wage earners or tenant farmers thoroughly acquainted with a monetary economy, rather than traditional peasants practicing subsistence agriculture. The first *gauchos* to enter the country in the seventeenth century were primarily interested in obtaining cattle hides for sale, and in the livestock areas this market orientation has persisted. The *gaucho* has become a paid ranch hand responsible for tending cattle or sheep.

The first farmers in the south and west were European immigrants, also familiar with a monetary economy, who were interested in producing food for the urban market. The agricultural regions continue to have a capitalistic orientation, with ownership or rental of land for money rather than crops or labor being the prevailing practice (see ch. 18, Agriculture).

At the bottom of the social hierarchy is a small marginal population of the very poor, who receive little benefit from the welfare state and subsist on the bare minimum of housing, food, and clothing. In the stockraising regions seasonal ranch workers who are able to find employment during only a small part of the year, such as sheepshearing or roundup time, live in small shack settlements of between 20 and 200 families known as *rancheríos*. These settlements often include the wives and children of ranch employees in cases where there is no provision for them to live on the ranch. In 1963 the total number of persons living in such circumstances was estimated to be about 60,000, or 10 percent of the rural population, but some estimates are as high as 20 percent of all rural residents (see ch. 2, Physical Environment).

Since 1945 shantytowns of tar-paper and sheet-metal shacks, known as *cantegriles*, have been developing on the outskirts of Montevideo and the interior towns of the livestock regions. The total population of these settlements is estimated at about 10,000, and the great majority live around Montevideo. Most of these slumdwellers are migrants from the interior livestock regions who are forced to seek work in the city. The majority subsist as rag and paper collectors, newspaper or flower sellers, janitors, porters, or day laborers. The distance between their houses and the city prevents wives and children from working close to the home, as they did in the country. The illiteracy rate in such settlements is high for Uruguay, and those who attend school remain only a few years. Most residents of the shantytowns have been accustomed to outdoor agricultural tasks and, because of their lack of experience and education, find the transition to regular urban employment difficult (see ch. 7, Living Conditions).

Regional Patterns

The variations in social structure in different parts of the country can be sorted into three typical patterns found in the capital city, in the agricultural area of the south and west, and in the rural livestock region of the north. The divisions depend on the proportional class representation, relations between the classes, and the economic basis of the society in each area.

Montevideo, with almost half of the national population, is the bastion of the middle class. Because of the extensive development of the secondary and tertiary sectors of the economy, thousands of middle class positions are available in the civil service, the nationalized enterprises, the public services, private industries, finance, and retailing. The large number of retired government employees and other pensioned white-collar workers swells the ranks of the middle class, making it, if not the numerically largest section of the population, the ideologically dominant one.

The national elites live almost exclusively in the capital city. Many wealthy landowners maintain seasonal residence in Montevideo. Political, financial, industrial, commercial, and religious leaders reside and operate in the capital, and representatives of foreign firms and interests usually prefer the cosmopolitan sophisticated urban environment. The upper class, however, forms a smaller proportion of the population of the city than of the interior towns or agricultural regions and exerts correspondingly less social influence.

The city has a large industrial working class represented by politically powerful labor unions. Pensions, minimum wage laws, and other welfare measures benefit much of the lower class, sustaining all but a very small group above the poverty level. Most of the population has adequate housing and food, and the city gives the visitor the impression of a prosperous, well-dressed, and adequately nourished society (see ch. 20, Labor Relations and Organization).

Montevideo has earned the country its reputation as advanced, progressive, and middle class. Its industries and business represent 80 percent of the capital, production, and number of workers and employees of the country. It is the center of the political and administrative system; controls the mass media, such as radio, television, and the press; is the hub of the transportation network; and dominates educational and cultural life (see ch. 8, Education; ch. 9, Artistic and Intellectual Expression; ch. 19, Industry; ch. 22, Finance).

A second regional pattern found in the agricultural areas along the southern coast and the Río de la Plata, is typical of about half the rural population. Agriculture in this region is intensive and relatively mechanized; many farms are organized into large plantations producing vast quantities of rice, sugarcane, flax, sugar beets, and other crops. Rich grazing areas are mixed with the cropland and, close to Montevideo and the interior towns, dairy and truck farms are common.

The small family farm is typical of this region. In cases in which the farm is of moderate size and the farmer has some machinery and capital at his disposal, he can be considered middle class, although this classification is not universally accepted.

Interspersed between the moderately sized farms are many small, directly owned pieces of land and a number of leased middle- and small-sized plots. Operators of these farms are generally lower in status than the medium-sized landowners and, together with the agricultural wage laborers, make up the lower class. The farms of some landholders are too small to support them adequately, and they are gradually being forced off the land by competition with large, mechanized farms. The situation of the small tenant farmer is also precarious, since his contract may not be renewed or his rent may be increased beyond his ability to pay. A marginal group of migrant agricultural workers on the lower fringe of society follows the harvests, ranging across much of the interior of the country and often into Brazil (see ch. 18, Agriculture).

Although the inhabitants of this region are engaged in agricultural work, their social and psychological oreintation is to the city. Production is aimed at the urban market, rather than toward the subsistence of the farmer himself. The farmers are largely of European immigrant extraction and tend to hold individualistic, typically urban values. These areas receive the public services of the city, the Montevideo daily press, and city-produced goods. The living standard is higher than in the livestock regions of the north. The inhabitants are generally well fed, and the percentage of inadequate housing, especially along the southern coast, is about the lowest in the country. Residence is either in isolated houses directly on the farms or in small settlements close to the fields.

The third regional pattern is typical of the extensive livestock-raising regions of the north and east, constituting perhaps 75 percent of the productive land of the country but only about 12 percent of the total population. The typical form of landownership is the large *estancia*, usually covering over 2,500 acres but staffed by a very few permanent employees. Usually a range foreman (*capataz*) supervises a geographical segment of the estate, assisted by a few rangers (*puesteros*) who are responsible for checking the livestock, repairing fences, branding cattle, and vaccinating sheep and cattle. Several hired workers do ranch work and a small amount of farming. In addition, migrant labor will be temporarily hired in seasons of peak activity, such as sheepshearing and roundup. Consequently, labor demands are minimal in comparison to the expanse of the land, and the population is very sparsely distributed (see ch. 18, Agriculture).

The *estancia* workers may live on the land, but their families are usually consigned to nearby settlements, which often take the form of *ranchoríos*. There they can be periodically visited by the men. Seasonal laborers and other underemployed ranch hands also live on the *rancheríos*. More progressive *estancias* provide housing, a school, and medical assistance for the workers and their families but, in general, although the *estanciero* respects the personal dignity of his employee, he feels little responsibility for his or his family's problems of housing or family relationships.

Lower class society in the rural areas is generally unorganized. Community life and activities are virtually nonexistent; attempts at self-government, interest in community affairs, concern with the preservation of law and order, or efforts to provide educational opportunities are extremely rare. In the *ranchenos* family life tends to be unstable and is plagued by boredom, drinking, and gambling.

About half of the upper class *estancieros* are absent for at least part of the year, since many prefer to live in Montevideo. The farms are often administered by paid managers who, together with the range foremen, perform middle-level functions but do not constitute a true, self-conscious middle class.

The existence of the archaic rural social structure in a progressive, modern country is comprehensible as a holdover from the eighteenth and nineteenth centuries. While the urban areas were undergoing major social and economic transformations, the rural livestock region remained practically untouched. The *gaucho* became a hired ranch hand, but the pattern of society organized into two classes separated by a wide gulf was unchanged. In 1970 the *estanciero* continued to act as a patron, providing whatever social, educational, medical, or legal services were available.

SOCIAL MOBILITY AND CHANGE

Because of an urbanized society and an expanding industrial base, Uruguay has had a highly mobile society in the past, but by 1970 mobility had lessened. A survey conducted in Montevideo and the rural areas between 1958 and 1962 revealed that, from a random sample of 1,718 male household heads, about one-fourth belonged to a higher class than their fathers, slightly over half had maintained the same class position, and approximately one-sixth were in a lower class than their fathers.

In the same period the percentage of individuals performing nonmanual work increased slightly, with a concurrent decrease in the proportion of manual labor. In general, the long-term trend is toward an increase in size of the upper and middle classes and a concurrent decline in the lower class.

Upward mobility is limited by the importance of personal and family connections in obtaining a job or social position. Selection for positions in the government or private enterprises is generally based on kinship, membership in a certain club or political faction, or friendship rather than on universalistic criteria such as standardized tests, educational level, grades, or experience. When such criteria are applied, the candidate has usually already been selected on the basis of personal relationships. Recruitment for the top professional, administrative, and executive positions in business and government occurs almost entirely from within the ranks of the upper class. Mobility is greater for the middle-status positions but decreases at the lowest levels of society, where individuals rarely move significantly higher than the level of their fathers.

Overcrowding at the upper levels of society decreases the chance for mobility, particularly for young, educated, middle class individuals. The long life expectancy means that many top positions are held for long periods of time by older men. Because the country is small and the economy is expanding slowly, it is unable to absorb the number of qualified applicants, and many are forced to emigrate. Some Uruguayans feel that the extent of foreign capital and investment in the country also limits their possibilities for advancement (see ch. 4, Population and Labor Force).

Education is the most common avenue for social mobility, and secondary academic school plays an especially significant role. Studies indicate that, if an indivudal exceeds the educational level of his father, he will probably experience some upward mobility, while a failure to achieve the same amount of education as the father will result in a decline in social status. A study made in Montevideo found that almost 50 percent of the residents were more extensively educated than their fathers, while only 10 percent had less formal education.

The level of educational attainment, however, is directly dependent on the economic and class position of the family. Even in government elementary schools, the dropout rate between the first and sixth grades in urban areas is 50 percent, in comparison to 80 percent in the poorer rural schools. Academic secondary education is highly valued as a road to middle class status, but for lower class and lower middle class families it is a heavy drain on the family resources, and many families are reluctant to permit entry into the secondary school unless they are sure that the child can go through to the university level. In a study made in Montevideo, it was shown that the children of upper class families are much more likely to finish academic secondary school than those of the lower class. A sample of a public high school revealed that 27 percent of the first-year class and only 13 percent of the last-year class were of the lower stratum of society (see ch. 8, Education).

Technical and vocational education is increasingly unpopular, since it leads to occupations involving manual labor, and is gradually being replaced by academic schooling in the aspirations of the lower middle and lower classes. If the child of a low-level white-collar worker fails in secondary school, his parents are likely to send him to a business school, where he will be trained to perform white-collar work even if at the lowest level. In Montevideo a working-class child with low or failing grades tends to stay in school longer than the child of lower middle class parents in a similar situation. The child of lower middle class parents is more likely to avail himself of the business school option, since the father's personal connections within the middle class will enable him to find a position for his son. In contrast, unless the working-class child finishes secondary school, he is likely to slip back into the lower class.

University education continues to be almost exclusively an upper and upper middle class prerogative. A 1960 university census indicated that at the time of matriculation 30 percent of the student body was upper class, 46 percent middle class, and 12 percent lower class. Since the dropout rate is higher for the poorer students, even fewer lower and lower middle class children gain university degrees than matriculate. In 1968 another survey indicated than 60 percent of the students were from Montevideo, 32 percent from the interior, and 8 percent from abroad. Of the provincial students, however, only 2.5 percent came from the rural sector, and almost none were from the poorest segments of rural society (see ch. 8, Education).

A person can also achieve higher status by landownership, by the transition from manual to nonmanual labor, and by an elegant life style. The noticeable display of material prosperity in socially accepted forms increases an individual's social prestige. Membership in high-status social clubs or associations and marriage into a more influential and powerful family are other avenues of social advancement.

Class consciousness is characteristic of the upper class and some segments of the lower class, such as the unionized industrial workers, but is generally lacking among the agricultural workers and peasants. Many middle class people in Montevideo and the interior towns are aware of their class interests as expressed through political ideologies of the Colorado Party and of their existence as a social category. The disparate nature of the middle class, however, prevents the entire social group from experiencing a unified class consciousness. In some cases the upper fringes identify with the upper class and, although the lower middle class may be anxious to emulate middle class ideals and habits, it often lacks the material means and education to lead the accepted middle class way of life.

There is some evidence that during the 1960's class differences had become accentuated in response to inflation, economic crises, and increasing domestic violence. Government employees experienced a significant drop in real wages between 1961 and 1966, and, in the same period, incomes of agricultural workers and laborers also decreased. The rampant inflation of the 1957—67 period was far more damaging to the middle and lower classes than to the commercial, business, and landowning elites. During the 1960's labor union activity was intense, producing increased political and class consciousness among the urban industrial working class and some unionized segments of the middle class, such as government employees (see ch. 20, Labor Relations and Organization).

The wage and price stabilization program of the late 1960's was beginning to improve the position of the middle and lower classes in 1970. Many lower class workers and some segments of the middle class, however, felt that the stabilization had been conducted at their expense to the benefit of the financial and business interests (see ch. 22, Finance).

FAMILY PATTERNS

The Emergence of the Modern Family

The upper class *criollo* family of the colonial period preserved many of the characteristics of the traditional Spanish family. Extended families made up of a large number of kinsmen who maintained close relations with one another were typical. The father was a dominant and authoritarian figure who controlled the family's economic and social existence, the future of his children, and the behavior of all family members. The wife's authority extended to household matters and the socialization, education, and religious training of the children, but in all areas she was ultimately subject to the wishes and decisions of her husband. Children were always desired, and large families were the rule.

The larger kin group played an important role in social and economic life. An individual relied on the assistance of family members in finding a good position and establishing himself in society. The family was the core of social life and often gathered to celebrate a baptism, first communion, marriage, or other important event in the life of a family member.

The lower class rural family in the same period was smaller and less cohesive. The nomadic *gaucho* often did not establish any permanent union, choosing instead a succession of temporary liaisons. Even if he formed a longstanding relationship, he usually did not reside permanently with his family, a pattern that continued to influence poorer rural families in 1970. Lower class urbanites also maintained close relationships with a more restricted circle of kin than the upper class, although a large number of children was common to all levels of society.

Commencing in the mid-nineteenth century, the effects of urbanization, secularization, and immigration served to undermine the norms and values supporting the traditional large-family pattern. In an urban environment children are an economic burden, since they are unable to contribute to the family livelihood as easily as a rural area. Furthermore, housing may be limited and food more expensive. The urban child needs an education if he is to find a good position in society, creating further drains on the family income.

In the late nineteenth century the influence of the immigrants was increasing. Many Uruguayans imitated the customs, habits, and life styles of the middle and upper class immigrants of the nineteenth and twentieth centuries; since a large portion of the higher status immigrants were French, German, British, or North American, their small-family tradition was introduced into the country (see ch. 5, Ethnic Groups and Languages; ch. 10, Religion).

The progressive education and emancipation of women during the late nineteenth and early twentieth centuries encouraged many middle and upper class wives to restrict the size of their families in favor of activities outside the home. By 1908 the average family had only three children, and many had fewer. The welfare measures of Batlle y Ordóñez gradually substituted state agencies for the extended family as the source of social security and insurance against economic crisis, thus reducing the individual's dependence on his larger network of kin. By World War I a large family was still considered the norm, but most urban dwellers, especially the growing middle class, had begun to restrict family size and to maintain close relationships with a fairly small circle of kin.

Structure and Function of the Family

In 1970 the average urban family consisted of a husband, his wife, and one or two children. Some 80 percent of the residential family units in Montevideo consisted of only parents and children. Working-class families tend to be slightly larger than those of the middle class. Upper class families are also typically somewhat larger and have been estimated to average six members.

The small family is partially a result of economic strictures, which affect the middle class in particular. Most moderately wealthy parents prefer to have only as many children as they can adequately feed, clothe, and educate. Urban living quarters are often too limited to accommodate large families. In the 1957—67 period inflation, the shaky economy, and the unreliability of the social security system further discouraged parents from increasing the size of their families. For many middle class families, a large number of children is a luxury they cannot afford.

Reduced family size is mostly a result of putting off marriage and of postponing having children until some time after marriage. Family planning is widely accepted among the urban middle and upper classes as well as large segments of the lower class. Although abortion is officially illegal, in 1968 the abortion rate was estimated to be three times the number of live births. In 1967 Uruguay had several private family planning associations and a family planning clinic in Montevideo. In 1962 a family planning symposium was held in Montevideo to discuss natural and artificial means of regulating conception, sexual education, premarital counseling, and assistance to a sterile or infertile couple.

Families in the interior towns and agricultural regions are similar to those in Montevideo in structure and size. The smallest urban communities, however, tend to have a birth rate almost double the national average.

The rural livestock regions are plagued by family instability and a lack of women. A family pattern in which the mother cares for a large number of children sired by several different men is typical of the poorer families in this region. Most families living in the communities of small houses on the fringes of *estancias* are of this type. Few marry formally; in some interior departments rates of illegitimacy range from 35 percent to as high as 69 percent of all births. As the children grow old enough to work, they are often forced to leave home in order to find jobs and, in many cases, migrate in their early teens. Most poor workers are financially unable to marry and, even if they were able, probably could not live with their families while they worked on an *estancia*. The very poor will occasionally give away their children if they are incapable of feeding and caring for them.

Rural migrants to the city and towns are predominantly women, since it is they who are generally unable to find an economic niche in the livestock region. The 1963 census reported that, on the average, there were 133 men to every 100 women in the rural interior. Males significantly outnumbered females in the five-to-nine-year age group. In the twenty-to-twenty-nine-year category, there were almost 150 men to every 100 women living in the countryside; in the fifty-five-to-fifty-nine-year group, the ratio was 175 men to every 100 women (see ch. 4, Population and Labor Force).

The family situation in the urban shantytowns is similar. Few adults marry, although they may maintain longstanding relationships. Families average about five members, but additional adults often live in each household. They are not always relatives; many are recent migrants or occasionally criminals hiding from the police. In general, the number of adults is larger than that of children.

The functions performed by the urban family have diminished, but in general it continues to be a stable, cohesive unit primarily concerned with the care, socialization, and early education of children. The state welfare measures relieve the family of financial burden of caring for aged, unemployed and, in some cases, sick members. A system of family allowances is designed as a wage supplement to assist poorer families, in particular, with the care of their children. A periodic allotment for each child under the age of fourteen, or the age of sixteen if he is attending school, is distributed to all families earning below a certain income level, and payments increase in direct proportion to the poverty level of the family (see ch. 20, Labor Relations and Organization).

The family continues to be an important center of social life, but in urban areas its members are increasingly involved in nonfamilial organizations, such as social and athletic clubs, community groups, and political associations, In rural areas such organizations are far less common and the family plays a correspondingly greater role in social events.

The family serves to establish an individual's position in society, assuming greater importance with each step up the social ladder. Elites are often interrelated by family ties, and even elective political offices tend to be held within large family groups. The concern with maintaining family position and prestige leads propertied middle and upper class individuals to avoid any risks to the family wealth, such as speculative economic ventures, and contributes to the typical middle class interest in security, stability, and moderation.

Family property usually passes to the children. If an individual dies intestate, illegitimate children receive a share amounting to two-thirds of that of each legitimate child. If the deceased was a legitimate child and he has no legitimate descendants, his estate is divided among his nearest ascendants, his spouse, and his natural children. If there are no relatives in these categories, the estate is distributed among the brothers and sisters and the adopted children or, in cases where none of these relatives survives, to adoptive parents, collateral relatives to the fourth degree and, ultimately, the state. The distribution of property to the heirs of a natural child who dies intestate follows approximately the same principles, although the parents who recognize the deceased as their child take precedence over adoptive parents. An individual can make a will and distribute his property generally as he wishes.

Family Relationships

Relations between husband and wife, while conforming to the pattern of male dominance, are affected by the relative quality between the sexes in the society at large. Men hold the dominant positions in society, but women are often involved in national life. The woman is generally considered capable of taking part in a business deal, a government enterprise, or a cultural event.

Since the late nineteenth century women have been encouraged to attend schools up to the university level, and in 1970 almost half the total school population was female. The professions have long been open to women; they are active in medicine, dentistry, pharmacy, and government administration. Women participate in even greater numbers in education, social work, and retail merchandising and almost monopolize nursing and home economics. In addition, they participate in political parties, labor unions, business associations, and civil groups and, in some cases, have assumed leadership positions. In 1964 it was estimated that 37 percent of all women in

Montevideo worked or studied outside the home and that women made up 31 percent of the total work force in the city. In the country as a whole, approximately one worker in four is a woman.

Women have extensive legal rights. They have full political equality, are able to own property, can hold a bank account in their own names, and may petition for a divorce with no proof required. In a few cases, women have held elected political office. In the 1967—72 term of the national legislature, there were two women in the Senate; the Chamber of Representatives has had female members for many years. In 1968 a leading woman politician was appointed minister of culture. The National Women's Movement for Social Justice and Peace was founded in 1968 to improve the social conditions of the country. Some women are skillful broncobusters and participate in the annual rodeo during Semana Criollo (Week of the Creole). Among lower class families, the woman may be an important breadwinner and, in some cases, is the only center of family life.

Relations within the family are usually harmonious and peaceful. It is generally accepted that older children dominate over younger, boys over girls, and husbands over wives. A 1964 survey of university students in Montevideo revealed that the large majority were satisfied with their childhood family life and wished their own family to be similar. Female students were particularly concerned about a further emancipation of the woman from the home. Most students believed their parents had prepared them adequately for life. Although many students were anxious to establish their independence, there was little indication of conflict or hostility between the generations.

A husband's relations with another woman are acceptable only if he behaves discreetly; he may appear in public with his mistress, but he must keep her far removed from his family and any social functions where wives are present. If he creates a public scandal or if he commits adultery in the home, it constitutes grounds for his wife to divorce him. On the other hand, any adultery on the part of a wife gives her husband grounds for applying for a divorce.

Extended family ties are most important at the top levels of society, decreasing in significance in the lower strata. The upper middle and upper class extended families may be united by common economic interest, such as family lands or joint family enterprises. Members of elite families are often proud of their ancestry and family traditions. Families usually choose to use both the paternal surname and the maternal maiden name to indicate their lineage. This practice is common, although not universal, at many levels of society.

Although family traditions are less important at the lower levels of society, the extended family still performs important mutual assistance functions. Relatives in a lower class family may exchange tools and equipment with one another, lend or borrow money, or care for one another's children. Among the rural poor, however, migration separates families and often renders contact with even the nuclear family difficult. The institution of ritual godparenthood seems to have only minor importance.

Marriage and Divorce

Civil, rather than religious, marriage was first permitted in 1837 and by 1885 was the only legally recognized form. If a couple wishes to have a church ceremony, they must first be married before a state official and four witnesses, then present the certificate to the clergyman performing the religious ritual. Only in extreme cases may the religious precede the civil ceremony. Men must be over fourteen years of age and women over twelve; until they reach the ages of twenty-five and twenty-three, respectively, permission of the parents or legitimate ascendants is required. The married couple generally holds property in common, although both retain the right to own property individually. In 1927 the marriage ceremony was officially amended so that the woman no longer promises to be obedient, but both bride and bridegroom vow to respect each other.

A large proportion of marriages are solemnized by a religious ceremony. The highest rate is found among the middle class, and the lowest rate is among industrial workers and small businessmen. Many couples establish a semipermanent union without any formal marriage ceremony. A large number are hesitant because of their suspicions of official formalities, their inability to pay the expenses, their lack of a cultural and pschological orientation toward marriage, or their ignorance of the advantages of a legally constituted marriage. In many cases a man is unable to obtain a binding divorce from a previous marriage.

Illegitimacy rates provide a rough indication of the frequency of nonformalized unions. The national average in the late 1950's was 29 percent of all births. Rates tend to be highest in the north and lowest in the farm regions of the south, such as San José or Canelones.

The country was early in legalizing divorce, voting it into effect in 1907. At that time a woman was permitted to sue on the grounds of cruelty and a man chiefly in the case of adultery. Acceptable grounds for divorce have since been expanded to include adultery by the husband in certain circumstances, attempted murder if it results in a criminal conviction, or voluntary desertion for over three years. A divorce is also permissible by mutual consent, with no reason given and no proof necessary.

According to divorce law, a husband is always bound to support the wife if she is not the guilty party, with the amount fixed according to his ability to pay and the needs of his wife. Ideally, she should be able to maintain the economic position she had during marriage. She loses this support, however, if she remarries or leads a depraved life. If either spouse is indigent, he or she may demand support payments from the other party. Custody of the children is determined by agreement of the spouses or, if they are unable to agree, by the decision of the judge. Both are liable for the maintenance and education of their children.

Divorce proceedings are long and expensive, especially in cases in which the divorce is requested on the basis of mutual consent or the wishes of the wife. Several hearings must be held over a long period of time. If the intention to divorce is not reiterated at any one of the established times, the proceeding is halted and cannot be resumed in the same form.

The frequency of divorce per 1,000 marriages doubled between 1935 and 1960. In the early 1960's about 70 to 85 divorces were granted for every 1,000 marriages performed each year.

Studies show that marriages are most likely to break up after from six to fifteen years, with the highest rate between six and ten years of marriage. Only about 14 percent dissolve before five years, and a very few couples separate after twenty-five years. In most cases divorce is a step toward a new union or the legitimation of an existing relationship. In 1960 the number of marriages in Montevideo involving at least one divorced person was 12 percent of the total number of marriages but 65 percent of the number of divorces in the entire country.

Childhood and Youth

Although the number of children in each family is small, they are greatly desired and well cared for. Most parents have their children baptized in the Roman Catholic Church during the first months after birth. At this time he is given a saint's name and acquires a godfather and godmother, who sponsor the child's baptism and promise to safeguard his development and religious training. The godparents are usually chosen by the parents and are individuals whom they respect and for whom they feel affection.

Usually, a child of unmarried parents will officially be recognized as a child of a particular person, although he continues to be an illegitimate or natural child. During their minority, natural children are given special legal protection. They can acquire legitimate status by the subsequent marriage of their parents or by adoption by a married couple if the biological parents are unknown. Both legitimate and natural children can be adopted by any person over thirty who is at least twenty years older than the child to be adopted. The child must first spend two years in the custody of the adopting person or family. The adoption of a minor requires the consent of his parents or guardian and, if he is over eighteen, his own consent as well.

Responsibility for the socialization of children rests on both parents, but the father is the primary disciplinarian and authority. The mother is freer to establish more sympathetic and indulgent relationships with her children, although she also will discipline them if necessary. The complete control a father has in a small town or rural environment is not always possible in the city. Urban children are likely to have more friends and activities outside the home, especially in connection with school functions, and the peer group assumes correspondingly greater importance.

Discipline among working-class families is likely to be inconsistent and arbitrary. Children may be left to their own activities except when they cause annoyance. In many poor families no father is present, making discipline even more erratic. Juvenile delinquency is becoming an increasingly serious problem, partially because of a lack of discipline in the home, unstable families, and early migration away from home (see ch. 23, Public Order and Internal Security).

Boys and girls are taught their sex roles early in life. As young children, they learn that boys dominate over girls. Boys are expected to be authoritative, strong, and aggressive. Girls are trained to be modest, retiring, deferential to male authority, and competent in the household tasks required of a wife and mother.

The first communion is usually regarded as an important step in the child's development. Many families also have a special celebration for their daughter's fifteenth birthday. Except for the relatively small number of children in private Catholic schools, Uruguayans attend coeducational schools and have opportunities for association with the opposite sex from their earliest school years. Although girls are more restricted than boys in their social life, they are increasingly free to date without chaperonage, especially in the urban areas. Single dates are acceptable in some cases, but most parents prefer double dates and group activities and generally want to know the young man before allowing their daughter to date him. Teenagers are free to attend parties, picnics, motion picture theaters, and other group activities. Middle and upper class children, in particular, are encouraged to behave properly in public, and girls are careful to preserve a good reputation.

Although young people are, to a large extent, free to meet their future marriage partners on their own, the consent and approval of parents are still important to most young people. Men generally marry in their late twenties and early thirties; the number who marry under twenty is negligible. Women marry slightly earlier, usually in their early twenties, and a small number marry under twenty years of age. After marriage, the ideal is to live apart from the parents, but in many cases housing shortages render this difficult. In general, parents maintain considerable influence over their children longer than they do in North American families. Women tend to have children in their twenties, although it is not uncommon for a woman to bear children until her late thirties.

CHAPTER 7

LIVING CONDITIONS

The conditions under which people lived in 1970 were substantially more satisfactory than those encountered in most parts of the world. The burden, however, of numerous and generous welfare and welfare-related government programs had contributed to an economic decline beginning in the mid-1950's. Real income suffered a corresponding decline, and there was a growth in popular unrest. Austerity measures were imposed in 1968 and real income turned upward in 1969 and 1970 but in 1970 some discontent was still evident. Even during the period of decline, however, the already superior conditions of health and sanitation had continued to improve.

Availability of medical care, access to stores, and variety of recreational outlets are at their best in Montevideo, and in 1970 about half of the population lived in the capital city. Amenities were fewer in the cities and towns of the interior and fewer still in rural areas. Less than a fifth of the population was rural, however, and even on the isolated farms and in the rural slum conglomerates living conditions were superior to those in similar places in many other countries.

With an economy based primarily on stockraising and agriculture, there is an ample and varied supply of food available to all except the relatively small sector with the lowest income. The average daily per capita intake of calories, as well as their protein content, rates among the highest in the world, although the diet is not always well balanced.

Ample diet coupled with good medical care, an extensive preventive medicine program, and generally satisfactory environmental sanitation have resulted in generally good health and one of the world's highest longevity rates. As in other Latin American countries, there is a substantial and increasing housing shortage, but in 1970, because of the country's low rate of population growth, it had not yet reached critical proportions. North American or European style of dress is customary, and clothing tends to be conservative. The reluctance of the wealthy Uruguayan to flaunt his wealth is illustrated by the fact that children customarily wear uniform smocks over their clothing while attending school.

The rather leisurely pace of the national life is reflected in short working hours in stores, offices, and banks and in an ample schedule of national holidays. This leaves considerable time for recreation, and recreational outlets are available, at least to some extent, to all of the population. Soccer is unrivaled as the nation's favorite pastime, but many other sports are popular. The inviting beaches, stretching for some 200 miles along the Río de la Plata estuary, are crowded in summer; social and sports clubs are numerous; games of chance are legal, and one or more of the various forms of gambling are indulged in by almost everyone; motion pictures, television, and radio are popular and available to much of the population; and legitimate theater, ballet, and symphony of good quality are presented in Montevideo. Most universal of the recreational outlets of gregarious Uruguayans, however, is social intercourse—ranging from the wild gaiety of Carnival week to casual conversations in bars and cafés between business acquaintances as well as the exchange of visits between relatives and friends. It is one of the major compensations of rural life that farms or ranch outposts are located near enough to neighbors living in the general vicinity that occasional visits may be exchanged.

The central element in the country's extensive and advanced welfare structure is its system of retirement and pension benefits. In one way or another, all Uruguayans—and some aliens—become eligible for benefits whether or not they have ever been gainfully employed. The amounts vary from meager to extremely generous. The welfare system also includes family benefits for low-income families. Conditions of employment benefits established either by law or collective contract are numerous. In general, public welfare and related programs are so comprehensive that private welfare activities are far less in evidence than in many other countries.

Several important criticisms have been leveled against the public program. The large number of retirement and family allowance plans, many operating entirely independently from one another and under separate legislative authorization with different rules and standards, has led to confusion, invited abuse, and often resulted in prolonged delays in making payments. In addition, the excessive number of people employed by the government (more than 20 percent of the labor force) is a kind of concealed welfare program.

The opportunities for early retirement are so extensive that in the late 1960s the number of pensioners was about one-fourth as large as that of the economically active population. Aware that the welfare system had gone beyond the country's ability to support it, the government in 1970 had already taken the first steps toward bringing order to its complexity and was studying means of revising the schedule of retirement eligibility—probably by advancing the minimum retirement age.

NUTRITION AND DIET

The people are among the best fed in the world. Although the adequacy and composition of nutrition and diet vary by region and by level of income, and the diet is often nutritionally unbalanced, starvation is unknown and serious malnutrition is rare. According to information available in 1969, there was an average daily consumption of 3,030 calories, as compared with the daily intake of 2,200 calories cited by a United Nations agency as an adequate worldwide average. The 3,030-calorie diet included up to 100 grams of protein daily. On the basis of a comprehensive 1962 survey conducted by the United States Interdepartmental Committee on Nutrition for National Defense, the nutrition was significantly deficient only in vitamins A and C and in thiamine, and it was calculated that an increase in the production of pork products and utilization of greater quantities of fruits and vegetables would result in a very satisfactory nutritional balance.

Meat is traditionally the most important item in the national diet (accounting for more than one-third of the national caloric intake), although the per capita consumption is unevenly distributed by locality and income group. Even though beef is the most popular, in parts of the interior sheep rather than cattle are slaughtered for local consumption. Lack of small-unit refrigeration would cause loss of beef through spoilage.

According to United States Department of Agriculture data, in 1967 the average per capita meat consumption of 227 pounds was the world's highest. It comprised 147 pounds of beef and veal, 20 pounds of pork, and 60 pounds of mutton, lamb, and other meats. Early in 1970, however, the government was endeavoring to increase the quantity of meat available for export; as a consequence, hotels and restaurants were prohibited from serving beef, veal, mutton, and lamb on Fridays, Saturdays, and Sundays.

In urban localities of the agricultural lowlands, particularly in Montevideo, eggs and fowl are readily available but of limited popularity. Fish and other seafood are good and plentiful (rock lobsters, in particular, are of good quality) but seldom appear on the table. Starches and milk and milk products are important diet components. For those who can afford a varied table, the pattern of consumption in Montevideo and most other urban centers is more a matter of custom than lack of availability of certain foods. In parts of the interior plateau, the diversity of available foods is less varied, and the diet consists primarily of starches, some meat, and a few fruits and vegetables.

Among countrypeople in particular, some traditional beliefs remain with respect to dietary rules that should be followed by expectant and nursing mothers. Meats, milk, fruits, and green vegetables are regarded as particularly desirable foods during the months before birth takes place; and spices, semolina products, fats, and all alcoholic beverages should be avoided. After birth takes place, lactation is believed to be stimulated by oatmeal with milk, milk taken as a beverage, beer, and salt; spices, alcoholic beverages other than beer, and nearly all green vegetables are regarded as detrimental.

Most characteristic of the country's dishes is the *asado*, the South American version of a barbecue. Frequently, it takes the form of *asado con cuero*—a yearling heifer, cooked in its own hide to retain the palatable and nutritious juices, eaten with bread and a green salad, sometimes accompanied by red wine. Another national dish is *churrasco*, grilled beefsteak cut into thin slices. Sausages, giblets, and black pudding are often added. *Parillada* is a mixed grill of varying content, usually consisting of such items as kidneys, liver, udder, pork sausage, and black pudding. It is prepared over a small container of charcoal.

A favorite and substantial dish of Spanish origin is *puchero*. Somewhat resembling a New England boiled dinner, it is a whole meal in itself and is a frequent menu item among families of modest income. It consists of meat cooked with vegetables, chick peas, and bacon and is frequently seasoned with a sauce of cayenne pepper and parsley. *Ensopado*, a dish similar to *puchero* but containing more liquid, is eaten primarily in the interior.

Another popular dish is *carbonada*, a meat stew with rice and fruits. *Costillas de papas* consists of barbecued spareribs cooked with onions, tomatoes, potatoes, and spices, and *milanesa* is a type of beef cutlet in which thin meat slices are seasoned and dipped in a mixture of breadcrumbs and eggs. They are pan-fried and may be eaten hot or cold. *Tallarines de pollo* is chicken cooked with noodles. One of the few main dishes not consisting largely of meat or fowl is *pascualina*, a vegetable pie in which spinach or Swiss chard is fried with onions in vegetable oil, then cheese, eggs, and seasoning are added; and finally, layers of biscuit dough are placed above and below the mixture to form a kind of sandwich that is baked until the crust is lightly browned. Another favorite is *tortilla de papa*—a potato omelet in which sliced potatoes are fried with vegetable oil, beaten eggs are poured over them, and then the mixture is fried on both sides; occasionally, potatoes are replaced by some other vegetable, such as spinach.

Breakfast is usually of the light European variety. *Café con leche* (coffee and milk mixed in equal proportions) accompanied by bread or crackers are the basic items. Frequently, the bread and crackers are spread with marmalade or cheese. A few well-to-do families add steak and potatoes. Fruit is not regularly a breakfast menu item.

For the large proportion of the population, the midday meal is the most substantial; served between 1:00 and 2:00 P.M. It may include a soup and a main dish combining meat, potatoes or rice, and vegetables. A side dish of salad may accompany it, and bread of the French or Italian variety is served. Dessert may consist of a milk custard, cheese with fruit preserves, cakes, pastries, or fresh fruits.

The evening meal, served not earlier than 8:00 and as late as 10:00 or 11:00 P.M., is usually less substantial than the midday one. Soup, bread, and dessert are sometimes omitted. Among lower income groups, the evening meal does not differ markedly from the breakfast, although beer or wine is frequently served with it. To fill the long gap between the noontime and evening meal, an afternoon tea or snack (*marienda*) is customary between 4:00 and 5:30 P.M. It consists of *café con leche* or tea accompanied by pastries, scones, or simply bread and marmalade.

For the well-to-do, dinner is an elaborate evening repast, featuring a variety of meat courses, sometimes as many as three. Spareribs, for example, may be followed by lamb and finally by beef tenderloin. Spaghetti, bread, green salad, and vegetables are frequent side dishes. A rich and popular dessert, *chajá*, may conclude the meal. It is a kind of ball-shaped spongecake filled with cream and jam and sprinkled with coconut.

The menu of the less affluent becomes simpler in proportion to income. The leftist press has asserted that even in Montevideo the poorest at times subsist principally on spaghetti and porridge. In rural areas the diet of the worker varies by region and occupation. Meat supplemented by bread is still the ranch worker's chief food, but the consumption of vegetables is increasing. Under the law, all rural workers must be provided food and lodging as a supplement to their wages (see ch. 20, Labor Relations and Organization). Batllistas (see Glossary) have urged that a healthy and adequate diet for them be defined and made compulsory.

Domestic wines and beer are good and produced in sufficient quantity to supply the demand. A cane alcohol is the principal domestically produced hard liquor, drunk mostly in the interior. Tea and coffee are popular, but the national drink is Paraguayan tea (*maté*). Enjoyed by all classes at all times of the day in town as well as in the country, it is made from an aromatic herb grown in Paraguay and Argentina and has stimulant qualities similar to those of tea and coffee.

CLOTHING

Clothing in Montevideo and other urban centers is distinguishable from that worn in North America only to the extent that styles for both men and women follow the European pattern. Men tend to be well dressed in a conservative manner, with dark colors predominating. Women who can afford to do so, dress with stylish conservatism but use dressier fabrics than those customary in most Latin American countries. Hats are seldom worn by either sex, but the Basque-inspired beret—usually of a dark blue felt—is often seen.

Although temperatures almost never drop below freezing, there is a pronounced seasonal change, and the use of sweaters and outer garments in winter and in the evening in all seasons is customary. On the beaches that fringe Montevideo and much of the southern and Atlantic coastline, however, inseason patterned sport shirts and shorts as well as abbreviated bathing suits are familiar sights. Businessmen, however, wear coats and ties during working hours. Urban women who can afford to do so wear fur wraps during the colder months. Women seldom appear in downtown streets in slacks or shorts. Blue-collar and rural workers and their families dress more simply at work, but few are without at least one set of best clothes for special occasions. At primary schools, administrators encourage students to wear smocks over the regular clothing in order that poor children, by virtue of their dress, will not be made to feel inferior to those with parents of higher income.

There is an extensive textile and clothing industry, and ready-made suits and dresses are available in wide variety. In urban centers, however, good-quality tailoring and dressmaking services at reasonable prices are available. There are shoemakers and shoe manufacturers, but shoe widths tend to be broad, and fitting for people with narrow feet is difficult.

A single exception to the conventionality of Uruguayan dress has been the survival of the colorful costume of the *gaucho*. Cowboys still frequently wear the traditional broad-trimmed flat *gaucho* hat and poncho, although the traditional ballooned, knee-length trousers inserted into boots have for the most part been replaced by more prosaic blue jeans. The raiment of the *gaucho* in his rustic splendor survives also in the numerous Montevideo social clubs that celebrate festive occasions dressed in *gaucho* costume.

Data concerning the percentage of income spent on food in the late 1960's are not available. An extensive survey in Montevideo in 1962 showed the expected inverse ratio between the amount of income and the percentage spent for food. It varied between 93 percent for families with six members in the lowest income group—100 to 500 pesos (for value of the peso, see Glossary) monthly—to 17 percent for families of three in the highest income group—over 4,000 pesos. Within each of seven income brackets enumerated, familes with four or five members spent the greatest proportions on food. The average monthly income of the families surveyed was slightly over 1,500 pesos. For families in this category, it was determined that the percentage devoted to food rose irregularly from 28 percent of the total for those with two members to 50 percent for those with seven members.

HOUSING

The rate of residential construction in the mid-1950's commenced a decline that was to continue for more than a decade. The fairly moderate rate of migration into the cities and a low rate of population growth, however, have prevented devlopment of urban slums comparable in extent to those that have sprung up in many other countries during recent years.

Nonetheless, the 1960's were marked by a growing housing problem. Rent controls, in effect throughout the period, discouraged residential construction in the private sector and maintenance of housing in existence; there was little activity by public housing agencies; inflation and an economic recession sharply limited the usefulness of the mortgage system and other sources of funds for housing construction in the private sector. Between 1961 and 1968 investment in construction dropped from 5.4 to 3.8 percent of the gross domestic product, a falling-off considerably sharper than that experienced by industry as a whole.

According to the 1963 census, the number of housing units exceeded the number of families. There were over 721,000 units in existence and about 701,000 familes, with an average of 3.7 persons per family. The number of units, however, included both the summerhouses of the well-to-do and virtually uninhabitable units in the last stages of disrepair. Estimates made in the mid-1960's indicated that, because of poor initial construction or deterioration of much of the available housing, the national deficit was between 85,000 and 100,000 units. Some 14 percent of the population as a whole was housed under substandard conditions; 15.5 percent of the urban and 17.8 percent of the rural houses were extremely deteriorated or uninhabitable. Some estimates, however, conclude that the proportion of marginal housing in the countryside was far higher.

Later refinements of the 1963 census recalculated the number of housing units at 667,000 with an occupancy of four persons per unit. Some 48.1 percent of the units had one or two rooms, 35.9 percent had three or four, 12.3 percent had five or six, and 3.4 percent had seven or more. Hallways and utility or storage rooms were not included in this count. No mention was made of the average floorspace per room or per unit. Some 47.3 percent of the dwellings were in Montevideo (where, in general, housing was best maintained and of the highest quality), 36.2 percent were in other urban localities, and the remaining 16.2 percent were rural.

To meet the needs of the low-income population, the National Low Cost Housing Institute (Instituto Nacional de Vivienda Economica—INVE) was established in 1948 to assist in the construction of low-cost housing. Some departmental governments also undertook direct action in the field of housing, but they, like the INVE, lacked sufficient funds. The Bank of the Republic and the Mortgage

Bank of Uruguay (Banco Hipoticário del Uruguay—BHU) extended loans for home construction and rehabilitation, but they also were hampered by limited resources. Between 1952 and 1961, 28 percent of the housing units were constructed by the private sector with public credits, 7 percent directly by the public sector, and the remaining 65 percent undertaken by the private builders without public assistance. Between 1955 and 1961 housing investment absorbed a yearly average of 6.4 percent of the gross domestic product. The resulting production of 11,900 units a year, however, was insufficient to meet the minimum requirement of 16,000 units.

In an effort to stimulate the sagging housing-construction industry, the Inter-American Development Bank (IDB) in 1962 granted a loan of US$8 million to finance 53 percent of the cost of construction of 4,100 units for low-income families. At the end of 1969, 2,203 units had been completed; 1,799 were under construction; and US$6.8 million of the total had been disbursed. Also in 1962, the United States economic assistance program had granted US$6 million for the same purpose.

The INVE and BHU joined forces with the departmental governments of Montevideo and Soriano in carrying out this pilot project made possible by the 1962 IDB loan. INVE was responsible for direct construction of low-cost dwellings, and BHU granted long-term mortgages at low rates with mortgage guarantees.

The immediately succeeding years were marked by a continuing increase in the overall shortage, and the National Development Plan for the 1965—74 period included as a major objective the construction of 320,000 new housing units, 45,000 to be built by the public sector. The building program, however, continued to stagnate during the late 1960's as private sector dwelling permits issued declined irregularly in numbers from 16,000 in 1960 to 12,000 in 1968 and to a preliminary figure of 11,000 in 1969. Public sector permits moved irregularly between a high of 1,026 in 1960 to a low of 41 in 1964. Permits issued in 1969 numbered 569 according to preliminary data. These figures represented totals well below the installed capacity of the construction industry, and in 1970 a government agency announced that 133,000 new units were needed at once in order to provide housing for people without accommodations habitable in accordance with the minimum standards of the country.

At the end of 1968 legislation was enacted establishing the National Housing Fund (Fondo Nacional de Vivienda) as a dependency of the Ministry of Public Works with authority to administer, coordinate, and control the activities of the housing agencies. It is financed by a 2-percent tax levied on salaries, wages, fees, and other sources of income, on the basis of a 1-percent contribution by employers and a matching 1-percent contribution by the National Housing Bank (Banco Nacional de Vivienda—BNV) and other banking and related entities. Plans for bringing the fund into operations were slow in being placed in effect, however, and at the end of 1969 it was estimated that its assets were about 1 billion pesos rather than the 3.6 billion anticipated, a circumstance that hampered envisioned housing investments during the first year.

In order to accelerate construction in June 1969 the executive branch ordered immediate issuance of invitations to bid on certain public housing plans. This decision to reinstate public projects after a virtual standstill of more than two years because of the refusal of constructors to continue operations without guarantees of payment probably reinvigorated production. During the stagnation period, however, construction costs had quadrupled, and in 1970 further incentives for builders were needed.

The 1968 law also established a savings and loan system and designated the BHU as its central element with authority to direct its operation. A further provision called for establishment of a unit adjustable to variations in the average wage index as indicated by the executive branch. The adjustment clause applies to all housing loans and to certain accounts in savings, bonds, and debentures. It also applies to mortgage loans granted by the BHU before enactment of the law. To achieve this end, an annual tax was to be levied on current loan balances at a rate equal to the percentage of variation the index indicated.

Not the least of the factors resulting in stagnation in the private sector of housing construction during more than a decade has been a system of urban rent control, in force since 1943. Without these controls, dwelling construction for rental purposes might have been more extensive. According to the latest data available in 1967, less than 15 percent of the urban housing units were rental properties. Increases have been permitted from time to time, and a general tripling of rents was authorized in 1967, but at the end of 1969 the rise in the cost of living in Montevideo since 1943 had been many times that of the generally allowed rental increases. Early in 1970, in some instances, rentals were reported no longer sufficient to cover taxes, but a further relaxation of controls might have meant multiple evictions and encouragement of real estate speculation. In mid-1970 a bill was under consideration before Congress that would in most cases prohibit eviction of low-income personnel, except for nonpayment of rent, until October 1972.

At the same time, the creation of a Fund for Rental Compensation and Acquisition of Housing (Fondo de Compensación de Alquileres y Adquisición y Construcción de Viviendas) was under consideration. It was to be supported by a tax equivalent to 2, 3, or 5 percent of the rentals (depending on the rental amount), half to be contributed by the lessor and half by the lessee. Some 65 percent of the proceeds were to be used by the BNV to finance construction of low-cost housing for sale or rental, and the remaining 35 percent was to be used to supplement rent payments of tenants unable to make the payments in full.

The same rental control system that has contributed to a stagnation in the construction of private individual housing has been a major factor in the growth of condominium apartments. During the 1950's and 1960's large and luxurious high-rises sprang up along the Rambla, the great avenue that skirts the Montevideo beaches, and a variety of more moderate condominiums appeared elsewhere. Construction of buildings of this type was encouraged in 1946 by promulgation of a law on cooperative building ownership.

Because of the lack of native forests, wood is seldom used as a construction material except for window frames, trim, and flooring. Latest data available in 1967 indicated that 35.6 percent of the dwelling unit flooring was of wood. This relatively heavy use of a scarcematerial for floors was in part accounted for by the popularity of parquet flooring among the well-to-do. It should also be noted that as a statistical category the term for wood (*madera*) included materials such as asphalt tile, linoleum, and other kinds of composition material. In the country as a whole, other floorings included 49.3 percent cement, 2.5 percent brick, and 12.2 percent earth. Flooring materials in urban areas outside Montevideo (no specific information was given for the capital city) included 65.8 cement, 3.7 percent brick, 18.0 percent wood, 11.9 percent earth, and 0.1 percent other. In rural areas 30.7 percent of the floors were cement, 8.2 percent were wood, and 44.7 percent were earth.

Statistical data are not available concerning materials used in construction of walls and roofs. Many of the better urban houses are fashioned with walls of small glazed bricks, a type of construction requiring considerable labor cost. Masonry walls are the most frequently encountered, and in large buildings reinforced concrete predominates. Roofs tend to be of tile. In most of Montevideo, residences and business establishments immediately adjoin one another in the traditional Latin American style. Modern trends are apparent, however, in the clean-cut designs of the new apartment buildings and private homes. In the large and prosperous suburb of Carrasco, tree-shaded streets and neatly trimmed lawns are the rule. Legislation enacted in 1916 requires that the houses in this locality by set back from the street and that all properties—even vacant lots—fronting on paved streets be fenced or walled.

More modest urban buildings often are made of lighter materials. These include sheets of fiber-cement, treated cardboard, and corrugated iron; roofs are made of thatch or loose tile. Efforts to popularize prefabricated panels in 1970 had not yet extended to a point where their savings in cost and convenience had become fully appreciated.

A part of the urban slum population of Montevideo lives in barracks-like masonry buildings called *conventillos*, large and dingy structures divided into cubicles affording little light and air. Most of the remainder live in *cantegriles*, primarily suburban squatter settlements made up of huts constructed of tarpaper, sheets of metal, or any available scrap material.

Data on the relatively small slum population of the country are incomplete and conflicting, but undoubtedly the greatest concentration is in the *rancheríos*, rural clusters of hutments occupied principally by dependents of livestock workers, who are not permitted to live on the estate with their families. They are housed in adobe barracks on the estate and visit their families weekly. The typical *ranchero* dwelling is constructed of mud-brick or wattle-and-daub with a thatched roof and mud floor. There is seldom sanitation of any kind. A type of temporary shack sometimes constructed by sugar workers is the *bendito*, in which two sloping roofs join like two hands in an attitude of prayer. Made of long branches of pine or willow, they are tied together with *cipo*, a flexible vine, and walled with straw.

HOLIDAYS AND BUSINESS HOURS

In 1970 there were eleven fixed national holidays, including some religious holidays retained with secular names. The dates were: January 1, New Year's; January 6, Children's Day (Epiphany); April 19, Landing of the 33; May 1, Labor Day; May 18, Battle of Las Piedras; June 19, Birth of Artigas; July 18, Constitution Day; August 25, Independence Day; October 12, Columbus Day; November 2, Day of the Dead (All Souls' Day); and December 25, Family Day (Christmas). Inauguration Day, occurring every five years on March 1, and the second Monday of August each year for tailor shop workers were also fixed holidays. The movable holidays were two days for Carnival during February or March and three days during Tourist Week (Easter Week). In mid-1970 legislation pending before Congress would eliminate January 6 as a holiday and shorten the Tourist Week holiday to two days.

Business hours vary, but many of the offices are open from 8:30 A.M. to noon and from 2:30 to 6:30 or 7:00 P.M., differences in weekday hours depending on whether or not they are open part of the day on Saturday. Many of the department stores are open from 9:00 A.M. to noon and from 2:00 to 7:00 P.M. Monday through Friday and from 9:00 A.M. to 12:30 P.M. on Saturdays. Banking hours are 1:30 to 5:30 P.M. in summer and 1:00 P.M. to 5:00 P.M. in winter. Government offices are open from 1:00 to 7:00 P.M. from mid-March to mid-November and from 7:00 A.M. to 1:00 P.M. the rest of the year. Banks and government offices are closed on Saturdays. Because dinner frequently starts as late as 10:00 P.M., the larger restaurants remain open until well after midnight.

The midday break is in part a consequence of the fact that the principal meal of the day is eaten at noon and in part indicative of survival of the traditional siesta. Shorter midday closings, however, are becoming increasingly frequent.

RECREATION

For a variety of reasons, recreation in Uruguay has become an art form. By world standards the people are among the most highly educated and, accordingly, among the best able to enjoy the numerous cultural outlets available to them. In addition, they are a highly gregarious folk who take particular pleasure in informal social intercourse, a circumstance that is significantly facilitated by the high degree of urbanization (see ch. 4, Population and Labor Force). Nearly everyone lives at least on the periphery of urban existence and enjoys some of its recreational advantages.

Unlike many developing countries where the isolated farm family of necessity turns to its own members for social concourse, many Uruguayan farmworkers live in small towns near their work rather than on the estates where they are employed and enjoy the opportunity of casual association with a variety of people. Even the rural poor have the opportunity for participating in some collective festivity, for virtually no one lives entirely outside the money economy. In so compact a country there are few localities where either an occasional community barbecue does not occur nearby or the nearest cinema is too distant for an occasional visit. Because of the variety of recreational outlets, it has become customary to describe the people as generally lighthearted and unwilling to take themselves too seriously.

The cities, particularly Montevideo, offer the greatest variety of recreational choices. In the towns as well as in Montevideo cups of coffee and conversation in sidewalk cafés are as universally popular as the evening strolls and casual street encounters with neighbors—customs that derived from the formal Hispanic promenade of an earlier era.

The ubiquitous transistor set has made radio programs available to almost everyone. In 1970 the latest available information indicated that virtually all of the Montevideo homes had radio sets and that in the countryside only a few dispersed housing units were without access to them. The ownership of television was significantly concentrated in Montevideo, with at least five out of six sets in or about the capital city. A majority of the provincial capitals had television stations, and only a few of the dispersed rural housing unit dwellers were too far from a crossroads store, café, or bar that they could not occasionally enjoy a television program. (see ch. 15, Public Information).

Family gatherings are important, and the active social life of the capital revolves in great measure around the home. In Montevideo and other urban areas, however, there are hundreds of social clubs that play an important part in the country's recreational life. Montevideo's Jockey Club, Club Uruguay, and several yacht clubs are sites of leading social events, but there are also social and sports clubs for people of more modest means. For a variety of aristocratic Montevideo clubs the high point of the year is Holy Week (Tourist Week in the secular Uruguayan nomenclature) when members repair to the countryside dressed in the traditional *gaucho* costume for *asados* and rodeo-like sporting events. Undoubtedly, the oddest of the myriad of Montevideo social club groups is the Parvenses. They exist for the purposes of general buffoonery and the deflation of well-known public figures regarded by the membership as stuffed shirts.

Carnival remains the annual high point of festivity. It occurs during the two days preceding Lent, although after its formal conclusion it tends to taper off rather than to cease abruptly, and during the Lenten season few give up pleasures for abstinence. During Carnival there is a profusion of public and private dances in hotels, homes, clubs, and in the streets. Montevideo, in particular, features flowered floats, and buildings are gay with streamers and colored lights. Parades with marchers wearing garishly colored masks and costumes clog the streets. A major feature is the *tablado*, a lavishly decorated temporary stage erected in each neighborhood. Painted musicians, clowns, dancers, and mummers perform. At Carnival's end substantial prizes are awarded to the best *tablado* presentations.

Gambling is legal and indulged in extensively. During January and February international horseraces are held at the Hipódromo Nacional de Maroñes on the northeast edge of the city. There is also a smaller track outside the city. There are gambling casinos in Montevideo and Punta del Este, roulette predominating in popularity. A National Lottery Administration has a monopoly on all forms of betting connected with the lottery and controls all raffles offering prizes in excess of amounts adjusted periodically to correspond to living costs. During the 1960's the number of raffles, in particular, proliferated. Many were for worthy causes, but the investment in them was reducing the disposable income of the average consumer to such an extent that in early 1970 legislation to curtail this increasing movement was under consideration.

Soccer (*fútbol*) is the national sport and is played throughout the country almost all year. The perennial national champions, Peñarol and Nacional, are subjects of public adulation, and the Uruguayan teams have often won world championships. In 1950, when the country was victorious for the fourth time, a national holiday was declared. Almost everyone is a soccer fan, and small boys may be seen playing it in the streets of cities and towns, perhaps using a ball improvised out of a wad of cloth secured by string. Basketball, volleyball, sailing, swimming, rowing, boxing, and *pelota* (a form of jai-alai) are popular, but they do not have the universal appeal of soccer. Bullfights and cockfights have been outlawed for many years.

More than 200 miles of beaches are government owned, and private construction on them is not permitted. Free to all, they are lavishly patronized. The beach season formally opens on December 8 in Montevideo. Throughout the summer months, sailboats are scattered along waters of the southern coastline, and the sands are crowded with beach umbrellas.

The more sophisticated of the cultural recreational outlets are confined to Montevideo. The principal theater company is the National Theater (Comédia Nacional), founded in 1947 under the auspices of the Montevideo municipal government. In the summer ballets are held in the Municipal Amphitheater of Montevideo. International artists appear regularly in the Teatro Solís, home of the Comédia Nacional. The government radiobroadcasting station in Montevideo in 1931 inaugurated a symphony that has since become the National Symphony. In addition, the government maintains a school of dramatic art and a school of the ballet.

Motion pictures are fairly popular; subtitled North American films predominate. In early 1970 it was estimated that there were 184 motion picture theaters; 56 of these (including most of the largest) were located in the capital. Of particular interest is the Annual Film Festival held at Punta del Este featuring outstanding recent films of various countries and attended by international film celebrities (see ch. 15, Public Information).

HEALTH

Public Health Administration and Finance

Under an appointive minister, the Ministry of Public Health maintains an extensive system for administration of the country's health program. Administration in the past has been heavily concentrated in Montevideo, but during the late 1960's some decentralization was accomplished. In this respect, the Constitution of 1967 assigned to the governors (*intendentes*) of the departments immediate supervisory responsibility for public health matters within their areas of jurisdiction.

During the late 1960's the General Health Office of the Ministry administered hospitals containing more than 77 percent of the hospital beds in the country, and the ministry was directly responsible for construction, repair, and remodeling of the public hospitals. Other state and state-associated entities supervised hospitals with 6 percent of the beds, and the remainder were in private or mutual care (*mutualista*) establishments.

Through the departmental governments, the ministry supervised the numerous departmental health centers, auxiliary centers, and polyclinics. Among its principal administrative elements, centered in Montevideo, were the Planning and Budget Office and departments of environmental hygiene, maternal and child protection, family planning, mental health, and nursing. Other operative units included those for pharmaceutical and technical matters. Among its other responsibilities were coordination and general supervision of the activities of related institutions, such as the National Medical School, the National Institute of Hygiene, the National Institute of Endocrinology, the Institute for Premature Children, and a colony for tuberculosis research.

The ministry regulated standards for the practice of medicine and paramedicine in all its branches; set conditions to be met by producers of food, beverages, and drugs; and maintained control of narcotics laws.

The Constitutions of 1934 and subsequent constitutional documents, including the Constitution of 1967, have stipulated that the government provide gratis the means of making available preventive care and treatment to those who are indigent or lacking in sufficient funds to provide for their adequate medical care. In addition, partial systems for insurance covering illness and medical care for personnel in a dozen sectors of employment have come into existence through separate legislative acts in the 1960's. Various union groups have obtained medical coverage through collective bargaining. Most of the medical protection, however, is provided by commercial insurance or by some forty small mutual protective associations that receive various forms of subsidies and loans from the government. In 1963 over half of the population of Montevideo participated in some kind of mutual association.

These mutual societies are supervised by the Coordinating Committee for Collective Medical Assistance, which is headed by the subsecretary for public health. Under a 1969 decree the committee was to ensure that the various collective health groups provide adequate and standardized services as prescribed by it. This was seen as a first step toward the establishment of a nationwide program of health insurance (*seguro del salud*).

Medical Personnel and Facilities

Because of the limited number of the surviving indigenous population, the widespread high level of education, and the general availability of medical services, traditional attitudes toward health have had little effect on medical practices. Nevertheless, in the mid-1960's midwives practiced extensively; and woodland herbs, such as chamomile, sarsaparilla, and quinine, were used frequently as rural home remedies.

It has become a cliché that Montevideo has a monopoly on the country's medical facilities and services, but in 1970 more than half the population lived in the capital city, communication systems in the small and compact country were good, and a rural health program had been emphasized during recent years. In 1966, however, the number of physicians in Montevideo per 10,000 population had been 11.4; the ratio outside the capital and the other larger cities (the remaining 45 percent of the population) had an average of 4.3 per 10,000.

The number of practicing physicians increased from 2,600 in 1960 to 3,300 in 1968 and to a preliminary report of 3,500 in 1969. This 34.6-percent growth during the nine-year period more than tripled the overall rate of growth of the population and resulted in a substantial emigration of young physicians who had completed their university training only to find no openings in their profession at home. Enrollment in the medical faculty at the University of the Republic, however, continued to increase at a fast pace during the 1960's. Moreover, the traditional concern in Uruguay over the excellence of its medical personnel is underlined by the fact that in 1968 some 51 out of a total of about 1,000 Pan American Health Organization (PAHO) and World Health Organization (WHO) fellowships awarded to Western Hemisphere countries for advanced training in medical and related studies went to Uruguayan students, an impressive number for the size of the country (see ch. 8, Education).

The superabundance of physicians has been offset by a shortage of nurses. Between 1960 and 1969 the number of graduate nurses more than doubled, but the increase in actual numbers was only from 300 to 610. In 1969 practicing physicians outnumbered graduate nurses by a ratio of almost six to one. It was therefore necessary to supplement the small corps of trained nursing personnel with auxiliaries, of whom there were about 3,800 in 1964—14 per 10,000 of the population. The rapid growth in the size of the small corps of graduate nurses during the 1960's was both encouraging and indicative of a change in attitude toward the nursing profession. In Latin America as a whole, nursing has never been a popular calling. The nurse, even at the graduate level, has not been well paid and has not enjoyed the prestige and social position accorded her in many other parts of the world.

The 1,250 dentists practicing in 1962 (the most recent date quoted in 1969 and 1970 publications) were generally well trained and their number in proportion to the population as a whole (4.8 per 10,000) compared very favorably with that in most other Latin American countries. A 1962 survey in Montevideo and in other parts of the country, however, found dental health to be far less satisfactory than health in general. Cavities were few in the teeth of people of all ages examined, but there had been many extractions, there was extensive evidence of peridontal (gum-related) disease, and oral hygiene seemed to have been largely ignored. The country's need appeared to be for more and better education in the care of teeth and gums than for more and better dentists.

The law requires that all pharmacies be operated personally by graduate pharmacists, with degrees issued or validated by the University of the Republic. The Medicaments Control Commission under the Ministry of Public Health has for many years controlled prices of medicines and monitored publication of advertisements concerning them.

The number of hospital beds increased from 12,135 in 1960 to 17,200 in 1968. In 1963 the ratio had been a very satisfactory average of 65 beds per 10,000 population, with 76 in urban and 54 in rural localities. Also in 1963 there had been seventy-eight hospitals, including seventy-two general institutions. There had been 16,935 beds; 11,867 general, 2,984 mental, and 2,084 tubercular. Institutions such as leprosariums and maternity and child hospitals were not listed separately. According to the most recent data available in 1969, the average period of stay was thirteen days. It applied to public health hospitals only and was for the year 1960.

In size and impressiveness the country's system of hospital installations is dominated by the Hospital de Clínicas, pleasantly located in Battle Park in downtown Montevideo, not far from the modern and privately run Italian and British hospitals. This twenty-story building, completed in 1950, has facilities for 3,100 patients. It is a government institution operated by the Medical School of the University of the Republic. A giant medical service center for low-income patients, it is also the country's principal center for medical research.

In the mid-1960's over half of the hospital beds were in Montevideo. A majority of those outside it were in the departmental capitals, but they were supplemented by auxiliary medical treatment installations; only in few instances were people located far from a medical facility. According to the most recent information available in 1970, the hospitals were supplemented by 17 departmental health centers, 25 auxiliary centers, and more than 130 rural polyclinics. Limited medical services were also provided on some of the larger rural estates. In addition, the Armed Forces Medical Services provides hospital and outpatient care for all military personnel and their dependents (see ch. 24, The Armed Forces).

Life expectancy at birth in 1965 was 67.9 years for men and 73.1 for women. For the 1965—70 years the weighted average for both sexes was about 70 years, one of the highest longevity rates in the world. The 1966 infant mortality rate of 42.7 per 1,000 was very low by global standards. There do not appear to be extreme variations in the mortality rates in the several parts of the country. In Montevideo the 1966 infant mortality rate was slightly higher than the national average, although the reported rate of illness and disease was highest in the northern departments. The annual death rate per 1,000 had risen from 7.6 in 1958 to 8.5 in 1960 and to 9.5 in 1967. A continuance in this increase could be expected during the 1970's, but in no sense could it be seen as a deterioration of the country's generally satisfactory health conditions. It is axiomatic that proportionally fewer births coupled with an increasing survival rate at all ages result in a rising death rate. In 1970 there was a trend toward a further decrease in an already low birth rate, heavy emigration of young people, and increasing longevity. An increasingly large proportion of the population was reaching advanced years, and senility and the diseases of old age were inevitably taking a proportionally greater toll of life.

During the 1963—67 period the principal causes of death were those characteristic of the more advanced countries. They included, in order of frequency, circulatory diseases, cancer and malignant tumors, vascular lesions affecting the central nervous system, accidents, and bronchitis and pneumonia. In general, the mortality rate in avoidable diseases, such as contagious and parasitic conditions, still accounted for 4.7 percent of all deaths. In particular, there was as high an incidence of infant diseases, cysts, and goiter. In 1966 the most frequently reported cases of notifiable diseases in order of incidence were scarlet fever, influenza, tuberculosis, infectious hepatitis, diphtheria, leprosy, syphilis, measles, and typhoid. Gains had been made in the campaigns against these diseases, or they were held to be at a standstill except in the case of syphilis, where the rate of incidence nearly doubled between 1958 and 1965.

Although the relatively low rates of endemic diseases, epidemics, contagion, and parasitic threats combine to make the need for preventive medicine less urgent than in many other developing countries, a substantial preventive program has been in existence for many years. It was, however, largely confined to Montevideo until the 1960's, when the government began to accelerate rural preventive activity. During 1969 some 230,000 vaccinations were given under the program, and 40,000 preventive clinical examinations were given to rural children. The teaching of proper health and sanitation is a regular part of elementary school training. Increasing emphasis on this practice in rural schools during recent years has been an important factor in the preventive medicine program.

With respect to preventive medicine campaigns as a whole, poliomyelitis vaccination has nearly completely eradicated the disease, the number of cases reported having dropped from 162 in 1958 to 2 in 1968. During the 1961—67 period over 735,000 immunizations were administered. From 1965 to 1967 a little more than 20 percent of the population had been inoculated against smallpox, and in 1968 the disease was considered eradicated. A campaign against jungle yellow fever began in 1948, when ninety-one positive cases were reported, and by 1968 the disease was considered eradicated. In 1966 tuberculosis remained the eighth most important cause of death, but a broad campaign against it had been in progress for several decades; between 1958 and 1965 the number of cases reported was down to 9.1 from 14.5 per 100,000 population. Malaria is listed by the PAHO as one of the diseases common to the South American continent that has either never appeared in Uruguay or has been eradicated. In an effort to cooperate in control of venereal disease, Uruguay is one of the fifteen Western Hemisphere countries to participate in an interlaboratory program of tests undertaken under direction of the WHO Library.

During the late 1960's leprosy remained a major health concern, but there appeared to be little danger of an increase in its incidence. Of 400 cases reported at the end of 1967, only 12.5 percent were hospitalized. The remainder were ambulatory and under surveillance, and the disease was considered under control.

Of particular importance during the 1960's has been the program to eliminate the *triatoma infestans*, a biting bug that is the transmitter of Chagas' disease. It represents a somewhat less serious threat than in neighboring Brazil and northern Argentina, but in 1969 it was estimated that the vector might be present in the walls and thatch roofs of as many as 57,000 houses of the coastal and northwestern provinces and to have infected at least 800 people. In 1969 about 700,000 people, primarily in rural areas, were considered potentially vulnerable.

The disease, which is virtually incurable, produces fever and lymphatic gland swelling and results in heart, esophagus, and colon malfunction. A death rate of up to 19 percent is reported, and its debilitating effect on the working force is also a matter of serious concern. In cooperation with PAHO, the country has initiated a program of periodic spraying with residual insecticides in and around houses in suspected areas.

SANITATION

Administration of the country's sanitation programs is primarily a responsibility of the Ministry of Public Works, although the Ministry of Public Health concerns itself in rural environmental sanitation through participation in educational programs and drilling wells in rural communities serving fewer than 1,000 inhabitants. Under the Ministry of Public Works, water supply and sewerage services are provided by the autonomous State Sanitary Works Administration (Administración de Obras Sanitarias del Estado—OSE), except that the sewage system in Montevideo is operated directly by the municipal government.

By 1970 the IDB had granted five loans totaling US$16.2 million to assist in the development of water supply and sewage systems. Two of the loans, the first in 1961, totaled US$8.2 million and were used to expand the water supply and sewage system of Montevideo with the OSE acting as executing agency. Implementation of these works had tripled the city's water supply by 1970, and existing facilities were expected to meet its demands up to 1980. In 1970 the city's sewage system was also being expanded by the installation of some forty miles of pipe in low-income districts.

In 1965 two IDB loans were granted for a total of US$3.6 million to assist in the construction of a central water supply facility capable of supplying resort areas located along the forty-three-mile coastal strip between Piriápolis and Punta del Este. Although the resident population of this area is only about 40,000, it reaches some 100,000 during the summer tourist season. During 1967 US$4.4 million was allocated for the development of water supply services to thirteen communities in the interior, including both departmental capitals and other urban centers widely dispersed throughout the countryside. Overall, the IDB loans will contribute to the construction of eighty-three water and two sewage systems expected to initiate or improve facilities available to about 60 percent of the country's population.

Also supplementing the domestic investment in public sanitation projects was a water purification plant in Montevideo, completed in 1964 with assistance of the Export-Import Bank of Washington. The installation has a 700,000-cubic-yard capacity. Other OSE projects during the 1960's included well-drilling, purification systems for river water, and laying of pipelines to carry water over long distances. It was contemplated that OSE-supplied *agua potable* (water suitable for drinking) would be available to all communities with more than 500 inhabitants by 1972 and that it would be available by that time to 90 percent of the country's urban and 70 percent of the rural population.

The supplier of almost all of the country's drinking water, OSE during the late 1960's acted as a pace setter in public relations, businesslike operations, cost-cutting, and customer service. The organization's plans included study of the possible installation of a desalination plant to draw potable water from the ocean. This program could serve as a model water system for other Latin American countries.

In 1970 Montevideo had the country's most extensive purification plant and water distribution system, but potable water was available also to the departmental capitals and other important population centers, such as Punta del Este and Piriápolis. In 1970, according to the latest available information, public water was available to about 85 percent of the population in Montevideo. Outside Montevideo, about 320 systems served 34 percent of the urban and rural population and 28 percent of the housing units. The principal difference between rural clustered (ten or more housing units per hectare, or 2.47 acres, of land) and dispersed (isolated) units was that the clustered units relied heavily on potable water from wells, while the dispersed units wells and cisterns produced water unsuitable for drinking without treatment. In the mid-1960's about 12 percent of the rural clustered and 14 percent of the rural dispersed units had no regular water supply of any kind. In many instances potable water was available only outside the housing unit. Even in Montevideo a sizable minority of the population lived in units without indoor facilities. An adjacent outdoor tap providing adequate quantities of *agua potable* was classified as having drinking water nearby.

Sanitary service is less extensive but roughly similar in distribution. In the mid-1960's about seventy percent of the Montevideo housing units were connected with a public sewage system, and in 1970 the city's sewage system was being expanded by installation of some forty miles of pipe in low-income districts. Some 18 percent of the population and 14 percent of the units in the interior cities and towns were served, but virtually none of the rural population had piped sewerage and 30 percent were without septic tanks or other regular means of disposal of wastes.

Facilities for the removal of human excrement ranged in the late 1960's from about 60 percent of the housing units in Montevideo with flush toilets and nearly 94 percent with some kind of cabinet facility, to no regular disposal facilities in some dispersed farm units and rural slums. Nowhere does improper disposal of human waste represent a real health hazard.

In Montevideo, in particular, sanitation standards are unusually high. Garbage and trash collection, a municipal responsibility, is sometimes criticized as being inadequate, but the streets usually appear clean and refuse does not accumulate conspicuously in yards and lots. In 1968 a study of the feasibility of depollution of the Montevideo beaches and coastal waters was initiated, and during the same year an air sampling station in Montevideo was placed in operation as part of the Pan American Air Pollution Sampling Network.

In Montevideo water and milk are drinkable, and no special care is required in connection with preparation of fruits and vegetables. In 1969 Great Britain imposed an embargo on importation of Uruguayan beef for sanitary reasons (see ch. 21, Trade). In general, however, food and beverage sanitation standards are high in the interior as well as in the capital city, although outside Montevideo and resort towns care is advised in preparation of salads and unpeeled raw fruits and vegetables.

WELFARE

The public welfare program is funded in part by public contributions and in part by contributions from workers and employers. It is government controlled, however, and its scope is so extensive and its provisions frequently so generous that the role left for voluntary welfare associations to play is marginal compared to that in most other countries. The overall public system meshes with welfare-related health and labor protection programs, but its core is the complex of retirement and pension funds (*cajas de retiro y jubilación*).

Although the operations of these funds—and the legislative authorizations upon which they are based—differ widely, certain principles are general to the four main funds. It is possible to retire with benefits from an occupation under one fund and take up a second career under another without forfeiture or suspension of pension rights under the first, thus eventually becoming eligible for two pensions. It is also possible for a person to qualify for and receive retirement benefits while continuing to work in an activity covered by a fund that pays his retirement benefits. Membership in an appropriate fund is mandatory, and the self-employed as well as those employed by others are required to participate; survivor benefits apply to family workers and their dependents.

Resources for the funds are established by employer and employee contributions, the government itself supplying the employer contributions for the 20 percent or more of the working force on the public payroll. In the late 1960's employers contributed to the funds an estimated average of 20 percent of gross earnings of employed personnel and withheld, for the same purpose, 12 to 19 percent of employee earnings. There were, however, wide variations. In the banking industry, which offered the most extensive benefits, employers contributed the equivalent of 23.5 percent of gross employee earnings and withheld from 8.5 to 16.5 percent of the gross payrolls. At the opposite extreme, employers of domestic servants contributed the equivalent of 5 percent of wages and withheld the same amount.

The intricateness of the system has made computation and collection of deductions and contributions difficult. During the mid-1960's some employers allegedly failed to file the required contributions on a timely basis. A net profit could be obtained by using the funds to make short-term loans and at the end of the year to pay the contributions plus penalties imposed. At the same time, the variety and volume of the paperwork involved have occasionally made it possible for employed personnel, either inadvertently or deliberately, to fail to contribute to the appropriate retirement fund yet eventually to receive benefits from it.

Because of these early retirement opportunities, in the late 1960's it was estimated that some 80 percent of the retirees were under the age of sixty, although many remained active in jobs covered by other funds. It was also estimated that the retirees numbered at least 250,000 (other estimates ran higher), as compared with a working force of a little over 1 million. With the increasing longevity of the population as a whole, the proportion as well as actual number of retired people could be expected to increase under the retirement system then in force.

The amount of basic retirement benefits varies from fund to fund, within the fund itself, by type of occupation, by length of employment, and by cause of retirement. In most instances it is based on the average wage earned during the last sixty months of active service, and the maximum is limited to a fraction—usually 80 percent—of the wages of active workers in corresponding jobs. Banking Retirement Fund retirees, however, may receive up to 100 percent.

In addition, special benefits for retirement or death, based on length of employment, are customary. These vary widely among funds. For example, personnel in industry and commerce are eligible only at the age of fifty after being employed for a minimum of thirty years; civil servants and teachers, only after thirty or more years of employment or if the years of employment plus years of age total ninety or more. On the other hand, there is no specific minimum service or age requirement for bank workers or for rural and domestic workers. In most instances the maximum benefit is eighteen monthly payments after forty or more years of employment. Bank workers, however, receive compensation equal to as many monthly payments as years of employment up to a maximum of thirty. In addition, their survivors receive a lump sum subsidy based on the decedent's years of service.

An effort was made in 1938 to bring some coherence to the program by merging four major funds as sections of a new Uruguayan Retirement and Pension Institution. In 1943 a fund for rural workers was established as an additional section of the institution. By 1948, however, social security in one form or another had been extended to most of the working population and their dependents, and the Retirement and Pension Institution had been divided into three separate elements. In 1970 there were seven systems in existence, including four main funds and three other funds operating under special systems.

The Industry and Commerce Retirement and Pension Fund, a catchall entity, covered, with certain exceptions, all persons, whether employers or employed personnel, who were engaged in any gainful and lawful activity and were not expressly assigned to some other fund. It included employers working personally in their own enterprises, employed personnel in industry and commerce, as well as public services administered by concessionaires, self-employed persons, and certain others. The oldest of the funds in continuous existence, its much-amended fundamental law in force had been enacted in 1919.

Pensions also vary between funds and, in some cases, are granted to family members and other dependents in case of declaration of absence, loss of right to retirement pay, or abandonment of home, as well as in case of death. In a majority of the main funds, pensions are limited to a maximum of 66 percent of the corresponding retirement pay, but in the case of survivors of bank personnel the pension may reach the equivalent of 100 percent.

One of the first in the Western Hemisphere to be initiated, the social security system has its roots in the mutual assistance associations of the mid-nineteenth century, which were also the forerunners of the organized labor movement (see ch. 20, Labor Relations and Organization). The first modern public welfare or social security entity was the pension fund for state teachers, established in 1896. It was followed in 1904 by a fund for civil service workers, and in 1909 pensions were introduced as welfare measures for the old and the disabled without means of support. During the 1920's and 1930's there were so many small funds of various kinds (the majority providing coverage for invalidity, old age, and death) that at one point two separate funds were in existence for benefit of employees of the Montevideo Jockey Club.

The Civil Servants' and Teachers' Retirement and Pension Fund covered all civil servants with the exception of bank employees and members of the armed forces. It included the members of government, personnel who worked for remuneration from the state, the decentralized services, the autonomous agencies, the departmental governments, and certain other categories.

The Rural Workers' and Domestic Servants' Retirement and Pension and the Old Age Pension Fund covered rural workers and domestic servants. It also covered owners of rural establishments who personally worked in them; technicians, employees, and workers occupied in rural tasks; caretakers and gardeners, servants, tailors, and seamstresses working in the employer's domicile; and certain others.

The Banking Retirement Fund provided coverage for personnel in public as well as in private banks. Included were the directors of government banks and their employees, owners of private banks who worked personally in their management, and employed personnel.

There were three other funds with systems of operation substantially different from those of the main four. The University Graduates' Retirement and Pension Fund covered those who practiced the liberal professions, excluding notaries, that required diplomas issued or approved by the University of the Republic. The Notarial Retirement and Pension Fund covered notaries and persons employed by them, and the Military Pension Fund covered retirees from the armed forces and their dependents (see ch. 24, The Armed Forces).

The Rural Workers' and Domestic Servants' Retirement and Pension and Old Age Pension Fund, in addition to its responsibility to retirees and their survivors, had been assigned the responsibility for administering the system of pensions covering any inhabitant of the country who had reached the age of sixty or was disabled, provided that he lacked means of support. Foreigners who had resided in the country for fifteen years or more were eligible. The pension was limited to a small fixed amount, the same for all persons in this category, and was subject to periodic adjustment.

In 1943 the government had also established a system of dependency allowances for principal wage earners in families in the lowest economic brackets among urban workers, the allowances to be administered by a variety of small equalization funds. Some coordination of the activities of these funds was achieved in 1950 by the establishment of the Central Family Allowances Fund, and in 1954 the system was expanded by the inclusion of rural workers. In 1970 the employers of industry and commerce contributed an average of 8.5 percent of the total amount of wages, rural employers paid 11 percent, and other employers paid 5 percent to the individual fund units administered by the central fund for payment of family allowances and other social security services for which the central organization was responsible. In the public sector the system was financed within the budget of the agency involved.

Under the system a small monthly allowance, fixed periodically under somewhat different legislative rules for the public and private sectors, was allotted to each dependent child, expectant wife, and dependent parent or aged relative living in the same household, if that family had an income below a basic scale, which was to be revised periodically. Seasonally unemployed estate workers could also receive corresponding dependency allowances. Amounts paid for children varied with the number in the family, those with the larger number receiving more substantial payments for each child.

The allowance ordinarily terminated at the age of fourteen but might be continued to sixteen under certain specified conditions and to eighteen if the child was disabled.

Welfare-related benefits applicable to certain worker categories—and sometimes for their families—included partial illness and medical care, work accident and occupational disease compensation, and unemployment and illness insurance (see ch. 20, Labor Relations and Organization).

Welfare activities for the young in 1970 were administered by the Children's Council, an agency established under the 1933 Children's Code. With broad responsibility for every phase of development and welfare of the young, it operated kindergartens, financed and operated school milk services, and maintained various holiday camps and homes. In addition, a 1964 law—confirmed by a provision of the 1967 Constitution—called for an apprentice-wages system to be administered by the Labor University with the aim of providing food, clothing, and transportation for minors enrolled in apprenticeship programs at the Labor University.

Generous and extensive as it has been, the public welfare system has suffered from a variety of difficulties. Distribution of benefits has not always been geared to needs. Retirement and other benefit payments have often been relatively high for persons with modest financial responsibilities, but protection of persons disabled early in life has tended to be inadequate. The same has been true of survivors of deceased wage earners, except that when the eligibility for a pension of a child or wife has become established, it may have proved to be very substantial.

In addition, the slow receipt of contributions, coupled with the excess of administrative personnel and cumbersome procedure, has often made it necessary for pension applicants to wait for a year or more before payments commence. Subsequently, payments have been several months late in coming to urban retirees and several weeks more to residents in the countryside.

As early as 1964 an International Labor Organization (ILO) mission had made a study in which it had pointed out the cumbersomeness and costliness of the welfare system and recommended an overall reform that would standardize and simplify administration and reduce benefits to a level conforming to the realistic financial capacity of the country.

Recognizing the undue complexity of the welfare program in complying with existing legal benefit requirements, the drafters of the 1967 Constitution prepared what was to become Article 195 of that document. It created the Social Welfare Bank as an autonomous agency with responsibility for coordinating the retirement services of the state and, in general, reordering the social security system. In order to free the new institution from political influences that had affected the welfare program in the past, Article 195 prescribed that its directors engage in no political activity beyond that exercising their right to vote during their terms of office and for some time after leaving office.

The initial specific functions assigned to the Social Welfare Bank were limited to assuming central control over the three largest retirement and pension funds—those of the civil servants and teachers, of industry and commerce, and of rural and domestic workers. The directorates of these funds were disbanded, and the organizations commenced to operate as sections of the bank. The funds retained their separate identities, however, and continued to operate under their own standards. In 1969 the bank—with some assistance from the ILO—had submitted the preliminary draft of legislation calling for future supervision by it of all social security services, whether provided by the state or by semiofficial or private bodies, and for standardizing and consolidating of the mass of welfare laws and decrees in force.

As reported in 1970, an International Monetary Fund staff team had noted that although Uruguayan social security costs during recent years had averaged about 7 percent of the gross domestic product (high by global standards), there was considerable popular dissatisfaction with the service performed and that benefits were often regarded as inadequate in comparison with the earnings of the actively employed. This was in large measure, however, owing to the excessive number of claimants under the system. It was recommended that a fruitful solution might take the form of advancing the retirement age and of redesigning the program to direct it more specifically toward those genuinely dependent on it for maintenance of income.

CHAPTER 8

EDUCATION

The educational system of the country is one of its greatest sources of pride. Although until the late nineteenth century schooling had played a relatively insignificant part in the development of the national life, by 1970 it had become a major focus of attention. During the years 1967 through 1969 educational expenditures of the central government were, as a percentage of the total central expenditures, the highest in Latin America and more than twice the Latin American average, a circumstance that heavily underlines the importance attached by the country to its public educational system. The private system, almost entirely confined to the primary and secondary levels, was small but compared favorably with the public program in organization and quality.

The public program is free for primary and secondary students. For those at the university level—although they must pay for books and other equipment—there are no tuition charges, and subsistence scholarships are available for the deserving needy.

During the 1960's the student population increased at a rate considerably more than twice the moderate national rate of population growth. By 1960 the number of Uruguayan young people who were attending or had attended school was already so substantial that qualitative improvement in their educational system had become a more pressing need. In 1969 the average amount of schooling for the population fifteen years of age or over was estimated at about five years. For those between fifteen and thirty it was close to twice this amount. In the 1960's rates of enrollment at all levels and in all kinds of schools were among the highest in Latin America. There was, however, a preference for academic and professional studies inconsistent with the country's economic and social needs. At the secondary level students showed a noticeable lack of interest in vocational training, and at the university level a superabundance of lawyers stood in contrast to lessening, but still serious, shortages of agronomists and veterinary surgeons.

Although rates of enrollment were high, dropouts and grade repetitions remained serious problems. The rates, however, appeared to be declining. The overall literacy rate was the highest in Hispanic America by a comfortable margin, and for more than a generation primary and adult school attendance had been so high that illiteracy had virtually been eradicated among people below advanced middle age.

Adult education consists in large measure of cultural enrichment programs, training for voluntary social work, and study schedules designed to improve working skills. In general, instructors have a high degree of competence, and the adult student body is of an educational order higher than that in most countries.

There are, however, some conspicuous deficiencies in the educational system. The number of classrooms was insufficient in 1970 and, although there was some new construction during the 1960's and a few large residences were converted into schools, the added space at best kept pace with the growth in the student population. As a consequence, in many schools classes were held in two or more four-hour shifts daily; and although the primary student-teacher ratio of about thirty or thirty-two to one approximated the Latin American average, nearly one-third of the class groups in the mid-1960's had more than forty students. Similarly, teaching aids and equipment, particularly in scientific and technical studies, were inadequate and in short supply.

Although administrative improvements were introduced during the 1960's, the different levels and kinds of schools were generally regarded as still operating too independently of one another. Urban primary schools offered courses leading to entry into either the general secondary or the technical-vocational system. Completion of the shorter rural primary system established eligibility only for entrance into some of the secondary agricultural schools. Graduates of the six-year general secondary school could apply for university admission. As a rule, entrants into the technical-vocational secondary schools found it necessary to choose a vocation after completing only four to six years of primary schooling. General secondary students had four additional years of grace. They were required to select their intended professions at the beginning of the preparatory cycle, the last two years of secondary school.

One basic characteristic of the system in 1970 could be attributed as much to circumstances of demography and geography as to defects in the system itself. Half of the population lived in Montevideo, and less than one-fifth was rural. The ratio of the student population to the nonstudent population in the same age group by physical location was significant principally at the university level, for the country's only university was in the capital city. Private schools with the best record of securing university admission for their graduates are in Montevideo, and the largest and best regarded technical-vocational schools are also located in the capital city, although the ratio of secondary vocational enrollment in Montevideo is not significantly higher than in the departmental capitals.

In rural areas, however, primary schools are relatively fewer, and the education they offer affords less access to further education.

Another characteristic of the educational system reflects the preference, by no means a national peculiarity, for professional, or at least white-collar, over manual occupations. In the Uruguayan wage structure, the blue-collar worker frequently is paid substantially more than his officeworker counterpart, but the social distinction of the white collar may overbalance in importance the size of the blue-collar paycheck. Primary graduates who enter technical-vocational schools often do so because they cannot find places in general secondary institutions. For those who are accepted by the university, the overwhelming preference is still for the traditional professions. Already surfeited with lawyers, the Uruguayan community finds about one-fourth of its university students studying law.

There have been some changes. In the badly needed fields of agronomy and engineering, the decade of the 1960's saw enrollments more than double. Overall, however, the university in 1970 was producing more professionals than the economy could absorb, and one result was massive emigration of people highly trained at public expense.

Administration of the educational program has been decentralized since the mid-1930's under a system providing considerable autonomy to the several educational levels. Deteriorating economic conditions culminated in 1967 in abandonment of the collegiate form of executive government and installation of a reform administration that took a stronger hand in administration of the schools. The years 1968 and 1969 were marked by increasing student and teacher unrest, including strikes, and the decade of the 1970's began in an atmosphere of explosive uncertainty for the educational community.

EDUCATION IN THE SOCIETY

During the period before independence, Jesuit and Franciscan orders provided formal schooling, available only to seminarians and the children of the elite. The first public education law was enacted in 1826, and as late as the middle of the nineteenth century only 30,000 students were enrolled in about thirty schools at all levels. The University of the Republic (often referred to alternatively as the University of Montevideo), in 1970 still the country's only university, was inaugurated in 1849 with a single department of studies, the nineteenth university to be founded in Latin America. The university had been preceded by schools of higher studies in philosophy, mathematics, medicine, and political economy as early as 1838.

José Pedro Varela, born in 1845, transformed public education. A friend and disciple of Horace Mann and of the Argentine educator Domingo Faustino Sarmiento, he was founder and later president of the Society of Friends of Popular Education and headed the General Administration of Primary Education. Two celebrated books that he wrote on education theory and practice led directly to the enactment of the 1877 Law of Common Education, establishing the principle that primary schools and teacher training should be free and secular and that primary schooling should be compulsory.

Never robust, and overworking himself, Varela died in 1879 at the age of thirty-four, but before his death he had interested scores of young people in teaching careers, raised the status of education in the public esteem, and laid the foundation for the tradition that a good and free public education was not the privilege but the birthright of every citizen. The general acceptance of this idea was the first major manifestation of the Uruguayan concept of the welfare state (see ch. 16, Political Values and Attitudes).

After Varela's death, legislation incorporated many more of his reform ideals, which were to attract the vigorous support of President José Batlle y Ordóñez. Local parent-teacher groups were founded to raise funds to supplement the meager teachers' salaries, and for more than ninety years these organizations have survived to coordinate local school leadership with the neighborhood public school systems.

For decades after Varela's passing, the school system remained highly centralized. Textbooks, lesson plans, and curricula were specifically prescribed for the country as a whole, and identical examinations were required for promotions from one grade to the next. Beginning about 1950, however, regional administrators were afforded progressively increasing opportunities to adapt course material and testing standards to local requirements. The mid-twentieth century saw the emphasis on rote memorization shift to a more effective use of library materials and other training aids, although in 1970 a major complaint was the relatively short supply of laboratory and other scientific teaching aids.

The extent to which the educational program is articulated to the needs of the country is debatable. By 1970 virtually all the children of primary-school age were receiving, or had received, some primary training. One statistical study showed that nearly 95 percent of the children between the ages of eight and nine were registered in the educational system. Secondary schools, however, were either academic or technical-vocational, with little provision for transfer between the two. All sectors of society tended to prefer the academic, and class distinctions between types of schools had lost most of their significance because lower middle class and working-class children were able to obtain free academic schooling. During the years since World War II, academic secondary education had been expanded at a rate much higher than technical and vocational education.

At the university level, too, prestige has remained as decisive a factor as preparation for earning a living. The social status of the skilled manual worker is rising, but as recently as 1969 a publication of an international organization described academic and technical-vocational schooling as systems totally apart, and during the 1960's dropout rates were approximately twice as high in the technical-vocational as in the academic programs.

Women play an important role in education. Coeducation, one of the primary objectives of José Pedro Varela has come to be a generally accepted aspect of the country's school system, although there remain a few female convent schools. Most of the data available on this matter in early 1970 were from the late 1950's. At that time virtually all of the kindergarten teachers and more than 90 percent of those in the all-important primary cycle were women. In the primary schools boys only slightly outnumbered girls, and in the basic cycle of general secondary school girls were in the majority. In the preparatory cycle there were more boys by a small margin. In technical-vocation schools about 40 percent of the students were girls, but in the basic adult education classes women made up only about 15 percent of the total. In 1965 about 40 percent of the enrollment in the University of the Republic was female; this percentage might have been higher had it not been for some reluctance to accept women in professions other than teaching and nursing.

All social classes have the same right to free schooling, but economic considerations are probably the principal cause for a far higher dropout rate among the children of lower income groups. The inability of the country's industry and commerce to absorb the continuing flood of newly graduated professionals has been cited as a major reason for the inflated rolls of the civil service and for the high rate of emigration of professional and skilled personnel (see ch. 4, Population and Labor Force). The government is aware of the lack of coordination between study program enrollments and the country's needs and, since 1967 in particular, has been endeavoring to extend, improve, and popularize practical study programs.

Although the government provides free education, all school systems enjoy a high degree of autonomy, and students tend to be highly vocal and sometimes militant adversaries. Student opposition to government has been a Latin American tradition since the famous liberal uprising at the University of Córdoba in Argentina during 1918. It is unusual in Uruguay, however, because of the extent to which the secondary students have rivaled the university students in their restlessness during recent years, particularly since 1967.

ADMINISTRATION AND FINANCE

Preprimary and primary schools and teacher-training schools preparing young people to teach at these levels are the responsibilities of the National Council of Primary and Normal Instruction. It consists of a director general, four other members, and a professional staff.

The National Council on Secondary Education is responsible for the general or academic secondary schools and for the Artigas Institute for Professors, a university-level institution preparing students for secondary-level teaching careers. On the council, a director general heads a board of six members. Three of these are chosen by the secondary teachers themselves and three by the councils of the primary, vocational, and university systems.

Under a director general, the National Council of Technical and Vocational Training is an administrative board including ten members nominated by the administrators of the several other educational systems, two by the teaching body of the Uruguayan Labor University, two by the executive branch of the government, and one each by the National Fine Arts Commission, the National Chamber of Industries, the Rural Federation, and the Rural Association of Uruguay. Board members serve for four-year terms. This council provides general guidance for the Labor University, a collection of the public industrial and agricultural secondary schools. It is less closely linked to the Ministry of Culture than are the primary and general secondary systems.

Limited independence of action was granted to the University of the Republic in 1935, and full autonomy came with the enactment of the Organic Law of 1958. The highest organ of the university is the General Directive Council, over which the rector presides as chairman. Some ten council members are nominated by the *facultades* (departments) and attached institutes and nine are nominated by the General Assembly of the Teaching Staff, the professions, and the students. Elections are for four-year terms.

Each of the university's ten *facultades* is governed by a twelve-man council under the chairmanship of the dean. Five members (at least three holding chairs) are elected by the teaching staff, three by alumni, and three by students. Terms are for four years, and incumbents are eligible for reelection after a two-year lapse. There is no regular schedule of meetings, which may be called either by the dean or by one-fourth of the council members.

The varying but considerable degree of autonomy granted after 1935 to the four public educational systems (primary and normal school, general secondary, technical and vocational secondary, and higher education) caused them to develop in different and uncoordinated ways. As a consequence, in 1963 the then Ministry of Public Education was instrumental in inducing the councils to establish a Coordinating Commission of Teaching Entities in order to rationalize and coordinate their activities. In the late 1960's, however, the informed consensus appeared to be that this goal was still far from achievement.

Within the country's departments, the Constitution of 1967 prescribes that regional educational administration shall be overseen by the governors (*intendentes*). Supervision of schools is carried out by a corps of specially trained inspectors, customarily graduates of the Artigas Institute for Professors with postgraduate training. The corps is so organized that an inspector assigned to a particular discipline supervises all teachers in his area engaged in that study. The function of the inspector is both administrative and technical. He guides and evaluates the work of teachers, organizes meetings and conferences, encourages the establishment of groups supporting education, publishes periodicals and notices, and engages in a miscellany of other tasks. In theory, at least, each school must be inspected at least twice a year. In Montevideo private schools are visited by special inspectors, but elsewhere both public and private institutions are monitored by public inspectors under an area director for each department.

Altogether, a high proportion of the government's public servants are engaged in the educational program. In 1966 about 20 percent of the civilian public positions, including those in government-owned corporations, were filled by teachers and administrative or service educational personnel.

The central government assumes all educational costs with the exception of those for certain books and other teaching aids at higher levels. Public education is financed by funds from the general national budget without supplementary contributions from local authorities. It is free at all levels, to resident aliens as well as to nationals. In addition, particularly at the primary level, parent-teacher commissions contribute funds for school activities but not for salaries. All such contributions are voluntary.

In 1966 resources were distributed more or less evenly in accordance with the number of students in the public schools. Special consideration, however, was given to schools located in areas with severe socioeconomic problems. Private schools are financed by tuition fees, gifts, and private funds. Those that provide free education for a number of children determined by several criteria are exempt from national and municipal taxes as an indirect subsidy for their services.

The country's financial contribution to its public educational program is generous, and the degree of generosity increased progressively during the 1960's. One statistical series shows central government educational expenditures as a percent of the gross national product to have risen, almost without interruption, from 2.5 percent of the total in 1961 to 4.4 percent in 1967 and to a provisional 4.8 percent in 1968. The 1968 figure was second highest among the eighteen Latin American countries, for which the average was 1.9 percent. As a percentage of total central government expenditures, the proportion rose irregularly from 16.1 percent in 1961 to 30.1 percent in 1967 before declining to a provisional 28.4 percent in 1968. The provisional 1968 proportion was the highest among the eighteen Latin American countries, for which the average was 13.2 percent. Peso expenditures rose from 8.26 billion (for the value of the peso, see Glossary) in 1961 to 13.22 billion in 1967 and to a provisional 14.32 billion in 1968. The index of expenditures on education, on the basis that 1961 expenditures equal 100, rose irregularly to 160 in 1967 and to a provisional 173 in 1968. Seven of the eighteen Latin American countries registered greater gains by 1968, but the Uruguayan figure was somewhat higher than the Latin American average of 154.

With the abandonment of the collegiate executive system of government in 1967 and the installation of an administration with a policy of fiscal austerity, the previously generous funding of the educational system took a new turn. Budgeted funds were either delayed or not forthcoming, and increasing concern was expressed by administrators at all educational levels. Early in 1970 a spokesman for the University of the Republic, commenting on the insufficient funds received since 1967, remarked that the institution had thus far been able to survive only be exhausting its stocks and by utilizing the credit that local commerce had granted. The Central Directive Council of the university early in 1970 was reported 2 billion pesos in arrears in monies budgeted since 1967. The cutting back on funds for public education was only part of the larger program to stem inflation and otherwise put the country's economic house in order, but in 1970 it was apparent that changes could be expected in the method of financing the school system. One suggestion under consideration was the charging of tuition, at least at the University of the Republic.

THE EDUCATIONAL SYSTEM

The government's educational authorities started in 1935 to grant considerable autonomy to both the individual schools and the school systems in what had been a highly centralized program. The systems involved were the preprimary and primary units, general or academic secondary schools designed to prepare students for college, technical-vocational secondary schools preparing students directly for skilled and semiskilled white- and blue-collar employment, and higher education, which consisted almost exclusively of the University of the Republic. Because the four types of school did not operate in effective concert, in 1963 the then Ministry of Public Education induced their directive councils to join in the Coordinating Commission of Teaching Entities in an effort to coordinate their administrative and teaching activities. Later in 1969, the National Board of Adult Education was added.

Public schools predominate both in number of establishments and size of enrollments at all levels. Higher education and teacher-training establishments are almost entirely public. There are, however, private preprimary, primary, general secondary, and a few secondary-level technical and vocational educational establishments. Incomplete information indicates that about 25 percent of the student population is enrolled in private institutions, many of them church-sponsored or ethnic schools in Montevideo. In 1969 some 72.1 percent of the population between the ages of fifteen and nineteen was enrolled, or had been enrolled in some kind of general or vocational secondary school. Enrollment had increased at an impressive 6.9 percent annual rate since the beginning of the decade.

The school year begins in March and continues to November or early December. There is some variation from this pattern in agricultural schools and in some university departments. Apart from the Southern Hemisphere summer vacation in December and January, there is a free week at Easter, two weeks in July, three to six days of spring vacation in September, and the national holidays (see ch. 7, Living Conditions). Ordinarily, about half the days of the year are days of school attendance. The school year is divided into three terms.

Making good education available to students at all levels is facilitated by the fact that half of the population lives in the capital city. It is here that the rate of school attendance is at its highest. Because they can live at home while attending excellent schools, residents of the capital have the best educational advantages. Satisfactory primary and secondary schools are usually available in the departmental capitals, but in the rural areas the school system, although of a relatively high calibre, remains in need of considerable improvement.

At all levels except possibly the university, the greatest problem is the inadequacy of buildings and of instructional materials and aids. Urban schools are frequently used to full capacity by two shifts of children. Secondary and industrial vocational schools are used by two or even three shifts, permitting the student only four hours of class time daily. Teaching personnel could be used for longer hours if more buildings were available—with corresponding salary increases. There was some classroom construction during the 1960's, and some large residences were converted into schools. These additions, however, have at best barely served to keep pace with the growth in enrollments.

Beginning in 1958 the several systems and, to an extent, the individual schools were allowed great freedom of action in designing their own operating rules, budgets, and curricula and were liable to government intervention only for the purposes of health, good morals, and public security. Unsettled circumstances of the late 1960's, however, saw firm government action against student and faculty activists at all levels and replacement of general secondary and technical-vocational councils by interventors.

Both the 1960 and 1968 school censuses show dropouts to have been greatest in the first grade, and the 40 to 50 percent of those who fail to complete primary school do so primarily for economic reasons. Among the upper classes, virtually all complete the six years of primary school. This represents a problem for the poor in a country where, in order to qualify for the position of elevator operator in some business houses, some schooling above the primary level is required.

Moderate by Latin American standards, the dropout rates are still high. In 1963 about 43 percent of the original primary school matriculants reached the sixth grade. In general secondary school the retention rate by the fourth year was 58 percent, and in secondary vocational training the third year retention rate was less than 27 percent. During the 1963 scholastic year, the primary dropout rate was 4.4 percent, the general secondary rate was 8.3 percent, and the technical and vocational rate was 11 percent. These referred not to students who failed to be promoted or who did not reenroll for the following semester but to those who discontinued their studies during the course of the year.

Preprimary and Primary Schools

Preprimary education is not mandatory, but in 1966 there was a preprimary school population of 22,267 children, over 41 percent of all children between the ages of three and five years. Public and private enrollments and numbers of boys and girls were both approximately equal. The total enrolled was nearly 40 percent higher than in 1958. Most of the establishments were in Montevideo and offered up to three years of preschooling to children between the ages of three and six. The teachers had attended the same normal schools that prepared teachers for the regular primary school system. Special kindergartens for children of working mothers, some of them functioning as day boarding schools, are maintained by the Children's Council, a public agency established in 1933 (see ch. 7, Living Conditions).

Primary enrollment of all kinds increased from about 320,000 in 1960 to 381,000 in 1967 and to a preliminary estimate of 400,000 in 1968. The 1968 figure represented 78.6 percent of the children five to fourteen years old. Other data indicate that in 1965 almost exactly 80 percent of the primary students were in public schools.

In general, the primary school system showed considerable progress during the 1960's. The average annual increase in enrollment of 2.9 percent was far higher than the 1.3-percent average annual demographic growth, and in 1966 some 94.5 percent of all children between the ages of five and fourteen either were in primary school, had graduated from primary school, or had received some education.

Under the law, children are required to complete primary school, except that in rural areas, where complete primary school facilities are frequently not available, withdrawal from school at the age of ten is permitted. The Constitution of 1967 enunciates also the principle of compulsory education at the secondary level; this, however, had yet to be implemented in early 1970, and the shortage of school classrooms made it appear unlikely that early implementation could be expected. A compromise solution under consideration in the late 1960's was extension of compulsory schooling to nine years.

Primary textbooks are prepared by private authors and published commercially. Teachers of lower grades, particularly the first grade, informally prepare textual material related to their particular needs and the studies followed during the year. There are no rigid governmental regulations concerning the preparation or content of primary texts. The National Council of Primary and Normal Instruction, however, furnishes guidance to the authors, is responsible for editing the texts, and fixes the sales prices of the books, which are furnished without cost to the students. For several years the primary schools have made extensive use of a comprehensive text for each grade; in other words, a single book includes all of the subjects of study. Beginning in 1963 school authorities distributed relatively more generous quantities of books and teaching aids to areas with particularly serious educational problems.

Children tend to start school at an age somewhat older than that customary in North America. During the 1961—64 period the largest number of children was in the nine-to-ten age group. This is in part explained by the fact that repetitions occur most frequently in the lowest grades, resulting in nine- and ten-year-old pupils in these grades.

There are two types of primary school, the complete and the

incomplete. The complete school is found in urban localities and offers a full six-year course of instruction leading to entry into any kind of secondary school. The incomplete, or rural, school offered only three years of schooling until 1958. During that year the number was increased to four, and by 1969 some rural units had established five-year curricula. There are also a few six-year rural schools. Because of this relative deficiency in rural education, country children anxious to attend most kinds of secondary school must travel to an urban area to complete their primary schooling, an undertaking beyond the means of those from poor families or those living in isolated localities. Some secondary agricultural schools, however, will accept children from incomplete primary schools.

Although more than 80 percent of the country's population in 1966 was urban, rural schools outnumbered urban by a ratio of more than two to one. Many of the country schools, however, were simple one-room affairs, with all classes taught simultaneously.

Numerous experimental and demonstration primary schools have been developed in Montevideo and other urban localities. There are experimental primary farm schools in several departments and, to meet the needs of children of migrant workers, there are a few mobile schools. Although primary school dropouts and grade repetitions represent the system's most serious problem, they are lower than in most Latin American countries and their rates declined during the 1960's. For example, between 1960 and 1968 primary enrollments increased by 23 percent and graduations by 50 percent; and between 1963 and 1965 the primary retention rate rose from 39 to 54 percent. In 1969, however, a Montevideo newspaper alleged that 54 percent of the urban and 88 percent of the rural students were failing to reach the sixth grade and that in the country as a whole some 40 percent of the first-year students were required to repeat that year.

There was general agreement that performance improved in higher grades. In 1963 there were 66,481 dropouts reported in the first grade and 25,109 in the sixth. In 1970, however, the National Council of Primary and Normal Instruction was continuing a program aimed at reducing the rate of repetition of the first grade and eliminating the problem of overage students in primary schools.

Teachers are well trained and competent, and the student-teacher ratio of thirty-two to one in 1968 was about average for Latin America. Since the mid-1950's the differences between public and private schools in student-teacher ratios have been minor, with the ratio more favorable in private schools in some years and in public ones in others. The shortage of classrooms, which also afflicts the secondary system, is a far more serious problem, which frequently results in crowding and multiple shifts. It is a problem, however, that is abating to some extent. It is estimated that in 1949 there were 122 children for each primary classroom; by 1967 the number had declined to 102. During recent years most of the new construction has been in the departments of Artigas and Colonia, where the worst shortages exist.

General Secondary Schools

From 1849 to 1877 the University of the Republic directly controlled the young secondary program. A measure of administrative independence was granted at that time, and in 1935 the National Council on Secondary Education was accorded under the law approximately the same degree of academic autonomy as that granted to the university. The general secondary schools, called *liceos*, offer academic courses during a basic cycle of four years and a university preparatory cycle of two years. Sometimes the basic four-year cycle is in an institution separated from the preparatory years, but as a rule the six years are elements of a continuing system with the university as its only goal. In the basic cycle the number of class hours ideally ranges from twenty-four to twenty-eight a week, but room crowding resulting from the shortage of classroom space often makes necessary a shortening in the number of productive work hours. The nine to twelve courses offered consist principally of languages, liberal arts, and sciences.

Courses taken in the preparatory cycle are selected in accordance with the university *facultad* in which the student proposes to enroll. In some instances, this choice must be made at the very beginning of the preparatory cycle in general secondary school at an age as early as sixteen. The general categories of preparatory study include law and social sciences, notarial studies, medicine, chemistry and pharmacy, engineering and surveying, and several others.

Completion of the basic four years coupled with the two preparatory years of general secondary school is certified by the *bachillerato* (certificate). As in the primary schools, the general secondary programs are centered on rote learning, a book-centered study, and strenuous homework. There is far less extracurricular activity than in comparable North American Institutions. Essentially, the general secondary school is designed to give the student the liberal arts background acquired in the first two years of North American colleges. At the university level he is expected at once to concentrate on his professional specialization.

If the student changes his preference in the selection of a specialty after receiving his *bachillerato*, he may have to repeat all or part of the preparatory cycle. The inflexibility of this system has been generally recognized by the educational authorities, and discussions between secondary and university authorities were initiated in 1969 with a view to planning ways to make the preparatory cycle a bridge rather than an obstacle between the two levels of education. One recommendation has been to expand the present restrictive preparatory program curriculum into three major study programs in order to provide a choice of enrollment in a far wider selection of university *facultades*.

General secondary student enrollment showed an unbroken increase from about 70,000 in 1960 to 109,000 in 1967 and a provisional 117,000 in 1968. Statistics for 1960 showed that 32 percent of Uruguayan children of secondary school age were actually in school. This percentage had risen from 24 percent in 1950 and was the highest of the eighteen Latin American countries. In the mid-1960's concentration on liberal arts studies remained high, but the 43.1 percent of time devoted to science-related studies was the highest among twelve selected Latin American countries.

Data released in 1969 by the Organization of American States reported general secondary school attendance by sex only through the year 1962. At that time 39,818 students out of a total of 75,958 were girls. Boys were in a slight majority in public schools, but girls heavily predominated in the private institutions, many of them convent schools. The average annual enrollment increase of 6.7 percent between 1960 and 1968 was substantially below the annual 11.4-percent average rise registered by eighteen Latin American countries, but in 1960 the proportion of Uruguayan children of secondary school age in school was already very high, and in 1968 it remained among the highest in the hemisphere.

General secondary entrance requirements are flexible. Under terms of the 1958 Organic Law of Secondary Education, public primary school graduates with grades of prescribed levels of excellence are granted automatic admission to general secondary school. Others, and all private primary school graduates, are required to take entrance examinations in Spanish, history, geography, and mathematics. Apart from the shortages of classrooms, general secondary schools feel most keenly the inadequate provision of materials and equipment for scientific studies, especially laboratories and laboratory equipment.

Detailed data on dropout and repetition rates were not available in 1970. It was reported in 1969, however, that during the mid-1960's about 40 percent of the general secondary students were failing to complete their courses of study. Allowing for some improvement in the retention rate, this figure seems roughly consistent with 1962 data showing that there were 20,971 students in the first general secondary year and 5,520 in the last year of the preparatory cycle. These figures do not of course, offer an entirely valid picture, since during the six-year period enrollments were increasing rapidly, and the considerable number of repeated years distorted the pattern. A high dropout rate from general secondary school, however, is indicated. The figures do show, moreover, that girls, who had maintained an enrollment about the same as boys during the primary cycle, at the secondary level dropped out at a far faster rate. Possible answers include early marriage and, in needy families unable to keep more than one child in secondary school, the greater potential earning power of the male, which gave him preference for retention in the classroom.

The heavy concentration of population in Montevideo has had a profound effect on secondary schooling, as it has on all other aspects of the educational system. In 1966 some 30 percent of the schools and 40 percent of the classrooms were located there. Most of the others were located in the departmental capitals. Among the best of the secondary general institutions were some urban private schools. These included: the Uruguay-American School; five British-operated institutions; a German, a French, and an Italian school; a secondary school in Carrasco operated by North American Catholic nuns; and the Crandon Institute of the Methodist Episcopal Missions Board.

The quality of instruction offered by the private secondary schools, in which Spanish must be taught at least as a second language, does not differ significantly from the public. In the late 1960's the student-teacher ratio was slightly more favorable in the public than in the private institutions, but the entrance rate of university applicants coming from private schools was more than twice that of those prepared at public institutions.

Public Montevideo high schools are the most numerous and have most of the capital's secondary students. Of increasing importance is the so-called pilot secondary school with a curriculum generally patterned on that of the United States. It has a five-year curriculum, including a fifth year of specialization in a technical or vocational field. This type of school is not intended primarily for students planning to go on to the university, but pilot high school graduates are eligible for matriculation in the university preparatory cycle. In this sense the pilot school represents a bridge between the general and the technical-vocational secondary systems.

A majority of the urban general secondary schools, however, are four- or six-year schools dedicated to preparation for higher education. Most of those in Montevideo who are enrolled in the four-year establishments and who desire further education at the university go to the Vázquez Acevedo Academic Institute. A preparatory-cycle school, it represents the principal access road to the University of the Republic and had a reported 1970 enrollment of almost 7,000 students.

The principal organization of students at the secondary level is the Council of Uruguayan Secondary Students, a large and active group closely associated with the principal student organization at the University of the Republic and with organized labor. It supports the political left, and secondary students—general and technical-vocational alike—are politically active to a degree seldom encountered below the university level. Activity by students and some of their teachers culminated early in 1968 in issuance of a decree replacing the National Council on Secondary Education and the National Council of Technical and Vocational Training with interventors (see ch. 13, Political Dynamics).

Technical and Vocational Schools

The public technical and vocational secondary school program became centralized in 1942 under a single autonomous agency misleadingly called the Uruguayan Labor University and a general directorate. Some of the schools affiliated with the Labor University had been founded as early as the middle of the nineteenth century, but they had been established for the most part as rehabilitation centers for juvenile delinquents, and it was not until the close of the nineteenth century that they were converted into institutions directed toward the teaching of practical skills for youths unable to aspire to professional careers.

In 1969 the secondary vocational schools reported a collective enrollment of 37,000 industrial and over 800 agricultural students. A Labor University general directorate figure released in 1969 estimated that there were 5,000 full-time or part-time teachers. The estimate was undated and did not differentiate between permanent and temporary staff, nor did it list the number of working hours. In 1966, however, an open invitation for people with technical or teaching backgrounds to apply for positions on the Labor University rolls resulted in a response by between one and two thousand applicants. In addition, in 1968 the Labor University council voted an additional 1,045 hours of class instruction, increasing the total by about 25 percent. At all levels of education, efforts are being made to attract full-time professors, but since most of the Labor University teaching staff is part-time, the increase in numbers of hours—and pay—was warmly welcomed.

Labor University schools usually offer courses of two or three years—although both longer and shorter ones are scheduled—and the combined graduation lists increased by about 75 percent between 1960 and 1968. In 1970 the most recent available data for enrollment by sex was for 1961, when nearly half of the students were girls, most of them industrial enrollees. Labor University industry is a catch-all sector that includes commercial and business studies, stenography, and dressmaking and designing, as well as the standard industrial vocational fields oriented toward male enrollment. Data from another source indicate that in 1967 there were twenty-three secondary agricultural institutions in rural and semi-rural localities teaching animal husbandry, milk production, soil conservation, and—more recently—poultry science.

In 1962 the government and the United Nations Development Program concluded an agreement to consolidate central statistical services and standards and methods, strengthen company training systems, and establish a teacher-training center for industrial educational personnel. By 1969 the agreement had been fully implemented. The United Nations' contribution was US$947,800 and the government's was the peso equivalent of US$1,130,440.

In most instances, Labor University entrants must have completed the full six years of primary school to establish eligibility for admission, but graduates of the shorter course, rural primary schools may go on directly to Labor University agricultural institutions after reaching the age of eleven.

Little information is available concerning the small, primarily church-operated private secondary vocational system. According to the most recent data available in 1970, there were four schools of unidentified character in 1966 with a total 1959 student body of 632.

The age of enrollment in Labor University units is ordinarily from twelve to fourteen years, and graduation is from fifteen to seventeen, ages that limit immediate employment opportunity because of the lack of technical and social maturity. As a consequence, experiments have already been made, on a pilot basis, in introducing a six-year curriculum including three years of basic, two years of scientific, and one year of prevocational education. There has also been talk of implementing a provision of the Constitution of 1967 making secondary education of all kinds, as well as primary education, compulsory. Montevideo secondary schools usually limit acceptance to students who have completed the six years of primary school and have reached the age of thirteen. Many institutions in the interior, however, will accept at the age of twelve children who have completed six primary years in urban areas or the shorter primary courses acceptable in the countryside. As a general rule completion of technical or vocational secondary training does not make the graduate eligible for university admission.

In 1962 the United States assistance program authorized a grant of US$1.2 million to the Labor University to promote agricultural education by construction and equipment of a Farm Mechanics School and improvement of equipment at several specialized agricultural schools. In 1963 it authorized another grant of US$207,000 to the Labor University to improve the machinery of the Institute of Mechanical and Electro-Technical Education.

More recently, the Labor University has prepared a project to improve and expand the technical education system by providing physical installations and improving teaching, technical, and administrative and accounting services. The project would also increase enrollment capacity and bring teaching methods up to date. In 1968, however, the same social unrest that had disrupted the general secondary schools affected the Labor University. Early in the year the Uruguayan Labor University Council, like its general secondary school counterpart, was replaced by interventors, and the decade of the 1960's drew to a close in an atmosphere of tense uncertainty.

There is a scattering of specialized public technical secondary schools outside the framework of the Labor University. The most prestigious of these is the National School of Fine Arts, with a five-year curriculum. Among the others are the National School of Music and the municipal schools of dramatic arts.

Among the outstanding agricultural schools are the Maldonado School of Silviculture, offering a two-year course to young people over the age of fifteen, and the Swiss Colony Dairy School, with courses of two and three years in dairy farming. Attrition rates as high as 90 percent are reported in industrial schools and as low as 20 percent in agricultural institutions. The relatively low rate in the latter is attributed to the fact that most are boarding schools where nonattendance is more difficult.

Statistics on enrollment in industrial schools indicate that in the late 1960's the Labor University administered six large industrial schools in Montevideo and forty-two other smaller units in departmental towns. Fields of concentration include carpentry, automobile and machinery mechanics, electricity, radio and television repair, construction industries, and shipbuilding techniques. The general classification of industrial studies includes also such fields as graphic arts, applied and decorative arts, a business school at Larranga, commerce (two years of general studies plus one year of secretarial training), and schools offering courses of varying lengths for certain female vocations. In addition to furnishing general direction and guidance to the individual schools, the Labor University provides vocational guidance and continuing education and training for those already at work.

Higher Education

The number of bona fide students in institutions of higher education during the 1960's was a matter for conjecture because of the difference between the number enrolled but academically inactive and the number actually attending class and taking examinations. In the academically active category, the number is estimated to have increased from about 15,000 in 1960 to between 18,000 and

21,000 in 1969. Ninety percent or more of the higher education matriculants attend the country's only university. The most recent available data on enrollment by sex, for 1960, indicated that females constituted almost 40 percent of the higher education enrollment.

Graduates of schools of higher education as a whole increased from 911 in 1960 to 1,400 in 1967 and to a provisional figure of 1,450 in 1968. In 1960 the rate of Uruguayan university completion was already one of the highest in the Western Hemisphere, but the ratio between higher education graduates and higher education entrants has been in sharp decline during the last generation. Data available do not make clear whether they refer to the University of the Republic alone or to all higher schools. However, the ratios between higher education graduates and higher education matriculants for the years 1942—44 and 1947—49 was reported at 56.0 percent, whereas for 1957—59 and 1962—64 it was a sharply lower 20.9 percent. From another source, roughly consistent figures for 1964 report a university retention rate in the major disciplines of 20.7 percent.

No university entrance examination is required, and there is no limit on the number of aspirants who can be accepted. The applicant usually must present a *bachillerato* awarded for successful completion of the two-year preparatory cycle of general secondary school, but for certain courses the Faculty of Humanities and Sciences accepts primary school teacher certificates. In the past the university has been status oriented and frequently described as a factory for professionals (*fábrica de profesionales*) designed for issuing diplomas rather than searching for enlightenment. During the 1960's this charge has become progressively less defensible with the enrichment in course offerings, particularly in the Faculty of Humanities and Sciences. There are no specific admission restrictions for valid certificate holders except in the schools of nursing and agronomy. The school year commences on about March 15 and concludes in November, although examinations may continue into December.

The sometimes considerable discrepancies in higher education enrollment figures in Uruguay are not difficult to understand. In 1969 it was estimated that as much as 19 percent of the higher education enrollment neither appeared in classes nor took examinations. Laboratory and seminar attendance is nominally required, but lecture and class attendances are seldom monitored, and failure to complete a course of study may result only in a failure to receive promotion.

The floating population of students who do not engage to any serious extent in study programs includes two elements. One is the status-seeker, usually a son or daughter of the well-to-do, who takes satisfaction in the right to use the title of *universitario* (university student). More important and probably more numerous are the activists, the students enrolled in order to participate in radical political activity. Ties between the University Students' Federation of Uruguay, the Council of Uruguayan Secondary Students, and the National Workers Convention have been close for a long time (see ch. 20, Labor Relations and Organization). The traditional estrangement between the Latin American university activist and the "establishment" has deep roots. Its particular intensity in Uruguay stems in part from the unusual degree to which a good education is available to so many at all levels of society. It is also undoubtedly in large part attributable to former President Batlle's philosophy of the welfare state, in which all people have not the privilege but the right to satisfactory living conditions.

Most university programs are aimed at the professions in courses of study running from as few as four to as many as six years (in medical studies). The general liberal arts background provided in the first two years of most North American institutions of higher education is found in Uruguayan secondary schools.

In 1968 the traditional Latin American disciplines remained the most favored. Among the new enrollees, law (including diplomacy and notarial studies) attracted 1,352 matriculants and medicine drew 552. Other disciplines with high new enrollments were humanities and sciences with 385, dentistry with 325, agronomy with 290, engineering with 237, and veterinary medicine with 110. The preference in disciplines differed from that of 1960 principally in that enrollment in law, agronomy, and veterinary medicine roughly doubled, whereas there was a pronounced decline in the industrial fields of engineering, chemistry and pharmacy, and architecture.

In the late 1960's a strong sense of tradition continued to affect the student's selection of his field of specialization. The increasing numbers of law students and graduates in some of the fields of engineering were aware that their futures were more likely to be in teaching or relatively low-paid bureaucratic assignments. Students in architecture, a diminishing but still popular faculty, readily acknowledged that the chances of finding employment in their chosen profession were minimal. At the same time, students continued to avoid mathematics.

It will be recalled that the student of a profession has acquired his liberal arts background during secondary school. There is no university-level premedical schooling and, after six years of medical studies, the medical student who successfully defends a thesis on some aspects of his intended profession is awarded the degree of doctor of medicine. The licentiate in law requires five years. After taking courses of varying lengths (usually four years or more), the successful candidate in another discipline may be awarded a degree in economics, architecture, mathematics, chemistry, pharmacy, biology, civil engineering or in some other field. In 1970 the most recent addition to the list of degrees offered was that of library science, added in 1959.

In 1967 for the first time consideration was given to a plan to restructure the university in the 1970's by establishing a central campus that would permit optimum use of teaching and physical facilities by related departments and disciplines. The restructuring would also provide better opportunity for postgraduate research and for doctoral programs in fields not yet represented.

The oversupply of university-trained personnel in many of the professions has resulted in a substantial emigration during recent years of the best educated young Uruguayan professionals. Adequate statistics are not available, and there is no evidence that industry and commerce have been seriously injured as a consequence of the loss of the skills of the emigré elite. The cost of their expensive and tuition-free education, however, has been lost (see ch. 4, Population and Labor Force).

The Department of Student Welfare gives assistance in a variety of ways. Able students from low-income families can obtain scholarships for living expenses in the form of tax-free loans. Free medical examinations and dispensary service are available, and students have access to the university-operated Hospital de las Clínicas, the nation's largest and best hospital (see ch. 7, Living Conditions). Sports are supervised by the National Commission for Physical Education, which maintains the university's playing fields.

The University of the Republic has had some autonomy since 1935 and full autonomy since 1958 under a program authorizing it to regulate election methods and machinery. The rector is elected for a four-year term (currently from 1968 to 1972). Election is by a board of seventy electors including thirty representatives of the faculty, twenty of the student body, and twenty of the alumni.

The highest university governing body, the Central Directive Council, is chaired by the rector and is made up of representatives of the faculties, the professions, and the students. Elected for terms of four years, the council is charged with supervision of general administration, policy formulation, research, teaching, approval of curricula, conditions for admission, and discipline.

Structurally, the fundamental element in the Latin American university is the *facultad*. Entirely different from the faculty in North America, it includes students, teachers, administrators, and the physical plant. It has a considerable degree of autonomy of its own. Each of the ten *facultades* of the University of the Republic has its own twelve-man council. Chaired by the dean, it has five teaching, three graduate, and three student members.

The university was founded in 1849 with the single Faculty of

Law and Social Sciences. With the establishment of the Faculty of Humanities and Sciences in 1945, the present number of ten was reached. All are located on the sixteen-building Montevideo campus with the exception of the Faculty of Agriculture, which maintains three units in the interior, the most important at Savago near Montevideo. The ten include law and social sciences, medicine, economic sciences and administration, dentistry, chemistry, and pharmacy, veterinary medicine, agriculture, engineering, architecture, and humanities and sciences.

There was an unbroken rise from 251 in 1960 to 1,070 in 1966 in enrollment in the country's higher schools of agronomy leading to the degree of agricultural engineer, specializing variously in agronomy, animal husbandry, or silviculture. In a nation so dependent on agriculture and stock breeding and on industries derived from these activities, the number of specialists remained deficient. Nevertheless, an Agronomy and Veterinary University City at Paysandú on the Río Uruguay, with a proposed capacity of 750 students, had been planned in 1969 for completion in 1972 as an affiliate of the University of the Republic.

Under terms of the Organic Law of 1958, academic research is a fundamental part of the university's mission. University researchers cooperated in programs conducted by outside learned societies, such as the Association of Engineers of Uruguay, the Chemical and Pharmaceutical Association of Uruguay, the Inter-American Childrens' Institute, and the Uruguayan Odontology Institute. In addition to the ten *facultades* of the University of the Republic, there are several small associated entities including the National School of Nursing, the National School of Music, and the National School of Fine Arts.

There is also a scattering of small institutions at the higher education level entirely independent of the University of the Republic. Most important of these is the Artigas Institute for Professors, which prepares most of the country's general secondary school teachers in three- and four-year courses. The Magisterial Institute of Higher Studies offers primary teachers further training to prepare them for headmaster, inspector, and other advanced primary teaching fields; the Institute of Philosophy and Letters of Montevideo offers two- and four-year postsecondary courses in philosophy and literature. There are also the armed services schools. The School of Public Administration, which opened its doors in 1963, has three-year part-time courses at two levels—those for civil-servant graduates of primary schools and those for secondary graduates.

Data from a 1968 census of the University of the Republic set off against occasional figures from a 1960 university census provide a partial profile of the typical university student. About one-third enter at or about the normal age of eighteen, another third enter at nineteen or twenty, and the balance are twenty-one or older at the time of first matriculation. Some 18,700 filled out the census questionnaires, but the number actively engaged as students was estimated at 15,000, the number attending classes or taking examinations in 1967 or 1968. Figures on 1968 enrollment suggested an increase of about 50 percent over 1950, the date of the previous university census. An accelerated dropout rate, however, reduced the 1960 to 1968 enrollment increase to about 30 percent. The higher dropout rate was particularly notable during freshman year and was attributed primarily to economic difficulties. Matriculation in a field of study not justified by a demonstrated aptitude for the course chosen was also an important factor.

Most of the programs were of four to six years duration, but the average time the successful student spent between matriculation and graduation was usually considerably longer. The low 1964 retention rate of 20.9 percent in the university's major disciplines could at least in part be attributed to the fact that 45 percent of the students held regular jobs and an additional 6 percent worked occasionally. Employees of most of the government departments and of the public corporations attended their offices half days only during much of the year, however, and as a consequence, many junior public servants were able to continue their studies at the higher level.

Ages of new enrollees at the University of the Republic are significantly higher for students from the interior, usually for economic reasons. Latin Americans at the university level tend to be considerably older than their North American counterparts, and a Latin American undergraduate thirty years or more of age is in no sense unusual. The Uruguayan higher education student tends to be somewhat younger than the Latin American average, probably because of the high degree of population concentration in Montevideo, but not to an extent so marked as to represent a significant exception to the general pattern.

Despite the free tuition, access to university education is largely limited to children of upper and middle income families, not because of design but because the only university is in Montevideo, where income is much higher than in the country as a whole and the need to supplement the family income by working, coupled with the minor expenses for books and fees, places college out of the reach of many. Adequacy of preparation for the university is probably also a major factor. In 1968 some 39 percent of the university students had come from private secondary establishments; exactly comparable data for public secondary school graduates were not available, but in 1962 only 17 percent of all general secondary students had been in private schools.

In 1968, 60 percent of the university population came from

Montevideo, 8 percent from abroad, and 32 percent from the interior—as the Uruguayan is accustomed to describe all parts of the country outside of Montevideo, where half the population lives. Of those coming from the interior, only 2.5 percent were from the rural sector, where nearly 20 percent of the total population lived (see ch. 4, Population and Labor Force). Despite the free tuition, a university education would have been virtually impossible for lower income families were it not for the 1,600 maintenance scholarships reported available in the 1969/70 school year.

The 1960 university census had reported, without revealing criteria, that 30 percent of the students came from upper class backgrounds, 46 percent from the middle class, and 12 percent from the lower class. The 1968 data reflected virtually no change in these proportions, although students of lower class origins showed a slight decline to 11 percent of the total.

In the late 1960's no clear polarization of the *facultades* had emerged, but most of the leftist-leaning students and teachers seemed to be attached to the Faculty of Law and Social Sciences, whereas conservative elements predominated in the business and industry oriented Faculty of Economic Sciences and Administration.

Uruguayan higher education maintains a variety of international relationships, political and apolitical, leftist and conservative. In fiscal year 1969 thirty-seven United States Information Agency (USIA) study grants included twenty-nine to Uruguayans and eight to United States citizens. During the 1969/70 school year the French embassy in Montevideo announced the availability of an undisclosed number of scholarships in France for Uruguayans. Because of the housing shortage in Paris, however, applicants were advised to seek enrollment in other French cities. In a different kind of international relationship, a regional interuniversity council brings together for consultations the national universities of Uruguay, Chile, Peru, and Argentina.

LITERACY AND ADULT AND SPECIAL EDUCATION

During a survey period covering the years 1960—65 Uruguay had the highest rate of literacy of eighteen Latin American countries. In 1963, the year of the most recent population census, the country was reported to have a literacy rate of 90.3 percent among persons fifteen years of age and over. Other isolated literacy statistics flesh out the general and comparative listing. In 1968 some 97 percent of the population over fifteen was reported literate, one of the highest rates in the world. A 1969 report by the Pan American Union showed virtually no differences between males and females in the literacy rate. The rate of student retention was so high that literacy training was no longer an important element in the country's adult education program, although an undetermined amount of functional illiteracy undoubtedly remained.

A 1968 study concluded that most of the 100,000 or more people living in the rural slum communities called *rancheríos* were probably functional illiterates, and another 1968 report indicated a high rate of outright illiteracy in the rugged and sparsely populated northwest, the stronghold of the outlaw Tupamaros (see ch. 7, Living Conditions).

Illiteracy is virtually confined to remote rural areas and to older age groups. At the time of the 1963 census the overall literacy rate of 90.3 percent for persons over the age of fifteen included a 92.2-percent rate among urban dwellers and an 82.8-percent rate among people in the countryside. Among the older segments of the population, 26.5 percent of the people aged sixty-five and older and 17.5 percent of those between fifty-five and sixty-four were unable to read or write. Among the younger age groups, however, only 4.6 percent of those between the ages of twenty-five and thirty-four and 2.7 percent of those between fifteen and twenty-four were illiterate. In 1963 the average schooling of the population fifteen years of age and older was five years. By 1970 it had increased a year or more; the older generation was dying off, and virtually all the younger was obtaining enough formal education to be considered marginally and even functionally literate.

Adult education is administered by the National Board of Adult Education, which was organized to systematize and coordinate a program inaugurated in 1967. In 1969 literacy and adult education classes were given at eighty-nine centers throughout the country but, with Uruguay's high literacy rate and high school attendance ratios, adult training took a particular form.

In many countries the core element in the adult training program is the evening course furnishing the rudiments of basic primary education or some measure of vocational training. In Uruguay there is little need of basic education in an already well-educated nation. Many public and private institutions, however, offer courses of study in cultural enrichment. Hospitals and welfare institutions give instruction to people interested in matters of social concern. Both from the university and from some secondary schools, intellectually broadening courses are available.

Binational centers play an important part. In 1967 nearly 4,000 students ranging in years from childhood to old age studied English under the Uruguay-United States Cultural Alliance at several locations in Montevideo and in the interior. Inaugurated in 1939, the program includes formal classes, radio instruction, and intensive English language courses distributed on tapes and records. The Anglo-Uruguayan Cultural Institute offers English language and literature courses in Montevideo and at branch centers. The French, Italian, and Brazilian governments also cooperate with associations of Uruguayan civic leaders in offering educational courses for adults. An institute sponsored by the Soviet Union mixes the study of Marxist ideology with language and cultural training.

In 1965 there were reported to be thirty-four special schools with 143 teachers and a student body of 2,851, not including schools in hospitals and for the retarded, an impressive gain over the enrollment of 441 reported for 1957. Boys slightly outnumbered girls. In 1970 the most recent available detailed and complete data (1962) showed an enrollment of 3,312, with 20 in a school for the blind, 270 in two schools for the deaf, 1,025 in thirteen schools for the mentally retarded and 1,997 in thirty-three other special schools. Many of these latter were seaside, mountain, and holiday home schools to build up the health of delicate children. Advances in the special-school system have been considerable, but much remains to be done. In the late 1960's it was estimated that there were about 14,000 handicapped school-age children in the country.

THE TEACHING PROFESSION

José Pedro Varela inspired many capable young persons in the late nineteenth century to direct themselves toward a career in education and to persuade successive governments to allocate to the public school system a progressively greater measure of budgetary support. Since his time, pedagogy at all levels has become an increasingly respected profession, although in 1970 it remained one of the least lucrative and one in which some teachers were paid for full-time work while others competed for the assignment of class hours because their stipend was computed on the basis of the number of teaching hours assigned.

The most recent comprehensive data available in 1970 indicated that in 1964 about 90 percent of the 11,000 teachers were female. The student-teacher ratio, which ranged downward by category of school from thirty-two to one, was slightly more favorable in the public institutions.

Most of the teachers were qualified graduates of the several levels of teacher institutions, representing a percentage that was perhaps the highest in Latin America. The success in recruitment of prospective teachers during the 1960's is mirrored by the growth in the number of normal schools, designed for the training of primary instructional personnel, from two in 1960 to nineteen by 1966. The new schools were small, but the number of graduates of the system rose steadily from 504 in 1960 to 880 in 1967 and to 967 in 1968. Enrollments increased from 2,681 in 1961 to 6,724 in 1966. In the late 1960's most of the rapidly growing number of new teachers were still in school. A single rural normal school had a 1966 enrollment reported at 28, and the normal school maintained by the Uruguayan Labor University had 130 students. No comprehensive normal school data on the sex of students are available, but it is known that females predominate by a very wide margin, except in the normal school in the Labor University system.

Systemized training for general secondary teachers was not available until 1949 when the Artigas Institute for Professors was established. The Faculty of Humanities and Sciences of the university now also trains secondary teachers. Here it should be noted that, whereas in North America the title of professor is reserved for the ranking personnel at the university level, the secondary teacher in Latin America also is customarily referred to as *profesor*.

Before the establishment of the Artigas Institute, vocational secondary teachers were almost invariably part-time personnel chosen at random and paid on the basis of hours devoted to teaching. An ample teaching schedule was a much prized objective, and its desirability had by no means disappeared in 1970, although the opportunities for full-time employment had increased during the course of the decade. In 1970, however, there was still a sufficient number of part-time personnel for the assignment of numbers of teaching hours to be the subject of many letters to the press and of an occasional editorial.

The Artigas Institute is a university-level institution, and Uruguayan Labor University professors hold what is considered to be the equivalent of a university degree. To qualify for a teaching appointment, Artigas Institute candidates must take competitive examinations in their fields of specialization, and preference for appointment is given to those achieving the highest examination marks.

At the university the teaching staff is appointed at any of the four levels. At the top are the titular professors (*profesores titulares*). They are followed in order by contract professors (*profesores contratados*) who have professorial rank but lack status, associate or adjunct professors (*profesores adjuntos*), and assistant professors (*profesores agregados*). The council of each *facultad* has authority to appoint its own teaching staff, a group that is the only one in the civil service not to have permanent status in most instances. The retirement age, sixty-five in some *facultades*, is later than that in most government occupations.

The principal representative of the teaching profession is the Uruguayan Teachers Federation, reported in 1969 to have thirty affiliated groups including primary, general secondary, Labor University, and University of the Republic affiliates. No reliable figures concerning its effective strength were available in 1970. In an effort to broaden its base of support, the Teachers Federation, at its 1970 Convention, voted to associate itself with educational administrative workers, blue-collar and service workers, normal school teachers, special professors, and other special categories associated with the teaching profession. The Teachers Federation moved also to establish effective integration with the National Workers Convention, the country's dominant and leftist central labor organization (see ch. 20, Labor Relations and Organization).

Between the mid-1950's and 1970 some pay raises were granted to teachers, but the teachers' unions were less successful than the industrial and commercial unions in gaining increases and, as a result, teacher purchasing power eroded at a faster rate. Under union guidance, a forty-eight-hour teachers' strike in 1963 was the first in history, and strikes since that date have occurred with increasing frequency, particularly in the secondary system. After 1967 the Teachers Federation was voluble in holding the government responsible for difficulties, largely financial, that had affected all levels of the educational system.

CHAPTER 9
ARTISTIC AND INTELLECTUAL EXPRESSION

A trend toward concentration on the sociological characteristics of the nation and on the direction of social change was apparent in 1970 in history and the social sciences. Research in the natural sciences was oriented toward meeting specific national needs; particularly outstanding work was being done in the medical and veterinary sciences.

Creative writing, the area in which the country's cultural expression has had its most vigorous development, was characterized by the superimposition of fantasy and metaphysical contemplation upon older literary styles, such as realism. Artists and musicians were generally following European trends, but *gaucho* (cowboy) folklore retained its popularity.

Montevideo, where the national university and most art galleries, theaters, libraries, and museums are located, virtually monopolized the nation's cultural life. Artists, writers, and scholars have traditionally enjoyed great respect. A number of families had been prominent over several generations in creative activities, but cultural expression was not the exclusive property of an elite; in terms of support, participation, and appreciation, it was broadly based.

The government has stimulated artistic and intellectual development through the sponsorship of such entities as schools of drama and ballet, a national symphony orchestra, a national theatrical company, and various research institutes. In 1969 the country was host to an international sculpture contest. The Uruguayan government provided the materials with which representatives of some six countries sculpted their entries in Montevideo's Franklin D. Roosevelt Park. The inter-American exhibit of painting, to be held every two years, was organized under the auspices of the Organization of American States, and its first exhibit was to be held in Montevideo in October 1970.

The first great impetus to cultural development was provided by the revolt against Spain. The colonial settlement on the Banda Oriental (East Bank) of the Río de la Plata generally lacked the resources and, until the first decade of the nineteenth century, the inspiration to engage in cultural activities. The revolutionary movement, however, aroused interest in patriotic poetry and drama.

Soon after independence was established, classic tendencies in literature gave way to romantic forms that were more easily adapted to the expression of the high ideals engendered by the revolution. While imitating French literary styles, Uruguayan novelists and poets called the attention of their readers to such native themes as the *gaucho* and the rapidly vanishing Charrúa Indians.

Philosophical trends and scientific pursuits were mutually reinforcing in the late nineteenth and early twentieth centuries, as those philosophers who favored an empirical approach to the appraisal of the human condition prevailed over those who clung to metaphysics. Essayist and lyricist José Enrique Rodó (1871–1917) saw in this development a menacing orientation toward materialism. In *Ariel*, a classic of Latin American literature, Rodó appealed to the youth of his country to uphold the spiritual values of their Spanish heritage.

Largely through the influence of Rodó a new literary movement, the first of Latin American origin, became popular in the early twentieth century. This movement, known as modernism, was characterized by simplicity of style and was particularly prominent in poetry. During the same period Florencio Sanchez, one of Latin America's most distinguished playwrights, introduced the social realist trend to the Río de la Plata region. Dramatists, novelists, and short story writers began to explore the conflicts between the *gaucho* and immigrant cultures and some of the seamier and more frustrating aspects of life in the city.

Poetry in recent years has tended to be highly individualistic. Novels and short stories have been enriched by the interplay of the real and the imaginary. Playwrights have made particularly effective use of irony and satire. Common threads running through the various genre have been a sense of the solitude of man and a mystical probing for meaning and purpose in life. Among the outstanding works in literary history and criticism are Carlos Roxlo's seven-volume *Historia crítica de la literatura Uruguaya* (Critical History of Uruguayan Literature), 1913; Alberto Zum Felde's *Proceso intelectual del Uruguay* (Uruguayan Intellectual Development), 1930; and Sarah Bollo's two-volume *Literatura Uruguaya, 1807–1965* (Uruguayan Literature, 1807–1965), 1965.

Beyond the folk culture of the *gauchos*, there was little development in art or music before the middle of the nineteenth century. The country's serious music has generally been of European inspiration, but the symphonic poems of Eduardo Fabini, Uruguay's most celebrated composer, dealt with national themes. Contemporary musical groups have done extensive work with stringed instruments and piano, but the use of wind instruments is not highly developed.

The country's early painters followed the European academic

tradition and depicted historic events. The works of figurative painter Pedro Figari and sculptor Juan Manuel Ferrari, who gained fame in the late nineteenth and early twentieth centuries, reflect the French impressionist trend. The influence of Joaquín Torres Garcia, who introduced abstract art to his country, continues to be important in sculpture and architecture as well as in painting. The modernist trend in architecture is particularly notable in the clean-cut, functional design of private homes, apartment buildings, and hotels constructed since the mid-twentieth century.

THE COLONIAL PERIOD AND THE REVOLUTION

The territory that was to become Uruguay did not support an important indigenous civilization. Whereas the colonial history of most of the Latin American countries spanned three centuries, that of Uruguay lasted scarcely more than a century. Furthermore, the colony was poor, neglected by the mother country, and scorned by the more prosperous settlement across the river at Buenos Aires. Thus, it was not until the first stirrings of the revolution provided a cause célèbre that a diversified national culture began to emerge (see ch. 3, Historical Setting).

A number of fortresses, public buildings, and private homes built during the colonial period are still standing, but few are of architectural interest. The General Artigas Fortress, on a hill across the bay from Montevideo, and the fortresses of San Miguel and Santa Teresa, in the north, have been restored and are preserved as historical monuments. The parochial church and municipal museum of Colonia are interesting examples of colonial architecture.

Montevideo's Plaza Constitución has two noteworthy buildings dating from the beginning of the nineteenth century. The *cabildo* (old municipal building), now housing the Ministry of Foreign Relations, has a neoclassical facade. The cathedral of Montevideo, across the plaza, is a stone and brick structure about 135 feet in height. Its three entrance arches are topped by a four-columned facade, and the dome is flanked by cupolas and turrets. Most of the painting and sculpture of the period consisted of undistinguished ornamentation for the churches.

Aside from the improvised and unrecorded verses of the *gauchos*, the colony produced little musical activity. The brothers José and Pablo Podestá became noted for their singing and guitar playing as well as their acting. It was not until 1824 that the first pianos were imported from Europe. Opera was first presented in Montevideo in 1830.

The first literary genre to grow out of the revolutionary movement was dramatic poetry in neoclassical form. The play *La lealtad más acendrada o Buenos Aires vengada* (The Highest Loyalty or

Buenos Aires Revenged) written by the priest Juan Francisco Martinez, was presented in Montevideo in 1807 to celebrate the reconquest of Buenos Aires from the Spanish.

The most celebrated literary figures of the revolutionary era were Bartolomé Hidalgo and Francisco Acuña de Figueroa. Many of Hildalgo's poems took the form of *unipersonales*, or verse dramas enacted by a single player to the accompaniment of appropriate music. All of these had patriotic content, and they were generally received with great enthusiasm. Hidalgo has been called the first of the "*gaucho* poets," as his works were influenced by popular *gaucho* verse forms.

Figueroa began his literary career as a monarchist, a position that led to temporary exile, but he later turned to verses in support of the revolution and composed the lyrics of the national anthem. In his odes, elegies, and pastoral and satiric poetry he remained faithful to cultivated classic norms.

NATIONAL CULTURAL DEVELOPMENT

Philosophy

To a great extent the country's intellectual development may be traced through the alternate stages of conflict and congeniality between the idealists and the pragmatists and between the metaphysicians, who exalted the spiritual values, and the scientists, who saw man not as a uniquely spiritual being but as one of many species of living things in evolution.

The romantic liberal ideas that provided the intellectual underpinning for the French and North American revolutions also stimulated the revolt of the Spanish colonies; it remained the dominant trend in social and political thought among the small Uruguayan intellectual elite for several decades after the country gained its independence. Philosopher Andrés Lamas (1820—91), like certain of his contemporaries in Argentina, felt that political emancipation from Spain was only the first step toward genuine national independence and that a far more important and difficult step was that of intellectual emancipation from Spain's authoritarian traditions.

Romantic liberal ideals such as democracy had little influence on political development in the country's formative years, as rival military leaders perpetrated a cycle of near-anarchy and repression. A permanent break in this cycle was anticipated when José Elluari was elected president in 1873 and a number of university men, known as the "Girondists of '73," were sent to Congress. But in 1875 Colonel Lorenzo Latorre seized power in an armed rebellion, and militarism once again became entrenched. The Girondists had failed because they idealistically sought to superimpose a democratic political system upon an uneducated society steeped in authoritarian traditions. Zum Felde has explained the failure in this way:

> It was an academy, not a parliament; a literary society is not an organ of government. Those men thought and discussed, with their backs to the country, mixing in lucid details the concepts and formulas learned in the classrooms or read in European writers. They did not deign to study their own national reality, nor did they face social and economic problems practically.

In the late 1870's a new generation of intellectuals, concentrated in the Ateneo del Uruguay (Uruguayan Athenaeum), sought to oppose the military rulers. In its early years the Ateneo group repeated the mistake of the Girondists, engaging in esoteric debate and ignoring the realities of the country, but gradually, under the influence of José Pedro Varela, a new approach to the moral and political regeneration of the country gained acceptance. Varela, impressed by the consequences of public education in the United States maintained that democracy and individual freedom could not be firmly established without an educated populace (see ch. 8, Education).

As there was no hope of dislodging the military from its firm grip on the government, Varela maintained that the military itself must be used as an instrument for the rehabilitation of the country. Thus he presented his proposals to Latorre, who received them enthusiastically, and the foundation of a free, compulsory, and secular education system was laid.

The new interest in education was accompanied by an influx of new ideas within the Ateneo, and the group was soon sharply divided between those influenced, for example, by rationalism in its idealistic form and those who rejected all a priori notions and sought empirical explanations for social phenomena.

By the beginning of the twentieth century the latter group was clearly dominant, but the fear of the idealists that human values would be overcome by material ones was not realized. The views of the great statesman José Batlle y Ordóñez, through whose efforts a new political and social order was established, were firmly rooted in humanism.

The eclecticism of Carlos Vaz Ferreira, the country's leading philosopher in the first half of the twentieth century, suggests the extent to which the moral and intellectual values, which in an earlier stage of the country's development appeared to be in conflict, have become fused. Although he placed great value on the scientific method, he suggested that empiricism is inappropriate to the study of the nature of morality. He contemplated reality without the tool of a system, and his books—the best known of which are *Lógica Viva* (Living Logic), *Moral para intelectuales* (Ethics for

Intellectuals), and *Fermentário* (Mind Vat)—tend to raise rather than answer questions.

Marxist thought, which has been gaining currency in recent decades, especially among university students, is best represented in the poems and essays of Emilio Frugoni. One of his most important works is *Ensayos sobre Marxismo* (Essays on Marxism).

The Natural and Social Sciences

Efforts in both the natural and social sciences have been directed primarily toward understanding the ecological and social characteristics of the nation and coping with its problems. Research in the natural sciences has been largely concentrated in physiology, agronomy, and the medical and veterinary sciences. Particularly outstanding work has been done in public health and preventive medicine.

The national university's School of Medicine has an international reputation for high professional standards and advanced techniques. Many other public and private institutions, such as the national institutes of hygiene, nutrition, endocrinology, and oncology and the Center for the Study of Gastroenterology, all under the Ministry of Public Health, have made important contributions to the country's high standards of health and medical care.

The Dirección General de Meteorologia (Board of Meteorology) has existed in some form since 1895. In 1970 it was participating in an air pollution detection and control program coordinated by the Organization of American States. The National Atomic Energy Commission was created in 1955 to promote the study of pacific uses of atomic energy.

The National Council of Scientific and Technological Research, created by law in 1961, promotes research through scholarships and publications. Seven of its eleven members are appointed by the executive and four by the national university. Its president, the noted surgeon Justo M. Alonso, has published more than 150 books and articles. In 1970 the council was promoting a study on parasites by the biochemist Israel Karc (b. 1925).

Sociology is predominant among the behavior sciences, and some of the best historical works in recent years have been sociologically oriented. Carlos Rama, one of the country's most noted scholars, has taught the theory of history, contemporary history, and sociology in the national university's School of Science and Humanities. Among his best known works are *Las classes sociales en el Uruguay* (Social Classes in Uruguay), 1960, and *Sociología del Uruguay* (Sociology of Uruguay), 1965. Another well-known writer on sociological subjects is Aldo Solari who, with Seymour Martin Lipset, wrote "Elites in Latin America."

In the 1830's, as the spirit of national independence developed, romanticism became fashionable in literary circles. Its exaltation of freedom and individualism and its emotional intensity seemed appropriate to the temperament of the times, and the focus on nature allowed the nationalists to develop local themes while conforming to European literary forms.

Alberto Berro was one of the first adherents of romanticism. He based his major work on a legend of the Charrúa Indians. Juan Carlos Gomez is generally considered the foremost lyricist of the generation despite his unpopular advocacy of the annexation of Uruguay to Argentina.

The second generation of romanticists, associated with the Ateneo del Uruguay, included the satiric poet Washington Bermudez, best known for *El Baturrillo Uruguayo* (Uruguayan Miscellany), and Elías Regules, who typically adopted *gaucho* themes. In addition to his seven-volume literary history, Carlos Roxlo wrote novels, biographies, and poetry.

The most famous Uruguayan poet of the nineteenth century, Juan Zorilla de San Martin, belonged to the third generation of romantic writers. He first achieved fame through the presentation in 1879 of his patriotic poem *La Leyenda Patria* (Legend of the Fatherland). Thereafter, his recitation of the poem became such a regular feature of national ceremonies that in 1880 a commentator remarked that a certain ceremony had been unique because "Dr. Zorilla de San Martin did not recite *La Leyenda Patria*." It is generally agreed, however, that his most distinguished work is the narrative poem *Tabaré*, first published in 1888. This complex work tells of the tragic life and death of Tabaré, an orphaned son of a Spanish woman and a Charrúa chieftain.

The most important prose writer of the late nineteenth century was Eduardo Acevedo Diaz, who wrote extensively on independence but whose greatest work was the *gaucho* novel *Soledad* (Solitude). A political activist, he spent much of his life in exile.

While romanticism continued to flourish, two new literary trends appeared around the beginning of the twentieth century. The school that became known as modernism, characterized by stylistic elegance and exoticism of subject matter, was the first to have its roots in Latin America. The founder of the modernist movement was the Nicaraguan poet Rubén Dario, but the Uruguayan writer José Enrique Rodó was a major force in popularizing the movement throughout the hemisphere. In Uruguay modernism became the dominant trend in poetry and strongly influenced the novel, the short story, and the essay, but it had little effect on drama.

Rodó, an idealist who revolted against the growing materialism of his times, is still considered Uruguay's foremost literary figure and one of the hemisphere's most influential writers. The humanistic philsophy expressed in his works, and particularly in his masterpiece, *Ariel*, published in 1900, combines the egalitarianism of Christian ethics with the Hellenic ideal of an order based on spiritual and cultural selection. In *Ariel*, which represents the farewell of a revered professor to his students, the young people are warned to shun the materialism of the United States, personified in the character Caliban, and cling to the spiritual and intellectual values of their Spanish heritage, represented by Ariel.

Julio Herrera y Reissig (1875—1910) is considered one of the best of the modernist poets, although his works were highly controversial during his short and turbulent lifetime. His poetry reveals great sensitivity as well as delight in the artful use of words and phrases, especially metaphors and similes. Most of his works were published in Montevideo in the decade after his death.

The literary movement that developed simultaneously with modernism was known as realism or, in more exaggerated form, naturalism. Strongly influenced by such writers as Emile Zola and Guy de Maupassant, Uruguayan novelists, short story writers, and dramatists took a closer look at their natural and social settings and sought to portray them with greater detail and accuracy. Thus novelist Javier de Viana strips the *gaucho* of his legendary heroism and portrays him in a state of degeneration, pushed and crowded by an advancing civilization.

The rural scene also inspired novelist Carlos Reyles, whose practical knowledge of ranching emerges, for example, in *Beba*, a psychological study of human and animal inbreeding. Most of his novels deal with *gaucho* life and other rural themes treated realistically, but the book considered by most critics to be his masterpiece is *El Embrujo de Sevilla* (The Witchery of Seville), in which he writes romantically of the historic Spanish city where his mother was born.

Horacio Quiroga, who is generally regarded as Hispanic America's greatest short story writer, found his inspiration in nature. The jungles of northern Argentina, where he spent several years, come to life with morbid intensity in such stories as "Anaconda," an account of a deadly fight among snakes. He wrote some ten volumes of short stories that were published between 1904 and 1925.

By the 1920's interest in both romanticism and modernism had begun to decline, and those with literary pretensions looked to newer trends, such as the avant-garde poetry in vogue in Europe. Since that time the trend has been toward greater diversity and individualism, both in literary style and in choice of subject matter.

Recent poetic works have shown tendencies toward introspection and a willingness to reveal innermost feelings. In the novel and the short story, realism has often been enriched by the inclusion of the fantasies and imagination of the characters. The various literary genre have been impregnated with philosophy and metaphysical probing, making the novel and the short story more complex and lyricism and drama more profound.

Sarah Bollo, poet and highly respected literary critic and historian, suggests that the idealistic views of the perfectibility of man entertained by earlier generations have been superseded by a sense of desperation concerning his very survival.

Among the older generation of contemporary poets is Carlos Sabat Ercasty, whose own pantheistic sympathies color his treatment of the ancient pantheistic peoples of South America. The poetry of Ildefonso Pereda Valdes has been inspired by Negro folklore. He has compiled an anthology of Negro poetry of the entire hemisphere.

The most famous of the country's many distinguished female poets is Juana de Ibarbourou. Her early works, in which she expresses a delight in life and love, are considered her best. Her later works are graver and more religious in tone. Referred to by critics since 1929 as Juana de América, she was named Woman of the Americas in 1953 by the Union of American Women.

A younger generation of poets includes Dora Isella Russell, whose style resembles that of Juana de Ibarbourou. Among her most popular works are *El Cantro Irremediable* (Irremediable Song), 1946, and *Los Barcos de la Noche* (The Ships of Night), 1954. In her more recent works, as in those of her mentor, melancholy has replaced exuberance, and she has bemoaned the solitude of man. This sense of human solitude and of the ephemeral and illusive qualities of life also pervade the works of Juan Cunha, Carlos Brandy, and Jorge Medina Vidal.

Contemporary works in prose include the nativistic short stories of Juan José Morosoli and Serafin Garcia and the harshly realistic regional and social novels of Enrique Amorim and Francisco Espínola. Amorim is noted for his portrayals of peasant life. Espínola's work, *Sombras sobre la Tierra* (Shadows over the Land), 1933, deals with the criminal underworld.

As Uruguay is overwhelmingly urban, some of the best of the contemporary novelists and short story writers have turned their attention to a penetrating study of their impressions of the quiet desperation of life in the city. Mario Benedetti in *La Tregua* (The Truce) creates characters inevitably Uruguayan but also generally recognizable in that they experience the frustration of man in a society overwhelmed by bureaucracy. He captures the deadening routine of the office and the emptiness of a family life in which the absence of relatives and neighbors makes every nuclear unit seem separate and isolated.

The special drama of rootlessness of the immigrant is a principal theme of Juan Carlos Onetti. In his *Tierra de Nadie* (No Man's Land) he explores not only the social fragmentation of city life but also the nature of the self and the process of alienation.

The Performing Arts

Theater

The construction of the Teatro Solis in Montevideo in the mid-nineteenth century gave impetus to the development of the dramatic arts. Most nineteenth-century works were imitative of Spanish trends and were highly moralistic. Among the most popular playwrights of the period were Heraclio Fajardo, best known for his *Camila O'Gorman*, and the dramatic poets Orosman Moratorio and Elías Regules.

Moratorio, whose work bore the pseudonym Julian Perujo, is noted for *Juan Soldado* (Juan, the Soldier), *La Flor del Pago* (Flower of the Village), and *Culpa y Castigo* (Crime and Punishment). Regules' best-known play is *El Entenao* (The Stepson). His plays were performed in Argentina as well as in Uruguay. Drama critic Samuel Blixen also wrote plays. His most famous work is a series of short plays deriving their titles from the four seasons.

The Uruguayan and Argentine theaters were closely linked until the mid-twentieth century, and several of the playwrights who were most successful in both countries were of Uruguayan birth. One of these was Florencio Sanchez, initiator of the social realist trend in the region and generally considered Latin America's most outstanding playwright.

Although Sanchez's short life was plagued with poverty and sickness and his life-style was that of Bohemian disorder, he wrote prolifically. His plays typically attack with harsh realism and dramatic vigor the social ills that afflicted Montevideo and Buenos Aires. Most of these problems—alcoholism, illegitimacy, racial intolerance, and fatalism—he traces ultimately to the curse of poverty. Another of his recurrent themes, developed, for example, in *M'Hijo el Dotor* (My Son, the Doctor), 1903, is that of the initial intransigence and ultimate degeneration of *gaucho* culture under the impact of immigration.

Ernesto Herrera and Otto Miguel Cione were among the contemporaries of Sanchez who followed the social realist trend. Like Sanchez, Herrera suffered from tuberculosis and lived much of his life in poverty. His best known play, *El León Ciego* (The Blind Lion), set during the civil war, deals with an old military leader who is abandoned by his colleagues for having outlived his usefulness. Cione's work was strongly influenced by European playwrights, such as Ibsen. He is particularly noted for *El Arlequín* (The Harlequin). Poet Edmundo Bianchi and prose writer Carlos Princivalle also wrote plays in the social realist style.

Despite the outstanding work of its dramatists, Uruguay, lacking a resident theatrical company, remained dependent upon Argentina for the development of its theatrical tradition until relations between the two countries were severed in 1945. In the early twentieth century President Batlle y Ordóñez had proposed the creation of an experimental school of dramatic arts, and actor Carlos Brussa had launched a movement to create a national theater. An independent company known as the Teatro del Pueblo (People's Theater) existed precariously from 1937 to 1947, but it was not until 1947 that the establishment of a permanent national theater became a reality.

The Comedia Nacional (National Theater), under the auspices of the municipal government of Montevideo and underwritten by the Ministry of Culture, aroused such interest in the dramatic arts that a number of new independent companies, both professional and amateur, came into being. The Comedia Nacional is the resident company of the Teatro Solis. Montevideo's municipal amphitheater and the open-air theater at Fray Bentos also offer splendid settings for dramatic productions. The government sponsors a school of dramatic arts in Montevideo.

Since the mid-twentieth century Uruguayan theater has reflected various European and North American trends. Critic and historian Alberto Zum Felde has experimented with philosophical drama. Francisco Espínola has been noted for his surrealistic works. Mario Benedetti—novelist, short story writer, critic, and poet—has also written plays, the best known of which is *Ida y Vuelta* (Roundtrip), 1958. He is especially skillful in the use of irony. Carlos Maggi is noted for the scintillating satire in such works as *La Biblioteca* (The Library), 1959, and Mauricio Rosencof's stridently social plays have been well received.

Music

Italian opera was an important stimulus to the country's early musical development, and most of the Uruguayan composers who became known in the late nineteenth and early twentieth centuries were Italian trained. The country's most famous composer, however, Eduardo Fabini (1883—1951), studied in Belgium. He experimented with many musical forms, including ballet music. He became known as a musical nationalist, as his symphonic poems were often inspired by the serenity of the Uruguayan countryside; *Campo* (Country) and *Isla de los Ceibos* (Island of the Ceibos) are among the most famous.

Among Fabini's contemporaries were Cesar Cortinas, who produced a number of piano sonatas and vocal compositions in his short life, and Leon Ribiero, a prolific composer in many musical forms. Luis Cluzeau Mortet, a pianist and a professor at the National Conservatory, is remembered for his chamber music, piano concertos, and symphonies.

Vicente Ascone, director of Montevideo's Municipal School of Music, like Fabini, has become known as a musical nationalist. Among other works, he composed an opera based on a Charrúa theme and the *Suite Uruguaya* (Uruguayan Suite) for orchestras.

Lauro Ayestaran has been among the most influential of the country's contemporary musicians. He received his training in Montevideo and devoted most of his career to the promotion of music in the public school system, particularly in the national university. He also wrote many books on the nation's music and assembled a large collection of recorded folk music.

German-born musicologist Francisco Curt Lange was a pioneer in the hemisphere-wide movement that became known as Americanismo Musical (Musical Americanism). Among other contributions to the movement, he edited and published, from 1934 to 1941, the *Boletin Latinoamericano de Musica* (Musical Bulletin of Latin America), a five-volume archive of Latin American musicology, and founded the Instituto Interamericano de Musicologia (Inter-American Institute of Musicology), made official by government decree in 1940. In 1970 the National School of Music was continuing the high professional level of musicological research inspired by Lange.

Among the younger generation of composers and performers, Hector Tosar Errecart and Leon Biriotti have been particularly successful. A child prodigy, Tosar Errecart had produced an imposing list of compositions by the age of nineteen, and in the 1950's he received national and international recognition for his neoclassical adaptation of *gaucho* folklore in *Danza Criolla* (Creole Dance).

Biriotti, composer and orchestral conductor, studied at the Municipal School of Music in Montevideo and was awarded a scholarship from the Karelyi Foundation for Studies in France. He founded the Orquesta de Arcos (Arcos Orchestra) of Montevideo and, in 1970, conducted that orchestra and the Chamber Orchestra of Musical Youth (Juventudes Musicales) of Uruguay. His many compositions include chamber music and pieces for orchestra, voice, and piano.

An important stimulus to musical development and appreciation is the Official Radio Broadcasting Service (Servicio Oficial de Difusión Radio-Eléctrica—SODRE). SODRE's orchestra, inaugurated in 1931, has become the National Symphony Orchestra. It has had a succession of distinguished directors and is highly regarded in the hemisphere. The country had no professional opera company in 1970, but foreign companies performed regularly at the Teatro

Solis. The National School of Ballet, sponsored by the Ministry of Culture, provided the opportunity for semiprofessional groups to perform regularly in Montevideo and provided a resident company for visiting ballet stars.

The Fine Arts

Painting

The first of the native Uruguayan painters to gain widespread recognition was Italian-trained Juan Manuel Blanes (1830—1901). His works, generally depicting historic events, are noted for their large size, dramatic style, realistic detail, and skillful use of color. Among his most famous canvases are *Episodio de la fiebre amarilla* (Episode of the the Yellow Fever) and *El juramento de los 33 orientales* (The Oath of the Thirty-Three). A museum named for him in Montevideo's Prado Park houses a collection of his works.

The European academic tradition, promoted by Blanes, gave way to impressionism under the influence of Pedro Blanes Viale (1879—1926), who studied in Madrid and Paris. He specialized in the portrayal of landscapes and scenes of festivities but also has two well-known historical scenes on exhibit in the Palacio Legislativo (Legislative Palace). The watercolor artist José Cuneo was also outstanding among the impressionists. His favorite subject matter was moonlit landscapes.

The first Uruguayan painter to achieve international fame was Pedro Figari (1861—1938), best known for his small studies in luminous pastel tones of life in Montevideo and the countryside. One of his most popular paintings, reminiscent of folk art, is *Flores Silvestres* (Wild Flowers). It depicts a Negro horseman, attired in top hat and tails, singing as he rides across the plain with his hands full of violets.

Although French influence was most prominent in the works of many early twentieth century figurative painters, the murals of Norberto Berdia, rendered in a dynamic, realistic style, reflected the influence of the Mexican revolutionary painters, and particularly of David Alfaro Sigueiros, who visited Uruguay in 1933. Berdia represented Uruguay in an international exhibit in Pittsburgh, Pennsylvania, in 1952.

The influence of Joaquín Torres Garcia (1874—1949) throughout Latin America, and especially in Uruguay, continued to be strong in 1970. Torres Garcia studied in Barcelona and later traveled widely in Europe and the Americas. While in Paris, from 1924 to 1932, he was largely responsible for founding the avant-garde *Cercle et Carre* review and, along with Kandinsky, Mondrian, Le Corbusier, and others, organized an exhibit of abstract art. When he returned to Montevideo in 1932, he opened an art school and continued publishing the review, which he renamed *Circulo y Cuadrado* (Circle and Square).

In the New World he developed an enthusiasm for the geometric symbolism of pre-Columbian art and, combining some of its characteristics with European abstract trends, he developed a new style that became known as constructive universalism. His paintings are characterized by the imposition of right angles and perfect geometric balance on figurative fantasies.

Among the painters who have carried on the abstract tradition are Miguel Angel Pareja and Julio Verdie. Other outstanding contemporary artists are expressionist José Echave and muralist and ceramist Carlos Páez Vilaró. The works of engraver Antonio Frasconi, internationally known for his woodcuts, and Luis A. Solari, noted for the bizarre enigmatic figures featured in his collages, were exhibited in the United States in 1970.

The gold medal for the best foreign entry at the Biennial in Florence, Italy, in 1970 was awarded to the twenty-eight year-old Uruguayan Henry Katser. The award-winning work, *In the Land of the Mirrors*, was a five-piece collection in which the attachment of colored adhesive paper to xeroxed copies of a single sketch created a kaleidoscope effect.

Sculpture

No sculpted works of any consequence appeared until the mid-nineteenth century, after the nine-year siege of Montevideo was lifted. The marble carvings of Italian-trained José Livi, including *Pieta*, modeled after Michelangelo's piece of the same name, and the *La Libertad* (Liberty) group in Montevideo's Plaza Cagancha, were among the earliest works of merit.

The expressionistic style of Juan Manuel Ferrari (1874–1916) reflects the influence of Rodin. Of his many works in bronze, the *Monument to Juan Antonio Lavelleja* at Minas is the most ambitious. The two most famous statues in Montevideo are *La Carreta* (Covered Wagon) by José Belloni and *Monument to a Gaucho* by José Luis Zorrilla de San Martin. *La Carreta*, blended into the landscape above a reflecting pool in José Batlle y Ordóñez Park, is dedicated to the pioneers of Uruguay. It takes the form of a bronze group of three yokes of oxen drawing a covered wagon, two free oxen, and a bearded horseman.

Zorilla de San Martin, son of the famous poet, Juan Zorilla de San Martin, is also sculptor of the *El Ultimo Charrúa* (The Last Charrúa) a representation of one of the indigenous inhabitants of the Banda Oriental, situated in Montevideo's Prado Park, and the obelisk at the head of Avenida 18 de Julio, commemorating the signers of the country's first constitution.

Uruguay's contemporary monumental urban sculpture is largely the work of Bernabé Michelena. His work, reflecting the extension to sculpture of Torres Garcia's constructive universalism, is characterized by concise forms stripped of unnecessary detail. Among his most famous works is the equestrian group *Monument to Bernardo O'Higgins* in Montevideo.

Eduardo Diaz Yepes introduced the country to sculptural abstraction. He is Spanish born, but after the Spanish Civil War he took refuge in Montevideo, married the daughter of Torres Garcia, and became a Uruguayan citizen. An eclectic sculptor, his work covers a vast array of styles, including cubism and expressionism, and he is particularly noted for his symbolic abstraction of objects, such as plants and shellfish. One of his best known abstract works is a seven-foot-high onyx monument in Sao Paulo's Ibirapuera Park.

Architecture

The atmosphere of political turmoil in the nineteenth century did not lend itself to architectual creativity. The most typical structure of the century was the complex of long, one-story buildings found on the *estancias* (large ranches or country estates). They were generally strictly functional in design, their facades devoid of decorative motifs. A more elaborate version of the traditional dwelling is the Estancia Santa Clara, built in 1904. Rich in variety, it combines elements of Romanesque, French Gothic, and French Second Empire inspiration.

The modern design of Antonio Bonet, characterized by long, low lines, is reminiscent of the traditional *estancia*. One of his typical works is a seaside house at Punta Ballena, built in the mid-1940's. Among its interesting features are low-pitched shell vaults and a long wooden cantilevered veranda. Bonet is Spanish, but most of his major works are to be found in Uruguay.

One of the most important public buildings constructed in the twentieth century is the Palacio Legislativo. This elaborately decorated neoclassical structure, designed by Cayetano Moretti, is a great source of pride to the people of Montevideo. The Palacio Salvo, an apartment and office building, is a landmark since it is one of the tallest structures in South America, but critics generally feel that its extravagant design and bulging tower are lacking in taste. The monumental building occupied by the Bank of the Republic is more cohesive in design but lacks the space necessary to set it off properly.

Architectural innovation has been given great impetus since the mid-twentieth century by the national university's School of Architecture. The buildings occupied by that school and by the School of Engineering are exemplary of the modernist trend. R. A. S. Bouret is prominent among the architects trained at the national university. One of his most noted works is the series of apartment houses along the beach in Montevideo known as Edifícios Ramla y Guayaqui. These simple elegant structures topped by butterfly roofs were constructed in 1952.

The most important influences on the country's proportionately large number of architects in 1970 were Le Corbusier's work; the so-called constructive universalism of Torres Garcia; the combination of modern and traditional design developed by Bonet; and the high technical standards promoted by Julio Vilamayó, former dean of the School of Architecture and collaborator in the design of the United Nations building in New York. The work of Guillermo Jones Odriozolo in Punta del Este, however, is more directly linked in style to that of Frank Lloyd Wright, and Eladio Dieste's designs reflect the influence of Mexico's Felix Candela. Dieste has experimented with self-supporting vaults and in the parish church of Atlantida achieved a harmonious relationship between a rusticated vault and undulating walls.

One of the most outstanding examples of contemporary Uruguayan architectural design is the office of the Pan American Health Organization in Washington, D.C. Constructed in 1965 and designed by Román Fresnedo Siri, it combines a curved facade that functions as the office building with a truncated cylinder serving as council chamber.

Folk Music and Crafts

Little remains of the culture of the seminomadic tribes, such as the Charrúa, that were the original inhabitants of the Banda Oriental. Shards of round-based pottery, decorated with impressed designs, and *tembetas*, resin and stone ornaments for pierced lips, constitute the bulk of archaeological finds. Early European settlers described the music of the Charrúa as toneless shouting and screaming (see ch. 5, Ethnic Groups and Languages).

The country's contemporary folk culture derives primarily from the legendary figure of the *gaucho*, his songs and dances as well as his costume and paraphernalia. To enliven the lonely life on the pampa, *gauchos* improvised verses—songs of love and adventure in the popular ballad form of Spanish folklore—that they sang around the evening campfire to the accompaniment of their own guitars.

Gaucho folk music gave rise to what has become the national dance of Uruguay, the *pericón*. A round dance in triple time, it is said to resemble the French minuet. Although the fullest development of *gaucho* music took place in Argentina, choreographic historians maintain that the *pericón* is distinctively Uruguayan. After a period of decline earlier in the century, an official arrangement of it for military bands was made in 1887, and it was featured by a theatrical company in 1889. Since that time its popularity has continued to spread, in urban as well as rural areas.

Most of the country's folk music forms, preserved from *gaucho* days or developed by an evolutionary combination of creole and African music on the waterfront, are shared with Argentina.

The melancholy *tango*—combining French, Spanish, and African folk influences—was a product of late nineteenth-century urban slum conditions. Although it originated in Buenos Aires, it has been equally popular in Montevideo; one of the best-known songs of this type, *La Cumparsita*, is the work of Uruguayan composer Gerardo H. Matos Rodríguiez. A popular composer and singer in 1970 was the Argentine Ruben Zarate, who had lived some thirteen years in Uruguay.

The country's handicrafts have been inspired almost exclusively by *gaucho* traditions. The most characteristic of these crafts, kept alive by the tourist trade, is *maté* carving. The *maté* (gourd), from which an aromatic tea made from a Paraguayan herb is sipped, is generally embellished with a figurative design. The most popular designs are romanticized pastoral scenes. Designs are produced by cutting away the dark wood of the surface to reveal the lighter wood of lower layers.

Other objects produced by the craftsmen include the *gaucho's* leather water-bottle, or *cantimplora*, and the famous *boleadoras*, lariats with balls attached at one end to trap the animal around the legs and bring it down. The *boleadoras* were inherited by early *mestizo* (see Glossary) *gauchos* from their native forebears, the Charrúa Indians.

Gaucho folklore is kept very much alive, despite the country's predominantly urban, cosmopolitan culture, through a plethora of clubs sponsoring activities typical of *gaucho* life and through celebration of the annual Semana Criolla (Creole Week). Semana Criolla, also known as La Semana de Turismo (Tourists' Week), coincides with Holy Week and is an official seven-day holiday, although in mid-1970 a bill to reduce it to two days was pending before Congress. The week's activities include exhibitions of national dances and contests in the improvisation of songs among the country's contemporary *gauchos* (see ch. 7, Living Conditions).

CHAPTER 10
RELIGION

Roman Catholicism is the dominant religion of the country, and in 1970 a large majority of the people were Catholics. The country was first settled by Spanish Catholics, and the imprint of the religion on the national culture is still clear. The Constitution of 1830, however, guaranteed freedom of worship for all faiths, and the Constitution of 1919 separated church and state.

The period of Spanish domination over the Uruguayan church was relatively brief since the country gained its independence less than two centuries after it was first settled by Europeans. The indigenous Indian population was too small and too fierce to attract substantial missionary efforts before the European occupation. Consequently, the church was unable to achieve the position of dominance and power it occupied in many Latin American countries colonized during the early sixteenth century. English and French secular philosophies were influential during the second half of the nineteenth century, particularly among the elites. The secular attitudes of the intellectuals gained popularity among the middle and lower classes in the early twentieth century. Many of the immigrants who arrived during the late nineteenth and early twentieth centuries were unsympathetic to the church.

The Uruguayan social reformer, José Batlle y Ordóñez, accelerated the secularization trend by his opposition to church involvement or influence in secular affairs, expressed first in his newspaper, *El Dia*, and later during his presidency. He promoted legislation designed to reduce the scope of ecclesiastical power, which culminated in the separation of church and state in 1919. Batlle's fundamental objective, the clear separation of ecclesiastical and spiritual institutions from governmental and political ones, remains the policy of the dominant Colorado Party.

In the 1960's the church was experiencing a thorough reform and renewal movement in conjunction with the new social philosophies articulated in the social papal encyclicals of the 1960's and the Second Vatican Council. Some clergy and laymen were opposed to the changes, but the majority favored working toward social reforms, such as the alleviation of the misery of the poor and the abolition of the injustices and inequities among the classes and between the capital and the interior. Some clergy and laymen were committed to reforming the political system and the distribution of wealth; others, to bringing greater life and vigor to the spiritual life of the church.

The church hierarchy consisted of 1 archbishop, 1 cardinal, 10 bishops, and almost 700 priests in 1969, with the priests fairly evenly distributed between the capital and the interior. The church was completely free of state control. Power to appoint members of the episcopacy resided exclusively in the church hierarchy.

Although Catholicism is an integral part of the national culture, actual rates of church attendance are low. Religious observance tends to be greatest among the upper classes and some segments of the middle classes and lowest among intellectuals and in the working classes. Women are more actively involved than men, particularly those under twenty or over sixty years of age. Many men regard religion as the responsibility of women. The rural poor generally have high respect for the clergy and strong religious faith, sometimes mixed with belief in local cults and influenced by spiritualism or Afro-Brazilian sects. The greatest respect for the church is found in the poor rural areas and among the urban upper classes, whose members are often educated in Catholic schools and have close ties to the priesthood.

Most of the institutions of society have been secularized, and religious observances, such as processions, pilgrimages, and festivals, are of limited importance. Religious instruction is not permitted in the public schools; divorce has been legal for over sixty years; civil marriage is compulsory; and cemeteries are under public ownership. Important religious holidays have been given secular names, emphasizing the nonreligious character of the celebration. To some extent the paternalistic welfare state has taken over many of the functions, such as education and social assistance, that were traditionally performed by the church. Consequently, it is possible for a young Uruguayan to receive little or no religious training outside his family.

Protestantism has grown rapidly in the mid-twentieth century. The rate of growth, five times the rate of population expansion, has been greatest among the evangelical adventist and pentecostal sects. In 1970 about 2 percent of the people belonged to one of the approximately twenty-five groups comprising the Protestant community. Protestantism tends to appear to the lower classes, although some denominations that have been in existence since the nineteenth century have developed substantially middle class congregations.

Because in many cases foreign churches provide substantial financial support and personnel, Protestantism tends to be considered non-Uruguayan. Many Protestant churches develop into isolated, self-contained subcultures with values and patterns of behavior not shared by the larger Catholic society.

The Jewish population is also small, amounting to less than 2 percent of the population. Most are fairly recent immigrants of Germanic, East European, and Iberian origin and have settled almost exclusively in Montevideo. The six synagogues in the city have large congregations.

HISTORICAL DEVELOPMENT

The Roman Catholic Church was never able to achieve the position of wealth, power, and influence in Uruguay that it had in many other Latin American countries, primarily because of the relatively late establishment of the church in the country. During the sixteenth and early seventeenth centuries, the period of the greatest missionary fervor of the church in Latin America, the country was almost entirely unpopulated except for nomadic Indian tribes. Many of these violently resisted the encroachment of the white men, rendering missionary work among them difficult. The first Jesuit missionaries entered the country in 1624 to establish Indian missions and were influential in imparting the Catholic religion and Spanish culture to the Indians of the northern region. The missions, however, never achieved the size or significance of similar communities in Paraguay. Not until the middle of the seventeenth century was the country effectively occupied by Europeans, and the capital city was not founded until 1726 (see ch. 3, Historical Setting).

By the eighteenth century the church in Uruguay, as in all of Latin America, was beginning to suffer from a shortage of priests, as the children of the upper class families began to enter the legal profession, the army, or the civil service rather than the priesthood. At that time the country was only an appendage of the diocese of Buenos Aires; not until 1878 was a separate diocese established for Uruguay.

In spite of these difficulties, however, the white population of the eighteenth and nineteenth centuries was largely *criollo* (see Glossary) and thoroughly Catholic. The Jesuits and, after their expulsion in 1767, the Franciscans opened Catholic schools in Montevideo, which educated the sons of the elites to serve in the army, the government, or the church. Visitors from Europe would invariably visit the cathedral in Montevideo and remark on the impressive religious processions and ceremonies that occurred frequently, often accompanied by fireworks, bonfires, and cannon. The "Thirty-three Immortals," led by Juan Antonio Lavelleja, began their attempt to win freedom for Uruguay in 1825 by praying at the shrine of the Madonna of Florida, a replica of Uruguay's official patron, the Madonna of Lujan (see ch. 3, Historical Setting).

The 1830 Constitution, promulgated soon after the country won its independence from Spain, recognized Catholicism as the official religion of the country and guaranteed the church government support, concurrently assuring freedom of worship for all faiths. In the same year Congress asked the president to petition the Holy See for a separate diocese for the Republic; Congress even offered to defray the expenses of an episcopal see but stipulated that the incumbent be an Uruguayan citizen.

Under the doctrine of Real Patronato de las Indias (Royal Patronage of the Indies), decreed in 1501 and 1508 by papal bull, the Spanish crown controlled the right of patronage over all Latin American churches. Consequently, many of the church prelates and priests were Spaniards or loyal to Spain, and many chose to return to their native country after independence was achieved by the colonies, thus aggravating the growing shortage of priests. The pope, uneasy about the new republics and under pressure from Spain, refused for several years to accept nominations from the new governments for church positions. The diocese of Buenos Aires, which had jurisdiction over Uruguay, was vacant for many years in the early nineteenth century.

During the late nineteenth and early twentieth centuries the position of the church was gradually eroded by the influx of European immigrants, the influences of secular European philosophies, and weak political support. The majority of immigrants came from Spain and Italy. A relatively small number of French and English settled in Uruguay, and their culture and secular ideas had a substantial impact on the country. Materialist and scientific philosophies of nineteenth-century Europe became popular among the intellectuals and professional leaders in the last third of the century. Intellectual clubs were organized to discuss the new philosophies. Freemasonry was also widespread among the elites, influencing many against the church.

In the same period the Colorado Party, associated with the urban, liberal, and immigrant sections of the country, adopted a stance opposed to church involvement in state affairs, advocating ecclesiastical neutrality in nonreligious matters. The Blanco Party, rural-based and more conservative, was sympathetic to the church and served as a defender of its prerogatives although in many periods its efforts were lukewarm. The Colorados, however, retained power from 1865 to 1958, assuring the predominance of their policies for almost 100 years.

In accordance with Colorado policy, a series of legislative actions gradually curtailed the sphere of influence and power of the church throughout the nineteenth and early twentieth centuries. In 1837 civil marriage was legalized. In 1838 Franciscan convents were closed, and the property was taken for public use; the primary motivation for this action was the desire of the country, because of its sparse population, to devote the maximum resources to the segments of society that produced families. In 1861 public cemeteries were removed from ecclesiastical control, and in 1880 justices of the peace were granted the exclusive right to register marriages and legitimate births, a prerogative previously reserved for the clergy. By 1885 the civil marriage ceremony was declared compulsory; church marriage alone was no longer recognized by the state. Many people continued to perform both ceremonies, but by 1921 only half of the civil marriages were consecrated by the church (see ch. 6, Social Structure).

In the 1870's the government established a comprehensive public school system, which gradually replaced the church-sponsored schools in importance. In 1909 all religious instruction in public schools was prohibited (see ch. 8, Education).

The government was generally unsympathetic to the church throughout the late nineteenth and early twentieth centuries. Juan L. Cuestas, president of the Republic at the close of the nineteenth century, attempted to place further restrictions on the church and to prevent the immigration of priests and friars. Although the Constitution of 1830 committed the state to support of the church, this was interpreted as purely financial assistance, and even the monetary contribution was steadily curtailed. By the end of the nineteenth century the contribution had dwindled to an insignificant amount. In 1892 the total annual grant was the equivalent of US$19,712 (see ch. 3, Historical Setting).

The leading figure in the secularization of the state was José Batlle y Ordóñez, president from 1903 to 1907 and again from 1911 to 1915. From 1886 to 1917 he conducted an active anticlerical campaign through *El Dia*, his daily newspaper. He persisted in spelling God without capitalization and referred to Pope Pius XII as Señor Pacelli in his newspaper. Significant statutes were enacted during the period of Batlle's influence that further curtailed the sphere of the church. A law permitting divorce was passed in 1907, despite a strong public objection by the Catholic clergy. In 1913 divorce was legalized in cases where a woman simply petitioned for separation, with no evidence of abuse required.

It is probable that the anticlerical and somewhat antireligious posture assumed by Batlle contributed significantly to the atmosphere of mild antagonism toward all religious endeavor typical of many segments of the country. By 1917 large sections of the middle and lower classes had adopted the nonreligious attitudes held by some intellectuals and professional leaders in the previous century. As early as 1912 church prelates foresaw the impending separation of church and state and gathered to discuss the restoration, rather than the maintenance, of religious faith in the country.

The Constitution of 1919 finalized the separation, eliminating a major source of friction by allowing the church to retain its ecclesiastical properties. Both sides saw the split as an advantage; the government achieved its goal of separation between the state and religion, and the church was freed from state control. A popular fund amounting to the equivalent of US$1 million was raised at the time to compensate the church for its loss of state support, indicating considerable sympathy among the populace for the church.

After the separation most of the population adopted a milder, less anticlerical attitude toward the church, and active participation in religious activities became increasingly restricted to the upper classes. In 1924 it was estimated that only 25 percent of the population were communicants in the church.

ORGANIZATION OF THE ROMAN CATHOLIC CHURCH

In 1969 the Roman Catholic establishment in the country included 1 metropolitan see or archdiocese and 9 suffragan dioceses: the Archdiocese of Montevideo and the dioceses of Florida, Salto, Melo, San José de Mayo, Minas, Tacuarembó, Mercedes, Canelones, and Maldonado. The country was further subdivided into 205 parishes, over a third of which were located in Montevideo. The episcopacy consisted of 1 cardinal, 1 archbishop, and 10 bishops, 1 of whom was an auxiliary to the archbishop. Many bishops were assisted by a vicar-general. A papal nuncio, appointed by the Vatican, maintained diplomatic relations with the country. The Constitution of 1919 confined the power to make ecclesiastical appointments to the church prelates free of government interference; this provision was not altered by the 1967 Constitution.

Of the 688 priests working in the country in 1969, slightly over one-third (257) were diocesan priests engaged in parish work, and almost two-thirds (431) were religious priests, members of religious orders. In 1969 the ratio of priests to inhabitants was about 1 to 4,200, which is high for Latin America. Slightly under half of Uruguay's professed Catholics and somewhat over half of all priests, diocesan and religious, live in Montevideo. The large majority of the diocesan priests work in the provincial capitals and the interior; most religious priests are concentrated in Montevideo. In 1969, 626 religious men (monks and lay brothers) and 1,955 religious women (nuns and lay sisters) were active in the country; about 60 percent of these resided in the capital city. In 1969, 60 seminarians were engaged in the study of philosophy and theology to prepare themselves for the priesthood.

Although the capital city dominates the nation, it does not seem to absorb a disproportionate number of the clergy. Most of the clergy in the interior, however, are located in small provincial cities rather than in distant rural settlements. Some of the more remote areas may be visited by a priest only once or twice a year.

The Uruguayan Episcopal Conference, established in 1966, functions as a forum for annual discussions and policy decisions by the whole episcopacy. The church is also a member of the Latin American Bishops' Conference (Consejo Episcopal Latino Americano—CELAM), an international organization that meets annually and maintains a permanent secretariat in Bogotá, Columbia. This organization has been in the forefront of recent attempts to reform the role of the church in society.

RELIGIOUS BELIEFS AND PRACTICES

In 1970 the large majority of people were Roman Catholics. About 70 percent had been baptized in the church. Estimates of the number of Catholics vary widely, ranging from the 1963 census figure of 62 percent to a 1969 estimate of 82 percent published by the Catholic church. Estimates made in 1966 vary between 65 percent and 78 percent. Surveys conducted in the late 1950's and early 1960's revealed that 67 percent of Montevideo residents and 58 percent of rural inhabitants were Catholics. The 1963 census reported that 39 percent of the population of rural Uruguay felt no allegiance to any religion.

In general, almost all Catholics have their children baptized, but fewer receive first communion, and still fewer attend Mass regularly. In Montevideo an average of about 10 percent of all baptized Catholics attend Mass on Sundays, and perhaps 7 percent attend regularly. Daily attendance is much smaller, amounting to less than 1 percent of the Catholic population, and is largely restricted to upper class parishes.

In rural areas the percentage of religious participants varies between 7 and 26 percent of the total population. It is lowest in the agricultural regions surrounding Montevideo, which have considerable social differentiation and clubs, unions, and associations; the highest percentages are found in the remote stockraising areas, which have a low population density and few social organizations (see ch. 6, Social Structure).

The upper and middle classes tend to be most active in the church in Montevideo and in the small provincial cities. Intellectuals, university students, and industrial workers usually have the lowest rates of church attendance. In most cases women are more actively involved in church than men. Many men feel that religion is the affair of women and leave religious observance and the training of children in the Catholic faith to their wives and mothers.

A relatively small isolated group of upper and upper middle class Catholics form a religious community and raise their children in the church. The community has its own schools, businesses, press, political party, medical assistance, and recreational facilities for the youth. Their attitude toward Catholicism is primarily defensive: they do not seek to influence or convert the outside community. Some Uruguayans have referred to this community as a Catholic ghetto (*ghetto católico*).

Catholicism is embedded in the national culture and consequently has some influence on the values, world view, and social life of most Uruguayans. Church ceremonies, such as baptism, first communion, marriage, and burial, mark the stages of life for many, particularly for the middle and upper classes in the small towns and the city. Some Uruguayans have hypothesized that the social consciousness and emphasis on social welfare inspired by Batlle y Ordóñez is, to some extent, a substitution of governmental actions for the spiritual and social concern usually found in the Catholic sphere (see ch. 11, Social Values).

Religious life for many people is concerned with coping with problems or satisfying specific needs. An individual may wish to aid a sick family member, to assure success in a business venture, or to gain protection from hostile forces. Participation in the ritual is expected to have intrinsic efficacy in solving problems. Usually the assistance of God is enlisted to solve a problem otherwise unresponsive to personal effort and initiative, almost always through the intercession of the saints and the Virgin Mary. The average Catholic has faith that the saints can and will help him. Often saints are regarded almost as real people, who are endowed with personalities and human characteristics and who can intervene at will in human affairs.

In remote rural areas, where little formal religious training is available, syncretisms of Catholic, African, spiritualist, and Spanish folk beliefs are prevalent. In the northern departments, the home of many Brazilian exslaves, Catholicism has been influenced by the Afro-Brazilian Macumba cults, derived originally from African religions and synthesized with spiritualist and Catholic doctrines. In some cults the priest serves as a medium who is possessed by the spirits, usually African deities overlaid with the names and characteristics of Catholic saints. During possession, the voice, gestures, way of walking, and thinking of the medium are profoundly altered. Through him, the spirits communicate with the faithful, giving advice and offering solace for personal problems. Spirits are also believed to be capable of rendering direct assistance. A diseased person may be cured by a medium who calls on a spirit to possess him and then transmits the healing power of the spirit and its suggested remediies to the sick person.

Other cults, often derived from belief in a particular saint, are found in rural areas. The cult of San Cono (Saint Cono) has been studied only in the department of Florida but is probably more widespread. The saint is believed to be capable of miraculous intervention in games of chance. The rural, uneducated poor tend to substitute superstitions for religious ideas; horoscopes and other non-Catholic religious beliefs are common among this group.

There is little social pressure on individuals to be active in or even to belong to the church, and support for religious endeavors is largely lacking in school, communal, and, often, family groups. A vast proportion of the school system is public, and teachers are not permitted to offer any form of religious instruction in these schools. If a child does not receive religious education in his family, it is probable that not other institution of society will provide it or encourage his involvement in the church (see ch. 8, Education).

Communal religious observances, such as festivals and processions, are rare and participation is limited. Although processions were popular and frequent in the past, they have been discouraged by the government on the ground that they distract schoolchildren from their studies. The Madonna of Lujan in Argentina has been the official patron of the country since 1887, but she is neither universally recognized nor widely popular. Since the 1950's pilgrimages have been made to the statue of the Miraculous Virgin on top of the Cerro de Verdún near the small city of Minas, but this is not a longstanding national tradition. Catholic clergy do not accompany funeral processions to the cemeteries, and cemeteries are not reserved to members of a single faith. In accordance with the growing secular trend, the government renamed all religious holidays in the early twentieth century. Christmas is called Family Day; Holy Week is Semana Criolla (Week of the Creole) or Tourist Week; Epiphany is Children's Day; and the Feast of Our Lady on December 8 is Beach Day. The religious holidays are widely celebrated but often only with a secular observance. In 1943 the president of the Republic publicly stated that he professed no religion.

Batlle y Ordóñez was strongly opposed to church influence in secular matters, but a leading contemporary literary figure, José Enrique Rodó, in his *Liberalismo y Jacobinismo* (1906) and other writings, objected to Batlle's anticlerical campaign and pleaded for his countrymen to maintain their spiritual, humanistic values and religious sincerity. His writings have had a substantial impact on the country and, to some extent, counteract the influence of Batlle on religious matters. The large fund raised by public contribution in 1919 to compensate the church also revealed considerable public support for the institution. Furthermore, at the time of separation the church was permitted to continue its educational and religious activities (see ch. 9, Artistic and Intellectual Expression).

On Beach Day the archbishop ceremoniously blesses the waters before the beaches are officially declared open. Some public leaders are devoutly religious, and the church's influence is still strong among more traditional upper and upper middle classes, but there is a general attitude of apathy and noninvolvement.

THE CHURCH IN SOCIETY

The Constitution of 1967 reaffirmed the complete separation of church and state, the freedom of all religions, and the exemption from taxation of all temples dedicated to worship. Since 1919 the church has been a significant, although not a major, factor in public affairs. The first Catholic political party was founded in 1872 by a bishop and was supported by the church. It represented an orthodox Catholic point of view and until 1912 concentrated on combatting the increasingly secular way of life in the country. In 1912 it was named the Civic Union and, under the influence of the social and political philosophy of the French Catholic philosopher and theologian Jacques Maritain, gradually became more involved in social issues and problems.

In 1962, after a conflict had developed between conservative and leftist wings of the party, it merged with a splinter group, took on a more leftist position, and renamed itself the Christian Democratic Party (Partido Democrático Cristiano—PDC). In the late 1960's the PDC advocated social transformation through democratic means, including a more equitable distribution of economic goods, to be achieved without eliminating private property rights. Some of the most radical political leaders, however, accused the PDC of being too conservative and reform-minded rather than revolution-oriented and claimed that it was losing its younger, more militant student and worker members; these leaders recommended an alliance with the Leftist Liberty Front (Frente Izquierd de Libertad—FIdeL) (see ch. 13, Political Dynamics).

The PDC serves as an avenue for political action by church prelates and lay leaders. It has always been small, and in both the 1962 and 1966 elections it received only 3 percent of the total vote, winning three seats for the party in the Chamber of Representatives. The small vote does not reflect the importance of Catholicism to the voting public, however, since most Catholics prefer to vote for the traditional parties regardless of their religious convictions (see ch. 13, Political Dynamics).

A Catholic-oriented newspaper has existed since 1878, when *El Bien Publico* was founded. In 1962 it was closed by a printers' strike but soon after was resurrected as *BP Color*, affiliated with the PDC. In 1968 it had a small circulation (see ch. 15, Public Information).

Lay organizations have long been important to the church, and in the 1960's, in conjunction with the church renewal movement, they have been particularly encouraged. In 1900 the Catholic Workers' Circle was organized and has since continued to provide social services for its members. The first Catholic labor unions were established in 1947. In 1970 a few were active, although in comparison with the secular labor movement they were of negligible importance (see ch. 20, Labor Relations and Organization). Catholic Action, the National Catholic Union for Social Action, the Catholic Family Movement, and the Associationof Catholic Fathers and Children are only a few of the many lay organizations working to improve the quality of family life, the training of children, and the state of society. The church has also encouraged the formation of social clubs, youth clubs, and workers' clubs in order to increase its influence and to attract people back into the church.

The role of the church in education is smaller than in many other Latin American countries because of the excellent public school system, although graduates from private secondary schools attend the university with a much higher frequency than do public school alumni. In 1969 the church operated 290 schools, ranging from the primary to advanced levels, with an estimated total of 82,000 students. Of the total number of students, 60 percent were studying in Montevideo; most of the rest were located in small cities in the interior, and almost none were in remote rural areas. In general, Catholic schools educated the children of the urban upper and middle classes and the progeny of the landowning elites. The contribution of these schools to Catholic education is lessened, however, by the fact that official curriculum requirements are so extensive that very little time is left for religious instruction. A large number of charitable institutions and hospitals, both in the city and the interior, are sponsored by the church (see ch. 8, Education).

RECENT TRENDS WITHIN THE CHURCH

The majority of the episcopacy and many of the clergy are in sympathy with the reform and renewal movement that has developed in the Roman Catholic Church in the postwar era. A major source of inspiration has been the papal encyclicals of the 1960's that deal with the church's responsibility for social justice and the importance of renewing pastoral life. Pope John XXIII's Mater et Magistra (Mother and Teacher, 1961) and Pacem in Terris (Peace on Earth, 1963), and Pope Paul VI's Populorum Progressio (The Development of Peoples, 1967) have been particularly influential. These encyclicals discuss the problems of colonialism, underdevelopment, and the dignity of labor, underlining the responsibility of the great powers and local elites in underdeveloped countries in stimulating social and economic reforms. The Second Vatican Council (1962—65) has given great reinforcement to the social action and renewal orientation of the church as well as the ecumenical and liturgical reform movements.

Within this broad context, the Latin American Catholic liberals have formulated an ideology centered on social justice for the deprived, basic institutional reform, and the importance of social action to extend Christian influence in the world. Some of the most radical refer to revolutionary reforms. These doctrines were fully enunciated and discussed at the Second General Conference of CELAM at Medellín, Colombia in 1968 and were subsequently adopted by the Uruguayan church. The Document on Peace, drafted at the conference, stated that peace is the product of a just order in which men can develop as men and in which their dignity is respected, their aspirations are satisfied, and their personal freedom is guaranteed. Furthermore, where there are unjust inequalities among men and nations, peace is violated. The conference also advocated defending the rights of the poor and the oppressed and urged the rulers and elite classes to eliminate the injustice, corruption, and insensitivity that endanger social peace. Another statement recognized the necessity for progress from subhuman living conditions to more human ones for each and every person, to be achieved through changes in the political and economic structure of society.

Statements by Pope Paul VI to the conference supported the liberals by recognizing the injustice of poverty and the living conditions of the poor, the exploitation of the less fortunate by the wealthy minorities, and the need for a reform of social structures, as well as increased social consciousness and willingness on the part of the elites to share the wealth in order to avert future crises. At the same time, the pope disappointed the radicals by stressing the necessity of gradual reform achieved through the existing institutions rather than a sudden or violent change or revolution of the kind proposed in the Marxist philosophies of some radical churchmen.

The Uruguayan church has been actively involved in the liberalization movement in the 1960's, and by 1970 conservative forces among the clergy were in the minority. The archbishop of Montevideo, Monsignor Carlos Parteli, his auxiliary bishop, and his vicar general were all sympathetic to the ideals expressed at Medellín and have been instrumental in spreading and implementing these doctrines. Monsignor Parteli has favored a change in the social structure that would contribute to a higher standard of living, adequate food, clothing, education, employment, and the possibility of family stability for all. He has also stressed the necessity of awakening people to their own human dignity.

Actions of the episcopacy and clergy indicate general support for the position of the archbishop. Since 1968 the Social-Theological Conference of the Archdiocese of Montevideo has been spreading the ideas enunciated at Medellín, including the need to educate the populace in *concientización*, or personal and political consciousness. In 1969 the Uruguayan Episcopal Conference issued a statement warning that social peace was in jeopardy as a result of national economic difficulties, violence by many strata of the population, the pursuit of their vested interests by the powerful few, and the abuse of power and arbitrary measures directed against some citizens. In an earlier statement the conference stated its opinion that all Uruguayans were in favor of order, tranquillity, and peace and of a true order, based on the individual and respect for his dignity and freedom.

After the 1969 meeting of the Uruguayan Bishops' Conference, a group of priests from the northern coastal departments presented a list of violations of social peace in their communities, including accusations against the government for specific actions it has taken. On the third march of the sugarcane workers from Artigas to Montevideo to assert their demands for land and decent living conditions in 1968, a parish priest gave them lodging in a parochial hall in a department in the interior, and some Catholic spokesmen publicly declared their support for the claims of the sugarcane workers. Many people were scandalized by these actions, claiming that the workers were being exploited by international communism.

A few members of the clergy have become more radical leftists. Some have asserted the need for armed struggle in order to accomplish social change and have even joined urban guerrilla groups. The large majority of the liberal clergy, however, is interested in accomplishing reforms gradually without recourse to violence.

Many clergymen and laymen are involved in the pastoral reform movement, which seeks to substitute a small parish community, in which the parishioners are drawn together by close social and religious bonds, for the aloof and formal atmosphere typical of the traditional, large parish. Other clergymen are attempting to bring new members into the church and to influence those usually isolated from church activities. Of particular importance are worker-priests, who take employment in factories in an attempt to reach the industrial working classes by sharing their lives and experiences.

Laymen are also actively involved in social action. The Christian Democratic Youth Movement held a world conference in Montevideo in 1969 to discuss the social and economic problems of the modern world. Uruguayan speakers stressed the desirability of combatting hunger, poverty, and exploitation and of achieving a communitarian form of socialism.

Other laymen are interested in pastoral and social welfare activities. Many engage in volunteer social assistance work; others work for a renewal of religious life within the parish. The Decree on the Apostolate of the Laity in 1965 and the statements of the Second Vatican Council have emphasized the spiritual responsibility of laymen to share in some pastoral duties, such as the teaching of Christian doctrine and the care of souls. In response to this encouragement, laymen have begun to participate more actively in efforts to create a parish community and to communicate their religious ideas to those who are indifferent to the church. In some parishes laywomen missionaries have undertaken block organization, in which they bring the families living on a block together for religious activities, festivals, plays, and sporting and social events.

The progressive church movement, however, has been accompanied by some friction both within the church itself and between the church and the state. Many devout believers resist the changes proposed by the liberals, fearing that the innovators will alter the church and destroy its unity. Many laymen and some conservative newspapers have expressed the fear that the church is being infiltrated by Communist ideas and subversive Communist agents.

Some members of the church hierarchy are also opposed to the new movement, believing that the church should remain substantially unaltered. In 1965 a conservative papal nuncio came into conflict with a group of young Catholics and was eventually recalled. When some liberal worker-priests stopped charging fees for baptisms and other services in 1969, they were strongly opposed by their bishop, although they were supported by their congregations. Minor conflicts have occurred between the church and the state as a result of critical comments by church prelates, sermons stating opposition to government policy, and participation of nuns in protest demonstrations.

OTHER RELIGIONS

About 2 percent of the population is Protestant, belonging to approximately twenty-five different sects and denominations. In 1968 the total number of communicants was estimated to be 15,400, and the total Protestant community involved in church activities was estimated at 40,000 to 60,000 persons. Protestants meet at over 300 places of worship and are served by some 250 ordained ministers and about 150 lay workers. The ratio of ministers to community members is about 1 minister to every 200 members. About half of the communicant members, or 12 percent of the total community of 60,000, attend church on Sundays.

Protestantism is relatively new in Uruguay; the first churches were established in the mid-nineteenth century. During the twentieth century the growth has been rapid, and in the 1960's the growth of

Protestantism was about five times the rate of population increase. The pentecostal and adventist sects have shown the fastest rate of growth and in 1965 represented almost half of Uruguay's Protestants.

Some Protestant denominations are primarily immigrant churches; they are an integral part of an ethnic community of foreign origin and recruit new members almost entirely from within the community. They tend to be endogamous and isolated and engage in negligible evangelical efforts. Typical is the Waldensian Church, the largest Protestant church in the country. Founded by Italian colonists in 1858, it claimed about 5,000 communicant members and a community of more than 13,000 people in 1966. One large Waldensian church is located in Montevideo; and the rest of the churches are in the coastal areas bordering the Río de la Plata. The Mennonite Church similarly consisted originally of refugees from Poland and Russia; in 1968 its community membership was about 2,000. The German Lutheran Church, with a membership of about 4,400, and the Anglican Church, composed of 300 member families, are also largely immigrant and foreign colony churches (see ch. 5, Ethnic Groups and Languages).

Most other Protestant churches were founded by missionaries with the goal of converting nonbelievers to the faith. Some, often referred to as historical churches, have been in existence for several decades and appeal primarily to the middle classes. Education is stressed and most historical churches run sectarian schools.

The Methodist Church, with a community membership of 5,000, is one of the largest of the traditional churches. The congregation is principally from the middle and upper classes and includes doctors, lawyers, and other professional people. Education and medical care are offered to members, and many are attracted by the opportunity to learn English. The Southern Baptist Convention, with a community membership of 5,000 in 1968, also operates several schools. The North American Lutheran, Mormon, Presbyterian, and Christian Science churches are of the same general category but are smaller.

The Young Men's Christian Association is large and influential in Uruguay and maintains branches in the interior as well as in the capital that provide recreation, social assistance, and cultural programs. The Young Women's Christian Association, affiliated with the parent organization in the United States, is somewhat smaller. They are both popular and well-attended, although not everyone who participates is Protestant. The Catholic church is establishing similar programs for Catholic youth.

Many churches and sects of more recent origin are committed to evangelism. The Church of God, the Assembly of God, the Swedish Free Mission, Seventh Day Adventists, Jehovah's Witnesses, the Salvation Army, and several smaller groups are actively involved in attracting new members and have experienced a very rapid growth in the 1950's and 1960's. Many of these churches tend to attract people of lower class background, occasionally even the very poor. The missionaries of some of the most evangelical churches preach on street corners and hand out leaflets to attract possible converts.

The Federation of Evangelical Churches of Uruguay (Federación de Iglesias Evangélicas del Uruguay) serves as an umbrella organization for most of the Protestant churches, including such major denominations as the Methodists, Waldensians, American Lutherans, Mennonites, German Lutherans, and the Salvation Army. The federation enables the Protestant groups to collaborate on problems of evangelism, education, contacts with the working youth, the defense of human rights, and relations with the government. Fourteen other ecumenical and international Protestant organizations exist in Uruguay.

In many cases conversion to Protestantism results in a radical change in life style and social status. Most churches stress the value of individual effort and achievement and the responsibility of each person for his actions and his faith; furthermore, education and an improved living standard are important in many churches. Consequently, there is a tendency for a lower class Protestant church gradually to assume middle class status as the congregation strives for education and success. Since a considerable portion of the congregations of the historic churches consists of members of long standing, including second-generation Protestants, they have generally acquired a middle class character.

Individual Protestant churches often become closely knit communities isolated from the larger Catholic society. The change of status estranges lower class converts from their home communities, and their religion isolates them from middle class Catholics. Members of a Protestant congregation often associate frequently with one another, share many social activities, and often marry within the group. They tend to develop their own subculture, which is centered on values and patterns of behavior at variance with the dominant Catholic forms. Although the festivals and activities of the Catholic church play a limited role in the country, the Protestant is excluded from these national events. Furthermore, Protestantism is considered something foreign and continues to be closely tied to foreign powers. In the late 1960's one-third of all missionaries were from foreign countries, and North American and European influence on the literature, architecture, and liturgy of most churches was marked. Many Protestant churches are still supported by financial assistance and personnel from North America.

Protestantism has had very little impact on the intellectuals or on the industrial classes. It tends to appeal to the middle classes and the poorer segments of the lower classes, which lack steady jobs and secure positions in society. Rural migrants, uprooted from their Catholic society and home environment, are likely to join the close, community-oriented Protestant churches when they reach the city. Principal doctrines of Protestantism, such as the priesthood of all believers and the right of private interpretation and judgment, emphasize the importance of each person and his equality with all other believers, ideas which appeal to those who feel oppressed and of marginal importance to society. Protestantism also appeals to former Catholics who find that the church is no longer satisfying them yet feel a religious vacuum. Protestantism competes with secular political movements, such as communism, for the loyalties of the discontented who seek a compelling ideology and a movement that will provide individual responsibility and meaningful activities (see ch. 6, Social Structure).

The attitude of the Catholic church toward Protestantism has been modified under the influence of the ecumenical decisions of the Second Vatican Council. Some Catholic seminaries in Latin America are now offering courses on Protestant doctrine and history and are expressing a new openness toward Protestant churches.

A few leaders of the Protestant churches have taken liberal positions on social and political issues. They emphasize the need for structural changes in society to accomplish economic advancement. Methodist leaders have acknowledged the possibility of a dialogue between Marxism and Christianity, stressing the necessity of understanding Communist ideals while admitting the various shortcomings of the ideology. Other Protestant leaders have also expressed their sympathy for Marxist ideals. They have expressed their support for the march of the sugarcane cutters on Montevideo in 1969 (see ch. 20, Labor Relations and Organization).

The Jewish population, estimated at between 40,000 and 50,000 in the late 1960's, is the third largest in South America. It represents between 1 and 2 percent of the national population and is primarily of Germanic, East European, and Iberian origin. Almost all Jews live in Montevideo; only 3 percent reside outside the city. They are divided into four communal organizations based on ethnic origin: East European Ashkenazic, German Ashkenazic, Hungarian, and Sephardic. Montevideo has six synagogues that serve the Jewish community; all have large congregations, but attendance tends to be low. The German synagogue, with 1,500 member families, has a weekly average of 200 persons (see ch. 5, Ethnic Groups and Languages).

In 1956 an ecumenical Judeo-Christian organization, the Jewish-Christian Conference of Uruguay (Confraternidad Judía-Cristiana del Uruguay), was established by a member of a prominent lay Catholic family. Relations between the Jewish and Christian communities are generally good. A group of Jews with leftist leanings has formed a Communist organization called the Jaime Zhitlovsky Cultural Organization.

CHAPTER 11

SOCIAL VALUES

The value system is based on traditional Hispanic culture but has been extensively influenced by the country's historical experiences, the character of the *gaucho*, or cowboy, and the ideals and philosophies of the nineteenth- and twentieth-century European immigrants. An emphasis on individualism, the importance of the family, a disdain for manual work, and fatalism are some reflections of the Hispanic traditions. In 1970 the focal values could be considered to be individualism, personal relationships and the family, social justice, security, and the enjoyment of life. Other social values are basically corollaries of these central principles. Although these ideals are not always followed, together they constitute the Uruguayan's blueprint for the social order, his standards of proper behavior, his image of himself, and his view of the world.

The country's early history as a frontier buffer state discouraged the development of the type of landed aristocracy characteristic of many other Latin American countries, favoring instead inhabitants with a rough, egalitarian outlook. The free and independent *gaucho* of this period accepted no authority above his own and followed only the dictates of his will. A certain arrogance typified the *gaucho*: he characteristically disparaged the law, emphasizing the importance of his personal courage, skill, and valor. He tended to be competitive and proud, unwilling to accept anonymity or inferiority. At the same time, observers have noted a quality of indolence or laziness in the *gaucho* character, possibly springing from the period when much of the land and livestock was not owned and existence was simple.

The European immigrants of the last century, although primarily of Spanish or Italian origin, contributed a more rationalistic, secular world view and the conception of a social order slowly changing under the impact of industrialization. Although Roman Catholic doctrines form an integral part of traditional Hispanic values, the influence of the church on the later formation of Uruguayan values was limited.

In spite of the prevalence of modern ideas in certain areas, such as the limitation of family size, secularization of political and educational institutions, and extensive political participation, most of the values remain traditional. The norms of an industrialized society are largely rejected because of a generally casual attitude toward the values of hard work, efficiency, and pragmatism. Particularly in the realm of family ties, personal relationships, work, and the symbols of social status, traditional ideas are still important.

The value system of the interior is more conservative than that of Montevideo. The rural upper class maintains its paternalistic role and respect for landownership and the produce of the land. The *estancia* (large ranch or country estate) owner with a long-established family position who is able to pursue a cultivated life of leisure is still widely respected.

In the urban environment the middle class serves as the dominant reference group for the norms of society, and some of its typical values, such as security, moderation, avoidance of risk, and the prestige of consumption, have spread to other segments of society. Inspite of some regional and class variations, however, the ethnic, racial, and linguistic homogeneity of the population has produced a relatively high degree of consensus on social values in all areas of the country.

THE INDIVIDUAL

The traditional Hispanic concept of individuality is the core of an interrelated complex of values and attitudes defining the nature of the self and of others, consequently affecting ideas about the conduct of social relationships and, to some extent, the nature of the social order. This concept is rooted in a belief in the inherent inner worth or integrity of every individual, regardless of his social position. The phrase *la dignidad de la persona* (dignity of the person) is a popular expression for this inner, almost spiritual quality. The concept is probably derived from the Roman Catholic idea of the soul, but it has lost most of its religious overtones and refers simply to a transcendental quality of all human beings. Each person is considered to be worthy of respect, not because of his conformity to social patterns, but because the individual is unique.

The country's *gaucho* heritage has amplified the importance attached to individualism and freedom. The personality of the independent and self-sufficient *gaucho* has become a popular ideal in modern society.

In order to ensure that the dignity of others is properly respected, patterns of courtesy and formality are emphasized in social behavior. Proper manners define how a person should treat others of equivalent or different social status in order to express a suitable regard for their integrity and individuality. Any slur to another's personal dignity is considered highly insulting, and a prompt and vigorous assertion of one's self is expected.

Derived from the value of individualism is an emphasis on individual judgment and opinion. In making a decision a person is expected to grant priority to his own personal feelings and wishes rather than to the opinions of his peer group. Another consequence of individualism is a disinclination to accept authoritarian political regimes or the intervention of political or other authorities in the sphere of social or private life. An individual is anxious to educate himself and to develop his creative aesthetic potential in order to realize his full inner worth and integrity. He is expected to express his inner self through strong feelings and an emotional involvement with life. If daily existence does not have a strong coloration of feelings, it is considered boring and flat, and even an ordinary incident is given an emotional meaning in the retelling to heighten its intensity.

The traits associated with the concept of the ideal man are summed up in the idea of *machismo*, or masculinity. The qualities subsumed under this ideal include physical strength and dominance, courage, self-confidence, and assurance, an orientation toward action, verbal facility, and sexual prowess. The man with *machismo* does not easily give up or admit that he is wrong. He tends to assume positions of leadership, either through direct action, as in the case of a military leader, or through his skill in verbal expression. Literary and oratory abilities are of primary importance to a lawyer, journalist, or politician, but the ability to speak well and forcefully is a significant asset for any leader. Even in private life, skill with words is a characteristic of the truly masculine person. The *caudillo*, or politically strong man is traditionally an individual who is able to attract followers through his *machismo*, including his skill at fighting, his masculine courage, and his facility with words.

A man wins esteem in his personal life through his sexual prowess, although in the middle and upper classes, he is expected to exercise discretion. Extramarital relations are accepted, but they must remain strictly separated from the sphere of home and family. If a man commits adultery in the home or in any way creates a public scandal, his wife is entitled to sue for a divorce. Among lower class men, relations with many different women are common (see ch. 6, Social Structure).

The ideal man responds quickly to any insult to his integrity or dignity, resorting in extreme cases to a duel. Even political differences have occasionally been settled by duels when personal pride became involved. In 1970 dueling was still legal and continued to occur occasionally.

The upper middle and upper class male is also expected to adhere to the role complex of the gentleman. Self-cultivation, leisure, generosity, and aesthetic sophistication are aspects of the ideal pattern. Wealth is not an end in itself but is valued as the necessary basis for a comfortable, gracious life. The gentleman ideally owns land or, if he must work, is a professional. Teaching a few courses at the university is taken as an indication of one's mental abilities and education.

Among all classes, but particularly in the upper levels of society, the ideal man is also a husband and father who takes his responsibilities and his obligations to his family seriously. He is the primary disciplinarian, the dominant personality, the provider, and the protector of his family (see ch. 6, Social Structure).

The image of the ideal woman is the opposite of the ideal man. Whereas men are self-assertive and dominant, women are expected to be submissive, retiring, modest, gentle, and affectionate. In more conservative families a woman's status is derived to a considerable extent from her husband and her family connections, and she is expected to regard her role as a wife and mother of primary importance. The husband makes all major decisions, but the wife is expected to handle minor problems and the daily administration of the household. She should be skilled and competent at domestic tasks and in providing a clean, comfortable home for her family. It is also incumbent upon her to direct the religious life of the family and, to some extent, the training of her children. A certain amount of self-sacrifice and abnegation for the sake of her family is regarded as a womanly virtue.

Traditionally, a woman was to be sheltered and protected within the home. This pattern is slowly breaking down in many urban areas as women become active in associations, civic groups, and clubs outside the home, but it is still idealized by some segments of the upper and middle classes. The economic contribution of lower class women is often essential for family survival, preventing them from adhering to the upper class ideal. Women of this group are usually more independent and self-reliant than women of higher status.

The country has a long tradition of educating women and providing them with access to professional and career opportunities. Women have extensive political and legal rights; they are generally accepted as equals in social and cultural life and sometimes in the political, business, and financial world. The school system is completely coeducational, and large numbers of women attend the university. Many young university-educated women in particular are anxious to develop a new, more emancipated conception of the woman's position in society.

Many of the values surrounding the ideal of womanhood and her social role have, however, proved resistant to change. A girl is almost always expected to marry and to place her family obligations before her career goals. The career woman is usually considered somewhat exceptional. Although divorce is legal and relatively easy for a woman to obtain, divorce rates are low, indicating a high value on preserving the marital relationship and the home.

HUMAN RELATIONSHIPS

Personal relationships are highly valued by the people and, in most cases, are vastly preferred to impersonal, functional connections. The average person likes to shop or work with people he knows personally, vote for an individual whose qualities of character he respects, and handle business arrangements through friends or kinsmen. The interpersonal relationship is generally regarded as highly attractive, dynamic, and satisfying. Enjoyment of friends through long conversations and visits is one of the principal pleasures of life. Uruguayans spend hours in sidewalk cafés in vigorous conversation, often discussing the ever-popular subjects of politics and soccer.

Close relationships with relatives and selected friends are of primary importanc. Only with these individuals can people establish a relationship based on the reciprocal appreciation of each other's self or *dignidad*. The greatest commitment of energy and involvement is therefore usually to the close circle of kin and friends; most people are far less concerned with more distant persons or the problems of the larger community. They may discuss the large ideological issues and difficulties facing the nation, hemisphere, or world, but this intellectual probing is rarely accompanied by emotional concern for, or active attempts to tackle, such remote problems.

The values of individualism and personal relationships are perfectly compatible, since each person is expected to be powerful, self-reliant, and influential in order to defend and protect the rights and interests of his family and close friends. Each person's freedom to act and express himself is respected, but these do not take precedence over his duty to his family.

Generosity and loyalty are expected between close friends and kin. Favors commonly exchanged within this group range from caring temporarily for one another's children to lending money or finding someone a job. Only persons who are related or feel particularly close can genuinely trust each other; people are much less likely to have confidence in strangers or a large impersonal organization whose reliability is founded on adherence to such abstract principles as honesty or fairness.

A network of family and friendship ties is of great importance in finding a job or in dealing with the government. An Uruguayan competing for a post in either the public or private sector will first seek out a friend or a friend of a friend who owes him a favor. Even when standardizing hiring procedures, such as a test, are put into operation, various personal criteria, including membership in the proper club or appropriate political faction, often bear on the decision. In interactions with the government bureaucracy, the intercession of a friend or kinsman may facilitate what would otherwise be a slow and intricate negotiation.

The family firm has persisted, in large part because employers wish to hire people they feel they can trust and who owe them personal loyalty. Many businessmen are also reluctant to sell stock in their companies to the public, thus placing partial ownership in the hands of complete strangers. In the rural areas the traditional paternalistic relationship between the *estancia* owner and his hired ranch hands is still strong. Some *estancia* owners feel a personal responsibility to provide some educational, legal, and medical services for their employees and exact personal loyalty in return.

In political life personal characteristics and relationships play a major role. Many voters will choose a candidate because of his personal qualities rather than his voting record or political views. Party factions are often identified with the name of their leaders as well as a certain policy, so that a group may be known as the Terristas or Batllistas (see ch. 13, Political Dynamics). Although José Batlle y Ordóñez molded his party around a powerful ideology, loyalty to his ideas has become intertwined with loyalty to him as a person, and at times his ideas are accepted almost as an article of faith.

Interpersonal relations tend to be ceremonial: good manners, courtesy, and polite behavior are emphasized, particularly in aspects of life where traditions remain strong, such as the family. Gift giving is popular and frequent, and hospitality is highly valued. A greeting between friends is likely to be ceremonious, gesticulatory, and voluble; it would be considered discourteous not to show human warmth even in a casual relationship. At the same time, Uruguayans are noted for speaking their minds frankly and directly, perhaps reflecting the influence of their rough *gaucho* forebears.

Proper, respectable dress is valued. Men tend to dress in a conservative European style. Although women often wear bright colors and occasionally short skirts, their dress also tends to be moderate. In 1969, at the height of the tourist season, the busdrivers of Montevideo refused to pick up any woman wearing bermuda shorts to protest the fashion, in spite of the objections of the city newspapers, the mayor's office, and the shorts-clad tourists, many of whom were Argentines rather than Uruguayans (see ch. 7, Living Conditions).

Although the people accept the fact that their country is socially stratified, little emphasis is placed on patterns of deference, and proper manners reflect the national ideal of democratic equality. The country's frontier and *gaucho* heritage have tended to minimize formal patterns of social differentiation. W. H. Hudson, writing in the late nineteenth century, noted that a landowner might sit down and talk with his hired shepherd without expecting deferential behavior, in spite of the social differences separating them. The liberal policies and reforms of Batlle y Ordóñez facilitated the development of egalitarian values. In modern Uruguay different social classes may share a café, restaurant, or school. Even in school all children must wear identical smocks to provide at least an outward appearance of equality. The Spanish practice of addressing a gentleman as Señor Don is abbreviated to Señor in written communications with people of all social classes.

THE SOCIAL ORDER

A belief in social justice is at the heart of a complex of values that define the nature of the ideal social order. All persons have the right to civil liberties, to participation in the political process, and to assistance from the state in times of need. These values, however, are compatible with a stratified society in which some classes are higher in status than others. The Uruguayan concept of equality is founded on the belief in the dignity of all men, each man's right to freedom, and the possibility that any man who strives to fulfill his inner self may also achieve high social position.

Historically, the *gaucho* prized his independence and freedom. The immigrants of the nineteenth and twentieth centuries brought with them European ideologies advocating equality, freedom, and justice. Thus the climate of opinion in early twentieth-century Uruguay was ripe for the innovative egalitarian ideas of Batlle y Ordóñez. His policies have gradually become accepted as a blueprint for the ideal social order by much of the country.

Various state policies have been adopted in an effort to realize the just society. Probably the most significant is mass public education, which theoretically provides equal educational opportunities for all classes of society (see ch. 8, Education). All members of society are expected at least to vote for their political leaders if not actively campaign for them or attempt to influence their decisions. A high percentage of the population votes in major national elections (see ch. 13, Political Dynamics). The extensive social welfare programs guarantee at least a minimal income for all members of society as well as financial assistance for the less fortunate, such as the unemployed, the poor, and the aged (see ch. 7, Living Conditions). State legislation has intervened in such diverse spheres as price supports for milk and rent controls in order to promote adequate nourishment and housing for all. Government labor legislation protects the rights of all working persons in the country. The fact that in many cases the ideals of social justice and individual freedom have not been fully implemented and the laws not adequately enforced does not diminish the importance of these values to the model of the ideal society.

A preoccupation with security and stability absorbs much of the population. These are of greatest importance to the middle class because of its unstable and uncertain economic situation, but an interest in security has gradually spread to large segments of all classes (see ch. 6, Social Structure). The state has taken on a paternalistic role and is expected to provide some measure of security to all members of society. A government job is especially desirable since it is almost impossible to dismiss a civil servant. The highest ambition of many young people is to get a government job.

There is a closely related tendency to rely on the government to take the initiative in solving major problems, including economic and social ills. Few individuals wish to risk the family wealth and foundation of security on a questionable economic venture or to advocate a radical change that might affect their own stable position. Instead, the common practice is to invest the family wealth in a home and land. Statistics indicate a high proportion of homeowners in all social classes, in spite of government legislation making renting financially advantageous. The quality of the house is less important than the fact of ownership since many are old or in poor condition. The value of security is reinforced by the importance of family and personal relationships since a man is expected to guard assiduously the economic basis of his family's well-being.

Although society was fluid and the middle class played an innovative role in the first third of the twentieth century, a resistance to change has become the norm of modern society. Particularly during the economic crisis beginning in the mid-1950's, the preservation of even a precarious status quo has become desirable. There is a tendency to advocate solutions that require changes and sacrifices from other groups without involving a corresponding disruption of one's own social community.

A spirit of moderation and compromise should govern the relation between persons and groups. As the noted journalist Carlos Maggi has explained, everything is settled incompletely and by conversation. In close personal relationships, open confrontation and competitiveness are rare. In the first half of the twentieth century there has been a tendency to settle political and labor disputes through the use of compromise rather than violent confrontation.

The Uruguayan's attitude toward himself and his country reflects the value of moderation. He sees his country in perspective, respecting it for its social and political accomplishments without having an inflated sense of national self-importance. Sword-rattling nationalism is almost nonexistent, and the military is usually regarded more as an internal peacekeeping and civic action agency than as an arm of foreign policy (see ch. 24, the Armed Forces). The national character is commonly thought to display traits of gaiety, humor, liveliness, an absence of prejudice, and an interest in the comfortable life.

Tolerance of other people and of other social groups is highly esteemed. The easy assimilation of foreign immigrants and the lack of racial discrimination testify to the widespread acceptance of this value. In general, individual idiosyncracies and differences of opinion are respected since each person is expected to remain true to his own *dignidad*. At the same time, people are often also tolerant of corruption and ineffective government and, in the past, have allowed inefficiency to persist until the national economy was on the verge of collapse (see ch. 22, Finance; ch. 5, Ethnic Groups and Languages).

The people share the traditional Hispanic respect for law and constitutional authority. In general, they believe that a problem can be effectively solved by the enactment of a comprehensive law and are less concerned with how adequately it is enforced. Many laws are extremely idealistic but difficult to apply. One example is the liberal pension system, which guarantees regular support for retired workers but is notoriously slow to initiate payments and is occasionally months in arrears (see ch. 7, Living Conditions).

The deep-seated traditions of individualism incline many to exercise their own judgment about compliance to a law. In many cases a law or regulation is regarded as something to be formally respected but avoided or delicately bypassed. Many tend to follow laws when convenient but reserve the right to disobey when obedience would conflict with another value, such as the welfare of the family. According to *gaucho* traditions, personal loyalty should stand above respect for a law.

The ideal that every group has the right to assert and defend its own interests is basic to the society. In the nineteenth century many groups chose to use violent means, and civil wars were frequent. Unanimity existed primarily on the point that the country should continue to exist as an independent entity. In the early twentieth century Batlle y Ordóñez succeeded in forging a broader national consensus, in which the goals of social justice and equality were widely accepted. Since that period the trend has been toward the increasing use of compromise rather than confrontation in forming national policy. The political history of the country reveals a tendency to substitute pacts between the two parties for violence as the method for settling differences. One attempt to put this theory into practice was the collegiate executive form of government in the 1952—67 period. In spite of the Colorado governments' preoccupation with the needs and desires of the urban groups, the governments have also respected the interests of the rural landed elite to the extent that no sizable attempts have ever been made to institute agrarian reform.

During the 1960's, however, in response to a grave economic crisis, the social solidarity and general acceptance of the social order have somewhat deteriorated. Violence rather than compromise has increasingly characterized the relations between interest groups. The frequency of strikes has increased radically, and some have been long and violent, as in the case of the meatpackers' strike in May 1969, during which the workers looted grocery stores. University student demonstrations have also become more violent, on occasion erupting into an actual armed conflict. The transformation of the urban guerrilla movement, the Tupamaros, parallels the transition to increased violence. Although the group originally projected a Robin Hood image, in the late 1960's and in 1970 it turned to more extreme activities, ranging from raids on banks, radio stations, and armories to kidnappings of political leaders and foreign diplomats and officials, and murder (see ch. 13, Political Dynamics; ch. 23, Public Order and Internal Security).

Another indication of the breakdown in acceptance of the social order is a widespread suspicion of the financial elite and political leaders, stemming from a fear that they have profited from the economic crisis and the frequent devaluations of the peso (for value of the peso, see Glossary) while the rest of the country has experienced a decline in real income. New men of wealth have appeared who are primarily interested in comfort and material prosperity, ignoring many of the traditional values. The *vivo*, or sharp person who believes that he can beat the system with clever, if occasionally dishonest, maneuvers, has become more common. There has been an increase in the number of bad checks written, a notable change for a people known for being conscientious. Many people have begun to lose confidence in the ability of the paternalistic state and their leaders to cope with major national crises.

ATTITUDES TOWARD WORK, WEALTH, AND MATERIALISM

The traditional Hispanic disdain for manual labor is widely accepted in the country. White-collar work is more prestigious than blue-collar, regardless of the income received for both forms of labor. A closely related belief is that livestock raising is superior in status to dirt farming. Until the European immigrants arrived in the nineteenth century, the potential for crop farming in the country was virtually ignored.

In spite of considerable industrialization, traditional Hispanic values concerning different occupations continue to dominate much of society. If the Spanish aristocrat has to work for a living, he traditionally chooses a profession in law, medicine, the church, the civil service, the military, or the arts. In 1968 almost half of the new students at the University of the Republic in Montevideo had enrolled in law and medicine, and only 7 percent in agronomy, 6 percent in engineering, and 3 percent in chemistry and pharmacy. Public employment continues to enjoy higher prestige than private.

The traditional distaste for science, technology, and mathematics is extensively accepted, and businessmen often remain aloof from such considerations. In Montevideo and other industrial centers, however, attitudes toward industrial and financial activities are changing slowly in response to a greater contact with industrialization.

The personalistic hiring system places less emphasis on the value of achievement and the development of technical skills than on personal characteristics. Leisure time is ideally devoted to cultural life rather than the development of new skills that would increase an individual's earning power. A man moves upward socially by cultivating his intellectual abilities rather than through business or industrial feats. Many Uruguayans work hard at projects that interest them but do not consider being efficient, keeping busy, and learning to conquer the material environment virtues in themselves. A common saying is that the clever person does not work but lives from the efforts of the stupid people who do.

Wealth is desirable because it enables a person to live a comfortable, cultivated life without the necessity of working or the burden of financial problems. It is almost essential for the existence of the gentleman. It is more esteemed to become rich through inheritance or a windfall than through diligent efforts. The "get rich quick" philosophy of the colonial Spanish settlers has a lingering appeal, as is revealed by the popularity of lotteries and gambling (see ch. 7, Living Conditions).

Leisure and the enjoyment of life are highly esteemed and have been developed to a fine art, particularly in the capital. Uruguayans love large and lengthy meals, an evening stroll, a chat over coffee, or a day in the sun. Sports are extremely popular, especially soccer, which is played by persons of all ages. Government employees regularly work a short day, enabling them to spend long summer afternoons on the beaches. The people enjoy jokes and witticisms and are generally lively and fun-loving. Fiestas, such as Carnival, are very popular and well attended. The country also has a rich and active cultural life, and many people are avid theatergoers and musiclovers (see ch. 7, Living Conditions).

The people share the common Latin American disdain for a pragmatic, utilitarian, and materialistic approach to life. In 1900 a Uruguayan, José Enrique Rodó, in his famous essay *Ariel*, composed a classic affirmation of the humanitarian and spiritual values of Latin America in contrast to the more pragmatic philosophy of North America. In his work he exhorted the youth to develop the integrity of their inner beings and to forge a truly democratic state in which all persons could grow according to their own capacity for love. Rodó hoped that Latin Americans would remain faithful to their humanistic traditions and values, their love of things of the spirit, their religious sincerity, and their idealistic politics (see ch. 9, Artistic and Intellectual Expression).

Rodó's works are still widely read, and Uruguayans have continued to extol humanistic, spiritual, and aesthetic values. At the same time, most are anxious to possess the luxury goods produced by modern industry, partly in genuine appreciation of the conveniences and value of the products and partly because of the prestige derived from conspicuous consumption. Middle class individuals are particularly avid consumers, frequently purchasing a washing machine, refrigerator, and television set; the possession of radios is almost universal. Their values have spread to most other segments of society. The vast majority of families of all classes have a radio, and about half also own a refrigerator.

The interest in consumption does not conflict with the humanistic, spiritual values of the country, however, since the goal of consumption is in large part the prestige derived from living a gracious and comfortable life and from the possession of wealth, which makes this possible. Furthermore, the disrespected norms of pragmatism, utilitarianism, and work apply only to the production, not the consumption, process. In a society with fairly fluid and undefined class lines, consumption of conspicuously expensive goods in a tasteful way has become a significant symbol of social status (see ch. 6, Social Structure).

FATE AND THE FUTURE

Although the average person feels competent and masterful in interpersonal relationships, he tends to adopt a fatalistic attitude toward the external world. He feels unable to bring physical reality under his control and powerless to affect the course of events in the external world. Even the concept of *machismo* implies dominance over other people rather than control of the physical environment. Fate is seen as an unrelenting force, against which man can do little.

One consequence of this belief is a love of gambling and games of chance. Since the future is uncertain and man is unable to control his ultimate fate, he prefers to reap the rewards of luck and concentrate on winning riches in the present rather than saving toward the future. The feeling that man is fighting a losing battle with fate contributes to a characteristic quality of *tristeza* (a sweet sadness or melancholy) and a preoccupation with death. In spite of the fact that man is doomed to succumb to fate, however, he owes it to his inner dignity to struggle valiantly. If an individual fails to achieve some goal after he has made a good try, he is considered to be the victim of fate and is not expected to feel guilty about his failure. Many resign themselves completely to the omnipotence of the forces of fate and let chance determine their destinies.

SECTION II. POLITICAL

CHAPTER 12

THE GOVERNMENTAL SYSTEM

In 1970 Uruguay was governed under the provisions of the Constitution of 1967, a document that placed executive power in the hands of the president and did away with the nine-man National Council of Government, which had governed the nation since 1952. The president was elected directly by the people by a simple majority of votes. During the twentieth century two political parties have been of significant importance, but each has been divided into several factions. A voter would select the faction of his choice and a list of candidates within that faction. The votes of all the factions were given to the party to which they belonged, and the presidency went to the candidate of the faction that received the most votes in the winning party.

The Constitution of 1967 was the fifth promulgated since the country declared its independence in 1825, and all four revisions have taken place in the twentieth century. The shift in executive power represented the second time the electorate had rejected executive authority by council rather than by an individual.

The bicameral legislature consisted of the General Assembly, made up of a thirty-one-member Senate and a ninety-nine-member Chamber of Representatives. The Vice President was also a member of the Senate. Members of both bodies were elected by the people but, although the Chamber of Representatives represented the nineteen political subdivisions of the country, members of the Senate were elected by the voters throughout the entire country and, therefore, represented the nation. The president appointed his cabinet, consisting of eleven members (who did not have to be members of the General Assembly), and also some members of the boards of directors of the several autonomous organizations that controlled government enterprises. Cabinet members could be removed from office by impeachment proceedings initiated by the Chamber of Representatives and approved by the Senate.

At the apex of the court system was the Supreme Court of Justice, followed by appellate and lawyer courts, and a series of electoral courts—one at the national level and one in each departmental capital. Political subdivisions consisted of nineteen departments, the smallest of which was Montevideo. Under the Constitution the departments were responsible for local administration, and executive authority was vested in the governors and departmental boards. The departmental boards appointed councils of five members to exercise authority in the municipalities.

Suffrage was granted to all citizens at least eighteen years of age, and the supervision of national, departmental, and municipal elections was exercised by the Electoral Court, consisting of nine members, of whom five were appointed by the General Assembly in joint session and two each were elected by the General Assembly from the two political parties having the highest number of votes. The Constitution contained sixty-five articles guaranteeing civil rights. The death penalty had been abolished in 1909. There was an extensive civil service organization, and its regulations were clearly defined in the Constitution. Permanent career status was achieved after a fairly short probationary period. It was estimated that civilian employees of the government represented as much as a fifth of the entire labor force.

THE CONSTITUTIONAL SYSTEM

Historical Background

The country's first constitution was promulgated in 1830, two years after Argentina and Brazil signed the Treaty of Montevideo signifying their renunciation of any further claim in the area. This constitution remained in effect until 1919, when it was rewritten by a convention that introduced substantial changes in the powers of the presidency (see ch. 3, Historical Setting).

Under the new system the president shared authority with the National Council of Government. The president was elected for a four-year term and controlled foreign relations, national defense, and agriculture. The nine-member council was responsible for the administration of industrial relations, health, public works, education, and the preparation of the budget. The members were the ministers of interior, foreign relations, finance, national defense, public works, public health, industry and labor, livestock and agriculture, and public education and social welfare. The Constitution of 1919 worked well during the time of prosperity after World War I, but when the depression came in the early 1930's the divided authority was unable to handle the economic problems resulting from the collapse of prices of the country's exports.

A third constitution, adopted by plebiscite in March 1934, abolished the National Council of Government and transferred its powers to the president. Presidential powers were limited, however, because the constitution required the president to appoint three of his nine cabinet ministers from among the members of the political party that received the second largest vote in the presidential election. That same party also automatically received 50 percent of the seats in the Senate.

In 1952 a fourth constitution was promulgated as the culmination of an effort to reestablish the National Council of Government and the plural executive power. This constitution was in effect until 1967 but did not serve to ameliorate the disastrous economic situation into which the country had fallen. The voters decided to return to the presidential system, and the fifth constitution, promulgated in 1967, created a strong presidency. It contained many of the provisions of the Constitution of 1952 but removed from the General Assembly some of its power to initiate legislation and provided for automatic approval of bills under certain conditions when the General Assembly failed to act. If, upon receipt of a bill, the president had objections or comments to make, the bill had to be returned to the General Assembly within a period of ten days. If sixty days elapsed without a decision by the General Assembly, the objections of the president had to be considered as accepted.

The Constitution of 1967

The Constitution of 1967 contains sixty-five articles primarily concerned with the rights of citizens. Section III defines citizenship and suffrage, and the next five sections cover the form of government, the responsibilities of the legislature, the introduction and passage of laws, and the relations between the legislature and the executive. Other sections define the duties of the executive, the cabinet, the judiciary, and the governors and departmental boards. Concerning national security, the president is required to take prompt measures in case of foreign attack or internal disorder, and the General Assembly, in joint meeting of the Senate and the Chamber of Representatives, can declare war; in peacetime it can designate the size of the armed forces. There is no mention of conscription in the 1967 Constitution.

Amendment Procedures

According to Article 331 of the Constitution of 1967, a constitution may be amended by any of four different methods. The first is upon the initiative of 10 percent of the citizens inscribed in the National Civil Register (a list of registered voters) if they present a detailed proposal that shall be referred to the president of the General assembly, to be submitted for popular decision at the next election. The second method consists of a proposal approved by two-fifths of the full membership of the General Assembly that had been presented to the president of the General Assembly and submitted to a plebiscite at the next election. In order to achieve an affirmative result through the methods outlined, a yes vote of an absolute majority of the citizens participating in the elections is required, and this majority must represent at least 35 percent of all persons inscribed in the National Civil Register.

A third method provides that senators, representatives, and the chief executive may present proposed amendments, which must be approved by an absolute majority of the full membership of the General Assembly. Any proposal that is rejected may not be renewed until the succeeding legislative period, and the same formalities must be observed. Amendments may also be made by constitutional laws that shall require for their sanction two-thirds of the full membership of each chamber of the congress in the same legislative period.

STRUCTURE OF GOVERNMENT

The Executive

The president and vice president are elected jointly by the people for five-year terms and may not be reelected until five years after leaving office. They must be native born, in full possession of their civil rights, and at least thirty-five years old. The Constitution of 1919 placed executive power jointly in the hands of the president and a nine-man commission. The Constitution of 1934 returned the power to the president. The plural executive system (with a nine-man council and no president) again came into being in 1952, and the 1967 Constitution returned power to the individual and created a strong presidency (see ch. 3, Historical Setting).

The president and vice president take office on the first of March succeeding the election, after taking the following oath in the presence of both houses of the General Assembly: "I promise on my honor loyally to fulfill the office that has been entrusted to me, and to guard and defend the constitution of the Republic." The president represents the state both at home and abroad. He is required to have published and circulated all laws and to see that they are enforced. At the beginning of each regular session of the legislature he informs that body of the state of the Republic and of any reforms and improvements that he considers necessary. Article 168 of the Constitution of 1967 places upon the president the responsibility for internal order and authorizes him to take prompt security measures in cases of unforeseen internal disorder.

The president is the commander in chief of the armed forces and has responsibility for ensuring the preservation of internal order and the maintenance of external security. He may decree the severance of diplomatic relations with another country and may declare war if arbitration or other pacific means to avoid it are unsuccessful. He appoints cabinet members, ambassadors, ministers, and other foreign service diplomatic personnel and confers military rank on members of the armed forces.

The president may not leave the country for more than forty-eight hours without authorization from the Senate. He may not be impeached unless found guilty of violations of articles of the Constitution or other serious offenses. Impeachment proceedings must be initiated by the Chamber of Representatives and followed by a Senate trial and, if impeachment is approved by a two-thirds vote of the total membership of the chamber, he shall be suspended from office while the Senate is investigating the case.

The Cabinet

In 1970 the president's cabinet consisted of eleven ministries, but the number could be modified by law on the initiative of the chief executive. According to Article 174 of the Constitution of 1967: "The President of the Republic shall allot the ministries to citizens who, by virtue of their parliamentary support, are assured of remaining in office." That is, those appointed by the president must have parliamentary support in order to remain in office. The ministries are: foreign relations; national defense; interior (including justice); economy and finance; livestock and agriculture; commerce and industry; public health; culture (including education); public works; labor and social security; and transportation, communications, and tourism.

The powers and authority of cabinet members are specified by laws passed by an absolute majority of both houses of the General Assembly. The qualifications for a cabinet post are the same as for election to the Senate; that is, cabinet members must be native-born citizens in full possession of their civil rights and at least thirty years old. When all the cabinet ministers meet and act jointly, the body is known as the Council of Ministers. Cabinet members may attend the sessions of the General Assembly, of either chamber, and of their respective standing committees. They may take part in debate, but they may not vote.

The principal duties of members of the cabinet are: to enforce the Constitution, laws, decrees and resolutions; to formulate and submit for the consideration of superior authority any laws, decrees, and resolutions they deem appropriate; to effect, within the limits of their functions, the payment of the national debt; to propose the appointment or discharge of employees of their departments; and to perform any other functions entrusted to them by laws or by measures adopted by the executive power.

The Legislature

Legislative power rests with the two-chamber General Assembly, which functions jointly or separately according to the provisions of the Constitution. The principal responsibility of the General Assembly is to enact laws relating to the independence, security, and decorum of the Republic, the protection of all individual rights, and the fostering of education, agriculture, industry, and foreign and domestic trade. In case of foreign attack the General Assembly can declare war and approve or disapprove, by an absolute majority of the full membership of both chambers, treaties of peace. It is also empowered to approve treaties of alliance or commerce or any other contracts with foreign powers that the president may make.

The General Assembly may create new departments by a two-thirds majority vote of the full membership of both chambers. It may decide the boundaries of the new departments, establish their ports of entry, and assign import and export duties. Each year the General Assembly designates the number of personnel for the armed forces, and the number of military effectives may not be increased except by an absolute majority of the votes of the full membership of each chamber. The assembly also may permit or prohibit the entry of foreign troops into the national territory and, in the former case, may determine the time of their departure. It may also permit the dispatch of national forces outside the country and set their time of return.

The General Assembly elects, in joint session of both chambers, the members of the Supreme Court of Justice; the Electoral Court, which exercises supervision over all electoral matters; the Tribunal of Accounts, which supervises national expenditures and the preparation of the national budget; and the Contentious-Administrative Tribunal, which hears pleas for the nullification of government acts that may be contrary to law. It creates or abolishes public offices, determines compensation and retirement regulations, and approves or disapproves the budgets presented by the president.

The General Assembly convenes on March 15 and remains in session until December 15. During the first fifteen days of each session a permanent commission of four senators and seven representatives is elected to represent the assembly when it is not in session. The commission also has the power to convoke the legislature in cases of emergency. In February 1970 the Permanent Commission of the General Assembly summoned a meeting of all cabinet members to discuss methods by which the state of siege that had been declared in July 1969 could be lifted (see ch. 3, Historical Setting; ch. 13, Political Dynamics).

In considering legislation the legislature utilizes a system of permanent committees to consider each bill. There are no joint conference committees, but the two chambers may meet to settle issues by a two-thirds vote. The public is permitted to attend the sessions of each chamber.

The Senate

The Senate consists of thirty-one members—thirty senators and the vice president. The senators are elected directly by the people for a five-year term, the entire nation representing a single electoral district. Thus, the senators represent the country as a whole. The vice president has both a voice and a vote in Senate deliberations and serves as the presiding officer of the Senate as well as of the General Assembly. If the vice president ever assumes the presidency, the presidency of the Senate is assumed by the senator heading the list of the party that received the most votes in the last election.

Senators are elected by a system of proportional representation. After an election, the votes for all parties are counted, and an electoral quotient is determined by dividing the total number of votes cast by thirty, the number of senators to be elected. The number of senators elected from each party is determined by dividing the total number of votes for each party by the electoral quotient. Candidates must be native-born citizens in full possession of their civil rights and at least thirty years old. Military personnel and public officials may not be candidates unless they resign their positions at least three months before the election.

When the Senate is in session a considerable amount of time is taken up with consideration of nominations for, appointments to, and removals from office submitted by the executive. In other respects the Senate and Chamber of Representatives have equal powers and duties, but impeachment proceedings must originate in the chamber.

The Chamber of Representatives

The Chamber of Representatives consists of ninety-nine members elected from the departments directly by the people. The number of representatives to be elected for each of the nineteen departments is decided by the Electoral Court, but each department has a minimum of two. In deciding the number of representatives the Electoral Court does not rely on population figures; it considers the number of votes cast in the previous election plus the number of new registrants.

Representatives are elected for five-year terms. They must be native-born citizens in full possession of their civil rights and at least twenty-five years of age. Officials of the executive, judicial, and electoral powers and governors and members of departmental boards are not eligible for election to the Chamber of Representatives unless they resign their positions three months before an election. The same restriction applies to civil service and military personnel, but it does not apply to university professors. Members of the Chamber of Representatives are prohibited from participating in enterprises connected with any public agency or governmental department and from representing third parties in negotiations with governmental agencies.

Among the most important duties of the Chamber of Representatives (in joint session with the Senate) are the election of the members of the Supreme Court of Justice, the Electoral Court, the Contentious-Administrative Tribunal, and the Tribunal of Accounts; the granting of pardons; and the settling of disputes concerning legislation on which the two houses disagree. The chamber also has the exclusive right of impeachment of members of both chambers, the president and vice president of the Republic, the cabinet ministers, and members of the Supreme Court of Justice, Tribunal of Accounts, and Contentious-Administrative Tribunal for violations of the Constitution or other serious offenses. Impeachment proceedings must be tried before the Senate.

Local Government

The administrative and legislative functions of each of the nineteen departments, with the exception of the public security services, are exercised by a governor (*intendente*) and a departmental board (*junta departmental*). The governor is responsible for the administration of the department, and the board carries out legislative functions, including approval of the departmental budget and judicial actions, such as impeachment proceedings against departmental officials, including the governor. The board sits in the capital city and takes office on the fifteen of February following an election. The departmental board of Montevideo has sixty-five members, and all the others have thirty-one.

In order to be a member of a board an individual must be at least twenty-three years of age, be native born or have been naturalized for at least three years, and be a native of the department or have lived there for at least three years. The board members hold office for four years; the governors are elected for five-year terms. A governor may be reelected only once, and the qualifications for election are the same as for senator, with the additional requirement that the candidate must be a native of the department or a resident therein for at least three years before assuming office.

A departmental board exercises jurisdiction throughout the entire territory of the department. It may issue decrees and resolutions that it deems necessary either on the suggestion of the governor or on its own initiative. It can approve budgets, fix the amount of taxes, request the intervention of the Tribunal of Accounts for advice concerning departmental finances or administration, and remove from office—at the request of the governor—members of nonelective local departmental boards. The board also supervises local public services and oversees public health and primary, secondary, preparatory, industrial, and artistic education.

The governor exercises the executive functions of the departmental government. He is required to comply with and enforce the Constitution and the laws and to promulgate and publish the decrees sanctioned by the departmental board. He prepares the budget, submits it for approval to the board, appoints the board's employees and, if necessary, disciplines or suspends them. The governor represents his department in its relations with the national government and other departmental governments and in the negotiation of contracts with public or private agencies.

Municipalities have local boards appointed, insofar as possible, on the basis of proportional representation of the political parties on the departmental board. Members must be natives or at least three-year residents of their municipalities. The president of the local board acts as mayor and carries out the board's resolutions.

The Judiciary

The Legal System

The Constitution provides that judicial power shall be vested in the Supreme Court of Justice and in such other courts as may be prescribed by law. The legal system is based on Roman law. Facilities are available to finance court costs for those without funds, but the jury system is not used. The death penalty was abolished in 1907 and replaced by penal servitude of from thirty to forty years.

In addition to the Supreme Court of Justice there are three civil appellate courts, one penal appellate court, one electoral court, and a series of lawyer courts (*juzgados letrados*). Each department capital has a departmental court, and each of the country's 224 judicial divisions has a justice of the peace court.

The Supreme Court of Justice

The Supreme Court of Justice was created in 1907 and is located in the national capital. It has original jurisdiction in all cases involving the Constitution, cases in international and admiralty law, matters relating to treaties and conventions, and cases against foreign diplomatic personnel assigned to Uruguay. The court has five judges appointed for ten-year terms by the General Assemby by a two-thirds vote of the full membership. The judges may not be reelected until after a lapse of five years following their previous term, and no individual may serve on the Supreme Court of Justice after reaching the age of seventy. A Supreme Court judge must be at least forty years of age, be a native-born citizen in full possession of his civil rights or a naturalized citizen for ten years with twenty-five years of residence in the country, and have ten years' experience as a lawyer or eight years' experience as a member of the judiciary.

The Supreme Court of Justice exercises directive, corrective, and economic supervision over all the various courts of the judiciary. It prepares budgets for the judiciary and transmits them to the executive for inclusion in the general budget, and it appoints judges to the appellate courts. In the exercise of its functions the court addresses itself directly to the other powers of the state, and its president is empowered to attend parliamentary committees, with a voice in discussion but with no vote.

Lower Courts

The four appellate courts, three for civil cases and one for criminal cases, are located in Montevideo. Each has three judges, and to be a member an individual must be at least thirty-five years of age, have been native born or naturalized for seven years, and have been a lawyer for at least eight years or have been engaged in a legal capacity for at least six years. Appellate court judges serve during good behavior or until they reach seventy years of age. These courts do not have original jurisdiction but hear appeals from the two lower court levels.

The Constitution states that the number of lawyer courts shall be established by law. In 1970 there were forty-seven. In Montevideo these courts included nine judges handling appeals from lower courts and all cases involving monetary amounts over 1,000 pesos (for value of the peso, see Glossary); three judges of treasury and administrative appeals; six judges of instruction and correction with jurisdiction over criminal matters; four criminal judges with appellate criminal jurisdiction; two juvenile court judges; and two judges of labor matters. Twenty-one lawyer judges (*jueces letrados*) serve in the eighteen other departments with original criminal jurisdiction, original civil jurisdiction in cases involving sums over 1,000 pesos, and appellate jurisdiction over decisions made by justices of the peace.

Each of the 224 judicial divisions of the country has a justice of the peace court. The justices are appointed by the Supreme Court of Justice for four-year terms. They must be twenty-five years of age, native-born citizens or naturalized for two years, and in full possession of their civil rights. Those serving in the capital must be lawyers; those in other cities and towns, either lawyers or notaries. Their jurisdiction is limited to cases involving eviction, breach of contract, collection of rent, and financial cases where the amount involved does not exceed 1,000 pesos.

The law recognizes only one category of lawyer (*abogado*). In order to practice an individual must first obtain the degree of doctor of law and social sciences from the Faculty of Law and Social Sciences of the University of the Republic in Montevideo. This degree is granted by the university after the successful completion of six years of studies. Candidates must be at least twenty-one years of age, must be listed in the Register of Lawyers maintained by the Supreme Court of Justice, must not be under indictment for a crime the penalty for which is corporal punishment, and must not have been convicted of a crime.

The Contentious-Administrative Tribunal

Article 307 of the 1967 Constitution authorizes the establishment of the Contentious-Administrative Tribunal, composed of five members. The qualifications necessary for election to the tribunal, the manner of appointment, remuneration, and term of office are the same as those established for the members of the Supreme Court of Justice. The tribunal hears pleas for the nullification of administrative acts executed by the government in the performance of its duties that are considered contrary to law or an abuse of authority. It also has jurisdiction over the final administrative acts of the departmental governments and of the autonomous agencies.

The functions of the tribunal are only to appraise the act itself and to confirm or annul it, without alteration. Its decisions have effect only in the cases before it. It may act in cases of conflict of jurisdiction based on legislation and upon differences that may arise between the executive, the departmental governments, and the autonomous agencies. The Contentious-Administrative Tribunal has a state attorney, who is appointed by the president. His qualifications, remuneration, and term of office are decided by the tribunal. He is heard at the final hearing of all matters within the jurisdiction of the Tribunal.

The Tribunal of Accounts

The Constitution prescribes the establishment of the Tribunal of Accounts of seven members whose elective qualifications are the same as those of a senator. The members are appointed by a two-thirds vote of the full membership of the General Assembly. Their term of office ends when the succeeding General Assembly makes new appointments, but they may be reelected.

It is the responsibility of the Tribunal of Accounts to deliver opinions and furnish information on budget matters, to supervise expenditures and payments in accordance with established law, and to certify as to their legality, appending pertinent objections whenever necessary. In the departmental governments and autonomous agencies officials acting under the supervision of the tribunal perform the same duties. The opinions of the tribunal cover all the organs of the state, including departmental governments, and an annual report must be rendered to the General Assembly. The tribunal is authorized to intervene in all matters relating to the financial activities of the organs of the state, departmental governments, and autonomous agencies and to report to the appropriate authority all irregularities in the management of public funds or infractions of budgetary and accounting laws.

Autonomous Agencies

The Constitution states that certain national industrial and commercial services shall be administered by boards of directors or directors general. The agencies performing these services shall have a degree of autonomy or decentralization determined by laws enacted with the approval of an absolute majority of the full membership of each house of the legislature. There are over twenty of these autonomous agencies or state corporations, and their boards of directors vary from five to seven members. Members are either elected by the Senate or appointed by the president with consent of the Senate, based on the personal and technical qualifications of the individuals.

The autonomous agencies may be divided into two general classifications: the first concerned with education, welfare, and culture; the second, with industry and commerce. In the first classification, autonomous agencies supervise the University of the Republic, the Labor University, and the councils for secondary and elementary education as well as the training for teachers. Others are concerned with radio, television, the theater, housing, welfare, and social security. In the second classification agencies supervise the waterworks, fishing industry, ports, national merchant marine, and the production of petroleum products, cement, alcoholic beverages, and electric power. In the commercial field autonomous agencies supervise the Central Bank, the Social Welfare Bank, the State Insurance Bank, and the Mortgage Bank.

A three-fifths vote of the full membership of both houses of the General Assembly is required for the passage of a law to allow the admission of private capital in the organization or expansion of the assets of any of the state autonomous agencies, and the contribution of private capital, if allowed, shall never be greater than that of the national government. The state may also participate in the industrial, agricultural, or commercial activities of enterprises formed by workingmen's cooperatives, if it has the consent of the enterprise. The autonomous agencies may not conduct any business not specifically assigned to them by law, nor may they expend any of their resources for purposes foreign to their usual activities.

ELECTORAL MACHINERY

The Electoral Court has broad jurisdiction over the election process. In addition to its jurisdiction over electoral offenses, it exercises directive, disciplinary, advisory, and economic supervision over electoral organs; renders the final decision on all appeals and controversies that may arise; and acts as judge of all elections, plebiscites, and referenda.

The court is composed of nine members and twice as many alternates. Five members and their alternates are appointed by a two-thirds vote of the full membership of the General Assembly in joint session. The other four members are elected by the General Assembly as representatives of political parties. Members of the Electoral Court may not be candidates for any public office requiring election by the people unless they resign and terminate their functions at least six months before the date of election.

The selection of the entire court takes place at the beginning of the legislative term, the members serving for about four years until the succeeding legislature selects their replacements. The court supervises the entire registration and voting process, registers parties and candidates, has final jurisdiction in all election disputes, and supervises the functioning of the various departmental electoral boards. It also supervises the National Electoral Office in Montevideo, which has the responsibility for organizing and maintaining the National Civil Register of all eligible voters in the country.

Before an election the General Assembly allocates a sum of money for the Electoral Court to distribute among the political parties. Funds are received in proportion to the number of votes a party received in the last election. These funds help to defray campaign costs. Party-proposed ballots must be presented to the Electoral Court at least twenty days before the election, and the parties are responsible for ensuring that each polling place has enough ballots for the expected vote. After the voting has taken place, the members of the balloting commissions make a preliminary count of the unchallenged votes at the polling places. Ballots are sealed in the ballot box and forwarded to the departmental electoral board. The boards send the departmental results to the Electoral Court for final verification. The Electoral Court may annul an election, although small irregularities that could not influence general results are not sufficient cause for this to take place.

All Uruguayans are entitled to vote if they are over eighteen years of age; if they have been inscribed in the National Civil Register;

and if they have not lost their citizenship by being under indictment on a criminal charge or serving a sentence that imposed exile or imprisonment. Voting privileges are also refused those who are insane or totally handicapped physically.

CIVIL RIGHTS

The Constitution spells out in detail rights guaranteed to the people, and these include the civil liberties found in most of the world's democratic constitutions. All persons are equal before the law, and no one may be arrested unless actually apprehended in the act of committing a crime. There is no death penalty. The expression of opinion on any subject by word of mouth, private writing, publication in the press, or any other method of dissemination is entirely free, but the author, printer, or publisher may be held liable for any legal abuses committed. No one shall be compelled to render aid to the armed forces or to permit his house to be used for billeting troops except by order of a magistrate, and in such cases indemnification shall be made for any loss incurred.

Heads of large families are entitled to compensatory aid if needed. Primary and secondary education is both free and compulsory. The right of peaceful and unarmed public meetings is guaranteed, and the exercise of this right may not be denied by any authority unless it would endanger public health, safety, or order. In no case shall brutal treatment be allowed in prisons, and they shall be used only as a means of ensuring that the inmates are reeducated, acquire a work skill, and become rehabilitated. Women have the same legal rights as men (including that of divorce), and illegitimate children possess the same legal rights as other children. The law recognizes the right of every person, performing labor or services as a worker or employee, to independence of moral and civic consciousness, just remuneration, limitation of the working day, a weekly day of rest, and physical and moral health.

The achievements of social legislation have been considerable, and social security, old-age pensions, a minimum wage, and unemployment benefits have been established by law. Social welfare is supported by many laws and regulations and by several administrative institutions. Most workers are covered by some form of social security, and eligibility for pensions and other benefits is ascertained under two systems—according to categories of workers and according to types of coverage. The types of coverage include pensions or retirement pay, health benefits, and survivorships.

Although every salaried and independent worker is theoretically affiliated with some social security system, there have been instances of evasion of worker contributions, which has increased the system's burdens. The increasing cost of operating the social security system is reflected in the steadily ascending rates of contributions on the part of employers and employees. In 1966 these rates were in the vicinity of one-third of basic pay.

THE CIVIL SERVICE

Article 59 of the Constitution requires the establishment of civil service regulations, the principles of which shall apply to the executive branch, with the exception of the military, police, and diplomatic officials, who shall be governed by special laws. The regulations also apply to the judiciary, the Tribunal of Accounts, the Contentious-Administrative Tribunal, the Electoral Court, and the autonomous agencies.

Civil service regulations establish the conditions for admission to the service as a career and regulate advancement to permanent status, promotion, weekly days of rest, annual and sick leave, grounds for suspension or transfer, and the various official duties. Departmental governments are required to adopt regulations for their own civil service personnel in accordance with the regulations applying to the national government. Article 67 requires that the general retirement and social security funds shall be organized in such a way as to guarantee to all workers, employers, employees, and laborers adequate retirement pensions and subsidies in case of accident, sickness, disability, and forced unemployment.

The Constitution states that civil service regulations shall be established on the basis that the official exists for the office and not the office for the official and that public officials are in the service of the nation and not of a political party. There are no exact figures on the number of government employees in the country, but an estimated fifth of the labor force is employed by the government, which operates twenty-two corporations.

CHAPTER 13

POLITICAL DYNAMICS

In early 1970 the several factions of the two major parties were undergoing realignments reflecting the positions of faction leaders in regard to the political and economic security measures that had been in effect over most of the previous two years. Jorge Pacheco Areco, president since December 1967, was a member of the Colorado Party. Certain elements of this party had withdrawn their support of the president. At the same time the president had gained support within the more conservative National Party (Partido Nacional, commonly known as the Blanco Party), through his economic policies and his firm actions against strikers and demonstrators.

The minor parties, appealing to workers and others who had been affected by inflation and austerity measures, were attempting to organize a united front against the Pacheco government. Their combined vote in the past had rarely amounted to more than 10 percent of the total vote.

The relative stability of the country's democratic system in the twentieth century has been attributed in part to racial and ethnic homogeneity, the high literacy rate, and the high level of mobility within the predominantly middle class social structure. The cleavage between Greater Montevideo and the rural interior has influenced party affiliation and political attitudes to a greater extent than have differences in social status and income. In 1970 the nine departments that constituted the interior were still the power base of the Blanco Party. The coastal region often holds the balance of power between Greater Montevideo and the interior.

The Roman Catholic Church and the armed forces, institutions that have strongly influenced political development in many Latin American countries, have had only minimal roles in Uruguay. Social welfare legislation and the patronage prerequisites of the major parties, however, have created an enormous body of pensioners and public servants who, in times of economic crisis, constitute a strain on the capabilities of the government and the political system. Governmental agencies as well as associational interest groups representing industrial, commercial, and financial institutions and the professions carry on vigorous lobbying activities directed toward both major parties and the executive branch. As the government is the principal employer, activities of the labor unions and federations have considerable political impact. Student organizations have little influence on their own, but they often lend weight to the demands of labor and other groups.

The two parties that have dominated the political processes throughout the country's history became known as the Colorados and the Blancos in 1835 when they fought over the issue of federal versus unitary government. In the nineteenth century their differences were expressed more often through armed conflict than through electoral competition.

Political stability, the beginnings of industrialization, and the establishment of a comprehensive social welfare system came about in the first two decades of the twentieth century largely as a result of the efforts of José Batlle y Ordóñnez, twice president of Uruguay and leader of the Colorado Party until his death in 1929. His formula for reducing conflict between the parties included ensuring minority party participation in government through proportional representation. In order to prevent the excessive accumulation of power in the hands of a single ruler, he proposed the creation of a plural executive.

The social welfare system developed by Batlle y Ordóñez, and expanded subsequently by his adherents in the Colorado Party has had far-reaching consequences for the stability and functional capability of the political system. It has limited the appeal of revolutionary philosophies and parties by co-opting their programs, minimizing social and economic stratification, and giving the majority of the population a stake in the existing system.

A compromise version of the collegiate executive (*colegiado*—see Glossary), adopted in 1919, was scuttled in 1933 when President Gabriel Terra assumed extralegal powers, but an authentic collegiate system, modeled after that of the Swiss, was established under a new constitution in 1952. With minority representation and a rotating presidency, however, the National Council of Government (Consejo Nacional de Gobierno) lacked the flexibility to cope with mounting economic problems. The Blancos were elected in 1958 to head the government for the first time in ninety-three years, but they were no more capable of dealing with the economic crisis through the plural executive than had been their Colorado predecessors. Thus, in 1967 the presidential system was reinstated, and the Colorados returned to power.

Almost all Uruguayans consider themselves either Colorados or Blancos from birth. The Colorado Party absorbed most of the European immigrants, who arrived in their greatest numbers around the turn of the twentieth century, and has generally catered to the interests of urbanites. The Blanco Party has been more rural and traditional in outlook and has been particularly attentive to the interests of landowners. Both parties, however, are highly factionalized and embrace persons of various political orientations and social backgrounds. Only three of the minor parties, the Socialists, the Communists, and a Catholic group, known since the early 1960's as the Christian Democratic Party, have maintained their following over a period of several decades. The Communist Party, since 1958 leading a coalition known as the Leftist Liberty Front (Frente Izquierda de Libertad—FIdeL), was the strongest of the minor parties in the 1960's.

Beset by inflation and other economic problems, a wave of strikes and demonstrations, and the activities of a bold urban guerrilla group known as the Tupamaros, the Pacheco government declared a state of emergency in June 1968 and imposed security measures allowing for extensive use of the executive decree to maintain order. By April 1970 there had developed a polarization of opinion cutting across party lines and a conflict of authority between the executive and legislative branches of government. That conflict, however, was set aside in August, when, after the kidnapping of two North Americans associated with the AID mission and a Brazilian diplomat and the murder of United States police adviser Dan A. Mitrione by the Tupamaros, the General Assembly temporarily granted sweeping powers to the executive.

PARTISANSHIP AND POLITICAL DEVELOPMENT

The two parties that have dominated Uruguayan political life since the country gained its independence were, in their early years, little more than feuding bands of *gauchos* (cowboys). The issue that provoked the initial major confrontation was federalism versus unitary rule. The federalist sympathies of General Manuel Oribe, who became president in 1835, led to a revolt by the forces of General José Fructuoso Rivera.

Oribe's forces, supported by merchants, landowners, and the high clergy, became known as Blancos (Whites) in reference to the white hatbands they wore to distinguish their own men from the enemy on the field of battle. Rivera's forces, representing more liberal urban elements, were distinguished by red hatbands and were designated Colorados (Reds).

The Pact of 1851 was the first of a series of political agreements alternately entered into and broken by the Blancos and Colorados in a century generally characterized by unremitting civil strife on the plains and in the cities. Of the twenty-five governments to which the country was subjected from 1830 to 1903, nine were overthrown, two were terminated by assassination and one by serious injury, and ten survived one or more attempted rebellions. Only three completed their legal terms of office free of extralegal threats to their authority (see ch. 3, Historical Setting).

Political stability came about in the first two decades of the twentieth century largely through the efforts of a single person. As president from 1903 to 1907 and 1911 to 1915 and the dominant figure in the Colorado Party until his death in 1929, José Batlle y Ordóñez guided a social transformation that reordered virtually every aspect of national life. The establishment of a comprehensive social welfare program, the encouragement of domestic industry, the improvement of working conditions, and the expansion of education contributed to the absorption by the capital city of the large numbers of immigrants from Europe as well as from the interior and the consolidation of the urban middle class power base of the Colorado Party. Batlle nationalized those enterprises he considered to be of greater social than commercial importance but avoided a major clash with the Blancos by leaving the large landholdings of the interior untouched.

Batlle's prescriptions for political stability included the sharing of power among the parties through proportional representation and a diffusion of the executive function so as to avoid undue concentration of power in the hands of a *caudillo* (political strong man). To achieve this diffusion, he proposed the adoption of a collegiate executive modeled after that of the Swiss system. This proposal provoked the first major split in the Colorado Party. The Blancos were hesitant to support a controversial proposal set forth by the strongest of their rivals, but when Batlle, the invincible votegetter, threatened to run for a third term if his plan were not adopted, the Blancos and dissident Colorados agreed to a compromise.

The electoral quotient system of proportional representation adopted in 1919 provided, in effect, for a combination of the party primary elections and the general election. Not only each party but also each faction was to acquire congressional seats in accordance with its electoral strength. For electoral purposes, the traditional party labels, Colorado and Blanco, were designated *lemas*, and the labels assumed by the various factions competing for predominance under each *lema* were designated *sub-lemas*. The *lema* system reinforced the trend toward factionalism that was already underway.

By 1930 each of the traditional parties had split into two factions. The Colorados who had opposed Batlle's collegiate executive had become known as the Independent Colorado group, and the Blancos who opposed the personalistic leadership of Luis Alberto de Herrera formed the Independent National group.

The compromise version of the collegiate executive, adopted in 1919, established the National Council of Administration (Consejo Nacional de Administración) but retained the office of president with limited powers. This arrangement survived until 1933, when Colorado President Gabriel Terra, frustrated by the inaction of the council in the face of soaring unemployment, entered into agreement with National Party leader Herrera to engineer a coup d'état. This compounded the factionalism within the major parties, as many Colorados found the authoritarian measures of Terra unacceptable, and many Blancos resented Herrera's collaboration with the Colorados.

A new constitution promulgated in 1934 restored presidential government, and most of the irregular powers that had been assumed by Terra were relinquished by his successor, President Alfredo Baldomir. Luis Batlle Berres, who assumed the presidency in 1947, proceeded in a stable political environment to advance the social legislation advocated by his famous uncle, Batlle y Ordóñez.

After the elections of 1950 the Blancos had despaired of gaining the presidency and had become disillusioned with their inability to influence the executive branch. Thus, leading Blancos and Colorados at last found themselves on the same side of the issue of the collegiate executive. A formal pact between the Batllista faction of the Colorados and the Herrerista faction of the Blancos on July 31, 1951, called for a plebiscite on constitutional reform. The plebiscite the following December drew less than half of the 1.1 million voters to the polls, but by a small margin the collegiate system was approved.

The presidency was abolished, but proportional representation was undermined, as representation on the National Council of Government was limited to the two major parties in fixed ratios. Six of the nine seats on the council were apportioned to the majority faction of the majority party, the other factions having no representation. Two of the three seats assigned to the minority party went to its leading faction and one to its second-ranking faction. The presidency of the council rotated annually among the six members of the majority party.

The intent of creating a homogeneous majority was subverted. Factions of the party that was expected to gain the majority of the council seats were not enthusiastic about having their votes counted toward electing candidates from another *sub-lema* list while they secured no representation. Thus, there developed a tendency for individual lists within the *lema* actually to represent a coalition. Such a list, when elected, remained divided within itself, and in the absence of a stable majority, agreement on policies had to be bartered for patronage. As a result, at a time when the prices for Uruguayan exports were dropping, the number of unnecessary employees on public payrolls was increasing (see ch. 17, Character and Structure of the Economy).

Public frustration growing out of the economic crisis of the 1950's was not channeled toward the unwieldy National Council of Government but rather toward the ruling party. General disillusionment with the factionally deadlocked Colorados, the defection of the Federal League for Rural Action (Liga Federal de Acción Rural —LFAR), and the adherence of the Independent Nationalists, through a new coalition, to the Blanco *lema* led in 1958 to one of the biggest political upsets in the history of the hemisphere; the party that had held power for ninety-three years was unseated.

In the preceding elections the moderate Independent Nationalists, alienated by the radical rightist leanings of Herrera, had refused to cast their lot with the Blancos. But in 1958 they entered into a coalition with a group of Herrerista defectors led by Daniel Fernandez Crespo. The coalition, Blanco Democratic Union (Unión Blanca Democrática—UBD), hoping to capture control of the parent party, adopted the Blanco *lema*.

The LFAR, whose members were commonly known as the *ruralistas*, called itself an interest group rather than a political party, but its leader, Benito Nardone, controlled thousands of votes. In 1954 the *ruralistas* had supported the candidacy of Luis Batlle, but in 1958 Nardone led his followers into a coalition with the Herrerista faction of the Blancos. Herrera swelled his ranks further by patching up a quarrel with Eduardo Víctor Haedo and his dissident faction. Meanwhile, the Colorado Party had been rendered impotent by the inflexible contention between the two major Batllista factions—List 15, led by Luis Batlle, and List 14, led by Batlle y Ordóñez's sons César and Lorenzo—and much of the Colorado rank and file had become impatient with their feud.

More than 1 million of the then 1.4 million voters participated in the election on November 30, 1958. The returns were roughly 500,000 votes for Blanco factions, 379,000 for Colorado factions, and 210,000 for minor parties.

Under the Blanco *lema* the Herrerista-Nardone-Haedo list prevailed. Herrera died only five weeks after the new government came to power, and Nardone, who assumed the presidency of the council, soon alienated most of his former allies with his strong man tactics. Thus, the Blanco majority, with splits and realignments pulling its factions in all directions, was no better equipped than its Colorado predecessor to cope with the country's mounting economic problems. In 1962 the Blancos, with a coalition of the UBD, Orthodox Herreristas, and followers of Haedo as their strongest list, were reelected, but by a margin of only 10,864 votes. Two of the minority seats on the council went to Luis Batlle's List 15 and one to César Batlle's List 14. A constitutional amendment to replace the collegiate with a presidential system was rejected.

During the second Blanco administration strikes and demonstrations became more frequent, inflation and unemployment increased, and the country approached bankruptcy. Meanwhile, the deaths of important leaders of both major parties contributed to further realignment and fragmentation of the party structures.

The death of Daniel Fernandez Crespo sparked a power struggle within the UBD, and the death of Nardone left the *ruralistas* without leadership. Among the Colorados, the vigor of the left-leaning List 15 was not seriously diminished by the death of Luis Batlle Berres; leadership of that faction was assumed by his son, Jorge Batlle Ibáñnez, and Alberto Abdala. The death of César Batlle left General Oscar D. Gestido in control of List 14, which united with other moderates to form List 123, the Colorado and Batllist Union (Unión Colorado y Batllista—UCB).

The 1966 election was a mélange combining candidacies and constitutional reform. The proposed new constitution would eliminate the National Council of Government and its counterpart departmental councils, substituting a president and departmental governors (*intendentes*), and the terms of all elected officials would be extended from four to five years. Seventeen presidential candidates were on the ballot, some running for both the presidency and, in case the new constitution was not approved, the National Council of Government (see ch. 12, The Governmental System).

More than 1.2 million of the approximately 1.5 million registered voters turned out on election day, November 27. The new constitution was approved, and the Colorados were victorious with 607,633 votes. The Blancos received 496,910 votes. The FIdeL coalition had 69,750, and the other minor parties combined accounted for the remaining 57,469 votes. Of the six factions submitting lists under the Colorado *lema*, Gestido's List 123 prevailed with 262,021 votes. Gestido died on December 6, 1967, nine months after assuming office, and the vice president, Jorge Pacheco Areco, succeeded him.

SOCIAL ENVIRONMENT

The homogeneity of the population and the lack of legal discrimination against such small minorities as do exist have contributed to the relative stability of the country's democratic system. An effort in 1937 to form the Autochthonous Negro Party (Partido Autóctono Negro) faded rapidly as most Negroes and mulattoes were already aligned with one of the two traditional parties and did not want to waste their votes.

There are no topographic features that would limit communication and transportation or encourage regionalism or separatism. There is considerable social mobility, and for several decades the population has been predominantly middle class. Extremes of wealth and poverty are not much in evidence. Pockets of poverty exist in the rural areas, but there are few highly visible slum areas or squalid shantytowns in the cities.

A 1960 survey found that Uruguay had 32 percent of its school age children, a higher percentage than any other Latin American country, enrolled in secondary schools. About 92 percent of the population is literate, and the people are generally well informed about national issues. The country has the highest per capita distribution of newspapers in Latin America and one of the highest in the world. Practically all factions of all parties have their own organs. Uruguayans tend to be joiners, and their political views and roles are often moderated by multiple interests and group affiliations.

The cleavage between urban and rural areas has had greater political significance than variations in income and social status. By 1900 Montevideo, with 30 percent of the country's population, had already gained a reputation for being the world's largest capital (excepting city-states) in proportion to the population. It retained that reputation in 1970, as about half of the population lived in Montevideo.

The spectacular growth of Montevideo in the latter part of the nineteenth century, primarily through European immigration, coincided with the consolidation of power by the Colorado Party. The party made such efforts to accommodate the interests of the immigrants that members of the opposition often referred to it derisively as the party of foreigners. All of the major economic sectors associated with urban life—commercial, professional, industrial, and labor—gravitated toward the Colorado Party. In addition, the truck farmers in the southern provinces who supplied foodstuffs for the great urban concentration identified with the interests of the city and of the Colorados.

The rural interior, the original stronghold of the Blancos, has retained something of the individualistic spirit of the *gaucho*, and attitudes toward property, religion, and government have remained relatively traditional. Agricultural laborers and ranch hands, tenant farmers, and small landowners have not recognized political interests distinct from those of the large landowners.

The "spheres of interest" arrangement that operated intermittently in the latter half of the nineteenth century allowed the Blancos to control the key offices, including that of chief of police, in four, and later six, of the interior departments. Control over elections by the chiefs of police, not coincidentally referred to as *jefes políticos* (executive magistrates or, literally, political chiefs), assured the Blancos representation in the Congress. In the twentieth century more sophisticated arrangements have assured minority representation, and the public security services are now centrally administered.

The Roman Catholic Church and the military establishment, which have greatly influenced political development elsewhere in Latin America, have had only a minor role in Uruguayan politics in the twentieth century. Never firmly established by the Spanish, the church came under attack from writers of liberal and social evolutionary persuasions around the turn of the century. The military had also lost prestige by that time as a result of its perpetual involvement in political conflict. What remained of the political power and influence of both institutions was sharply and deliberately curtailed by José Batlle y Ordóñez. In recent years the more liberal Catholic prelates and lay leaders have articulated their interests through the Christian Democratic Party and a few Catholic labor unions and the more conservative ones through the Blanco Party or the Christian Civic Movement.

The all-volunteer army, the largest of the services, has generally been smaller than the national police force, which it has backed up in times of disorder. Until the late 1960's even this role was insignificant; a 1962 study revealed that from 1946 to 1960 the country had the lowest incidence of domestic violence in Latin America. As late as 1963 the military budget amounted to only 1 percent of the country's total budget. Since the mid-1960's, however, the political role of both the police and the army has been expanded as these bodies have been called upon to quell guerrilla activities and labor and student unrest and, since June 1968, to enforce compliance with the security measures.

The development of a large bureaucracy as a result of social legislation, the nationalization of industries, and the patronage requirements of a highly factionalized two-party system have fostered a tendency among rank and file members to think of their parties as potential sources of benefits rather than as organizations proposing alternative programs. Uruguay's leading sociologist, Aldo Solari, pointed out in 1967 that particularistic criteria, such as kinship, friendship, or membership in certain clubs or political factions, continued to prevail over universalistic criteria, such as standardized examinations, in the selection of government employees.

As a result of free medical services (Uruguayans have the longest life expectancy in the hemisphere) and generous retirement policies, less than half of the population over fifteen years of age is economically active. It has been lamented that, whereas in many countries the contemporary generation makes sacrifices for future generations, in Uruguay the contemporary generation sacrifices for past generations. Furthermore, at least one-fifth of the labor force is employed by the government. As long as the economy was healthy this produced no major strain on the political system, but since the mid-1950's the bureaucracy has continued to swell as the economy declined. Attempts to prune the bureaucracy in the name of austerity have not been successful, and unemployment resulting from failure of private enterprises has put severe pressure on the government, as the government is expected to supply jobs when all else fails. In the late 1960's the government's difficulty in distributing pensions and welfare benefits on schedule contributed further to a climate of social unrest.

POLITICAL PARTIES

The Colorado and Blanco parties together have generally received about 90 percent of the vote. Affiliation with one of the two major parties, or *lemas*, is a part of one's family heritage and, despite the ease with which parties may organize and present candidates for election, no other party has gained a significant voice in government since the country won its independence. Three small parties have in recent decades accounted for about 10 percent of the vote. In addition, various other parties have appeared on the ballot, but they have usually been transient personalistic or special interest groupings or splinters of larger parties.

The actual pattern of interactions in Uruguayan politics is far more complex than a simple two-party system. The *sub-lemas*, or factions, of each major party have their own leaders, candidates, and organizational structures. Furthermore, new parties that have developed independently may incorporate themselves as *sub-lemas* of the traditional ones. The various *sub-lemas* reorganize and shift in relative strength with each election as politicians move from faction to faction because of personal quarrels, rivalries, and ambitions. Significant ideological differences have also existed from time to time among some of the factions in each party.

Some of the minor parties have followed the lead of the major ones and sought to enhance their electoral chances through coalitions. The leftist coalition FIdeL has been gaining strength since it was organized in the late 1950's, and in 1970 most of the minor parties were seeking to establish electoral pacts or were advocating a broad popular front approach to challenging the traditional parties in the 1971 elections.

Campaigns are funded in part by government subsidies proportioned among the parties and factions in accordance with their voting strength in the previous election.

The Major Parties

Certain broadly defined ideological differences between the major parties still exist, but more apparent in their maneuverings are political expediency and allegiance to persons and traditions. The Colorados have traditionally been more liberal than the Blancos. There are liberals and conservatives in both parties, however, and in Congress the respective left wings of both parties often line up in opposition to the respective right wings on important votes. The Colorados were more anticlerical in the early twentieth century, but this distinction lost most of its significance as both parties broadened their bases of support. The urban-based Colorados have been considered more cosmopolitan in outlook than the rural-based, tradition-oriented Blancos, but each party has been highly nationalistic in its own way. The most important distinction in the twentieth century has been that the followers of Batlle y Ordóñez, who have generally been in the majority in the Colorado Party, have been more willing than the Blanco leadership to undertake political, social, and economic innovations.

Both parties, despite internal fractionalization, maintain the structures typical of more cohesive modern parties, including conventions, party steering committees, and caucuses. The fundamental units of the factions of both parties, are the community clubs, which are guided and controlled by the professional politicians.

For almost half of the twentieth century the Blancos were cast in the role of the loyal opposition with little hope of gaining control of the government, but since the early 1950's support for the Blancos and Colorados has been more evenly divided. Although the rivalry between them remains intense, there appears to be a concensus among the leaders in favor of preserving the predominant position of the two parties.

The Colorado Party

Throughout most of the twentieth century the policies and organization of the Colorado Party have reflected the influence of José Batlle y Ordóñnez. Internal dissension has also been largely related to the forcefulness of his leadership and the radicalism of his ideas. Fragmentation has resulted not only from opposition to his leadership and his program but, since his death, from differing interpretations of his philosophical position.

In the 1966 election the most important factions were Lists 15, 123, 515, 99, 315, and 10. All traced their origins to Batlle. List 15, known as Unity and Reform (Unidad y Reforma), is one of the oldest and has generally been considered the most liberal of the *sub-lemas*. It was the majority faction from 1946 to about 1960; it placed second in the 1966 elections, but by 1970 it had regained its majority position. Jorge Batlle, who assumed leadership after the death of his father, Luis Batlle, in 1964, continued to lead the faction in 1970.

List 123, Colorado and Batllist Union (Unión Colorado y Batllista), as the leading faction in 1966, elected Oscar Gestido to the presidency and Jorge Pacheco to the vice presidency. List 123 was formed in 1962 as an alliance of List 14, originally formed by César Batlle about 1950, with several other factions. One of these was List 515, Colorado United Front (Frente Colorado de Unidad), which had defected from List 15 in order to support Gestido.

Both List 99, Evolution and Government of the People (Evolución y Gobierno del Pueblo), and List 315, Torch of Batlle (Antorcha de Batlle), splintered off from List 15, the former in 1962 under the leadership of Zelmar Michelini and the latter in 1966 under the leadership of Amilcar Vasconcellos. List 10 was a small faction headed by the constitutional lawyer Justino Jiménez de Arechaga. He was drawn into Pacheco's cabinet in 1968. Lists 10 and 313 favored a continuation of the collegiate system, but all of the others supported the return to a presidential system.

The Blanco Party

The Blanco Party (officially the National Party) has also been strongly influenced by a single individual. The fragmentation that began to take place in the 1930's was largely a reaction against the policies and personalistic leadership of Luis Alberto de Herrera, who dominated the party for much of the twentieth century. When the Blancos assumed control of the government in 1959, for the first time in almost a century, they were divided into two large factions, the strongest of which was led by Herrera. His death that same year led to further cleavages in the party.

The main factions that competed in the 1966 elections were the Blanco Democratic Union (Unión Blanca Democrática—UBD), the Orthodox Herreristas (Herreristas Ortodoxos), the National Popular Movement (Movimiento Popular Nacionalista—MPN), the Blue and White (Azul y Blanco), and the Rocha Movement (Movimiento de Rocha). The divisions among these factions were not ideological; they represented the strategic maneuvers of various leaders to optimize their power positions.

The Orthodox Herreristas, the MPN, and the Blue and White, led respectively by Alberto Heber, Martín Echegoyen, and Víctor Haedo, had all been incorporated into the UBD when it held the majority position on the National Council of Government in 1962. The Rocha Movement was a group put together on the eve of the elections by party leaders from the coastal department of Rocha. It incorporated elements from the UBD, the MPN, and the Blue and White factions and supported the candidacy of UBD leader Alberto Gallinal. All of these factions supported a return to the presidential system.

The Minor Parties

The Leftist Liberty Front

The Leftist Liberty Front (Frente Izquierda de Libertad—FIdeL) is a coalition of a number of leftist, primarily Marxist, groups and parties, the oldest and largest of which is the Communist Party. The Communist Party was founded in 1921 but drew little attention until about 1946. FIdeL has been gradually but steadily gaining strength since it was organized in 1958. It received 2.7 percent of the vote in 1958, 3.5 percent in 1962, and 5.7 percent in 1966. Its following derives largely from students, intellectuals, and labor groups. Its influence has been more notable in labor union activities than in elections, as Communists in the 1960's generally held some 80 percent of the strategic union leadership posts. The Communist Party has been led since the 1940's by Rodney Arismendi, and Luis Pedro Bonavita has been president of FIdeL since it was founded. Both men are journalists.

The Catholic Parties

The Catholic Party, founded in 1872 and initially representing the institutional interests of the church, became known in 1912 as the Civic Union; increasingly influenced by the Christian Social movement, it officially became the Christian Democratic Party (Partido Democrático Cristiano) in 1962. Modeled after the party of the same name in Chile, it is led by Américo Plá Rodríguez and supported by a majority of the university students. It received 3 percent of the vote in 1962 and again in 1966.

Some of the more conservative Catholic groups from the original Civic Union, under the leadership of Venancio Flores, broke away from the Christian Democratic Party in 1964 and formed the Christian Civic Movement (Movimiento Cívico Cristiano—MCC). Its vote in 1966 was insignificant.

The Socialist Party

The Socialist Party was founded by Emilio Frugoni in 1910 but lost most of its following to its offshoot, the Uruguayan Communist Party, after the Russian revolution. When part of the membership joined FIdeL in 1962, Frugoni's sector organized a coalition known as the Popular Union (Unión Popular) and succeeded in electing two deputies. It had a small following at the time of professionals, intellectuals, students, and workers. By 1967 the Popular Union had disintegrated, and the Socialist Party consisted of little more than a few thousand Maoists; in 1968 President Pacheco declared it illegal.

INTEREST GROUPS

Governmental Entities

The government entities that manage a substantial part of the country's economic affairs often exert influence on the executive and legislative branches to protect their interests and enhance their positions. Among the most important of these are: the transportation agencies, such as the Administration of State Railroads (Administración de los Ferrocarriles del Estado—AFE) and the Uruguayan National Airlines (Primeras Líneas Uruguayas de Navegación Aérea—PLUNA); the National Administration for Fuels, Alcohol and Cement (Administración Nacional de Combustibles, Alcohol, y Portland—ANCAP); the Electricity and Telephone Corporation (Usinas Electricas y Telefonos del Estado—UTE); and state banks, such as the Bank of the Republic (Banco de la Hipotecário del Uruguay). Proximity to the actual policymaking structures gives these agencies considerable leverage (see ch. 17, Character and Structure of the Economy).

Private Enterprise

Special interest pressure groups of the private sector generally maintain contact with the leadership of both major parties and seek to influence the autonomous government agencies as well as the executive and legislative branches.

Organizations representing landowners and ranchers are usually more cohesive than those representing commerce and industry. The Rural Association (Asociación Rural), founded in 1871, is oriented more to technology than to politics, but it has a reputation for defending rural traditions and exerts considerable influence, both formally and informally, on policymakers. The Rural Federation (Federación Rural) and the Federal League for Rural Action (Liga Federal de Acción Rural—LFAR), on the other hand, are almost exclusively political in orientation. Both are noted for vigorous lobbying activities, and the LFAR, whose members were commonly known as the *ruralistas*, actually functioned as a political party in the 1950's and early 1960's, collaborating with the Colorados in 1954 and with the Blancos in 1958 and 1962.

The political interests of retail merchants and wholesale distributors are represented by the National Chamber of Commerce and its departmental and local affiliates. The League of Commercial Defense (Liga de Defensa Comercial) and the Mercantile Chamber of Products of the Nation (Cámara Mercantil de los Productos del País) also lobby effectively for private business. The National Chamber of Industries (Cámara Nacional de Industrias), speaking for the nation's manufacturers, concerns itself in particular with policies relating to export-import regulations and quotas. The chamber's pressure was largely responsible for the abolition of the Export-Import Control Board in 1959, and its leaders consulted at length with President Gestido's minister of industry and commerce and minister of finance before new controls were adopted in 1967.

The Association of Textile Industries of the Interior (Asociación de Industrias Textiles del Interior) speaks for provincial industrialists but coordinates its efforts with the National Chamber of Industries. Provincial interests are also represented by the Federation of

Commercial and Industrial Entities of the Interior (Federación de Entidades Comerciales e Industirales del Interior).

The Association of Banks represents bank management from both the public and private sectors in dealing with the Union of Bank Employees. Most of the professions have their own lobbying groups, as do certain mutual-aid societies organized to protect the health and welfare of their members.

Organized Labor

Labor union development was slow in the first three decades of the twentieth century, partly because the government of Batlle y Ordóñez preempted the causes the unions might have championed and seemed to eliminate the need for collective action. In 1915, for example, Uruguay became the first country in the hemisphere to establish the eight-hour workday. The ranks of organized labor began to swell, however, in response to the economic depression of the 1930's.

In 1940 the Communist-oriented General Workers' Union (Unión General de Trabajadores—UGT) brought together 40,000 members from thirty-one individual unions. A second federation, the General Confederation of Labor (Confederación General de Trabajo—CGT), inspired by the Peronist movement in neighboring Argentina, began to grow in the 1950's, but at its peak had no more than 3,500 members. The Confederation of Trade Unions of Uruguay (Confederación Sindical del Uruguay—CSU), made up of unions that rejected both communism and Peronism, had become by 1956 the largest and strongest federation in the country, but it began to decline after 1958 as its members defected to the One Center of Workers (Central Unica de Trabajadores—CUT) that replaced the defunct UGT.

The Communist-led labor federation, again under a new label, the National Workers Convention (Convención Nacional de Trabajadores—CNT), by 1967 had built its membership to 290,000, while the CSU had dropped from a high of 71,000 in 1962 to 10,000. Smaller federations included the Uruguayan Trade Union Action (Acción Sindical Uruguaya) with a Christian Democratic orientation, the Federation of Uruguayan Transport Workers (Federación Uruguaya de Trabajadores de Transporte), and the Regional Workers Federation of Uruguay (Federación Regional de Trabajadores del Uruguay). Far-reaching changes were underway in the labor movement in 1970 (see ch. 20, Labor Relations and Organization).

Since the government is the major employer, all union activities tend to have political repercussions. Government attempts to curb inflation by freezing wages were countered by some 700 strikes in

1966 and many others in 1967. The security measures imposed by President Pacheco in 1968 included the stationing of police on the grounds of corporations that had been the targets of strikes and demonstrations. In early 1970 the CNT was continuing to build its numerical strength and had been joined by students, teachers, and various parties and factions in calling for a popular front to counter what they saw as the increasingly repressive actions of the government.

University Students

Organizations and movements of university students have little direct influence on government policy, but they have been effective in drawing attention to the sources of popular discontent. They have given support to the demands of labor generally, and of teachers in particular, for wage and salary increases.

Student groups of the various colleges of the University of the Republic, the country's only recognized degree-granting university, are organized into the University Students' Federation of Uruguay (Federación de Estudiantes Universitarios del Uruguay—FEUU). The Christian Democratic movement controls the student organizations in a majority of the colleges, and the Communists, Socialists, and anarchists control the rest. Political militancy is most pronounced in the College of Law and the College of Social Sciences.

In early 1970 the FEUU, the Council of Uruguayan Secondary Students (Consejo de Estudiantes Secondarios Uruguayos—CESU), the Uruguayan Teachers Federation (Federación Uruguaya de Magisterio—FUM), and the CNT were attempting to develop a strategy for combating the government's replacement by its own appointees of the elected councils administering secondary and trade schools and its encroachment on university autonomy (see ch. 8, Education).

CLANDESTINE MOVEMENTS

Uruguay has not been free of the guerrilla activity that became common throughout Latin America in the 1960's. Sporadic incidents have been staged by groups appearing under various labels, but only one organization, the National Liberation Movement (Movimiento de Liberación Nacional—MLN), popularly known as the Tupamaros, has had real political significance. The success of the Tupamaros in attracting activists, collaborators, and sympathizers in a country noted in the twentieth century for its abhorrence of political violence may be attributed in part to the general alienation and discontent, especially among the youth, provoked by severe economic problems and the restraints imposed on civil liberties in the late 1960's.

The Tupamaros, deriving their name from the Inca rebel, Tupac Amaru, who in 1780 led the last uprising of his people against the Spanish, initiated their activities primarily, but not exclusively, in Montevideo in the early 1960's. They gained publicity and sympathizers for their revolutionary cause through robbing banks and casinos and distributing portions of the take in poor neighborhoods, stealing and exposing confidential records that embarrassed public officials, and cleverly eluding the police. One of their most widely publicized operations was the kidnapping in October 1969 of Gaetano Pellegrini Giampietro, a prominent banker and newspaper publisher. He was released unharmed after seventy-three days in exchange for a ransom equivalent to about US$60,000 privately paid to a meatpackers' clinic and a state primary school.

The ideological orientation of the Tupamaros has been described as "new left" Marxism. Estimates of their numerical strength in late 1969 and early 1970 ranged from 500 to 1,000 with an additional 2,000 to 5,000 collaborators. The group's membership consisted largely of students but included workers, intellectuals, professionals, members of the clergy, and public employees as well. It has been reported that women make up roughly one-third of the group. Authorities have confirmed that the Tupamaros maintain contact with clandestine organizations in Argentina and Brazil.

By early 1970 the national police force had been expanded and, with the help of the United States AID mission, trained and equipped to deal with guerrillas, and authorities asserted that many of the Tupamaro leaders had been arrested. Nevertheless, Tupamaro activities became even more audacious. In April they carried out the biggest robbery in Uruguayan history and assassinated Hector Moran Charquero, head of the country's police intelligence branch and of a newly formed police group known as the Special Brigade.

In late July the Tupamaros kidnapped Judge Daniel Pereira Manelli, who had handled most of the recent cases involving members of their group. The judge's wife was assured that all they wanted was a "long chat," and he was released unharmed after a week in captivity. Before his release, however, two more kidnappings took place. The victims of the July 31 kidnappings were Dan A. Mitrione, head of the public safety division of the United States AID mission, and Aloysio Mares Días Gomide, consul and first secretary of the Brazilian Embassy. On August 7, Claude Fly, a soils expert employed by International Development Services, Inc. of Washington, D.C., and working under an AID-funded contract with the Uruguayan Ministry of Livestock and Agriculture, was seized from his laboratory to join the other foreign envoys in Tupamaro captivity. Meanwhile, during the first week of August some sixty suspected Tupamaros, including a lawyer, Raul Sendic, reputedly the founder and leader of the group, had been arrested.

The Tupamaros, who had been demanding the release of all political prisoners in exchange for the release of their captives, informed the Uruguayan government that, unless their demands were met by noon on August 9, Mitrione would be killed. President Pacheco stood by his pledge never to negotiate with the Tupamaros, and the Tupamaros then proceeded to carry out their threat. In the aftermath of the murder, it was decreed that information concerning Tupamaro or police activities had to be cleared by the Ministry of Interior before release. It was reported, however, that despite the largest police and military manhunt every carried out in the country, yielding hundreds of arrests, Días Gomide and Fly remained in captivity at the end of August.

THE PACHECO GOVERNMENT

By early 1970, in response to the increasingly authoritarian measures employed by President Pacheco to combat inflation and domestic disorder and in anticipation of the 1971 elections, factions of both of the major parties had undergone considerable reshuffling.

The Pacheco government was plagued during its first year in office by strikes of employees in both the public and private sectors, sympathy strikes and demonstrations by students and teachers, general unrest among pensioners whose checks did not arrive on time and were devalued by inflation, and the activities of the Tupamaros. It responded in June 1968 by declaring a state of emergency and imposing security measures restricting some of the civil liberties Uruguayans had enjoyed throughout most of the century. The security measures were lifted in March 1969 but were reimposed four months later.

Wages, salaries, and prices were frozen intermittently. Public employees were prohibited from striking; strikes in the private sector and demonstrations were made illegal unless special government permission had been secured in advance. Leaders of illegal strikes and demonstrations were subject to arrest without court order or warrant. The government dealt with strikes of bank employees in 1968 and 1969 by drafting the employees into the military and threatening them with court-martial if they refused to return to work. In 1970 the government temporarily closed down some newspapers that criticized its intervention in the secondary and vocational educational councils.

Measures such as these, along with the increasing visibility and influence of the police and the army in the political processes, had tended to polarize the population. The president had gained support across party lines from landowners and from members of the industrial, commercial, and financial communities but had aroused the resentment of some workers, bureaucrats, students, and intellectuals.

Realignments within the Colorado Party had left President Pacheco's List 123 a minority faction, but he had maintained a tenuous alliance with the majority faction led by Jorge Batlle. Vasconcellos and Michelini, leaders, respectively, of Lists 315 and 99, were opposing the president, especially in regard to the security measures, but some important figures had disassociated themselves from those factions and were supporting the president. List 515 had split into two groups, one supporting the president and the other supporting the vice president, Alberto Abdala, who had defected from Batlle's List 15 and announced his intention to run for the presidency in 1971.

The Blancos had succeeded in March 1970 in uniting all of their factions, with the exception of a Herrerista group led by Echegoyen, in a single convention, designated the United Directorate (Directorio Unico), which had elected Heber as its leader. Echegoyen was basically in support of President Pacheco's policies, and a number of Blanco businessmen, bankers, and industrialists who approved of the manner in which the president had dealt, for example, with the striking bank employees, had begun to refer to themselves as Blancos Pachecistas.

Venancio Flores, leader of the Christian Civic Movement, had declared himself in support of the president and had been appointed foreign minister (until replaced by Jorge Peirano Facio in April 1970), but most of his following had been reabsorbed by the Christian Democratic Party. The Christian Democratic Party, FIdeL, some smaller parties, and dissident elements of the traditional parties advocated the formation of a united, or popular, front to oppose the president and seek a repeal of the security measures.

A crisis of authority developed in March 1970 when the president nullified a proposal, adopted by a margin of one vote by the Permanent Commission of the General Assembly (Comisión Permanente del Poder Legislativo), to revoke the security measures. The commission responded by convoking a special session of the General Assembly, but it then became apparent that many of the legislators were not prepared to force a confrontation between the legislative and executive branches of government. A motion to remand the controversy over the security measures to the Constitutional, Legislative, and Legal Commission (Comisión de Constitución, Legislación, y Código) for consideration and recommendations failed for lack of a quorum, and the issue remained unresolved until the murder of Mitrione by the Tupamaros on August 10 prompted the General Assembly to frant to the executive the power to suspend all individual guarantees for twenty days.

CHAPTER 14

FOREIGN RELATIONS

Uruguay was one of the earliest proponents of a hemispheric organization based on the principle of the sovereign equality of nation-states. It adheres to the Inter-American Treaty of Reciprocal Assistance and has been an enthusiastic participant in the Organization of American States (OAS), the Latin American Free Trade Association (LAFTA), and the Alliance for Progress. It was a charter member of both the League of Nations and the United Nations. Through these and other international organizations it has championed the principles of national self-determination, the pacific settlement of disputes, respect for human rights, and economic cooperation.

As a small country situated between the two giants of South America, Uruguay has in the twentieth century depended to a large extent upon international and regional organizations and treaties and the rivalry of its neighbors for the maintenance of its security. In 1970 the government of Jorge Pacheco Areco was appealing to the OAS to establish collective measures for dealing with the kidnapping of diplomats and with other guerrilla activities. The primary focus of the country's foreign policy, however, was the expansion of foreign trade, especially within LAFTA, and the development, in cooperation with neighboring countries, of the industrial power potential of the basin of the Río de la Plata.

In the nineteenth century internal and external policies were inextricably interwoven. As national political groups took advantage of the expansionist ambitions of leaders in Argentina, Brazil, and Paraguay and looked to them for support in overcoming their domestic rivals, the country was the site of frequent international conflict. In the twentieth century, however, its territorial integrity has generally been respected; its foreign relations have been more stable, and its foreign policies have had greater continuity. Foreign policy initiatives since the first presidential term of José Batlle y Ordóñez (1903—07) have been directed primarily toward the establishment of international law designed to protect the interests of small states.

Relations with Argentina and Brazil have continued to be affected by the orientations of the Colorado Party toward Brazil and of the Blanco Party toward Argentina. The Colorado Party, ruling continuously from 1865 to 1959, maintained particularly amicable relations with Brazil. Relations with Argentina were strained in the 1940's and early 1950's when that country was under the authoritarian rule of Juan Domingo Perón. Since 1955, however, as is normal for a buffer state, Uruguay has generally sought to maintain a delicate balance in its relations with the larger countries on its borders and has cooperated with each of them in trade and development projects.

Policies concerning diplomatic and commercial relations have generally been pragmatic. In 1970 the country maintained embassies in almost all countries of the Western Hemisphere and of both Western and Eastern Europe but only a few in Africa and Asia. Most of the country's interactions with African and Asian nations have taken place in the forums of international organizations.

Despite occasional disagreement on specific policies, relations between Uruguay and the United States have always been friendly. The two countries have entered into several bilateral treaties that have served as models for such treaties between the United States and other Latin American nations. The country has maintained strong ties with a number of Western European countries. French cultural influence has been most in evidence, but British ties have been more important in economic and political matters. There was some friction between Uruguay and the Soviet Union in the 1960's, and several Soviet diplomats in Montevideo, charged with involvement in fomenting strikes, were expelled, but commercial and cultural contacts have remained strong.

The president is the supreme commander of all the armed forces and is charged with the preservation of external security, but he can declare war and conclude treaties and conventions only with the approval of the Congress. The country's commitment to the settlement of disputes through arbitration or other peaceful means and its determination to seek the social and economic integration of the Latin American states are contained in the Constitution of 1967.

HISTORICAL BACKGROUND

The long struggle, first between Portugal and Spain and later between Brazil and Argentina, for possession of or control over Uruguay was launched in 1680 when a Portuguese expedition arrived in the estuary and set up an encampment on the site of the modern town of Colonia. Although the area known as the Banda Oriental (eastern bank of the Río de la Plata estuary) had been the last region to be claimed by Spain and Spanish settlement was sparse, the authorities at Buenos Aires, obliged to protect the waterway for Spanish trade, repelled the invaders (see ch. 3, Historical Setting).

The Spanish and Portuguese cooperated in 1911 in defending the Spanish garrison against the rebel junta that had assumed control and declared independence in Buenos Aires. After the Argentines had driven out the Spanish and the nationalist forces of José Gervasio Artigas had driven out the Argentines, however, the Portuguese again invaded and drove Artigas into exile. In 1821 Brazil, Portugal's new world heir, formally annexed the Banda Oriental. But the British, concerned lest hostilities between Brazil and Argentina over possession of the territory disrupt their valuable commerce with the Río de la Plata ports, intervened and in 1828 prevailed upon Brazil and Argentina to sign a treaty recognizing Uruguay as an independent republic (see ch. 3, Historical Setting).

Independence, however, by no means brought an end to foreign intervention. By 1835 civil war had broken out between the forces of President Manuel Oribe, supported by the Argentine ruler Juan Manuel de Rosas, and those of former President José Fructuoso Rivera, supported by the Brazilian Empire and Argentine exiles. Oribe's forces, known as the Blancos (Whites), and Rivera's forces, known as the Colorados (Reds), became the country's dominant political parties, and the orientations of the two groups toward Argentina and Brazil, respectively, continued to influence partisan struggles and foreign policies throughout the nineteenth century and the first half of the twentieth.

Uruguay continued to be the target of Argentine sorties until the fall of Rosas in 1852, the last phase being the nine-year (1843—52) siege of Montevideo, in which the Blancos and Argentines bombarded the Allied Colorados and Brazilians. The international character of the struggle was amplified by the intervention of France and England and the participation of the Italian patriot Guiseppe Garibaldi, who entered the fight against Rosas.

Internal political strife in Uruguay precipitated the War of the Triple Alliance (1864—70), in which Paraguay fought the allied forces of Argentina, Uruguay, and Brazil. In 1865 the Brazilians helped Colorado leader Venancio Flores to unseat his Blanco rival in the presidency. The Paraguayan ruler Francisco Solano López drove his forces across Argentine territory to aid the Blancos, thus provoking a tripartite alliance against Paraguay. The defeat of Paraguay and the Blancos left the Uruguayan government firmly in the control of the Colorados, a circumstance that prevailed for almost a century (see ch. 13, Political Dynamics).

Intermittent internal political strife persisted until 1904 but without the stimulant of overt foreign intervention. The statesmanship of Batlle y Ordóñez, which contributed to internal political stability and a restructuring of the national society in the early twentieth century, also led to greater stability in international relations and a reorientation in foreign policy. Batlle stressed international cooperation as the foremost defense of the independence of small nations. At the Hague Peace Conference in 1907 he proposed the establishment of an international organization similar in structure to the subsequent League of Nations.

At the outset of World War I Uruguay proclaimed its neutrality, but in 1917 the government protested against the German notification of unrestricted submarine warfare; when Brazil declared war, Uruguay's foreign minister announced that no American country that in defense of its own rights should find itself in a state of war with nations of other continents would be treated as a belligerent. The government had hoped that the American republics would reach agreement on concerted action. When no such understanding had been reached by October 1917 it proceeded to sever diplomatic relations with Germany and revoke its own neutrality decrees with regard to the Allies.

Uruguay became a charter member of the League of Nations and from 1923 to 1926 served on its council, where it was particularly active in promoting arbitration of disputes and relief measures for children and the aged. In 1927 Montevideo was host to the first league conference to convene in Latin America, a conference devoted to the planning of public health programs.

From the beginning of World War II the sympathies of the government lay with the Allies, and as early as December 1939 the danger posed to the South American continent became apparent, as the German battleship *Graf Spee* and the British cruisers *Ajax*, *Archilles*, and *Exeter* engaged in battle off the coast of Uruguay. The *Graf Spee*, refused refuge in the harbor of Montevideo, was scuttled just outside the harbor, and its crew found refuge in Argentina. German anger culminated in 1940 in a Nazi plot to overthrow the Uruguayan government.

When the United States entered the war on December 8, 1941, Uruguay declared its solidarity with the Allies. At the Third Inter-American Foreign Ministers' Meeting in Rio de Janeiro in January 1942, it joined several other Latin American states in severing relations with Germany, Italy, and Japan. The Emergency Committee for Political Defense, authorized by that meeting, was headquartered in Montevideo. On February 15, 1945, Uruguay formally declared war on the Axis powers.

In the postwar period Uruguay, through active participation in international organizations, has continued to defend the rights of small states and to seek peaceful solutions to international conflicts. The country's reliance on procedures for pacific settlement is evident in the fact that there is no conscription and the military budget has generally amounted to less than 10 percent of the total budget.

WESTERN HEMISPHERE AFFAIRS

Regional Cooperation

Throughout the twentieth century Uruguay has been one of the strongest supporters of inter-American regional organizations and has been host to many of the hemisphere's most consequential conferences. Montevideo's first international conference, the Congress on Private International Law, which met in 1888—89, in fact antedated by one year the launching of the Pan American movement under United States initiative. That congress drew delegates from Argentina, Bolivia, Brazil, Chile, Paraguay, Peru, and Uruguay, who negotiated multilateral treaties on international commercial law, civil law, penal law, procedural law, and trademarks and patents.

The country took the lead in attempting to harmonize the functions of the inter-American system with those of the League of Nations. In 1920 President Balthasar Brum proposed the establishment of an American league of nations, based on the principle of sovereign equality among the Latin American republics and the United States, to cooperate with the league at Geneva but to have authority and responsibility to deal with peculiarly American problems.

Before the formalization of such an organization in 1948, Uruguay often assumed the role of mediator in the inter-American system. In 1929 and from 1935 to 1938 the country coordinated the efforts of the Pan American Commission of Neutrals to conciliate the Chaco War between Bolivia and Paraguay.

Uruguay participated in the several meetings of foreign ministers that took place during World War II and, at Rio de Janeiro in 1947, along with the other nineteen Latin American states and the United States, signed the Inter-American Treaty of Reciprocal Assistance. The treaty asserted that an attack on any American state would be considered an attack on all and that the other states were bound to assist, individually or collectively, the state attacked.

At the Ninth International Conference of American States, convened in Bogotá, Columbia, in 1948, the various institutions, procedures, and expedients that had evolved over a sixty-year period were incorporated into a regional organization of general competence, designated the Organization of American States (OAS). In 1956 Uruguayan diplomat José A. Mora was elected by the OAS council to an interim term as secretary general. He was later elected to a full ten-year term, which he completed on May 18, 1968, having served in the highest post of that organization longer than any other person. In 1970 the seventy-two-year-old Mora was chosen to head a newly formed commission to resolve the lingering dispute that plunged El Salvador and Honduras into a border war in July 1969.

One of the earliest among the important inter-American conferences held in Uruguay was that of 1933, which became known as the Good Neighbor Conference. At that time concern over past United States intervention in the Caribbean area was mitigated, as Secretary of State Cordell Hull pledged the United States to a new era of neighborliness and nonintervention in the internal affairs of other nations in the hemisphere.

After the creation of the Inter-American Development Bank (IDB) in 1959 and acting upon the recommendations of the United Nations Economic Commission for Latin America, several of the Latin American nations met in Uruguay in 1960 and signed the Treaty of Montevideo, which created LAFTA. The purpose of the association, which in 1970 included Mexico and all of the South American states except Guyana, was to achieve free trade among the signatories through average annual tariff reductions and complementation agreements. LAFTA is headquartered in Montevideo (see ch. 21, Trade).

When in 1961 United States President Kennedy, building upon a proposal set forth by Brazilian President Juscelino Kubitschek in 1958, announced his advocacy of an Alliance for Progress, the site chosen for the final drafting and signing of the charter was Punta del Este, Uruguay. The charter called for a 2.5-percent annual per capita increase in the economic growth of the Latin American nations, to be generated by a total annual investment in the area over a ten-year period of US$10 billion. United States grants and loans were to account for 10 percent of that commitment. Uruguayan Minister of Finance Juan Eduardo Azzini presided over the conference.

From April 12 to April 14, 1967, Uruguay was host to a conference of the heads of state of the OAS nations, the only such conference to take place in the 1960's. A resolution drawn up at that time called for the realization of a Latin American common market by 1985.

The country's policies in regard to intrahemispheric security issues have varied in accordance with internal political configurations and with the immediate circumstances of international incidents. In 1945 the Colorado government, having offered asylum to a large number of political exiles from Argentina and being uneasy about the intentions of that country's authoritarian ruler, reversed its traditionally strong stand for nonintervention and proposed to the American republics the adoption of a policy of multilateral intervention in support of democratic principles and human rights. The proposal was approved by the United States but decisively rejected by the majority of the Latin American nations.

In 1955, upon request by the OAS council, Uruguay made aircraft available to the inter-American committee that was seeking to repel an invasion of Costa Rica by Nicaraguan forces. In 1960 the country supported the adoption by the OAS of collective sanctions against the Trujillo government of the Dominican Republic. It also supported the suspension of the Castro government from the OAS in 1962, collective action against Cuba during the missile crisis later that year, and collective sanctions, including the severance of diplomatic relations, in 1964.

In 1965, however, the Blanco government, which had been in power since 1959, voted against collective backing by the OAS of the United States intervention in the Dominican Republic. That intervention had been extremely unpopular in Uruguay, and the Blancos were facing a difficult electoral test the following year.

Relations with Neighboring Countries

The circumstance of being a buffer state has strongly influenced the country's foreign policy. In recent years Uruguay has tried to maintain a scrupulous balance in its relations with Brazil and Argentina, not allowing either country to appear to be exerting greater influence or gaining greater advantage in its relations with Uruguay than the other. When one of the giants has been judged to be attempting to take unfair advantage in its dealings with Uruguay, Uruguay has discouraged such practice by leaning toward the other.

The historic affinities of the Colorado Party for Brazil and of the Blanco Party for Argentina were particularly notable during World War II. The Colorado government, like its northern neighbor, favored the Allies and offered refuge to political exiles from the pro-Axis government of Perón in Argentina, whereas the Blanco opposition, under the leadership of Luis Alberto de Herrera, maintained close ties with the Peronists in Argentina and evidenced sympathy for Germany. As the Constitution of 1934 had guaranteed to the Blancos half of the thirty senate seats, the government was unable to lend support to the Allies until President Alfredo Baldomir, in 1942 dissolved Congress. Argentina retaliated by blocking trade and restricting the passage of tourists. Relations between the two countries remained tense until the fall of Perón in 1955.

Relations with both Brazil and Argentina since 1960 have been generally amicable and marked by cooperation on important projects. In 1960 an agreement was reached among the governments of Uruguay, Brazil, and Argentina on the utilization of the waters of the Río Uruguay, and in April 1969 the governments of Paraguay and Bolivia joined them in signing a treaty for the joint development of the basin of the Río de la Plata.

The agreement was almost undermined earlier in the year as a result of Brazil's resentment of the ban placed by Argentina and Uruguay on its fishing in the Río de la Plata and by the reemergence of the historic controversy between Argentina and Uruguay concerning territorial rights in the river. The Argentines have claimed that the boundary follows the deepest channel, whereas the Uruguayans have maintained that it lies in the middle of the river. The most recent dispute arose when Uruguay called for international tenders for the exploration and working of offshore oilfields in the estuary and on the continental shelf in the Atlantic.

The good will of the Pacheco government has been cultivated by the governments of both Argentina and Brazil with loans, invitations to official visits, and the like, and President Pacheco has attempted to act impartially, but the river boundary dispute with Argentina and Brazil's support for the Uruguayan position caused some observers to perceive a measure of deviation from that policy. The Argentine foreign ministry in fact accused President Pacheco's government of adopting a pro-Brazilian attitude.

Argentina and Uruguay continued to cooperate on other matters, however, and after a meeting between President Pacheco and Argentine President Juan Carlos Onganía in March 1970 at the site of the Paysandú-Colón bridge, the first to link their countries, the demarcation issue, though unresolved, ceased to be highly divisive. The following month Uruguay agreed to support Argentina's candidacy to serve on the United Nations Security Council.

Meanwhile, ties with Brazil remained strong. In May 1970 agreement was reached on terms for the joint Brazilian-Uruguayan development of the Sete Quedas, or Guaira Falls, hydroelectric scheme, expected eventually to produce 10 million kilowatts of power, and President Pacheco met with Brazilian President Emilio Garrastazu Médici to dedicate an international highway linking their countries.

Relations with the United States

Relations between Uruguay and the United States have always been amicable, despite disaccord on certain trade and security policies and a Uruguayan national literary tradition abounding in anti-United States sentiment. The latter phenomenon has been built largely upon the foundation laid by José Enrique Rodó in his famous book *Ariel*. This book, published in 1900, launched an energetic attack on the "materialistic" North American way of life as opposed to what he viewed as the humanism and spirituality in Latin traditions (see ch. 9, Artistic and Intellectual Expression).

A satisfactory formula to resolve the difficult issues involved in the construction, with financial assistance from the United States, of air and naval bases in Latin America during World War II first emerged in negotiations between the United States and Uruguay. It was agreed that the bases would remain under Uruguayan sovereignty and would be manned by Uruguayans but with technical assistance from the United States. The first of a series of bilateral treaties of friendship, commerce, and economic development negotiated between the United States and Latin American nations after the war was signed with Uruguay on November 23, 1949. This treaty, which served as a model for subsequent ones, guaranteed free introduction and withdrawal of capital, free introduction of executive and technical personnel by United States firms, equality of treatment of property and personnel, just compensation in the event of expropriation, liberalizing of exchange controls, and other measures designed to promote private investment.

United States economic and military aid to Uruguay in the form of loans and grants from fiscal year 1946 through fiscal year 1969 totaled US$162.2 million. About 25 percent of that total, primarily in the form of loans, was extended in 1968 alone. This sharp increase may be attributed largely to supplementary food shipments under the provisions of United States Public Law 480 and an agricultural sector loan. In fiscal 1970 the United States and Uruguay agreed to a US$15 million capital goods import loan.

The United States has been one of the largest purchasers of Uruguayan beef and wool and has replaced Great Britain as the major supplier of imports. United States tariff and quota policies, however, have sometimes been a source of friction between the two countries.

On issues brought before the OAS, Uruguay has generally voted with the United States. At the Tenth Inter-American Conference in Caracas, Venezuela, in March 1954, Uruguay voted for a resolution that declared that the domination of the political institutions of an American state by the international Communist movement constituted a threat to the sovereignty of the American states. This resolution preceded by three months the overthrow of the government of Jacobo Arbenz in Guatemala. Uruguay supported the United States position on the various collective measures directed against the Castro government in the early 1960's but opposed the United States on collective intervention in the Dominican Republic in 1965. It has also opposed the creation, proposed since the Dominican Republic intervention, of an inter-American peacekeeping force.

RELATIONS WITH WESTERN EUROPE

The country has maintained strong cultural and commercial ties with several Western European countries. Approximately 75 percent of the population is of first, second, or third generation European descent. Most of the immigrant population came from Spain and Italy, but the influence of the small English and French communities has been great. German cultural influence was also quite notable until the uncovering in 1940 of a Nazi subversive plot, involving a considerable proportion of the local German population, resulted in a surge of anti-German sentiment (see ch. 5, Ethnic Groups and Languages).

Batlle y Ordóñez spent the four years (1907—11) between his two terms in the presidency in close observation of European institutions. The collegiate executive system (*colegiado*—see Glossary) he proposed, which was established in compromise form from 1919 to 1933 and in full from 1952 to 1967, was modeled after that of the Swiss (see ch. 3, Historical Setting).

Despite the country's largely Spanish heritage, relations with Spain were cool for many years after Generalissimo Francisco Franco assumed control of the government in 1939. Uruguay opposed Spanish membership in the United Nations and even Spanish participation in the activities of the specialized agencies on the grounds that Franco's government was established with the help of the Axis powers, that it was totalitarian in nature, and that a government that denies fundamental rights to its own people is ill equipped to deal with internationl issues, such as labor, culture, and refugees. Relations improved during the 1960's, however, partly as a result of commercial factors. In 1967 the Spanish government conferred the Grand Cross of the Order of Isabel la Católica on Uruguayan Foreign Minister Hector Luisi in recognition of his contribution to relations between Spain and Uruguay.

Although French cultural influence has been paramount, economic and political ties with Great Britain have been crucial to Uruguayan development since the British guaranteed the creation of the buffer state in 1828. Railroads constructed by the British in the last quarter of the nineteenth century provided the initial impetus to economic development. The purchase of the railroads by the Uruguayan government, begun in 1915, was completed in 1948. Since that time the United States has replaced Great Britain as the country's principal supplier, but in 1969 Great Britain continued to be the largest national market for Uruguayan exports. Thus, the announcement in May of that year that as of June 14 Great Britain was closing its market to Uruguayan boned meat, pending improvements in the hygienic standards of slaughterhouses and in inspection services, was a source of considerable alarm. The export quota for 1969 was met before the ban took effect, and Uruguay has attempted to carry out the prescribed improvements, but in May 1970 the ban remained in effect (see ch. 21, Trade). Other important trading partners among the Western European countries have been West Germany, the Netherlands, France, Italy, Sweden, Belgium, and Luxembourg.

RELATIONS WITH EASTERN EUROPE

In 1926 Uruguay became the first Latin American nation to extend recognition to the Soviet Union. In December 1935, in response to the charges by Brazilian President Getúlio Vargas that Soviet diplomats accredited to Montevideo had been organizing subversive activities in Brazil, Uruguay broke off relations. Four years later the country supported the expulsion of the Soviet Union from the League of Nations.

Friendly relations with the Soviet Union were renewed during World War II as a result of the common struggle against the Axis, but relations were chilled once again by the Soviet blockade of West Berlin. Suspicion of Soviet activities was reflected in the proposal by the Uruguayan representative at the United Nations that international aggression be defined to include subversive agencies in foreign countries trying to undermine their institutions. Diplomatic relations between the countries, however, remained intact.

Trade between Uruguay and the Soviet Union and other Eastern European countries increased significantly during the 1940's and 1950's. The level of trade with those countries rose from 5 percent of Uruguay's total foreign commerce in the early 1950's to 16 percent in 1958 and 1959. In 1958 the country was so short of hard currency reserves that it temporarily shifted much of its petroleum imports from Western countries to the Soviet Union, which was willing to trade on a barter basis. In 1960, however, when Uruguay refused to increase its petroleum imports, the Soviet Union stopped buying Uruguayan wool, and trade with other Eastern European countries also temporarily declined.

In 1960 Uruguay was one of only four Latin American countries that exchanged diplomatic representatives with the Soviet Union. Relations with the Soviet Union in the 1960's were marred by the economic decline in Uruguay, accompanied by frequent strikes and other disruptive activities by the Communist-dominated labor unions. The first secretary of the Soviet embassy, Mikhail K. Samilov, was charged with subversive activities and declared persona non grata by the National Council of Government in January 1961. In 1966 the council declared four more Soviet diplomats, accused of fomenting strikes, personae non gratae, and in October 1968 three administrators of the Soviet embassy were accused of interfering in industrial strikes and were likewise expelled. Another source of friction in 1968 was the Uruguayan allegation that Soviet fishing vessels had violated its territorial waters.

In February 1969, however, Uruguayan Vice President Alberto Abdala traveled to Moscow, was received by both Premier Aleksei N. Kosygin and President Nikolai V. Podgorny, and signed a trade agreement amounting to the equivalent of US$20 million, under which Uruguay was to buy heavy equipment and to sell agricultural products and some consumer goods (see ch. 21, Trade). In reciprocation of Abdala's visit, a group of Soviet legislators visited Uruguay in May 1970.

Relations with other Eastern European countries have usually been cordial. The publications and conferences of the Uruguayan-East German Cultural Association have been well received by those who favor a reduction in cold war tension. Luis Hierro Gambardella, minister of culture under President Oscar D. Gestido and President Pacheco, has served on its binational board.

The Romanian minister of foreign affairs, on the occasion of his visit to Montevideo in November 1968, signed an agreement providing for cooperation in educational matters and proposed a similar agreement concerning cultural affairs. In May 1970 President Pacheco announced his intention of visiting Romania, along with several Western European countries, the following October.

In 1970 negotiations were underway for accelerating trade with Czechoslovakia. It had recently exported to Uruguay large amounts of small arms, especially machineguns, for use by the police.

INTERNATIONAL COMMITMENTS

The country's commitment to international organization as a means of promoting peaceful multinational solutions to disputes dates back to the Second Hague Peace Conference in 1907. Several of the proposals set forth by Batlle y Ordóñez at that conference were incorporated in both the Covenant of the League of Nations and the Charter of the United Nations.

The country played an important role in the League of Nations and in the development of the Permanent Court of International Justice. One of its delegates to the league, Alberto Guani, was elected president of both its council and its assembly. A declaration was issued by the government of Uruguay in 1921 recognizing in broad terms the compulsory jurisdiction of the court, subject only to reciprocity. This declaration was still in force in 1970, according to Article 36(5) of the Statutes of the International Court of Justice, and was the oldest acceptance of the compulsory jurisdiction of the court. Uruguay was also a party to the Pact of Bogotá (1948), which makes acceptance of pacific settlement procedures obligatory among the ten Latin American states that had ratified it.

After the Moscow Conference in 1943, where the need for a general international organization was conceded, the Uruguayan minister of foreign affairs, José Serrata, set up an advisory commission on postwar problems, including those related to international organization. That body of distinguished scholars and statesmen envisioned an organization of far greater competence than that which emerged as the United Nations. They called for the abandonment of the absolutist notion of sovereignty and the conversion of the world into a legal unit capable of enforcing its decisions. They recommended the coexistence of regional pacts and the world organization, provided the former operated within and was complementary to the latter; they assumed that the domination of a powerful nation within a regional unit would be mitigated in a regime of universality.

Uruguay became a charter member of the United Nations in May 1945, but its delegates to the San Francisco Conference were disturbed by the predominant position assumed by the great powers and by the omission of reference to a number of principles they considered fundamental. Since that time the country has striven to expand the powers of the General Assembly and to promote within the organization greater concern for international law and justice, human rights and liberties, and social welfare.

In accord with these concerns Uruguay has opposed colonialism and championed self-determination of nation-states. It has maintained that independence should not be denied to a nation because of a lack of human skills and economic resources, smallness of territory, or backwardness of social institutions and has asserted that the United Nations has the obligation to prepare disadvantaged nations for self-government. Uruguay was among the first countries to vote in the United Nations for the establishment of a Jewish state and was the first Latin American state officially to recognize Israel.

Reflecting on the failures of the League of Nations, the country initially took the position that membership in the United Nations should be universal and participation obligatory, but that position was soon modified with regard, for example, to Communist China and Spain. The Uruguayan representative took the position in 1950 that Communist China had demonstrated by its conduct that it was not disposed to comply with the principles set forth in the Charter of the United Nations. That position remained unchanged in 1970. In 1952 Uruguay voted to bar Spain from membership in the United Nations Educational, Scientific, and Cultural Organization (UNESCO). It has maintained, however, that decisions concerning the representation of states should be the prerogative solely of the General Assembly.

The country's adherence to the principal of collective security and its desire to expand the role of the General Assembly were cited on the advent of the Korean crisis as its reason for joining with six other countries in sponsoring the Uniting for Peace resolution. Uruguay made available 70,000 blankets and the equivalent of US$2 million to the United Nations forces during the Korean conflict.

In principle, the country has strongly advocated disarmament, but it has insisted on the establishment of guarantees and controls accepted as binding on all as the first step toward that goal. It initially had misgivings about the motivations that gave rise to the Nuclear Non-Proliferation Treaty. Pedro Berro, Uruguayan delegate to the United Nations, expressed in September 1968 the opinion that in promoting this treaty the superpowers were only defending their own interests and that the small powers must do likewise. Uruguay, however, ratified the treaty in June 1970. Uruguay was also a party to the Latin American Nuclear Free Zone Treaty (1967).

The country has consistently attached great importance to the functions of the United Nations specialized agencies. Among those agencies in which it was particpating in 1970 were: the International Bank for Reconstruction and Development (IBRD), the International Monetary Fund (IMF), the International Labor Organization (ILO), the Food and Agriculture Organization (FAO), UNESCO, the International Telecommunications Union (ITU), the Universal Postal Union (UPU), the World Health Organization (WHO), the World Meteorological Organization (WMO), the United Nations Development Program (UNDP), the International Atomic Energy Agency (IAEA), the United Nations Council on Trade and Development (UNCTAD), and the Economic Commission for Latin America (ECLA).

The country has adhered to the General Agreement on Tariffs and Trade (GATT) since 1953. In 1961, however, Uruguay's representative delivered to the GATT council a condemnation of policies of the industrialized countries; he suggested if they did not remove numerous discriminatory barriers and restrictions, some of which were illegal under the terms of the general agreement, and take action to mitigate the deteriorating terms of trade for producers of primary products the foundations of the general agreement would be irretrievably undermined. Fifteen countries were specifically charged with illegal practices. A special panel formed to investigate the charges found eight of those countries guilty and directed them to make amends. All but one of the eight responded by modifying the offensive policies. Uruguay has benefited to some extent since the late 1960's from the International Grains Agreement, a price support arrangement for wheat, and from membership in the International Wool Textile Organization.

MACHINERY OF FOREIGN RELATIONS

Under the Constitution of 1967 responsibility for the country's external relations is shared by the executive and legislative branches. The president is designated supreme commander of all the armed forces, but only in the case of unforeseen foreign attack is he authorized to take prompt measures on his own accord. Even in repelling an unforeseen attack, he is required to give an account of his actions and intentions within twenty-four hours to a joint session of the General Assembly or, during its recess, to the Permanent Commission; the decision of the legislators in regard to subsequent actions is final (see ch. 12, The Governmental System).

Congressional approval is required for a declaration of war, and the Constitution further specifies that such a declaration is authorized only after arbitration and other pacific means of avoiding war have proved unsuccessful. It is the responsibility of the Congress to permit for a specified period of time, or to prohibit, the entry of foreign troops into the Republic or the dispatch of national forces beyond its borders. Congress is empowered to approve or disapprove, by an absolute majority of the full membership of both chambers, treaties of peace, alliance, or commerce and conventions or contracts of any nature that the executive may conclude with foreign powers.

The president has the power to receive diplomatic agents, to authorize foreign consuls to exercise their functions, and to decree the severance of relations. He is to appoint consular and diplomatic personnel, but the consent of the Senate or, during its recess, of the permanent commission is necessary for the appointment of chiefs of missions and for the dismissal of diplomatic and consular officers. As the posts of ambassador and minister in the foreign service are regarded as positions of personal responsibility to the executive power, Senate approval is not required for the conferring of those titles, but it is required for the assignment of persons holding those titles to specific posts. Senate approval is not required for their dismissal (see ch. 12, The Governmental System).

There are no entrance examinations for the foreign service and no formalized standards in regard to education or experience. Most appointments, therefore, are made on the basis of criteria such as kinship, friendship, or political influence. A law passed in 1967, however, specified that a few of the lower level positions are to be filled by students from the national university's college of economics.

In 1970 the Ministry of Foreign Relations employed 300 persons in Montevideo and 240 in foreign posts. The country maintained embassies in every Western Hemisphere state except Haiti, where it had a consulate, Cuba, Jamaica, Tinidad-Tobago, and Guyana; and in every European state except Iceland, where it had a consulate, Finland, Luxembourg, Eire, Albania, and East Germany. In addition, it maintained embassies in India, Israel Lebanon, Japan, Australia, Nigeria, and the United Arab Republic and consulates in the Republic of South Africa and Hong Kong. Plans were underway for establishing additional consular offices in Africa and Asia. Permanent delegations included those to both the New York and Geneva offices of the United Nations and to FAO, UNESCO, GATT, OAS, and the European Economic Community.

The Constitution states that the Republic shall seek to attain the social and economic integration of the Latin American states, especially through the mutual protection of their products and raw materials and the effort to make their public services complementary. It further asserts that the state shall guide foreign trade by protecting with all the means at its disposal the productive activities that create exports or replace imports and shall promote investments, preferably from public savings, to achieve this purpose.

Jorge Peirano Facio, foreign minister in mid-1970, indicated that his primary goal was the promotion and diversification of foreign trade; to this end he announced plans for the establishment of a Board of Foreign Commerce and an Interministerial Commission comprising the ministers of foreign relations, commerce and industry, and economy and finance to coordinate and set guidelines for government activities.

GOVERNMENT POLICIES

Upon being sworn in on April 2, 1970, Peirano stated that Uruguay's fundamental problem was foreign trade. With the sole exception of 1966, the country had sustained a trade deficit every year since 1954. The payments due international creditors in fiscal year 1970 from the Bank of the Republic and the Central Bank amounted to the equivalent of US$45.7 million, and the servicing of the US$450 million external debt was expected to absorb more than half of the trade receipts (see ch. 21, Trade).

The controversy with the International Monetary Fund (IMF) that had been a major concern of all Uruguayan governments since the late 1950's was at least temporarily resolved in 1970. President Pacheco had urged the IMF to solicit international assistance for his country, but the IMF had insisted upon the prior adoption of measures that the Pacheco government considered politically unfeasible. After having devalued the peso three times, President Pacheco in early 1970 resisted IMF pressure for a further devaluation. By May the issue had been resolved without devaluation, and Uruguay was granted an IMF standby agreement of US$13.7 million as the country had maintained a favorable trade balance for the first quarter of the year.

The Pacheco government has attempted to counteract the British ban on the country's meat exports by presenting a common front with Argentina and Brazil, which have been similarly affected by the ban. In April 1970 representatives of the three countries met in Buenos Aires to seek agreement on a proposition to present to the British.

Meanwhile the government had been able to obtain some sizable loans in 1970, including a total of US$6 million in development loans from the Inter-American Development Bank (IDB) and US$15 million in capital goods import loans from the United States. Negotiations for a loan of US$16 million from the IDB for modernization of the meatpacking industry were nearing completion in May 1970.

In order to stimulate the local fishing industry and to preserve sea-bottom and subsoil resources, President Pacheco on December 29, 1969, promulgated Law No. 13,833, advancing the country's maritime border to 200 nautical miles. In May 1970 eight other Latin American nations claiming the 200-mile limit—Argentina, Brazil, Chile, Peru, Ecuador, Panama, Nicaragua, and El Salvador—attended a meeting in Montevideo called by Uruguay to discuss the formation of a common front on issues pertaining to territorial waters and the exploitation of maritime resources.

Another issue on which the Pacheco government was seeking collective action in the hemisphere was that of dealing with guerrilla activity generally and the kidnapping and ransom of diplomats in particular. A Uruguayan proposal to bring this matter to the attention of the OAS General Assembly in its next extraordinary session was incorporated into a resolution passed on May 13, 1970, by the Juridico-Political Commission of the permanent council of that organization.

CHAPTER 15

PUBLIC INFORMATION

In 1970 mass media played vital roles in the lives of the people. In a country with a remarkably high literacy rate the great majority read daily newspapers, most of which were published in Montevideo. Leading Montevideo dailies are national newspapers in the sense that they are delivered quickly to all parts of the country. Since many newspapers are associated with political parties or factions whose positions are presented in their columns, a reader seeking an unbiased view of the political scene may read a number of papers every day. In most dailies a notable amount of space is devoted to sports.

Radio stations blanket the country with newscasts, music, entertainment, educational programs, and advertising. Almost every home has a receiver and, along with sets heard in village squares and cafés, portable transistor sets have increased the number of listeners to encompass most of the population. Television networks, first established in the early 1960's, disseminate news, entertainment, and advertising. The viewing public is estimated at about one-third of the total population.

The most widely read periodicals are Spanish-language editions of foreign magazines. Uruguayan magazines and journals are few in number. Likewise, the number of book publishers and booksellers is limited. In 1970 gathering places such as cafés, restaurants, and bars continued to serve as centers for the exchange of information, ideas, and rumors.

The Constitution guarantees freedom of speech and freedom of the press, and Uruguay has been noted for the extent to which these rights have been respected. Under the limited state of siege declared in June 1968 certain newspapers were closed temporarily for violation of security measures. In 1969 a law was decreed that forbade newspapers to print stories about planned demonstrations or strikes; it also restricted general criticism of the government and reporting on certain forms of political controversy and the armed forces.

In 1970 the importance of the issue of freedom of the press was illustrated by events following the closing of the newspaper *El Debate* and the Communist daily *El Popular* for five days. A senator engaged in an acrimonious debate with the minister of interior, who was subsequently summoned to appear before the Senate to explain the order under which the newspapers were closed.

Among the foreign governments conducting informational and cultural activities in the country in 1970 were the United Kingdom, France, Italy, West Germany, the United States, and the Soviet Union. Programs included maintenance of binational centers, support of schools, distribution of materials to radio, press, and television, and arrangements for student exchange.

NEWSPAPERS

The country may be described as a nation of newspaper readers. One reason for the continuation of the party system over the years has been the existence of one or more newspapers supporting almost every permanent party or faction in the country. Thus the citizen who wishes to obtain a clear picture of political developments must read more than one daily regularly.

In 1970 nine Montevideo dailies and the leftist weekly *Marcha* were sold throughout the nation. Because of the short distances between the capital and provincial centers, morning editions of Montevideo newspapers can be read almost anywhere in the country on the day on which they appear. Montevideo newspapers account for an estimated 90 percent of the total sales of daily papers for the entire country. As a consequence the papers published in the interior concern themselves primarily with matters of local interest. One of the best-known provincial dailies is *El Telegrafo* of Paysandú. Many of the others in the interior have faced economic difficulties.

Leading newspapers in Montevideo in 1970 were *La Mañana*, *El Dia*, *BP Color*—all morning—and *Acción* and *El Diario*—both afternoon. *El Popular* was a Moscow-oriented Communist daily (see table 5).

La Mañana, a Colorado Party newspaper founded in 1917, was progovernment. It had an estimated circulation of 25,000 in 1970. Its principal appeal was to middle and upper income groups —businessmen and landowners. *El Dia*, the second oldest newspaper in the country, founded by Batlle y Ordóñez in 1886, supported an important wing of the Colorado Party. It had served as a powerful weapon in the journalistic campaigning of Batlle, who, in the late nineteenth century, attacked authoritarian governments. In 1920 acrimonious rivalry between Batlle and Washington Beltrán, codirector of an opposition Nationalist Party newspaper, led to a duel in which Beltrán died (see ch. 13, Political Dynamics).

In the late nineteenth century and the early twentieth century *El Dia* supported strikers who sought shorter hours and higher wages, advocated legalization of divorce, publicized Batlle's ideas on constitutional reform, and published articles of an anticlerical nature.

*Table 5. Leading Uruguayan Newspapers, 1970**

Title	Estimated Circulation	Remarks
El Diario	55,000	Colorado Party; photographs, sports, news, entertainment.
El País	35,000	Blanco Party (Beltrán faction); conservative appeal.
El Día	30,000	Colorado Party (traditional Batlista); founded by José Batlle y Ordoñez.
La Mañana	25,000	Colorado Party; progovernment.
BP Color	25,000	Catholic Action; all-color tabloid.
Acción	15,000	Colorado Party (list 15—Unity and Reform); liberal appeal.
El Popular	12,000	Communist Party daily; Moscow line.
Marcha	18,000	Leftist intellectual weekly.

*All published in Montevideo.

Source: Adapted from *Political Handbook and Atlas of the World, 1970* (Eds., Richard P. Stebbins and Alba Amoia), New York, 1970; and *Editor and Publisher International Year Book, 1970,* New York, 1970.

In 1970 its appeal was primarily to middle and upper income groups—businessmen and white-collar workers, including public service employees (see ch. 10, Religion; ch. 20, Labor Relations and Organization).

El Pais, with an estimated circulation of 35,000 in 1970, was a Blanco newspaper founded in 1918, which appealed to middle and upper income groups—businessmen, intellectuals, and white-collar workers, including public service employees. *BP Color*, a Catholic Action organ associated with the Christian Democrats, derived from the oldest newspaper in the country, *El Bien Público*, founded in 1878, which over the years took a special interest in problems of the interior and in analyzing political and economic developments. An all-color tabloid, *BP Color* had an estimated circulation of 25,000 in 1970.

Acción, an organ of the Colorado faction List 15—Unity and Reform (Unidad y Reforma)—founded by a nephew of Batlle y Ordóñez, appealed to middle income groups and had a circulation of about 15,000 in 1970. *El Diario*, an independent organ of the Colorado Party, was established in 1906; it appealed to some middle and lower income groups, including sports fans. *Marcha*, a leftist weekly, was read by students, artists, and intellectuals. Founded in 1931, *El Debate*, organ of a small faction of the Blanco Party, appealed principally to the hard core of its own political party (see ch. 13, Political Dynamics).

The press is served by the National Information Agency (Agencia Nacional de Informaciones—ANI), which receives service from Buenos Aires. Foreign wire services include: the Associated Press

(AP) and United Press International (UPI), both of the United States; (Prensa Latina) of Cuba; Reuters of England; French Press Agency (Agence France Presse); National Press Agency (Agencia Nazionale Associata—ANSA) of Italy; and Telegraph Agency of the Soviet Union (Telegrafnoye Agenstsvo Sovietskogo Soyuza—TASS).

In 1970 reporters were organized in an interpaper organization called the Uruguayan Press Association. Because of the infiltration of this organization by leftist elements, some members were endeavoring to form a new association. Publishers and owners belonged to the Press Association of Uruguay (Asociación de la Prensa Uruguaya) and to the Newspaper Association of Uruguay (Asociación de Diarios del Uruguay).

Newspaper circulation dropped sharply in 1967, when the price per copy increased almost 100 percent after a press strike that lasted 114 days. Before this the total circulation of daily and weekly Spanish-language newspapers published in Montevideo was an estimated 413,000 and the estimated number of newspaper readers throughout the country was 1.5 million.

Newspapers derive revenue from advertising and, in many cases, financial backing from political parties and factions. Advertising is placed through a number of advertising agencies, some of which also serve as space brokers in the field of television.

The format of dailies is similar to that of European and North American newspapers. In many cases editorial content presents the views of the political group that backs the paper. Coverage of international news is extensive. In most newspapers great prominence is given to sports—particularly soccer. Some newspapers publish a Sunday supplement.

A large number of comic strips are of North American origin. "Blondie" appears under the caption "Vida Conyugal" (Married Life); "Mary Worth" becomes "María de Oro" (Mary [with the heart] of Gold); "Henry" is presented as "Cero Pelo" (The Hairless One); and "Bringing Up Father" appears as "Educando a Papa."

RADIO

A total of seventy radio stations—twenty-seven in Montevideo and forty-three in the interior—broadcast to an estimated 2,380,000 listeners in 1970. Twenty-three of these stations operated with 10,000 watts or more. The number of receiving sets was estimated at 950,000. One network, the Official Radio Broadcasting Service (Servicio Oficial de Difusión Radio Eléctrica—SODRE) was operated by the government. One of the SODRE stations in Montevideo—call number Cx—6—used a 50,000-watt transmitter. Other powerful stations were Radio Carve, with 50,000 watts, and Radio Oriental and Radio El Espectador, with 25,000 watts each (see table 6).

Table 6. Major Uruguayan AM Radio Stations, 1969

City	Station name and owner	Symbol call letters	Wave length (in meters)	Frequency (in kilocycles)
Montevideo	Radio Eléctrica (SODRE) Servicio Oficial de Difusión*	CX6	461.50	650
	Radio Sarandi Corporacion de Publicidad S.A.	CX8	434.80	690
	Radio Oriental Luis A. Artola	CX12	389.60	770
	Radio El Espectador Difusoras del Uruguay S.A.	CX14	370.40	810
	Radio Carve Sadrep Ltda.	CX16	352.90	850
	Radio Libertad Sport Difusoras del Uruguay S.A.	CX18	337.10	890
	Radio Montecarlo Maria E. Salvo de Romay	CX20	322.60	930
	La Voz del Aire Sadrep Ltda.	CX24	297.00	1010
	Radio Eléctrica (SODRE) Servicio Official de Difusion*	CX26	285.70	1050
	Radio Imparcial Walfrido Figuerira Moran	CX28	275.20	1090
	Radio Nacional O.R.O.S.A.	CX30	265.50	1130
	Radio Sur Cia. Uruguaya de Publicidad S.A.	CX32	256.40	1170
	Radio Eléctrica (SODRE) Servicio Oficial de Difusión*	CXA4	48.98	6125

Table 6. Major Uruguayan AM Radio Stations, 1969—Continued

City	Station name and owner	Symbol call letters	Wave length (in meters)	Frequency (in kilocycles)
	Radio Montecarlo Maria E. Salvo de Romay	CXA20	48.86	6140
	Radio Carve Relays CX16 S.A.D.R.E.P. Ltda.	CXA13	48.74	6155
	Radio Sarandi Corporación de Publicidad S.A.	CXA71	31.53	9515
	Radio Monte Carlo Maria E. Salvo de Romay	CXA72	31.27	9595
	Radio Eléctrica (SODRE) Servicio Oficial de Difusión*	CSA6	31.19	9620
	Radio Sarandi Corporación de Publicidad S.A.	CXA68	25.24	11885
	Radio Eléctrica (SODRE) Servicio Oficial de Difusión*	CXA10	25.21	11900
	Radio Eléctrica (SODRE) Servicio Oficial de Difusión*	CXA18	19.64	15275
	Radio Eléctrica (SODRE) Servicio Oficial de Difusión*	CXA18	19.54	15355
Tacuarembó	Difusora Zorilla de San Martin Luis S. Dini	CXA140	214.30	1400

*Government owned. SODRE—Servicio Oficial de Difusión Eléctrica (Official Radio Broadcasting Service).

Source: Adapted from Foreign Broadcast Information Service, Broadcasting Stations of the World, Part I: Amplitude Modulation Broadcasting Stations According to Country and City, Washington, 1969.

The first government station was operated by the Ministry of War and Marine. Under a law promulgated in December 1929 SODRE was created, and in April 1930 it initiated daily programs of eleven hours of music. In 1931 SODRE started broadcasts of symphony programs, which won recognition outside the country. SODRE's principal objective was to serve educational and cultural needs; and the station broadcast courses in geography, history, science, and literature, both for schools and for the general public.

Although a notable proportion of the people are newspaper readers, radio has become a major medium for distribution of news and ideas and for the formation of public opinion. An estimated 98 percent of urban and rural homes had at least one set in 1970. Types of programs—music and entertainment—are similar to those in Western Europe and North America. Several stations in Montevideo are owned by or affiliated with newspapers, and radio advertising has become a profitable business. Most of the commercial stations depend on advertising for their basic revenue. Groups of people listen to broadcasts in cafés and other gathering places, and the advent of the transistor radio has generated a dramatic increase in the number of individual radio listeners.

Under the provisions of Law No. 8390 of November 1928 and subsequent regulatory decrees, commercial broadcasting stations must obtain from the minister of national defense a license, which may be revoked at any time. In 1970 radio broadcasting was regulated by the Directorate of Radiocommunications (Dirección de Radiocommunicaecions) with headquarters in Montevideo. There was no prior censorship of programs. Broadcasters were organized in the National Association of Uruguayan Broadcasters (Asociación Nacional de Broadcasters Uruguayos—ANDEBU).

TELEVISION

In 1970 there were nineteen programming television stations, all using a 525-line definition (see table 7).

Television stations were first established in the early 1960's, and in 1963 a group of businessmen, recognizing the interest in television in rural districts, formed an association to promote the establishment of stations in the interior. In 1966 the first four channels in the interior were assigned to Fray Bentos, Minas, Pasa de los Toros, and Rocha. The station built in Fray Bentos had a 500-watt transmitter and a radius of a little over thirty miles.

In 1970 television was a powerful force in the public information field. The viewing audience was estimated at 1 million. Programs included educational television, news, documentaries, and entertainment. Among imported programs shown by Montevideo stations in early 1970 were "Dragnet," "Panorama USA," "Mission Impos-

Table 7. Uruguayan Television Stations, 1969

City	Owner of station	Channel	Video-audio power (in watts)	Frequency video-audio (in kilocycles per second)
Artigas	Tele Artigas	A3	500	61250
	SODRE TV Servicio Oficial de Difusión*	A12	316000	205250
Colonia	SODRE TV Servicio Oficial de Difusión*	A6	10000	83250
Fray Bentos	Río Uruguay TV Maria E. Salvo de Romay	A12	1000	205250
Melo	SODRE TV Servicio Oficial de Difusión	A8	316000	181250
Mercedes	SODRE TV Servicio Oficial de Difusión*	A5	75000	77250
Minas	Luis Segui Gonzalez	A13	....	211250
Montevideo	Monte Carlo TV Maria E. Salvo de Romay	A4	32000	67250
	SODRE TV Servicio Oficial de Difusión*	A5	5000	77250
	Saeta TV Soc. Anom. Emissoras de Tele y Anexos	A10	2500	193250
	Teledoce Damaso Larranga S.A.	A12	64000	205250
Paso de los Toros	SODRE TV Servicio Oficial de Difusión*	A2	100000	55250
	Rodriguez, Tarde, Evangelesti y Landoni	A9	....	187250
Paysandú	SODRE TV Servicio Oficial de Difusión*	A10	316000	193250

Rivera	SODRE TV			
	Servicio Oficial de Difusión*	A5	100000	77250
Rocha	Ing. Francisco Elices Elorza	A7	....	175250
Salto	SODRE TV			
	Servicio Oficial de Difusión*	A6	100000	83250
	Affiliated: Damaso Larranga S. A.	A8	....	181250
Tacuarembó	SODRE TV			
	Servicio Oficial de Difusión*	A13	316000	211250

*Government owned. SODRE—Servicio Oficial de Difusión Eléctrica (Official Radio Broadcasting Service).

Source: Adapted from Foreign Broadcast Information Service, Broadcasting Station of the World, Part IV: Television Stations, Washington, 1969.

sible," "Cisco Kid," "The Virginian," "Abbott and Costello," and "Bonanza."

Television programs from other parts of the world are received via satellite through the ground station outside Buenos Aires, from which they are transmitted by microwave to the SODRE transmitter in Colonia.

PERIODICALS AND BOOK PUBLISHING

Popular periodicals are Spanish-language editions of *Reader's Digest*, *The Economist*, *Visión*, and *Life*. Locally published magazines are limited in number and in circulation. Western European and Argentine magazines are read, along with official publications from Communist bloc countries.

Writers have found outlets in a number of reviews, but it has sometimes been necessary for them to finance their own books. In 1966 some 266 books were published in Uruguay. Of these 115 were classed as literature; 64 were in the field of social sciences; 33 were on geographical and historical subjects; and the rest were on philosophy, religion, philology, pure science, applied science, and the fine arts.

In 1970 there were over 200 public libraries in the country. The National Library, founded in 1816, had more than 200,000 volumes, including a sizable historical collection (see ch. 9, Artistic and Intellectual Expression).

In 1970 there were a number of commercial publishing houses in Montevideo. The publications department of the University of the Republic also produced books. The number of bookshops in Montevideo was small, but ten or twelve firms imported and exported books. Booksellers belong to the Uruguayan Booksellers' Association (Asociación de Libreros del Uruguay) (see ch. 9, Artistic and Intellectual Expression).

MOTION PICTURES

In 1970 there were 184 motion picture theaters, 56 of them in Montevideo. Total seating capacity was estimated at 134,000. Although the number of theaters had declined—from 223 in 1963—motion pictures were still a popular form of entertainment.

The government produces documentaries and educational films, and the local industry produces newsreels and a few features. The great majority of films shown are imported from the United States, Mexico, France, Italy, Great Britain, and the Soviet Union. Feature films from a number of Soviet satellite countries are also exhibited.

Films that are cut by the censors in Buenos Aires may be shown uncut in Montevideo, with the result that Montevideo theaters draw a number of Argentine patrons. Early in 1970 one feature film was advertised with the announcement that the censor in Buenos Aires had cut eight minutes but that the uncut version was being shown in Montevideo; and another feature was advertised under the heading "Prohibited in the United States. Received Without Cuts."

In 1970 feature films shown in Montevideo included *The Yellow Submarine*, with the Beatles; *Staircase*, with Rex Harrison and Richard Burton; *Chitty Chitty Bang Bang*, with Dick Van Dyke; *Good Evening, Mrs. Campbell*, with Gina Lollobrigida; and *John and Mary*, with Dustin Hoffman and Mia Farrow. Other films were of European, Latin American, and Japanese origin.

ACTIVITIES OF FOREIGN GOVERNMENTS

In 1970 the United Kingdom maintained thirteen bilateral cultural centers, granted scholarships for study in the British Isles, and supported a school. The French government operated a cultural institute, awarded scholarships, arranged visits of artists and lecturers, sponsored some twenty branches of the French Alliance (Alliance Francaise), and supported three schools.

The Italian government maintained a cultural center, offered scholarships, brought in cultural presentations, and supported a school. Similar activities were carried out by the government of West Germany.

The United States Information Agency (USIA) provided programs for domestic radio and television stations, and extensive use was made of Voice of America rebroadcasts. USIS also made materials available to newspapers and prepared an intellectual quarterly *Facetas*, which was sold on newsstands. Sixteen-millimeter films were distributed to various organizations, and thirty-five-millimeter films were shown commercially. An Information Center had a 25,000-volume library, and the Binational Center in Montevideo enrolled several thousand students. During fiscal year 1969 educational exchange grants were made to twenty-nine Uruguayans and to six professors and students from the United States.

In 1970 Communist governments conducted informational and cultural activities through eight embassies and three news agencies —News Press Agency (Agentsvo Pechati Novosti, commonly known as NOVOSTI), TASS, and Prensa Latina. There were twenty-three Communist-line associations, seven of which were binational centers sponsored by the Soviet Union. Some materials from the Soviet Union and Communist China entered the country via international mails. A considerable number of publishing houses and bookstores in Montevideo produced and sold pro-Communist materials. Three radio stations habitually followed Communist lines.

There was considerable travel between Uruguay and Communist countries by Communist leaders, students, educations, and labor groups. Communist nations also sent cultural attractions and trade missions. Communist influence was apparent in the University of the Republic, where student organizations were, for the most part, controlled by well-organized Communist and leftist minorities (see ch. 8, Education; ch. 9, Artistic and Intellectual Expression).

CHAPTER 16

POLITICAL VALUES AND ATTITUDES

In 1970 the general agreement on national goals and how they should be pursued that had given the country an outstanding record of political stability appeared to be weakening. In the twentieth century, development of the habit of compromise between the major parties had prevented a recurrence of the violent partisan conflict that was endemic in the nineteenth century, and the security provided by the welfare state until the 1960's had limited middle and lower class alienation. The pluralistic democratic system had filtered individual and group demands through accepted political institutions. Thus the most powerful, as well as the least satisfied, elements of society had usually been willing to seek their political goals within the bounds of the legal order.

By mid-1970, however, economic difficulties were eroding many of the benefits of the welfare state; an urban guerrilla group, comprising persons of all social classes, was operating boldly; and the security measures that had been in effect over most of the preceding two years had generated much opposition to the government. Supporters of the government maintained that rule by decree under the security measures was necessary to enforce austerity and to maintain order, but many opponents alleged that established political processes and highly prized civil liberties were being undermined.

The development of a nationalistic tradition strong enough to override regional and partisan loyalties was largely a twentieth-century phenomenon. In the nineteenth century the involvement of foreign interests in internal political competition posed an obstacle to national cohesion. The spread of education and the beginnings of a national literary tradition around the turn of the twentieth century, however, enhanced national self-awareness, and the initiatives of President José Batlle y Ordóñez in economic development and in the restructuring of the social and political order in the first two decades of the century laid the basis for general agreement on national goals.

Uruguayans place a high value on nonconformity and individual freedom of expression. The great diversity in what is regarded with pride as characteristic of the country is revealed in the almost universal admiration for such dissimilar national figures as: José Gervasio Artigas, rugged *gaucho* (cowboy) and revolutionary fighter; José Enrique Rodó, literary defender of spiritual values; and José Batlle y Ordoñez, astute politician, institution builder, and secular reformer.

Uruguayan nationalism gives human values precedence over material values. The people regard their nation as civilized and politically sophisticated and one that has built its reputation on serving as a pacesetter in social reform and international cooperation.

Most citizens take an interest in the political processes, are aware of national issues, and are affiliated with one of the two major parties. The identification of inhabitants of the rural interior with the Blanco Party and of the predominantly immigrant population of Greater Montevideo with the Colorado Party was firmly established by the beginning of the twentieth century. Party affiliation generally passes down through the family, and the migration from rural to urban areas has increased the Blanco following in the capital city. Differences in social structure and unequal distribution of government services and controls between city and country, however, have tended to perpetuate the regional partisan division.

The large urban middle class population, the high literacy rate, the effectiveness of the information media, and the important role of the state in the daily lives of most of its citizens have fostered a highly politicized culture. It is common for the people to organize in defense of their interests and to seek to influence the government through party leaders. A large majority of the eligible voters customarily cast their ballots, and there is a high level of year-round participation in party and interest group activities.

The parties are fragmented, but the complex electoral system, providing for proportional representation among factions as well as parties, has served to preserve the essentially two-party system. The minor parties are increasingly resentful of the monopolistic position of the traditional parties, but the honesty of the elections is not seriously questioned. Despite the intensity of electoral competition, the results are generally accepted as the legitimate expression of popular will.

DETERMINANTS OF POLITICAL VALUES

Social Development and Political Sophistication

The country's relatively small size and population, its ethnic homogeneity, the high level of social integration, and the predominance of the middle class in the social structure have contributed to national unity and to a broad agreement on certain fundamental beliefs and values. A government popularly elected by the majority, but with minority representation, freedom of expression and of assembly, and the right of all parties to participate in elections have been among the widely shared values. The middle class preoccupation with security is reflected in government policies that have rarely been challenged by the wealthy, and the middle and upper classes generally concede the obligation of the government to provide for the basic necessities of all its citizens.

At the same time, a keen political consciousness has been generated by: the degree of urbanization; the high literacy rate; the high level of education generally; the abundance and large circulation of newspapers and other periodicals presenting widely varying points of view on political issues; the proliferation of associations representing all types of economic, cultural, and civic interests; and the ease with which political parties or factions may be formed and candidates presented. Individuals have generally felt free, if not obligated, to promote their interests and make known their convictions through active participation in politics.

The public school system, the communications media, the prolonged and noisy political campaigns, and the omnipresence of government have combined with family traditions and the rural-urban cleavage in influencing political orientations. Though most Uruguayans are Roman Catholics, the church has had only limited impact on attitudes toward secular institutions. Religious affiliation has not been a prerequisite for a successful political career.

Since the beginning of the twentieth century the military has not been regarded as an acceptable instrument for altering domestic power relationships. The coup d'etat of 1933 was headed by civilian President Gabriel Terra, and an important supporting role was played by firemen. A few military officers have obtained high positions in government, but these positions generally have been acquired through family or party ties rather than as a result of military prestige or power.

The two traditional parties, which together claim the allegiance of a large majority of the population, are highly fragmented. The electoral system, however, which combines the primaries with the general election and allots elective offices through proportional representation to factions as well as parties on the basis of their voting strength, has allowed a broad spectrum of views to be represented without bringing about the disintegration of the two-party system. Furthermore, the tradition of *co-participación* (sharing of power and spoils between the majority and minority parties) that has developed since the late nineteenth century has contributed to the acceptance of the legitimacy of individual administrations and of political institutions generally.

Regional Imbalance and Partisanship

The national society is often referred to as a closely knit community, but there is a gulf in living standards and attitudes between

Greater Montevideo and the rural interior. The elites of city and country are united by bonds of kinship as well as interlocking economic interests and political responsibility. University ties and common membership in various clubs and associations facilitate contact among elites from different parts of the country with various political interests and philosophies.

The communications media of the capital penetrate virtually all parts of the interior, and the *estancieros* (members of the landowning class) are usually well informed on national issues. Nevertheless, since independence there has existed in the rural areas an attitude of suspicion and resentment toward the capital, which dominates all aspects of national life. Citizens of Montevideo, on the other hand, tend to exhibit a colonial attitude toward the people of the interior.

Party affiliation around the turn of the twentieth century was generally determined by the rural-urban cleavage The Colorado Party catered to the needs of the urbanites and made it possible for the large numbers of European immigrants to become incorporated into the social, economic, and political life of the capital. Commercial and professional, as well as labor and bureaucratic, sectors benefited from Colorado policies and aligned themselves with the party.

The rural elites were able to maintain their landholdings but nevertheless were forced to bear much of the economic burden for the institutionalization of the welfare state in the capital; this burden served to entrench the rural power structure within the Blanco Party. Loyalty to their landlords and animosity toward city dwellers limited the development of class consciousness among the rural poor and secured their support for the Blanco Party.

The greater interest of the Colorado Party, in power from 1865 to 1959 and since 1967, in its urban power base and the control of the more conservative, rural-oriented Blanco Party by the landowning class have meant that the greater part of the national budget has been spent in the capital and its environs and that the services and benefits available to the lower classes in Montevideo have only belatedly and partially been extended to the interior. The rigid social structure and the virtual lack of a middle class to bridge the gap between landowner and worker have inhibited the development of community organization in the rural areas.

Respect for the human dignity and independence of spirit of the individual, a basic tenet of the *gaucho* tradition, is manifest in the relationship between landowner and worker, but this personal egalitarianism is not carried over into economic and political relationships. As the landowners have little economic use for the families of their hired hands, the families are not allowed to live on the *estancias* (large ranches or country estates), and the landowners assume no responsibility for their well-being. These families have generally settled in rural shantytowns knows as *rancheríos*, where living standards have often been very low. Those who have found these conditions intolerable have migrated to urban centers, particularly to the capital. An important exception to this pattern was the protest movement by the sugar workers of Artigas. After a series of marches and demonstrations, they were able to prevail upon the National Institute of Colonization to expropriate, in April 1970, about 75,000 acres of unused land on a large *estancia* for redistribution to the sugarcane cutters under a cooperative system.

In both life-style and political attitude, the provincial cities, the truck farming region on the outskirts of Montevideo, and the coastal area represent a transitional zone. In recent decades rural-urban migration and investment by landowning families in commercial and industrial enterprises have increased the Blanco following in the cities.

Affiliation with one of the two traditional parties has become a part of one's family heritage, generally transmitted by the father, and individual political views find expression in the choice of a liberal, moderate, or conservative faction. Each faction maintains neighborhood clubs through which the professional politicians inform and, when appropriate, activate the rank and file members. Members in turn look to faction leaders for favors, such as jobs and help in circumventing bureaucratic red tape.

Leaders move from faction to faction with relative ease and as, the loyalty of the rank and file members to a particular leader is generally greater than to the faction itself, the size of the various factions of both parties is often in a state of flux between elections. A shift from one of the traditional parties to the other or to a minor party, however is a serious matter and may result in considerable friction among relatives and friends.

When members of one party find themselves in agreement with the policies of the other party and in disagreement with the majority position of their own, they may form temporary pacts with the opposition and cross party lines in voting on issues or candidates, but they are careful not to cast doubt on their loyalty to the parent party. For example, the many Blancos who supported Colorado President Jorge Pacheco Areco in 1970 on the perpetuation of the controversial security measures referred to themselves as Blancos Pachecistas.

The minor parties—the Christian Democratic Party and the traditional Socialist and Communist groups, as well as more recently formed groups adhering to Maoist and Castroite interpretations of Marxism—have usually drawn their support from students, intellectuals, and labor leaders. Their appeal has been limited, however, because the Colorado Party, until the late 1960's, championed the rights of labor and the disadvantaged.

ATTITUDES TOWARD THE NATION

National Cohesion

In the nineteenth century Uruguayans had only a tenuous foundation upon which to erect a national tradition. The country had its revolutionary heroes—Artigas, Juan Antonio Lavalleja and his "Thirty-three Immortals," and others—but its independence had to be underwritten initially by Great Britain, and its sovereignty and territorial integrity continued to be jeopardized by the expansionist designs of its neighbors. Its own political leaders were so divided that each of the two major parties was willing to take the risks to sovereignty involved in enlisting the support of foreign armies rather than accept defeat by their domestic rivals (see ch. 3, Historical Setting).

Even when the government changed hands through elections rather than force, fraud was generally suspected, and the exercise of authority was not necessarily regarded as legitimate by the defeated group. When the Colorado and Blanco parties finally came to terms after the War of the Triple Alliance (1864—70), their formula for coexistence within the national territory did not call for cooperation in the overall functions of government but rather for an arrangement whereby the Colorados controlled most of the country from Montevideo and the Blancos ruled almost autonomously in four, and later six, interior departments.

It was not until the 1870's that education became a matter of national concern and a truly national literature began to emerge. Among the first poetic appeals to patriotism to gain lasting fame was *La Leyenda Patria* (Legend of the Fatherland), written by Juan Zorilla de San Martín in 1879. The classic of Uruguayan literature, *Ariel*, by José Enrique Rodó, was published in 1900; his assertion of the humanistic and spiritual preeminence of the Latin over the Anglo-Saxon heritage has remained a source of inspiration to his countrymen. Novelists Eduardo Acevedo Diaz and Carlos Reyles and philosopher Carlos Vaz Ferriera also contributed greatly to the growing sense of national identity and self-awareness in the late nineteenth and early twentieth centuries (see ch. 9, Artistic and Intellectual Expression).

The foundations of the modern state and of the governmental institutions and political traditions that are the greatest source of pride to most contemporary Uruguayans were laid in the first two decades of the twentieth century under the sponsorship of Batlle y Ordóñez. His egalitarian philosophy and his ideas concerning the responsibilities of political parties to each other and to the state and of the state to its citizens established the first solid basis for national unity.

Nationalism

Poet and essayist Gaston Figueira wrote of his people in 1967, "No somos patrioteros" (We are not exaggerated patriots). Uruguayan nationalism is generally low key, neither militant nor defensive. Carlos Maggi described his countrymen in 1961 as a people who "do not aspire to greatness, or to anything absolute, but who desire that things shall be kept in good, human proportion and that the human values shall be treated with proper respect." One of the terms most commonly used by Uruguayans to characterize their nation is "civilized." They take pride in the fact that many of the social welfare measures now taken for granted throughout the hemisphere were first introduced in Uruguay and that they have an outstanding record of democratic government and respect for civil liberties.

Uruguayans are quick to laugh at themselves and to concede their shortcomings. They often attribute the economic malaise of the last two decades in part to a distaste for both austerity and hard work. They note that they desire freedom and comfort but are generally disinclined to accept personal sacrifice.

The differences in life-style between city and country have resulted in differences in concepts of the nation and in manifestations of nationalism. Urbanites, especially citizens of Montevideo, are often described by their rural countrymen as cosmopolitan in attitude. The generally keen interest of the urban population in foreign affairs, however, might be interpreted as an extension of nationalism, as an active international role is an important aspect of the national self-image (see ch. 14, Foreign Relations).

Inhabitants of the rural areas are largely isolated from the abundant cultural advantages of the capital and deprived of many of the benefits of the welfare state enjoyed by their urban counterparts. They generally find referral points for nationalistic sentiment in the heroic struggles of the independence movement, in natural phenomena, such as the scenic landscapes, and in national symbols rather than in twentieth-century political institutions and governmental and cultural achievements.

Symbols of the Nation

The flag, adopted in 1830, has four blue horizontal stripes on a white background. In the upper-left corner is a golden sun emitting sixteen rays. This sun, with human facial features, is called the "Sun of Mary" and symbolizes the country's independence. The "Sun of Mary" also crowns the nation's shield. The shield, an oval wreathed by branches and decorated in blue, green, and gold, is divided into four sections. In these sections are depictions of a horse, a cow, the scales of justice, and a small mountain topped by a fortress. The comment of one of Magellan's sailors upon seeing that mountain, "Monte vide eu" (I see a mountain), is cited as the source of the capital city's name. The national flower is the scarlet blossom of the ceibo tree.

The national anthem begins with the phrase "Orientales, la patria o la tumba" (Uruguayans, our country or death). With music composed by Fernando Quijano and lyrics by Francisco Acuña de Figueroa, it was first sung in Montevideo in 1845.

Holidays with national historical significance are: the Landing of the Thirty-three, April 19; the Battle of Las Piedras and Armed Forces Day, May 18; the Birthday of Artigas, June 19; Constitution Day, July 18; and Independence Day, August 25. Columbus Day, October 12, is celebrated throughout the Western Hemisphere. Other national holidays include: New Year's Day, January 1; Children's Day, January 6; Carnival, February and March; Tourist Week (Easter Week); Labor Day, May 1; All Souls' Day, November 2; Beach Day, December 8; and Family Day, December 25.

ATTITUDES TOWARD THE STATE

Although the state remains a remote entity to many in the rural interior, it is an important force in the daily lives of most of the people. In 1970 approximately 20 percent of the entire population was directly dependent upon the state for its livelihood, through civil service jobs, pensions, or welfare. In addition, the state had assumed the obligations of regulating the prices of staple foods and of ensuring decent working and housing conditions and adequate medical and other services for all of its citizens (see ch. 7, Living Conditions).

Some wealthy people, especially the producers of agricultural products for export, have resented the extent of state controls, but even the most conservative Uruguayans take for granted a great number of social welfare measures and an extent of government involvement in the economy that elsewhere in the hemisphere would be considered quite radical. The people commonly regard themselves as stockholders in the state. Even though they are annoyed by the delay and inefficiency inherent in the workings of a large bureaucracy and are aware of the economic problems involved in maintaining a remarkably large public payroll while production is declining, they continue to look to the state as the employer of last resort and as the guarantor of their economic security. Furthermore, the state has traditionally been considered a protector rather than a usurper of individual freedom.

The strongest link between the individual and the state is the political party or faction, as it is generally the professional politician who is most capable of cutting across bureaucratic red tape to secure a favor or expedite a service for his client. Furthermore, political patronage has formed the basis for the distribution of government jobs.

ATTITUDES TOWARD THE POLITICAL SYSTEM

Uruguayans approach political contests in much the same spirit as that in which they approach a soccer match—with exhilaration and sportsmanship, but with deadly seriousness. Campaigns are carried out with a great deal of noise and fanfare. Sound trucks, banners, posters, and handbills are used abundantly in the interior cities as well as in Montevideo, and neighborhood faction clubs are active around the clock.

Humor is a common attribute of political life. Cartoons tend to be uninhibited, and an occasional eccentric adds a light touch to the campaign. Invective is also common in political discourse, and insults have sometimes led to duels, which were still legal in 1970. Nevertheless, tolerance is generally exhibited for even the most unconventional views.

Since the beginning of the twentieth century, with the exception of the authoritarian rule of Gabriel Terra from 1933 to 1938 and the "state of emergency" rule by Jorge Areco Pacheco since 1968, all political parties have been allowed to function legally and participate in elections. The Communist Party, heading a coalition of leftist groups, continued to function in 1970. The Socialist Party was outlawed in 1968; in 1951 when its founder, Emilio Frugoni, was arrested in Argentina and deported to Uruguay, a civic reception, at which the traditional parties were represented, was given in his honor.

Although a few families, such as that of Batlle y Ordóñez, exercise a large influence in the political system, a great many people participate in party and interest group activities throughout the year. Between elections, neighborhood faction clubs conduct "schools for citizenship" to attract new adherents and to keep their members informed on issues of public policy. The clubs also serve as social and cultural centers. Lobbying is carried on vigorously by groups representing everything from big business to welfare recipients and, until security measures were imposed in June 1968, demonstrations and political strikes were a common feature of national life.

Most people identify themselves with a political party, generally one of the traditional ones, and those persons who identify themselves as independents usually profess an interest in politics. With certain exceptions, all Uruguayans over the age of eighteen have the right and legal obligation to vote, and most of them do.

More than 80 percent of those eligible actually voted in the presidential elections of 1926 and 1930. As a result of Terra's authoritarian rule, many people boycotted the 1938 elections, and voter turnout dropped to 56 percent. Since that time it has risen steadily—to 65 percent in 1946, 70 percent in 1950, 77 percent in 1962, and 80 percent in 1966. The complexity of the electoral system is often criticized, but charges of electoral fraud are not heard. President Alfredo Baldomir (1938—43) once remarked: "We have the costliest electoral system per capita on the continent, but it is cheaper than revolution."

In 1970 comments on the country's democratic tradition were often accompanied by expressions of embarrassment over the extralegal assumption of power by Terra in 1933 and assertions of the need for vigilance against such an eventuality. One of the primary concerns of Batlle y Ordoñez was institutionalization of safeguards against *caudillismo* (one-man rule—see Glossary). The *colegiado* (see Glossary) system in effect from 1919 to 1933 and from 1952 to 1967 was designed as such a safeguard, as were many of the powers and watchdog functions allocated to the legislative branch of government. A few politicians, such as Blanco leader Luis Alberto de Herrera, have demonstrated an authoritarian bent, but in so doing they have alienated many members of their own parties (see ch. 13, Political Dynamics).

Electoral laws encouraging the proliferation of factions and of candidates for public office have provided relatively easy access for members of the upper and middle classes to roles of political leadership, and the exercise of such leadership is highly prized. Although *caudillismo* is considered an anathema to most Uruguayans and demagoguery generally has little appeal, personalism is important at all levels of the political process. Friendship, kinship, and loyalty to individual leaders have often overshadowed issues in determining the composition of factions or coalitions; the names of certain leaders are commonly used to identify factions and subfactions, such as Batllista, Herrerista, and Pachecista.

The people generally respect their governmental institutions and take pride in their political system, but they do not hesitate to criticize them. A frequently cited problem is that, although the system responds to the various organized and articulated interests, response is in piecemeal fashion and often at the expense of an integrated program based on calculations of priorities. The diffusion of power among faction leaders tends to neutralize the political parties as formulators of policy, and minor parties complain that the electoral laws and the tradition of *co-participación* allow the major parties to monopolize the system.

ATTITUDES TOWARD THE GOVERNMENT

In 1970 attitudes toward the government were sharply polarized, and both supporters and opponents alleged that some of the nation's most cherished traditions were in jeopardy. There were indications that agreement on such fundamental values as freedom of expression and acceptance of the legitimacy of governmental actions was being eroded.

The electoral swing toward the Blancos in 1958, after ninety-three years of Colorado rule, and the swing back to the Colorados in 1966, as well as the abandonment of the plural executive in favor of a presidential system, had indicated a general awareness that the nation was confronted with serious problems. Overstaffing and inefficiency in government had been joked about and denounced, and it was widely recognized that in its paternalistic role the government had overextended itself economically. Although many people were speaking in the abstract of the need for austerity, neither as individuals nor as members of interest groups were they advocating austerity for themselves.

When the Colorados returned to power in 1967, there was evidence of social unrest, especially in the ranks of organized labor and among pensioners whose real incomes were steadily declining and whose checks were often late in arriving. Economic uncertainty had engendered some sympathy for the Tupamaros, an urban guerrilla group that initially became noted for robbing banks and casinos and distributing portions of the take among the poor.

The security measures imposed by President Pacheco in June 1968, including price and wage controls and prohibitions of strikes and demonstrations, had allowed him to carry on a highly successful campaign against inflation, but the perpetuation of rule by decree and the use of such measures as press censorship to repress dissent had polarized public opinion. Those to whom economic growth and stability and civic order were of most immediate concern, strongly backed the president's actions, but others, who placed higher priority on civil liberties and political pluralism or who considered themselves particularly disadvantaged by the austerity program, were largely alienated from the government.

This divisiveness had resulted in considerable reshuffling in the party system as many members of the traditionally more conservative Blanco Party supported the president, and organized labor and other urban groups that had served as a base for the Colorado Party were making common cause with the radical left. The police and the armed forces, as a result of their role in enforcing the security measures and their increasing outspokenness on policies, had somewhat diminished their reputation for being apolitical. The Catholic hierarchy was critical of the security measures and, on May 28,

1970, canceled the traditional Corpus Christi procession as a gesture of solidarity with other groups whose public marches had been banned.

One of the developments most disturbing to both supporters and opponents of the government has been the rising level of violence in political life. Both guerrilla activities—such as the theft by the Tupamaros on May 29, 1970, of some 700 weapons from a naval training center and the July—August kidnappings of two American advisers and a Brazilian diplomat and the murder of one of the Americans—and allegations of the use of torture by police on political and other prisoners, reported in June by a Senate investigating commission representing all parties, have caused concern in a nation that has taken pride in its reputation for nonviolence and political maturity.

SECTION III. ECONOMIC

CHAPTER 17

CHARACTER AND STRUCTURE OF THE ECONOMY

In 1970 production of livestock for meat and wool continued to form the basis of the economy. The agricultural sector provided about 15 percent of the gross national product (GNP), employed about 18 percent of the labor force, and generated from 80 to 90 percent of the country's foreign exchange earnings. The country's principal natural resource was its rich agricultural land. Around 70 percent of the area was used for raising livestock; 1970 estimates set the number of sheep at about 20 million and the number of cattle at around 8 million. The processing of agricultural and animal products accounted for about half of the country's industrial output; industry generated about 32 percent of the GNP and employed about 26 percent of the labor force. About four-fifths of the consumer goods sold were produced domestically.

The standard of living was relatively high. The labor force was literate; it contained a substantial element educated to the middle school level as well as a strong nucleus of skilled and professional workers. The country, moreover, possessed some reserves of unutilized capacity, and specialists believed that substantial gains in economic well-being could be obtained from a more efficient utilization of the country's resources—the land, the abundant fisheries, and the natural tourist attractions. The existing capacity for processing agricultural products was said to be underutilized and could be expanded at relatively little expense.

Until 1968 national economic policies had been designed basically to maintain the level of consumption. This goal had been achieved but only at the cost of accelerating inflation and declining investment. The government that came to power on March 1, 1967, had concluded by the end of 1967 that the process of inflation had developed to a stage at which it was no longer susceptible to control by purely fiscal and monetary restraints. This forced the government to take unprecedented action in the form of direct controls over wages and prices that were imposed in mid-1968. The adoption of severe stabilization measures in 1968 halted the wage-price spiral (see ch. 20, Labor Relations and Organization; ch. 22, Finance).

In 1969 the GNP rose by 5.3 percent in real terms or by 4 percent per person, the largest rate of increase recorded in sixteen years. Exports of goods and services, including foreign exchange earnings from tourism, grew by 12 percent in 1969, after an increase of 13 percent in 1968, and exceeded the equivalent of US$200 million for the first time since 1956. The country's net international reserves in gold and foreign exchange as of the end of March 1970 exceeded US$90 million for the first time since 1961. Agricultural and livestock production increased by 15 percent in 1969, and industrial production rose by 5 percent following similar increases recorded in 1968.

The government's economic analysts, in releasing these figures, emphasized that the rates of increases in production recorded in 1969 were based on the extremely low levels of economic activity registered in 1967 and 1968. They pointed out that the GNP in 1969 was below the 1966 level and that the GNP per person in 1969 was 12 percent less than in 1956; expressed in constant United States dollars, the GNP in 1969 was equivalent to US$1.7 billion, and the GNP per person was equivalent to about US$595.

Data through the first five months of 1970 indicated that economic recovery was continuing. Net foreign exchange reserves in May 1970 were US$39 million higher than at the beginning of the year. Tax revenues in the first five months of 1970 were 41 percent higher than for the same period of 1969. The higher level of tax receipts reflected the 9.4-percent increase in domestic prices through May 1970, higher rates of taxes, the increased level of economic activity, and some improvements in tax administration.

The government published in June 1970 a national development plan for the 1971—75 period. The plan recommended that the country work during this period toward an annual rise in real GNP per person of 4 percent, an annual increase in real GNP of 5 percent, and an annual growth in exports of 10 percent. These projections were based on proposed targets for increases in exports of meat and meat derivatives, leather and leather products, all other agricultural products except wool, and miscellaneous exports as well as an estimated 10-percent annual increase in foreign exchange earnings from tourism. The plan stated that the government would propose revised foreign trade policies and administrative, fiscal, and monetary reforms designed to achieve these goals.

The country in 1970 had a mixed economy in which both the public and private sectors participated; through 1970 a wide variety of economic activities was incorporated within the public sector. A large group of special agencies and autonomous entities, both within and alongside the ministries, had come into being. The autonomous entities performed commercial and industrial as well as some traditional functions for the government, through largely autonomous boards of directors. The resulting complexity of the public sector created difficulties in administration (see ch. 19, Industry; ch. 22, Finance).

Partisan political influence and pressures to provide and share public jobs were said to have led to considerable overstaffing of a part-time and poorly paid public service (see ch. 12, The Governmental System; ch. 13, Political Dynamics; ch. 20, Labor Relations and Organization). Control of autonomous public agencies was dispersed among various political subgroups in such a manner that they were operated less efficiently and also independently of any coordinated control (see ch. 13, Political Dynamics; ch. 22, Finance). A complex and uncoordinated system of controls over the activity of the private sector further interfered with incentives to investment and the efficient allocation of resources (see ch. 21, Trade).

The principal decentralized agencies in 1970 were: the National Administration for Fuels, Alcohol and Cement (Administración Nacional de Combustibles, Alcohol y Portland); the State Electric Power and Telephones Administration (Administración General de las Usinas Eléctricas y los Teléfonos del Estado); the Administration of State Railroads (Administración de los Ferrocarriles del Estado); the National Port Administration (Administración Nacional de Puertos); the Uruguayan National Airlines (Primeras Líneas Uruguayas de Navegacíon Aérea—PLUNA); the State Oceanographic and Fishing Service (Servicio Ocenográfico y de Pesca); the Mortgage Bank of Uruguay (Banco Hipotecário del Uruguay); the National Land Settlement Institute (Instituto Nacional de Colonización); and the State Sanitary Works Administration (Administración de Obras Sanitarias del Estado) (see ch. 7, Living Conditions; ch. 18, Agriculture; ch. 21, Trade; ch. 22, Finance).

Another important characteristic of the country's economic institutions was the role of the urban sector. About 50 percent of the population lived in Montevideo, and another 20 percent resided in other cities of over 10,000 persons; this distribution of the population, together with the electoral system of proportional representation, was a basic factor in shaping national economic policies (see ch. 4, Population and Labor Force; ch. 12, The Governmental System; Ch. 13, Political Dynamics).

ECONOMIC TRENDS AND FORCES

The country possessed an exceptionally favorable endowment of resources in relation to its population; this ratio had resulted in the country's attaining one of the highest standards of living in the world's developing nations (see ch. 7, Living Conditions). Through 1968, however, this standard of living had been declining for more than a decade; the economy had in many respects expended its stock of resources accumulated in the past. There was in 1970 a growing recognition that only a drastic reorientation of economic goals and economic behavior could reverse the trend of a deteriorating economic environment.

The framework of economic institutions had considerable influence in making fiscal controls and administration relatively ineffective. The Ministry of Economy and Finance had not had the necessary authority to control the financial operations of a large and important proportion of the public sector located in the autonomous agencies (see ch. 22, Finance). The government found the tax system seriously deficient. Despite the general preoccupation with public welfare, successive governments had been unable to levy direct and progressive taxes to an appropriate extent. Among the reasons for this situation were the concentration on public expenditure rather than taxation as a means of redistribution of income, tax administration publicly described by the government as inefficient, and the widespread use of taxes on exports of animal products that were borne directly by the landowning group (see ch. 18, Agriculture; ch. 22, Finance).

The resulting system of taxes was inflexible in response to changes in money income. The tendency, furthermore, to obtain increases in revenue through the enactment of new taxes, rather than through raising existing taxes or through improvements in tax administration, had resulted in a superfluity of taxes. One tax, moreover, was often superimposed on another; wool, for example, bore twenty-three different taxes.

Efficiency in the utilization of tax revenues was further substantially curtailed by the partial or total earmarking, or identification, of the proceeds of many taxes for specific public expenditures. Such earmarked taxes amounted on the average to more than 20 percent of regular tax revenues (see ch. 22, Finance).

The export taxes were levied on the main export commodities—meat, wool, and hides (see ch. 21, Trade). These taxes were easily administered and were relatively adjustable to expanding needs for revenue. They were used as the main fiscal device to meet short-term fiscal crises. An important restriction on the flexibility of these taxes was their interrelationship with the foreign exchange rate (see ch. 21, Trade; ch. 22, Finance). With inflation forcing costs to rise, maintenance of the rates of export taxes at constant levels would have required periodic adjustment of the foreign exchange rate. The rates of export taxes had in fact varied widely with several massive but irregularly timed devaluations of the currency through April 1968 (see ch. 22, Finance).

Consumption by the public sector had remained for twenty-five years relatively constant at approximately 12 percent of the GNP.

The disposition to maintain public consumption despite declining levels of revenue had brought public savings to very low levels, which through the 1960's averaged less than 1 percent of the GNP. The magnitude of public investment had as a result been severely constrained. Moreover, the distribution of investment resources in the public sector had been made without systematic examination of economic priorities. A mechanism for the planning of public investment by means of which the activities of the government and of autonomous agencies could be made consistent with broad objectives of national economic policy was absent; decisions on public investment were therefore made primarily for short-term political reasons, often with a predominantly urban orientation (see ch. 22, Finance).

Investment had been concentrated in a domestically oriented expansion in manufacturing, encouraged by a very high level of protective tariffs, import surcharges, and a generous policy of tax exemptions (see ch. 19, Industry; ch. 21, Trade). Consequently, there existed in 1970 a high-cost manufacturing sector characterized by a large number of small firms, inefficient management, and a considerable amount of excess capacity. Imports of consumer goods had been reduced in volume by this policy, but they were replaced to a sizeable extent by a heavy dependence on imports of intermediate goods and replacements of capital goods (see ch. 21, Trade),

The country's livestock sector, which traditionally had been the main source of exports, was neglected. Rural development policies were concentrated on crops rather than on pasture improvement and livestock (see ch. 18, Agriculture). Government policies tended to constitute deterrents to cattle producers. The practice of levying relatively high export taxes on traditional livestock products depressed profit margins and effectively maintained the livestock sector as an extractive industry utilizing the natural pastures extensively (see ch. 18, Agriculture; ch. 21, Trade).

During the 1960's the country's GNP grew by only 0.2 percent annually, but the GNP per person declined by 1 percent annually. The rate of fixed investment declined to 13 percent of the GNP as compared with an average of 19 percent in the previous ten-year period. Flight of capital from the country and inadequate fiscal policies reduced the availability of domestic savings, and the net inflow of foreign capital declined sharply. The flight of capital became especially great in the mid-1960's, reaching an annual average level of the equivalent of approximately US$50 million during the 1962—65 period. Imports were reduced from an average level of 19 percent of GNP to 14 percent of GNP. The net foreign exchange reserves of the banking system declined from a peak level of the equivalent of more than US$300 million at the end of 1953 to a debit balance of the equivalent of US$92 million at the end of 1965 (see ch. 21, Trade; ch. 22, Finance).

The annual increases in the price level began to accelerate during the 1960's. With the increased pace of the inflation, the inflexibility of regular tax revenues in responding to changes in nominal income, and the rigidity of real consumption by the public sector, the government tended to become increasingly dependent on export taxes. The outcome was a great decrease of investment in the livestock sector, except for participants in the pasture-improvement program financed by loans from the International Bank for Reconstruction and Development (see ch. 18, Agriculture; ch. 21, Trade).

The instability of the economy reached acute proportions in 1965. The situation temporarily eased in 1966 when the government was able to avoid an increase in civil service salaries and wages because of a constitutional prohibition of such increases in election years. In 1967, however, the government's fiscal deficit soared to 3 percent of the GNP, and the pace of the increase in the domestic price level rose to 135 percent (see ch. 12, The Governmental System; ch. 22, Finance).

The government in power in mid-1970 had faced short-term fiscal and balance-of-payments crises from the onset of its assumption of office on March 1, 1967. The granting of a 90-percent increase in the wages of public sector employees by the outgoing government, retroactive to the beginning of 1967, was not accompanied by creation of adequate new sources of regular tax revenues or by a devaluation of the foreign exchange rate, which would have permitted an increase in export taxes (see ch. 21, Trade; ch. 22, Finance). This led to substantial recourse to Central Bank (Banco Central) financing of the government's fiscal deficit in 1967, and the rate of inflation accelerated.

A substantial flight of capital from the country had exhausted the meager foreign exchange reserves of the Central Bank. The foreign exchange market was closed in July 1967, and stringent import controls were introduced, including complete prohibitions of the importation of major categories of goods. On November 6, 1967, the peso (for value of the peso, see Glossary) was devalued by more than 100 percent from 90 pesos per US$1 to 200 pesos per US$1. After this devaluation there was a substantial return of capital to the country.

Late in 1967 the government imposed tight fiscal and monetary restrictions. The rate of inflation in the first six months of 1968, nevertheless, was as high as in the last six months of 1967, resulting in an increase in the price level over these twelve months of 183 percent (see ch. 22, Finance). On April 29, 1968, the government was forced to devalue the peso by another 25 percent from 200 pesos per US$1 to 250 pesos per US$1. Effective June 26, 1968, the government instituted direct controls on wages and prices (see ch. 20, Labor Relations and Organization; ch. 22, Finance). The increase in prices during the last six months of 1968 was restrained to 1.5 percent.

These measures created a short-term equilibrium; they did not, however, by themselves attack the underlying factors responsible for the prevailing inflation and stagnation. The government was able in 1968, however, to reduce its subsidy payments and payments to the decentralized autonomous agencies. An important element in this reduction was the limitation by the Ministry of Economy and Finance of the automatic transfer of certain earmarked, or assigned, revenues to other government agencies; this transfer accounted for more than half of the total subsidy payments by the national government. By retaining certain revenues formerly transferred automatically, the national government succeeded in reducing the ratio of earmarked revenues to total regular revenues from 26 percent in 1967 to 14 percent in 1968 (see ch. 22, Finance).

In 1968 the government succeeded in reversing the trend of increasing fiscal deficits through a series of stabilization measures more stringent than those applied in the past. Returns from the export taxes were increased by more than 300 percent in nominal terms; these taxes constituted 19 percent of total tax revenues in 1968 as compared with 11 percent in 1967.

One effect of the increasing pressure of fiscal problems was a substantial reduction in the burden of the social security system on the national economy (see ch. 7, Living Conditions). This had been accomplished by gradually reducing the real value of annuity payments. Annual adjustments in nominal annuity values had been kept less than proportionate to the corresponding increases in the cost of living, and in 1968 the annual adjustment was suspended entirely (see ch. 7, Living Conditions).

Expansion of credit to the private sector by the monetary authorities tended to be limited to the amount remaining after the needs of the public sector and payments on the foreign debt were satisfied. The stock of credit outstanding with the private sector had declined from 30 percent of the GNP as of December 31, 1963, to 11 percent of the GNP as of December 31, 1968 (see ch. 22, Finance).

After the substantial improvement in monetary performance achieved in 1968, the government adopted a 1969 budget designed to contain deficit financing by the monetary authorities to 4.4 billion pesos; in mid-1970 estimates put the deficit in a range between 6.5 billion and 10 billion pesos. The monetary authorites responded to this situation by intensifying their efforts to control the credit operations of the commercial banks and by cutting to a minimum the expansion of credit to the private sector (see ch. 22, Finance).

NATIONAL DEVELOPMENT PLAN, 1971–75

On June 4, 1970, the director of the National Office of Planning and Budget (Oficina de Planeamiento y Presupuesto) delivered to the president of the Republic a national development plan for the 1971–75 period entitled Strategy for Development (Una Estrategia para el Desarrollo). The plan contained a brief survey of the status of the economy as of mid-1970, a diagnosis of the country's basic economic problems, broad outlines of the government's proposals for resolution of these problems, a statement of suggested goals of national economic development, and a catalog of proposed instruments for the effective realization of these goals.

The plan proposed that the country accept the following as economic development goals for the 1971–75 period: an annual increase in exports of 10 percent, an annual rise in the GNP of 5 percent in real terms, and an annual growth in real GNP per person of 4 percent. These objectives were regarded as the most important elements of the plan.

The plan based these projections on assumed structural characteristics of the economy. These characteristics could be comprehended, according to the plan, by a review of the country's economic history during the 1942–68 period. From 1942 through 1950, when the country's economic growth in real terms was almost 6 percent, exports rose by about 9 percent annually, and 22 percent of the GNP was exported. In 1951 the prices of the country's exports had begun to fall on world markets, and during the years 1956–58 the country had entered a period of economic stagnation that persisted through 1968.

The plan stated that the government's development policy was based on two fundamental premises. The first premise was that the country must seek the stimulating force for its economic development in its export sector; this premise arose out of the country's economic history, the special characteristics of the country's economy, the small size of the country, and the evolution of the country's economic relations with other nations. The second premise was that economic development was a process of increasing the productivity of the country's national resources; this premise embodied an economic proposition believed by the framers of the plan to be universally valid.

To achieve the goal of improving the quality of the country's resources and organizing their more efficient use in production, the plan laid down three basic principles: the nation could not guarantee to each individual continuity in the work in which he or she was currently engaged; businessmen could not expect that the government either would guarantee a continuing expansion of their activities or would support inefficient business operations; and the public sector must become more efficient.

The plan noted the importance of earning foreign exchange from the export of goods and from tourism and stated that this factor had been assigned highest priority in the country's long-term economic development policy. The plan warned that the structure of the country's economy in 1970, if unaltered, could keep the country indefinitely in a sort of static equilibrium and that this condition of stagnation must be replaced by an economic structure that would promote economic development.

The plan cited four Latin American countries that had achieved an average annual rate of economic growth of 5 percent through the mid-1960's and noted that the ratio of exports to the GNP in these countries had ranged from 21 percent to 39 percent. The plan asserted that the proposed strategy for development should be based on exploitation of existing and potential opportunities for vigorous growth of the country's exports; it further recommended that in view of the size of the country its economy should be opened to world trade.

The plan set proposed targets for annual increases in the major categories of exports of goods. These were 15 percent for meat and meat derivatives, 16 percent for leather and leather products, 13 percent for all other agricultural products except wool, and 16 percent for miscellaneous exports; the plan estimated that the value of exports of wool and wool textiles during the 1971—75 period would remain constant. Receipts from tourism were expected to increase by 10 percent annually over the 1971—75 period.

For components of the GNP other than exports, the plan projected annual increases of 5 percent in private consumption, 1 percent in public consumption, 11 percent in investment, and 13 percent in imports of goods and services. These estimated movements of the major components of the country's GNP would lead to investment reaching 20 percent of the GNP in 1975, or almost double the 12-percent rate that prevailed during the 1965—69 period.

The instruments for achieving the plan's objectives were divided into two broad categories. The first concerned measures to promote and provide incentives for exports; the major action proposed in this field was the removal of the taxes on exports of meat and wool. The second category consisted of a group of measures designed to increase the productivity of the country's national resources; the measures included proposed reforms of financial institutions, revision of foreign trade policies, and a program to promote greater efficiency in the public sector.

The plan stated that the government would reserve for the public sector activities in which state monopolies already existed, such as electric energy, petroleum refining, and railway transport; that the government would favor the expansion of private investment in sectors, such as fishing and cement, in which there existed efficient private organizations; and that the government planned no public investment in new sectors. The government would continue to treat direct foreign private investment in a nondiscriminatory manner; the government would particularly welcome foreign investment that would increase the country's industrial potential and would represent a significant transfer of technology.

The plan declared that the government would propose to the General Assembly fiscal and monetary reforms aimed at curbing tax evasion, simplifying the tax structure, increasing saving, and strengthening the country as an international monetary center. The government also recommend to the General Assembly enactment of legislative measures necessary for the creation of development banks and financing corporations.

In the field of foreign trade policy, the plan called attention to the projected increase in imports during the 1971—75 period and asked that imports be regarded as a contribution to the country's economic development rather than as a necessary evil, as had been the attitude taken in the past. The plan stated that the government intended to reduce most of the import surcharges that had been imposed to protect domestic industry.

The plan pointed out that a substantial portion of the nation's savings was channeled into investment through the public sector and that an increase in national productivity would be achieved in relation to the extent that the allocation of resources via this means became more efficient. The plan established standards for the control and evaluation of the national government's budget and announced administrative reforms designed to increase efficient implementation of the budget.

An appendix to the plan discussed the government's policy on incomes and wages. The appendix stated that the government was formulating a transitional three-year policy to become effective January 1, 1972, and that the government would continue to rely until that date on the mechanism of the Commission on Productivity, Prices and Incomes (Comisión de Productividad, Precios e Ingresos), established by Law No. 13,720 of December 16, 1968.

CHAPTER 18

AGRICULTURE

In 1970 agriculture provided about 15 percent of the gross national product (GNP) and employed about 18 percent of the labor force. Agricultural products accounted for between 80 and 90 percent of the total value of the country's exports. The country's economy continued to be based on agriculture, particularly livestock. About 70 percent of the land area was devoted to raising livestock, accounting for more than two-thirds of the total agricultural production of the country; crop farming, however, had increased in importance in the 1960's. Estimates for 1970 placed the number of sheep at about 20 million and cattle at slightly more than 8 milllion. The livestock population had been relatively static since around 1920, productivity being below optimum levels, since ranchers had been slow to adopt modern methods of production. Around 3 percent of the land area is natural woods and forests; timber resources are limited (see ch. 2, Physical Environment). Considerable fish reserves are accessible to the country, and exports on a small scale began in 1969.

The stagnation in the agricultural sector that has prevailed since 1950 was traceable chiefly to the unfavorable prices received by producers of major farm products. The foreign exchange and export-tax policies pursued by the government through 1967 had discouraged productive investment in agriculture. The 1965—74 National Economic and Social Development Plan (Plan Nacional de Desarrollo Económico y Social de la República Oriental del Uruguay, 1965—74) proposed major policy and administrative reforms to improve agricultural conditions.

In 1970 agriculture was still based for the most part on extensive production methods. Unit yields for crops and livestock were low, reflecting the failure to apply modern techniques on a broad scale. Programs for the agricultural sector proposed by the government aimed at raising yields and emphasized expanded production and research services, supervised credit, land reform, and product and input prices that would provide an incentive to increase production. A tax on the minimum output that could be required from farms was enacted in late 1968; during a three-year transition period, this tax would gradually replace the previous levies on foreign trade in agricultural products (see ch. 22, Finance). A pasture improvement program initiated in 1960 had been successful in demonstrating the profitability of improving pastures and modernizing the care and management of cattle and was being extended in 1970.

LAND USE AND DEVELOPMENT

Ninety percent of the country's total land area was classified as agricultural land, according to government publications issued in 1967. These gave the total area devoted to agriculture as almost 42 million acres, of which over 36 million acres were classified as arable pasture or permanent grassland. Slightly more than 3 million acres were planted for harvest. The balance of the country's agricultural land was classified either as natural woods and forests or as other land in farms. Grains for human consumption and cattle fattening occupied most of the area planted to crops for harvest. The government's plans for development of the agricultural sector through 1974 called for the area in crops for harvest to increase, with a corresponding decline in the area devoted to pasture, and for the remaining area in pastures to be improved.

The government estimated in projections published in 1967 that there existed in the country a potentially arable area of somewhat over 8 million acres, assuming that recommended agrarian reform measures were adopted and that the soils were also managed so as to protect them from erosion and improve their natural fertility. The potentially arable area was below the estimated maximum cultivable area, projected at from 13 million to over 16 million acres. This maximum cultivable area, according to the government's agricultural planners, should be used in rotation between crops and pasture, so that in any one year the maximum area that could be devoted to annual crops would total between 7 million and 10 million acres, or approximately 17 to 23 percent of the country's agricultural land.

The principal production areas for wheat and corn are in the south and west, extending roughly along the southern littoral from the department of Maldonado through the department of Colonia and from there northward along the flood plain of the Río Uruguay through the department of Salto. In the case of the sugar and oil crops, the production areas are concentrated along the Río Uruguay, the single exception being an area devoted to sugar beets extending from the seacoast of the department of Canelones northward into the departments of Florida and Lavalleja. Most of the country's rice is grown under irrigation in the Laguna Merín basin (see ch. 2, Physical Environment).

Cattle are evenly distributed throughout the country, but the dairy breeds are heavily concentrated in the south. Sheep are not raised on small farms in the extreme west and southwest; they are, however, widely distributed elsewhere.

The single land improvement program being carried out in 1970 was a pasture improvement plan initiated ten years earlier with financing provided by a loan from the International Bank for Reconstruction and Development (World Bank) and expanded in 1964. Under this program some 1,400 ranches serve as demonstration points from which knowledge and experience in modern pasture production would spread throughout the farming community. Ranchers participating in the demonstration program were expected to follow the government's recommendations. These were that each ranch be subdivided into some twelve to fifteen fenced and watered paddocks, that a fodder reserve be established for feeding animals in seasons of slow growth of grass, and that an agreed percentage of the ranch's pasture be improved by application of fertilizers and planting of better grasses. These ranchers received loans to help finance the improvements and technical assistance and supervision from qualified technicians.

The Honorary Commission on the Livestock Plan (Comisión Honoraria del Plan Agropecuario) had technical responsibility for the pasture improvement program. The commission and its experts, including advisers from New Zealand and Australia, had tried different methods of pasture improvement and through 1970 had achieved notable success. In addition to the conventional plowing of pastures before seeding and fertilizing, the commission had tried implanting legumes and fertilizer in the existing grass cover by means of a special machine; this method is known as sod seeding. The commission had also experimented with oversowing, that is, dropping pellets of seed and fertilizer on the ground either by topdressing equipment or from airplanes. By the mid 1960's the commission had determined which method should be used in the different parts of the country and had also accumulated information about the legumes and grasses best suited to the country's agricultural conditions.

In response to widespread demand for extension of the pasture improvement program, the government requested and obtained an additional loan from the World Bank in 1965 (see ch. 21, Trade). The loan was used to include an additional 2,600 ranchers in the pasture improvement program and also provided financing for the importation of such production essentials as livestock, seeds, fertilizer, subdivisional fencing, corrals, and machinery for an additional 1,000 ranchers who would prepare ranch-development plans with the aid of the Honorary Commission on the Livestock Plan but would arrange their own local financing. These 3,600 ranchers were expected by 1970 to have started improving about 1 million acres of pasture.

The pasture improvement program had aroused the interest of landowners in the direct management of their land. They had found that full use of new pasture-management opportunities required a considerable amount of daily close supervision and important decisions that could only be handled by owners themselves or by highly qualified managers. This realization reportedly had led a number of participating ranchers to live on their properties or to spend much more time on them than previously, to take personal charge of the pasture improvement program. In contrast, the refusal of a group of landowners to utilize the new techniques, had induced the Honorary Commission on the Livestock Plan to advocate fiscal measures that would penalize underutilization of grazing lands.

LAND TENURE

About 50 percent of the country's agricultural land in 1970 was operated under contractual arrangements of some type, including cash rentals, sharecropping, and various mixed forms. Tenure classes included owner-operator, renter, sharecropper, owner-renter, and all other forms of tenancy. The category of all other forms of tenancy includes mixed tenancy arrangements, such as owner-sharecropper and renter-sharecropper, which includes squatters.

Law No. 12,100 of April 27, 1954, as modified by Law 12,116 of July 2, 1954, remained in 1970 the basic legislation covering contractual land tenure. The laws recognized the right of every rural producer to a minimum period of stability on the land occupied and to determine the work to be performed. The legislation regulates in detail the periods for leases or sharecropping, dispossession, amount of rent, improvements, and limitations on areas leased. Law No. 12,100 provides for a minimum contract of five years, with an additional three-year extension at the request of the tenant. The landlord may oppose this three-year extension if he or his immediate family wishes to operate the land directly for a period of at least two years. Even if the landlord does not oppose the extension, the law provides that the renter must bring his request for extension before the local judiciary six months before the expiration of his contract. Subsequent to the promulation of Law No. 12,100, there have been periodic temporary extensions by the government of the expiration dates of rental contracts. Such governmental actions have lengthened the contractual protection of most tenants.

Also provided under Law No. 12,100 is the requirement that the landlord provide certain basic improvements on the land, such as fencing, sheds, housing for the renter and his family, and a potable water supply. If the landlord does not comply with these obligations, the renter is legally entitled to make these improvements, and the landlord must reimburse him up to a maximum amount of 20 percent of the fiscal value of the holding. The renter may, however, exercise this prerogative only once during his tenancy, regardless of the time period involved.

Rental prices are negotiated between the two contracting parties and are subject to renegotiation every two years. If the two parties cannot agree, the renegotiation is taken to court; if the court raises the rent by more than 30 percent, the tenant is free to break his contract.

Governmental data available in 1970 indicated a tendency toward reduction in the number of rental agreements and consequently a trend toward more extensive production practices as contracts expired and were not renewed. The data further suggested that landowners had moved to increased direct management, increased use of idle lands, or a combination of the two.

There was evidence in 1970 that in some cases landlords had abandoned the use of written contracts while continuing the rental agreements. Under the provisions of Law No. 12,100, such action was punishable by a fine equal to one year's rent, this fine to be paid by the landlord to the renter. The law also provided a legal procedure, however, whereby the landlord might rent the use of his pastureland for less than one year, including extensions of the original agreement, without a written contract. The possibility existed in 1970 that this procedure was being used as an alternative to longer term written contracts in the presence of the risk and uncertainty of inflation (see ch. 22, Finance).

In 1970 a small number of large farms and a large number of small ones continued to characterize the country's farmholdings. The latest available data indicated that of farms larger than 2½ acres, 4.9 percent had 2,500 acres or more each and comprised some 62.4 percent of all land in farms. At the other extreme, almost 30 percent of the counted farms had less than 25 acres and made up only 0.7 percent of the total farm area.

Landownership was in 1970 more highly concentrated than farm sizes would suggest. Many landowners possessed two or more farms, which might be operated separately or subdivided for renting as farm units or parts of farm units. Increasing numbers of landowners had been incorporating their properties, largely into personal or family agricultural societies, to benefit from the tax exemptions and privileges granted such societies and to prevent the division of landholdings through inheritance. The most recent data available in 1970 indicated that almost two-thirds of the country's agricultural land was controlled by only 3,000 enterprises.

AGRICULTURAL PRODUCTION

Livestock Production

The country's farming is concentrated on the production of cattle for meat and milk and of sheep for wool. In the late 1960's livestock products accounted for more than two-thirds of the value of agricultural output and nearly nine-tenths of the value of agricultural exports. Wool was produced mostly, and beef partly, for export.

Wool

The latest available estimate in 1970 of the number of sheep was 19.7 million head. Sheep breeds have shifted from an earlier predominance of Lincoln, Merino, and Romney Marsh to the Corriedale, in accordance with a continuing trend toward breeds that produce good meat as well as wool. The quality of the stock had been well maintained on the larger ranches, but little attention has been paid on the smaller farms to culling out inferior animals. Wool production in 1970 was expected to be 75,000 metric tons. There appeared to be a declining interest among ranchers in sheep raising, mainly because of the high costs of production, high taxes, and low prices obtained for wool in the local market. Other reasons for the expected low production were the dry weather during the first four months of 1969 and the poorer health condition of the flocks resulting partly from the higher costs of pesticides.

Of the total value of livestock products, wool has generally contributed about 30 percent. Production of lamb and mutton has been relatively unimportant, accounting for only about 5 percent of the total value of livestock production.

Beef

Beef, including veal, accounted in the late 1960's for about four-fifths of the red meat produced in the country. Beef was also far in the lead among the red meats consumed and exported. The number of cattle in the country was estimated in 1970 at about 8.5 million head. Production of beef and veal during 1970 was projected at about 275,000 metric tons. The value of output of beef and veal has generally been about 40 percent of the total value of all livestock products, making beef and veal the most important products within the livestock group. Production of beef had remained almost constant for thirty-five years through 1970, the index of beef production in 1970 being only 4 percent above the 1935—40 base figure of 100.

Total per person consumption of red meats during calendar year 1969 amounted to about 213 pounds, a slight reduction from the total per person consumption of 252 pounds recorded in 1968. Higher prices of meat in the local markets, because of the strike of refrigerator plant workers, and government action curtailing beef consumption and cattle slaughter for local consumption had been the main reasons for the decrease (see ch. 20, Labor Relations and Organization). In 1969 the government prohibited the slaughter of beef cattle for domestic consumption for a one-month period, from September 15 to October 15; domestic sales of beef were also banned during this period. The measure was adopted because of a shortage of finished cattle and the government's desire to conserve the available supply for export. Before the prohibitive action, domestic sales of beef had been banned for three days a week.

Beef consumed in urban centers other than Montevideo and in rural areas comes mainly from municipal slaughterhouses. Slaughter of cattle on farms is restricted by the moderate climate prevailing most of the year; the beef is eaten at once or preserved by drying it in the open.

Most of the cattle are beef breeds. The Hereford predominates, accounting for more than half of all cattle in the late 1960's; Shorthorn and Aberdeen Angus are also important beef breeds. The latest available data in 1970 indicated that dairy breeds made up only 7 percent of all cattle. Crossbreeds are numerous and include crosses with the wild cattle of colonial days (see ch. 3, Historical Setting). Imports of the best animals available have resulted in good foundation stock.

Milk

Commercial production of milk averaged 798 million quarts annually in the mid-1960's; commercial output accounted for more than two-thirds of the milk produced. Commercial production was estimated by the Milk Producers' Cooperative (Cooperativa Nacional de Producción de Leche), a government agency established in 1935. The cooperative has the exclusive right to provide milk for Montevideo, and more than a fifth of the nearly 10,000 commercial dairy farms send their milk to the cooperative to supply the fluid milk sold in the national capital. Prices are fixed at farm, wholesale, and retail levels. Members of the cooperative have a daily sales quota for which they receive the fixed price. Milk sent in excess of the quota and used mostly for manufacture brings lower prices. Fluid milk sold in the capital is pasteurized (see ch. 7, Living Conditions).

Some milk plants in the interior also buy from producers on a quota basis; others buy on the basis of quality and butterfat content. Producers may sell raw milk to retailers for direct distribution to consumers, as well as to milk plants for pasteurization (see ch. 21, Trade). Producers also make a substantial part of their milk into butter and cheese. Commercial output of dairy products in 1967 included 2,100 metric tons of butter, 3,200 metric tons of cheese, and 2,500 metric tons of canned milk.

Other Products

Hides, skins, and tallow are the most important livestock byproducts. Production of tallow, used largely in the domestic soap and shortening industries, averaged about 24,000 metric tons annually in the mid-1960's (see ch. 19, Industry). Hides and skins were also important export items (see ch. 21, Trade). Output depended on the commercial slaughter of animals. Annual average production in the mid 1960's included almost 1.5 million cattle hides and calf skins and 3.1 million sheep and lamb skins.

Output of both eggs and poultry increased substantially in the 1960's. Annual average production was about 360 million eggs and nearly 6,000 metric tons of poultry meat.

Crop Production

Among crops produced in the country, the cereal grains have been the most important, both in total value contributed and in area devoted to their production. Data available in 1970 indicated that approximately 62 percent of the cultivated acreage was sown to cereal grains. Through 1970 cereals had consistently contributed from 30 to 60 percent of total crop value. The cereal group is composed of wheat, corn, oats, barley, rye, and rice. The second most important crop grouping has been the oil crops, consisting of sunflower, oil flax, and peanuts. The sugar crops are beets and cane.

Wheat

The country's major staple food grain, wheat, has led among harvested crops in area sown. In 1970 the estimated total area sown was 336,000 acres, and output was expected to be 403,000 metric tons. The country was expected to be self-sufficient in production and consumption of wheat in 1970.

Output of wheat had declined in the early 1960's because former high-cost producers had abandoned wheat growing as a result of the less remunerative prices maintained by the government in those years compared with the prices of previous years. Since 1963 the system of guaranteed minimum prices for wheat instituted in 1945 had been supplemented by a government loan program designed to encourage the use of better production techniques. Loans were made to wheat farmers for operating expenses, such as seed, fertilizer, pesticides, and harvesting. Improved production techniques for wheat were also emphasized in the 1965—74 development plan. The government believed that unit yields could be raised substantially and costs lowered sufficiently to permit the country's wheat to compete successfully on world markets (see ch. 21, Trade).

Wheat is grown mostly in the south and west on farms of over 250 acres. In the late 1960's an estimated 15 percent of the wheat seeded was of recommended varieties of certified seed produced at the country's major agricultural research station maintained by the

Ministry of Livestock and Agriculture. Preliminary fertilizer recommendations have been developed for wheat, and government policy had encouraged the use of fertilizer on wheat in the 1960's; in the late 1960's an estimated 16 percent of the country's wheat was fertilized.

In 1970 production of wheat appeared to be highly mechanized. Bulk handling of the harvest was not widely practiced, however, and a large percentage of the grain went to the market in bags. Harvesting took place from November through February almost everywhere by combine; bulk transport from the field, introduced in the mid-1960's, had begun to spread in the departments of Colonia and Soriano.

Rice

Rice is a major export crop and is second only to wheat as a food crop. Both output and exports of rice have tended to increase since 1960; estimates for 1970 projected a production of somewhat over 96,000 metric tons of rice, equivalent to a little over 64,000 metric tons of milled rice. The 1970 output was expected to be produced on over 87,000 acres. Commercial production of rice was in 1970 relatively new. Through 1960 the government prohibited imports of rice, except for seed, and controlled producer prices. Since 1960 prices have been fixed between the small, independent ricegrowers and the large rice mills, which own and operate large farms, extend production credit to independent growers, and buy nearly all their output.

Most rice is produced by independent growers who rent medium-sized to large farms. Growers usually cultivate the land for three years and then move to new and more fertile fields. On large, owner-operated farms, rice is rotated with pasture to rebuild fertility of the soil and to eradicate weeds. Rice is planted in November and harvested from March through July, mostly by combine.

Corn

In 1970 corn remained the principal feed concentrate grown in the country. Corn was grown in all parts of the country, but the concentration of growing was heaviest in the south. A large percentage of the corn area was cultivated by small holders for on-the-farm use. There were few large commercial growers of corn, although the crop was of major importance in area. Pesticides were seldom used in the production of corn, despite the often serious attacks by insects and the constant problem of weeds. In general, throughout the country the harvesting of corn was not mechanized. In the marketing stage, most grain was transported in burlap bags rather than in bulk.

Production of corn for 1970 was estimated at nearly 186,000 metric tons from approximately 528,000 acres. The country's agricultural planning authorities contemplated in 1970 that corn for feed would ultimately be replaced by grain sorghums, which were considered better suited to the country's climate; their forecasts for 1974 placed corn output at 55,000 metric tons, compared with 149,000 metric tons for grain sorghums.

Other Cereal Grains

The country produces oats, barley, and a little birdseed. Grain sorghums increased in importance during the 1960's, output rising from 1,000 metric tons in 1961 to an estimated total of nearly 59,000 metric tons in 1969 on almost 104,000 acres. Small amounts of rye for food and some barley for malting are also produced. Oats are planted more for forage than for harvest as grain. They rank first in popularity among annual grains sown on arable pasture but in the 1960's gained favor as a feed grain. Output of oats for 1970 was predicted at 60,000 metric tons on about 188,000 acres.

Oil Crops

Flaxseed and sunflower seed follow grains in importance among cultivated crops. Peanuts are grown also but in small quantity. Flaxseed is important in the country's export trade. Exports are chiefly in the form of linseed oil for industrial use, plus cake and meal for livestock feed. Sunflower seed and peanuts are grown almost entirely for the domestic edible-oil market, although a substantial part of the residues from pressing for oil are exported as cake and meal. Oil output from these seeds is usually supplemented by small quantities of imported edible and industrial oils. For 1969, production of sunflower seed was estimated at a little over 65,000 metric tons on 225,000 acres.

Sugar

Both sugar beets and sugarcane are grown in the country, but beets account for more than four-fifths of total sugar output. Production of refined sugar from domestic sources reached a high of 57,000 metric tons in 1969, but imports of raw sugar were expected to reach 59,000 metric tons in the same year; Brazil is the country's principal source of raw sugar (see ch. 21, Trade).

ROLE OF THE GOVERNMENT

Through mid-1970, despite the relative lack of emphasis it had placed on the agricultural sector of the economy, the government had long given some assistance to agriculture in an effort to diversify production and become more self-sufficient. The government protects farmers against competition from foreign producers and establishes support prices or direct subsidies for various crops and livestock products. The government also operates through the National Subsistence and Price Control Council (Consejo Nacional de Subsistencias y Contralor de Precios) to control consumer prices under the authority of Law No. 10,940 of September 19, 1947, which gave the government broad powers to regulate the prices of articles of prime neessity. The council operates its own stores throughout the country and also controls the prices of fruits and vegetables in the daily street markets of Montevideo and other urban centers (see ch. 7, Living Conditions; ch. 21, Trade).

Governmental aid to agriculture in 1970 included not only price support but also some limited programs to improve farming techniques. To finance these programs, a small share of the total taxes collected on agricultural exports in the 1960's had been used largely for fertilizer subsidies and also for better seed, cattle improvement, agricultural research, and the agricultural extension service, which was still at an early stage of development in 1970.

In 1970 the government fixed minimum support prices on grapes, sugar beets, sugarcane, beef, wheat, cotton, and milk. Subsidies were paid to plants slaughtering cattle for export or local consumption, for locally grown cotton, and for reducing the price of fertilizers; the subsidy on fertilizers was administered by the Agricultural Development Plan Commission (Comisión del Plan de Desarrollo Agropecuario) of the Ministry of Livestock and Agriculture.

Under Law No. 12,670 of December 17, 1959, and Law No. 13,048 of April 26, 1962, the government was directed to fix, in relation to the physical volume of goods, an amount in pesos (for value of the peso, see Glossary) to be deducted from the proceeds in domestic currency for exports of wool of all types, linseed and linseed oil, sunflower seed and sunflower oil, peanuts and peanut oil, sunflower seed and sunflower oil, peanuts and peanut oil, wheat and its byproducts, beef of all kinds and prepared in any form, and cattle hides and sheep skins. Prices paid to farm operators for these products had been determined principally by the foreign exchange deductions levied under this legislation. The decline of these prices through 1968 had been caused by the continual increase in these foreign exchange deductions through the successive devaluations of the currency (see ch. 21, Trade; ch. 22, Finance). The primary objective of the imposition of the foreign exchange deductions had been to attract resources needed to finance the national budget; in the second half of 1968 the government adopted a policy designed to promote intensive techniques in agricultural production and, over a period of three years, to enable farmers to achieve a substantial improvement in domestic prices that would be equivalent to those offered in the international market.

Law No. 13,695 of October 30, 1968, established a new tax covering minimum required production of farmland; during a three-year transition period, this law would replace the system of foreign exchange deductions on exports of basic agricultural products. The essential principle of the law is based on the minimum required production per acre for each of the agricultural holdings in the country. The productive capacity of holdings would be determined by a new entity, the National Agro-economic Land Commission (Comisión Nacional de Estudio Agro-económico de la Tierra), taking into account location and types of soil. On a provisional basis and for the 1968—73 period, the law set the average production capacity of the country per acre at about 227 pounds of beef, 44 pounds of mutton, and 29 pounds of wool. This average productivity, valued in terms of average prices, which are fixed by the government for each of the products, determines the basic income of each agricultural operation. The income so determined is subject to a minimum progressive tax rate of 25 percent, with a maximum of 50 percent; the law authorizes deduction by the farm operator of up to 30 percent of the tax for reinvestment. The basic income for each of the agricultural operations in the country is to be obtained by multiplying the minimum required production per acre for each farm by the total number of acres per farm, excluding wooded areas.

Agricultural Research

The Ministry of Livestock and Agriculture maintains in the department of Colonia the country's principal agricultural research and extension center; the center has the formal title of Alberto Boerger Center for Agricultural Studies (Centro de Investigaciones Agricolas Alberto Boerger) but is known as La Estanzuela. The station in 1970 was continuing its work on agricultural production problems, using the combined efforts of specialists in the areas of soils and soil fertility, plant breeding, plant pathology, seed production, pasture improvement, and livestock improvement. The center operated some 3,250 acres of land, complete with livestock buildings and equipment, and had a professional staff of about sixty-five persons.

The ministry also operated the Miguel C. Rubino Veterinary Research Center, known as the Rubino Institute. This center is located in the department of Canelones and was established as a result of the government's concern regarding the problems of animal disease and parasites. The center employed about 130 persons, of which around 45 were assigned to a special hoof-and-mouth disease control program. The staff of the center are mostly members of the

Faculty of Veterinary Medicine of the National University (Facultad de Veterinaria de la Universidad de la Republica) (see ch. 8, Education). Laboratory facilities included a modern hoof-and-mouth disease laboratory, a laboratory for virus study, and a central laboratory for research in microbiology, parasitology, and nutrition deficiencies.

The Faculty of Agriculture of the National University (Facultad de Agronomía de la Universidad de la Republica) had in 1970 about 200 acres of land, of which 160 acres were available for research and the remainder was occupied by buildings and grounds. The Faculty of Agriculture also operated three experimental stations located in Paysandú, Salto, and Cerro Largo. The Faculty of Veterinary Medicine of the National University had a staff of about 160 professional persons. In addition to the Faculty of Agriculture and the Faculty of Veterinary Medicine, there are nineteen agricultural schools at the secondary education level, of which thirteen conduct general agricultural programs and six concentrate on special areas of agriculture; the schools include the dairy industries school at Colonia Suiza, the school of poultry farming in Florida, the farm machinery school in San José, the wine school in Canelones, the forestry school in Maldonado, and the livestock school in Durazno.

Land Resettlement

The official agency in charge of the distribution and management of land owned by the government continued in 1970 to be the National Land Settlement Institute (Instituto Nacional de Colonización). As of December 31, 1969, the number of settlements was 114, covering a total of about 903,000 acres composed of 2,350 farms with an average of 300 acres each. These are located throughout the country except in the departments of Rocha and Montevideo. In 1963 the institute announced a four-year program for distributing 625,000 additional acres to small farmers, of which over 135,000 acres were distributed in 1969.

Agricultural Development

The Decree of January 27, 1960, amended on March 17, 1960, created the Commission for Investment and Economic Development (Comisión de Inversiones y de Desarrollo Económico) which with assistance from the Organization of America States, the Economic Commission for Latin America, and the Inter-American Development Bank, issued in October 1965 a comprehensive national development plan covering the 1965—74 period (see ch. 17, Character and Structure of the Economy). A major portion of this national plan was the agricultural development plan (1965—74), which proposed policy and administrative reforms for agricultural programs. It included general outlines for ten major farm programs: research, extension, certified seed, agrarian reform, farm credit, and programs aimed at raising yields of grains, oilseeds, sugar, wine grapes, and livestock. It contained seven proposals for legislation relating to the agricultural sector; through mid-1970 three of the proposals had been enacted into law. They were: Law No. 13,663 of June 14, 1968, establishing the policy to govern the manufacture, commercial sale, and exports of fertilizer; Law No. 13,664 of June 14, 1968, establishing the policy to control the production, certification, commercial sale, and imports and exports of seeds; and Law No. 13,667 of June 18, 1968, declaring a national interest in soil conservation and reclamation and conservation of surface water and ground water (see ch. 2, Physical Environment).

AGRICULTURAL ECONOMICS

Through 1970 the farmer or rancher with money to invest generally had not elected to invest in the intensification of his current operation; investments in improved technology and in the employment of yield-increasing inputs, such as fertilizer, pesticides, improved seeds, and artificial pastures, had been through mid-1970 quite limited in the country's agriculture. To explain this situation, the argument had been advanced that the large landholders had as a goal a consciously or unconsciously predetermined level of income that would permit the desired standard of living. Given the large expanses of relatively productive land, minimal land taxes, and low labor costs under the prevailing system of operation, this desired level of income had been readily achieved without the need to intensify production through increased productive investment and the use of modern agricultural technology.

Another explanation often cited for the low level of agricultural investment had been that the effects of the government's policy regarding the agricultural sector in the form of export and sales taxes, the manipulation of the multiple foreign exchange system that prevailed until 1960, import taxes, and controlled prices on agricultural products had provided little incentive for widespread adoption of technology that would require investment in fertilizer, machinery, pesticides, and other agricultural inputs.

A third possible explanation was that investment in additional land had been economically attractive and had proved to be an effective protection against inflation (see ch. 22, Finance). Covering the 1940—66 period, data on land prices in nine of the country's nineteen departments tended to support the hypothesis that investors had used land purchases as a hedge against inflation and had sought opportunities to buy land in areas requiring minimal investment in technological inputs and managerial time.

In 1970 the government was engaged in gradually changing from the system of retention of proceeds from exports of agricultural products to a tax system based upon the productive potential of the land. Taxes on the agricultural sector included export, land, transaction (or sales), import, and income taxes (see ch. 22, Finance). The system had been complex and uncoordinated in its objectives and, because of deficiencies in administration and lack of public support, the collection rate had been low. The personal income tax was in 1970 a relatively new introduction into the range of taxes affecting the agricultural sector. Because of multiple allowable deductions and a low presumed productivity of the land, however, this tax still played a very minor role in mid-1970.

CHAPTER 19

INDUSTRY

In 1970 industry supplied about 32 percent of the gross national product (GNP) and employed about 26 percent of the labor force. Light industry was predominant, and the processing of agricultural and animal products accounted for about half of industrial output. From the standpoint of value, the most important products were foodstuffs, beverages and tobacco, textiles, metallurgical and mechanical products, chemicals, and petroleum and coal derivatives. Domestic manufacturers provided about 80 percent of the products sold as consumer goods.

Aside from the wool and meat-processing industries and such auxiliaries of the cattle industry as tanning, most industries were dependent on imported raw materials. This was true of the manufacture of cotton textiles, of metalworking, and of petroleum refining. Other sizable industries were the manufacture of nylon, rayon, and other synthetic fibers and the manufacture of cement. The state was engaged in industrial activities, in some cases as a monopoly and in others in partnership with private companies. State enterprises were important in the output of petroleum, cement, and power; the most important was the National Administration for Fuels, Alcohol and Cement (Administración Nacional de Combustibles, Alcohol y Portland).

The country's lack of coal and oil resources made development of its hydroelectric potential important. Apart from marble and various construction materials, the country's mineral resources were few and undeveloped. There was, however, considerable interest in the country's deposits of iron ore (see ch. 2, Physical Environment).

MANUFACTURING

In 1970 the food, beverages, and tobacco group remained the most economically significant category of manufacturing, contributing about 33 percent of total value added in manufacturing industries; of this total, the meat-processing and dairy products segments accounted for 31 percent (see ch. 18, Agriculture). Next in importance was textiles, with about 17 percent of total value added. Metal products was third, with around 16 percent of total value added by manufacturing. The other major category of manufacturing was the group consisting of chemicals and chemical, petroleum, and coal products, which generated over 12 percent of total value added. The balance of 22 percent of total value added by manufacturing was divided among the other manufacturing categories: clothing and footwear, wood products and furniture, paper and paper products, printing and publishing, leather and leather and fur products, rubber products, nonmetallic mineral products, basic metals, and miscellaneous manufacturing industries.

Another indicator of the relative importance of each category of manufacturing in the industrial complex was the percentage distribution of employment by major groups of manufacturing industries. The food, beverages, and tobacco group was first, with over 21 percent of total employment, closely followed by clothing and footwear with over 19 percent, and metal products with nearly 19 percent. Fourth in importance was textiles with 10 percent of total employment. The wood products and furniture group and the chemicals and chemical, petroleum, and coal products group each had about 8 percent of total employment; the balance of 15 percent was divided among the remaining manufacturing categories.

Meat Processing

In mid-1970 the meat-processing industry was concentrating its attention on modernization. In 1969 there occurred a four-month strike of packinghouse workers because of management's decision to stop supplying each worker about 4.4 pounds of meat each day; a ban by the United Kingdom on imports of meat from the country, effective June 14 of that year, and a shortage of finished cattle that resulted in a prohibition of slaughter from September 15 to October 15 (see ch. 18, Agriculture; ch. 20, Labor Relations and Organization). During the monthlong prohibition of slaughter, 1,800 tons of beef were imported from Argentina to help supply domestic demand and stabilize prices (see ch. 21, Trade). The strike of packing plant workers in the spring and summer of 1969 had closed the larger meatpacking plants. The small plants employed new personnel, continued to operate, and maintained the country's exports of meat.

The meat-processing industry urgently required modernization. The industry comprised three large older plants (built in 1918, 1924, and 1928) and fourteen small plants of more modern construction. All the plants were in 1970 considering remodeling and installation of new equipment. A shortage of financing and the difficulty of importing equipment, however, were handicapping the process of modernization (see ch. 21, Trade; ch. 22, Finance). International lending agencies were in mid-1970 reported to be considering making loans to the industry for modernization and were making broad studies of the possibilities of providing financing.

There were slaughtering and meatpacking plants in Montevideo, Paysandú, Canelones, Fray Bentos, Salto, and Artigas. The capital had four important refrigerator plants, and one large plant was located in Fray Bentos.

Some of the packing plants, primarily the three largest ones, had in mid-1970 been in some difficulties in the livestock market because of their delays in paying farmers for previous purchases (see ch. 18, Agriculture). The government was taking steps to resolve this situation and to avoid similar problems in the future. The government was also working to strengthen the meat inspection service as a move toward getting approval to ship meat to both the United Kingdom and the United States (see ch. 14, Foreign Relations; ch. 21, Trade).

Textiles

In 1970 the country's textile manufacturing group continued to rank as the largest manufacturing segment after meat processing. It was divided into two main manufacturing sections, one comprising those firms working with natural raw materials, such as wool and cotton, and the other consisting of those firms working with man-made materials, such as cellulose, acetate, polymers, polyesters, and other chemical products. The industry as a whole employed 14,000 workers, and about 90 percent of the firms were located in and around Montevideo (see ch. 4, Population and Labor Force). Approximately 450 individual firms operated 3,626 looms (2,505 automatic) and 216,000 spools (89,532 combing spools and 126,468 carding spools). Since most of these firms were very small, 98 percent of the weaving and related functions were performed by medium- and large-sized firms. Five dominant companies operated integrated plants processing greasy wool—the raw wool obtained from live animals and which has not been scoured—into finished products; they also produced cotton and synthetic yarns that were woven into textiles for the domestic market.

The textile manufacturing section working with natural raw materials included a category of firms producing wool tops—combed loose ropes of wool, ready for spinning. This textile manufacturing category consisted of twelve factories that employed 2,200 workers and could produce slightly over 155,000 pounds of output daily. Most of the mills producing wool tops processed raw wool for the export market only, but some prepared wool tops for domestic consumption. Approximately 35 percent, or 28,000 tons, of the country's total output of raw wool was converted into wool tops, the rest being exported in the form of greasy wool, scoured wool, and noils—the short fibers removed during the combing of the wool and spun into yard for cloth.

Technical guidance and financial incentives have been provided by the government to promote the growth of textile manufacturing. Through mid-1970 the major trends registered in textile manufacturing had been toward increased exports of woolen textiles, increased processing of textile materials, and increased blending of natural raw materials with synthetics, mainly polyester. There had been a growing interest among textile producers toward investing their profits outside textile production—in the production of polyfoam and polyurethane goods, for example, and in new activities in the fields of tourism, construction, and services. The country was in 1970 self-sufficient in the production of textiles.

POWER RESOURCES

In 1970 the country's installed electric capacity amounted to 519,059 kilowatts, of which 250,000 kilowatts were thermal, 236,000 kilowatts hydraulic, and 33,059 kilowatts diesel generated. Output of electric power for 1967 was estimated at 1.8 billion kilowatt-hours, of which 1.4 billion originated from thermal sources; this total allowed an annual per person output of 700 kilowatt-hours, well above the Latin American average of 440 kilowatt-hours. The two most important sources were both on the Río Negro: the 128,000 kilowatt Rincón del Bonete hydroelectric station, with four units of 32,000 kilowatts each, and the Rincón del Baygorria station, with three units of 36,000 kilowatts each (see ch. 2, Physical Environment).

The country had in 1970 aerial electric power transmission lines as follows: 824 miles of 150,000 volts, 1,072 miles of 110,000 volts, 120 miles of 60,000 volts, and 293 miles of 30,000 volts. The State Electric Power and Telephones Administration (Administración General de las Usinas Eléctricas y los Teléfonos del Estado), which had a monopoly of public utility electric power and telephone services throughout the country, was expanding the country's electric generating capacity through projects using thermal and diesel generation. The agency was considering the possibility of using peat moss as fuel for the thermal electric power.

Three major hydroelectric projects were being considered by the government. The first was a joint venture between the governments of Argentina and Uruguay to be located at Salto Grande on the Río Uruguay; the project was to be completed before the winter of 1979 under the terms of an agreement signed by the two countries' presidents in July 1968 (see ch. 14, Foreign Relations). In late 1969 the two governments signed a contract with a Canadian consulting firm for a final feasibility study of the Salto Grande hydroelectric project and related works; the Canadian firm was expected to make several important modifications to the original study done in 1963 by a French firm. The project was estimated to cost the equivalent of US$400 million.

The second hydroelectric project under consideration in 1970 was the large Palmar hydroelectric complex on the Río Negro; the government announced a call for bids on this project on November 14, 1969. Through the first quarter of 1970, seventy companies from seventeen countries had submitted bids. The project included six generator-turbines of seventy-five-megawatt capacity each, of which four would be installed in the first stage of operation. The complex would include, in addition to the powerplant, a spillway dam with ten sluice gates, a highway bridge, and two substations in Palmar and Montevideo. The project was estimated to cost the equivalent of about US$150 million and would approximately double the country's installed electric capacity.

The third project is the Laguna Merín hydroelectric project on the border with Brazil (see ch. 2, Physical Environment). The mixed Uruguayan-Brazilian commission responsible for its development in the third quarter of 1969 invited bids for the construction of a dam on the Río Olimar Grande to irrigate 97,500 acres for ricegrowing (see ch. 18, Agriculture). The associated hydroelectric station was expected to have a capacity of 14,000 kilowatts; construction was expected to begin in the early 1970's and take two years. The government hoped to finance the cost of the equivalent of US$21.5 million, which included outlays for irrigation, by assistance from the Inter-American Development Bank (see ch. 22, Finance).

Crude oil was imported and refined at the refinery operated by the National Administration for Fuels, Alcohol and Cement in Montevideo, which had a capacity of about 2 million gallons daily. In 1967 the refinery processed slightly over 482 million gallons of crude oil; almost half of the output was fuel oil, and about 20 percent was automotive fuel. The refinery also produced turpentine, plus crude oil derivatives, such as kerosine, diesel oil, and miscellaneous petroleum products. These included liquified petroleum gas that was manufactured, bottled, and distributed by the National Administration for Fuels, Alcohol and Cement. Since the introduction of liquefied petroleum gas in 1958, demand had exceeded the supply that the national agency had been able to provide. Bottled gas was available both in Montevideo and, in more limited amounts, elsewhere in the country. Through the first half of 1969 piped gas produced from coal and coke by the privately owned Montevideo Gas and Dry Dock Company (Compania del Gas y Dique Seco de Montevideo) had been available only in Montevideo, but in the third quarter of 1969 the company was forced into liquidation, reportedly because it had not been permitted to raise rates to cover rising costs.

On May 28, 1968, because of the interest that had developed in possible offshore petroleum deposits, the president approved a decree regulating the exploration and exploitation of hydrocarbon fields. The decree stated that full rights to offshore deposits of liquid hydrocarbons, combustible gases, solid fossil fuel, and bituminous rocks belonged to the state and could be exploited only by the state and only through the National Administration for Fuels, Alcohol and Cement. The Ministry of Commerce and Industry could authorize geological and geophysical topographic studies; the authorization would be valid for only a one-year period and would generate no rights with respect to later exploration and exploitation. Public invitations were issued in December 1968 for foreign firms to bid on offshore petroleum exploration and in January 1969 for the development of mineral deposits along the coast; the projects signified changes in official policy, authorizing foreign companies to seek petroleum in the country's coastal waters and allowing a government entity to form a joint venture with foreign organizations.

Two United States firms responded to the invitation to bid on offshore petroleum exploration; the government rejected their bids as unsatisfactory. The government, nevertheless, remained resolved to develop whatever offshore petroleum existed and rearranged its exploration program into three distinct stages. In September 1969 a new public invitation was issued for a six-month geophysical survey and, in the second quarter of 1970, the government was planning to award the contract to perform the survey. After completion of the geophysical survey, public invitations for bids for the subsequent phases of exploration and extraction would be issued.

In January 1969 the president issued a decree authorizing the construction of an oil terminal on the country's eastern coast. The project was designed to allow large supertankers to deliver crude oil to the country. Because the port of Montevideo was too small and congested to handle such traffic, smaller, older tankers had to be employed with resulting high freight costs. A preliminary study on the proposed terminal was completed in March 1969; the study focused much of its attention on the choice of a site and the installation of a floating terminal. Four locations along the coast in the department of Rocha were considered. The terminal would consist of a large buoy, technically referred to as a singe-point mooring, that would receive crude oil from 100,000-ton supertankers and transfer the oil through floating hoselines to a tank farm on shore.

A British petroleum company was awarded in 1969 a contract to supply the equivalent of US$50 million in crude oil to the country during the 1970—74 period, with an option to supply the country's needs for crude oil for an additional year. The contract included a provision for a loan equivalent to US$7 million to the National

Administration for Fuels, Alcohol and Cement for the improvement of docks and other facilities for handling oil tankers.

MINING

Production from the mineral sector made up less than 1 percent of the GNP in 1970; there had been until the late 1960's a general absence of known deposits of valuable minerals in the country (see ch. 2, Physical Environment). Before 1969 marble, building stone, and gravel had been the only known valuable mineral deposits. In 1970, however, there was considerable interest in possible development of iron ore deposits found in the late 1960's. The deposits at Zapucay in the department of Durazno were believed to contain some 400 million tons with an ore content of over 40 percent. Deposits estimated to contain 100 million tons of 40 percent ore had been found at Valentines on the borderline of the departments of Florida and Treinta y Tres; the initial cost of the development of these was projected at the equivalent of US$17 million. A deposit of uranium had been discovered in local clay along the Río Negro in the department of Durazno, and uranium ore had also been found at Amarillo in the department of Cerro Largo.

The government was in 1970 actively seeking foreign companies to help develop a deposit of about 3 million tons of heavy minerals, including ilmenite, rutile, zircon, and monazite, located on the Atlantic coast at Aguas Dulces, 175 miles northeast of Montevideo in the department of Rocha (see ch. 2, Physical Environment). The composition of the heavy minerals was reported as 60 percent ilmenite, 5 percent zircon, 1 percent rutile, and 0.6 percent monazite. Annual extraction could reportedly reach 70,000 tons of heavy minerals for forty years; an investment of the equivalent of about US$3 million would, according to the government's estimates, realize an annual production of the equivalent of over US$1 million. The government announced in 1969 that participation in the entire process of development of the deposit, from dredging to mineral purification, could be shared with one or more foreign enterprises, the type and extent of activities to be arranged mutually between company representatives and officials of the National Administration for Fuels, Alcohol and Cement.

CONSTRUCTION

In 1970 construction generated about 3.5 percent of the GNP and employed 5 percent of the labor force. Construction output had fallen by 4 percent in 1969 to reach its lowest total in four years; in 1968 output had risen by slightly over 1 percent. Employment in construction had reached about 50,000 persons in 1970 (see ch. 4, Population and Labor Force). Activity in construction had diminished since 1960, measured by the number of dwelling permits issued; in the private sector the total had fallen from 16,000 in 1960 to 13,000 in 1968, or a drop of nearly 19 percent, whereas in the public sector the total had declined from 1,026 in 1960 to 350 in 1968, or a decrease of 66 percent (see ch. 7, Living Conditions). The contribution of construction to the GNP had contracted from 6 percent in 1960 to the 3.5 percent figure registered in 1970; the value of output in construction had shrunk annually by an average of over 3 percent during this period.

ROLE OF GOVERNMENT

In 1970 the government's policies, basic laws, and regulations continued to reflect the system established early in the 1900's by President Batlle y Ordóñez. This system promoted state enterprises. The Constitution of 1967 devotes a separate section to provisions regarding the autonomous entities and decentralized services; the prior Constitution of 1952 had included a similar section with identical wording in some sentences and paragraphs (see ch. 3, Historical Setting; ch. 12, The Governmental System; ch. 16, Political Values and Attitudes).

Law No. 8764 of October 15, 1931, established the National Administration for Fuels, Alcohol and Cement and gave it a state monopoly over activities connected with the alcohol industry and trade and over fuels. An enterprise that is not an autonomous entity or decentralized service but which is governed by public law is the National Packinghouse (Frigorífico Nacional); this enterprise was given a monopoly on the slaughter of beef and mutton for Montevideo under Law No. 8282 of September 6, 1928. This monopoly includes the supply for ships in the port of Montevideo by decrees of June 7 and June 14, 1954. Law No. 4273 of October 21, 1912, gave exclusive rights to the autonomous entity known as the State Electric Power and Telephones Administration to supply electric power to the public; Law. No. 8767 of October 15, 1931, gave exclusive operation of telephone and cable communications to this agency (see ch. 21, Trade).

Article 188 of the 1967 Constitution authorizes the state to participate in industrial enterprises with the free consent of the enterprise and under mutually agreed conditions, provided the General Assembly has approved such participation. A similar provision had been included in the Constitution of 1952. The government has particpated in the Uruguayan Tire Factory (Fábrica Uruguaya de Neumáticos Sociedad Anonima), which produces pneumatic tires, rubber goods, foam plastic, and footwear. In a study to ascertain the country's ten largest industrial firms using the criteria of authorized total capital, actual capital, and number of employees, the

United States embassy found that on an overall basis, this company ranked as the largest industrial firm in the country.

Article 85 of the 1967 Constitution empowers the General Assembly to grant monopolies. In 1970 monopolies established under laws pursuant to this constitutional provision included the National Administration for Fuels, Alcohol and Cement, the National Packinghouse, and the State Electric Power and Telephones Administration.

Article 168 of the 1967 Constitution authorizes the executive to grant industrial privileges according to law (see ch. 12, The Governmental System). An industrial privilege may be granted to new industries when the industry to be established would manifestly benefit the national economy; an industrial privilege grants the right to operate an industry to the exclusion of competitors and may be accompanied by certain tariff protection if this would be advantageous to the national economy (see ch. 21, Trade). The privilege is granted, without extension, to large industries for nine years and to other industries for four years.

In 1970 industrial wages and prices continued to be controlled by the Commission on Productivity, Prices and Incomes (Comisión de Productividad, Precios e Ingresos) established by Law No. 13,720 of December 19, 1968. The commission is composed of nine members—five appointed by the government, two representatives of employers, and two representatives of labor; it was empowered to fix minimum and maximum wages, adjust wage increases governed by industrywide agreements, fix maximum prices for essential goods and services, and act as an arbitrator in labor disputes (see ch. 20, Labor Relations and Organization). Since the government already had substantial price control powers over most essential goods and over salaries of the public sector and had set minimum wages in almost all segments of the economy, the main effect of the legislation was to allow the government to establish a wage policy for the private sector (see ch. 22, Finance). Public-sector employees received an increase of nearly 50 percent in salaries and fringe benefits effective January 1, 1969; employees in the private sector were granted an 8-percent increase in wages in December 1969, and public-sector employees were authorized a 10-percent increase in salaries in January 1970, raises in family allowances being approved in both cases (see ch. 20, Labor Relations and Organization; ch. 22, Finance).

CHAPTER 20

LABOR RELATIONS AND ORGANIZATION

Organized labor in 1970 represented up to one-third of the total labor force of roughly 1 million. It was loosely organized, however, and estimates as to its strength varied substantially. Wages and prices have been under periodically revised controls since 1968 in order to slow the rise in the cost of living and bolster the sagging economy; and other conditions of employment, such as vacations, unemployment insurance, and retirement, were numerous and generous. Accordingly, there was little scope for collective bargaining.

A general decline in the real income of workers that had commenced in the mid-1950's continued until 1969, when a modest upturn was registered. The decline had the effect of encouraging a sharp rise in union membership, an increase in strikes, and a shift to the Left in union ties. In 1970 the dominant central labor organization—like its immediate predecessors in the constantly shifting pattern of organized labor—was affiliated with the Moscow-oriented World Federation of Trade Unions (WFTU).

The early governments paid little attention to legal protection of the interests of working people. This posture changed abruptly in 1903 with the election of José Batlle y Ordóñez as president. A believer in the protection of the working classes, he encouraged the enactment of legislation dignifying and giving rights to labor. Mutual aid societies had existed since the middle of the nineteenth century, but it was under Batlle that the first real federation of labor unions were formed.

Batlle's encouragement and protection of the labor movement became a policy supported by subsequent administrations. Uruguay has been a forerunner in establishing rules that limit the length of the workweek and protect workers with respect to conditions of employment in general.

During the first half of the twentieth century an anarchistic attitude—imported from Europe—resulted in loosely affiliated collections of unions that often changed affiliation from one central group to another. In addition, enactment of so much legislation granting benefits and protection to the working man limited the effectiveness of organized labor and inhibited its early growth.

Because of the abundance of laws and regulations protecting

labor, the strike rather than negotiation has tended to be organized labor's first recourse in the event of a labor dispute. Accordingly, the strike is an instrument to impose pressure on government rather than on management. For this reason, a regular practice is the demonstration general strike. Strikes are traditionally important bargaining weapons.

In the mid-1960's comprehensive minimum wage laws and a variety of fringe wage benefits had been in effect for many years, but the removal of the collegiate executive (*colegiado*—see Glossary) and the continued progress of a runaway inflation in 1967 were followed in 1968 by a partial wage-and-price freeze and the institution of maximum wage limits (see ch. 12, The Governmental System). The immediate response was a spate of strikes, but in late 1969 and early 1970 the rate was lower and, for the first time in many years, real income was rising. The post-1967 government had resorted to severe measures, including the mobilization of some striking worker groups. But at the beginning of 1970 this policy had been accompanied by a modest upturn in the economy and a decline in the rate of inflation.

CONDITIONS OF EMPLOYMENT

Recruitment

The government operates a considerable number of labor exchanges combined with unemployment compensation units for industrial workers. These are agencies associated with various entities of the executive branch. Among the areas of employment served are maintaining sewers and markers in the port of Montevideo, stevedoring at coastal and river ports, wool and hide warehousing, wool washing and sheepskin processing by personnel not on monthly salaries, and glass industry work. A labor exchange system for packinghouse workers and for cattle handlers and receivers in the national livestock market includes a labor pool. The companies may hire personnel directly but must first call upon registered workers. With respect to maritime and port workers in general, employers have limited freedom in selecting registered workers; except for a few in each enterprise, workers are called up strictly in turn.

Recruitment for the civil service and for the twenty-two state corporations is based on examinations that may be written or oral, qualifying or competitive. In the commercial sector, recruitment is by private agency, newspaper advertisement, or word-of-mouth. In the rural areas the superabundance of the labor supply makes hiring a matter of first-come-first-served, although the Artigas sugar-workers' union exercises some control over recruitment practices.

Working Hours, Days of Rest, and Vacations

The basic work schedule calls for a regular working day of not more than eight hours and a six-day week with a maximum of forty-eight regular hours for manual and forty-four for office and professional workers. It does not include administrators, managers, and other executive personnel. Neither does it preclude the holding of two or more jobs. A legal option, seldom exercised, is that five hours of continuous work must be followed by two hours of rest; alternatively, four hours of work by one and a half hours of rest. These options are exercised with progressively less frequency but show that—in principle at least—the traditional noonday siesta continues to exist to a great extent.

The working force, as a general rule, is entitled to twenty working days of paid vacation after the first year of service. Staff members with five or more years of service with the same employer (leave seniority eligibility is not transferable) qualify for one more day of annual vacation with the completion of each four years of unbroken employment. Vacation credits do not accumulate; they must be taken within twelve months after they are earned. A majority of the worker-management agreements stipulate that workers must take these vacations in not more than two uninterrupted periods of a minimum of ten days.

Sunday is a compulsory day of rest, except on special occasions. Saturday in 1970 was still a working day, but the practice of making it a holiday or a half day was becoming customary. Public holidays for which workers are entitled to full pay include January 1, May 1, July 18, August 25, and December 25. In addition, work comes to a virtual stop during the carnival days that immediately precede Lent and during Holy Week (currently called Tourist Week). It is during these periods of general celebration, however, that vacations are most frequently scheduled (see ch. 7, Living Conditions).

There are a number of variants and proposed variants to the pattern. The civil service and public banks work a thirty-hour week, and some public agencies are reported to go on a shortened schedule in summer. According to the system reported in effect in 1970, civil servants were said to be on a 7:00 A.M. to 1:00 P.M. schedule during the summer and a 1:00 P.M. to 7:00 P.M. schedule during the winter. This would be thirty-six-hour schedule but does not take into consideration time off for meals. Working hours in the rural sector depend on seasonal pressures. During the harvest season workers may be employed regularly in the fields twelve hours a day or more. In mid-1970 the mounted police were reported briefly on strike in protest over twelve-hour workdays that had been in effect since the imposition of security measures (see ch. 13, Political Dynamics).

Work of Women and Minors

The country has ratified a majority of the International Labor Organization (ILO) conventions with respect to the employment of women and of minors, and the Constitution of 1967 specifies that the labor of women and minors under the age of eighteen shall be specially regulated and limited.

The employment of minors under the age of fifteen, the general minimum age for employment in industrial and service activities, is not widespread. In exceptional instances, however, they may work after the age of twelve under the supervision of the Children's Council, an autonomous government agency, if they have completed their compulsory education. Children under the age of twelve may not engage in agrarian occupations during the school year. In unhealthful, dangerous, or exceptionally fatiguing work—and in night work except for domestic service—eighteen years is the minimum. In rural areas, however, a young person of sixteen may receive less pay than an adult for equally rigorous work. In theatrical work, employment is permitted ordinarily only for boys over the age of sixteen and girls over eighteen, but employment at earlier ages may be authorized by the Children's Council. The same age minimums, subject to approval by the Children's Council, apply to variety theaters, cabarets, and cafés where entertainment is offered.

Working minors (under the age of eighteen) must present evidence of the completion of the years of elementary education required in the locality in which they live, evidence of physical fitness, and evidence of registration with the Children's Council. The medical examination must be repeated annually until the age of eighteen is reached. Persons under the age of eighteen may not work more than six hours daily and must be given two hours off during the midday period. Exceptions permitting adults to work longer hours than those regularly prescribed are not available to minors. A maximum of four hours daily in manual training is permitted for children under the age of fourteen.

Working children under the age of eighteen have the exclusive right to receive and manage their own wages, without interference from their parents or guardians, and those sixteen years of age or older have the right to present themselves in court on their own behalf in order to force payment of wages. Employers of minors have a special responsibility to provide guidance with respect to regulations and satisfactory working conditions. Failure to meet these obligations is subject to administrative fines and may in some cases be considered a criminal offense.

Female workers are required to discontinue work for a period of six weeks before and six weeks after childbirth. In cases of illness related to pregnancy and certified by a government authority, this period may be extended for the time indicated by the authority. During the nursing period, the mother is entitled to discontinue her work for two daily half-hour periods for nursing purposes. A woman discharged after pregnancy is entitled to six months of wages in addition to normal discharge indemnity.

In general, women may not be employed in the repair or cleaning of dangerous machines or in the use of poisonous, caustic, or otherwise dangerous materials. Where jobs permit, women must be provided with chairs in order that they may sit while at work. The country has subscribed to ILO conventions prohibiting the work of women in mines and limiting female nightwork in industrial enterprises. Beginning in 1945, salary councils were advised by executive order to apply the principle of equal pay for equal work to the two sexes, except that a differential of not more than 20 percent could be established because of differences in productivity or other similar circumstances. In addition, the Constitution of 1967 calls for equal pay for equal work by men and women.

Wages

In addition to the regular wage, all employees are entitled to receive a Christmas bonus equal to one-twelfth of their earnings for the year ending November 30. Family allowance contributions are payable by employers, usually at the rate of 8.5 percent of the total payroll, and by workers at 0.5 percent of their individual earnings. Payment to farmworkers is 11 percent of the aggregate wage plus a food and housing allowance. Employers are responsible for work-incurred injuries and illnesses and must carry insurance to cover the loss of earnings as well as medical and funeral expenses. Most workers are eligible for unemployment compensation, and there is a comprehensive pension program (see ch. 4, Population and Labor Force; ch. 7, Living Conditions).

Income tends to be highest in manufacturing and lowest in agriculture. Even unskilled rural workers are protected by minimum wage laws that inhibit somewhat their exploitation by employers, but minimums are lower than those in industry and difficult to enforce. Rates for common laborers made effective in February 1969 ranged from 234 to 328 pesos (for value of the peso, see Glossary) per day. Agricultural wageworkers are considered socially inferior to small farmers but superior on the economic scale because lodging and food are provided by the employer.

Wage earners have fared relatively badly during recent years. Beginning in about 1955, increases in wages in general fell irregularly behind the rise in the cost of living, even though they were frequently adjusted. For example, one large meatpacking plant granted increases ranging from 10 to 50 percent of basic wages seven times between August of 1964 and March of 1967.

On the basis of a wage index base of 100 in 1961 for the manufacturing industry, wages dropped irregularly to 95.9 in 1967 and 91.2 in 1968 before recovering to 96.7 in 1969. Wages of public employees, which had fared relatively worse than wages in the manufacturing sector in the early 1960's, rose from a base of 100 in 1967 to 109.9 in 1969.

Before 1968 wage rates were set for different industries, professions, and worker categories by management-labor negotiations leading to contract or by awards (*laudos*) of salary councils on which management, labor, and the government were represented. More of the various rates were fixed by awards than by contract. All awards and those collective contracts that were confirmed (*homologado*) by the appropriate government agency had the force of law.

In mid-1968 a state of emergency was declared, and the government imposed a limited wage-price freeze fixing wages at their June 26 level. At that time legislation was introduced that resulted in December in the creation of the tripartite Commission on Productivity, Prices, and Incomes (Comisión de Productividad, Precios e Ingressos—COPRIN). The basic functions of COPRIN were to centralize control over prices of basic commodities and to exercise the wage controls that had been in effect since June of that year.

The legislation made the decisions of the salary councils and the norms prescribed by the collective contracts subject to review by COPRIN and to adjustment by the Council of Ministers. In effect, COPRIN became the controlling arbiter of wage matters. The same process was prescribed in the periodic fixing of maximum and minimum wages even in the absence of an award or collective contract. In practice, with certain exceptions under the system, the maximum and minimum wage figures have been identical. Wage levels under awards or contracts were already in effect in mid-1968 and, as a general rule, these have been increased periodically by fixed formulas. It was originally anticipated that the life of COPRIN would be of limited duration, probably two years, but in mid-1970 no plans for its termination had been announced.

At the end of 1969 upward adjustments of 25, 12 and 6 percent were authorized for those with monthly wages below 40,000 pesos. COPRIN announced that the wage freeze would be selectively relaxed for companies able to demonstrate increases in productivity.

Workers fared relatively poorly during recent years until there was a moderate upturn in real income in late 1969 (see ch. 22, Finance). Beginning in the late 1950's the periodic increase in wages fell irregularly but progressively behind the rise in the cost of living.

Between 1961 and March of 1969 real wages in the manufacturing sector declined from an index base of 100 in 1961 (the Montevideo cost of living serving as indicator) to 93.8 in March 1969. On the same basis, real wages in the construction industry were at 83.8, and in commerce they were at 74.3. Government wages were at 85.8 percent in real values at the end of 1968 in comparison with the 1961 base.

The pattern of decline was irregular by years and by business sectors. During 1967, for example, the government index had stood at 103.2; in August of 1967 it had reached 110.5 for commerce, although in the same month of 1968 it had plummeted to 68.2. The irregularity of the pattern of wage movement in relation to the cost of living is further illustrated by the fact that in current values the cost of living during 1967 was up by 135.6 percent as industrial wages were rising 85.5 percent. In sharp contrast, 1969 was marked by a rise of 14.5 percent in Montevideo living costs, and industrial wages were up by an average of 17.7 percent for the year.

In December 1969 private sector wages were increased, and it was anticipated that there would not be another general adjustment at least until late in 1970. The December increase consisted of a 7-percent increase in basic wages and a 6-percent rise in family benefits. Public sector wages were also raised by an average of 13 percent, the increase occurring in January 1970, but the family allowance proportion was irregular and considerably smaller in the public than in the private sector.

In mid-1970 the most recent general wage increase had been made effective on December 1, 1969, and was applicable to all employed persons in the private sector with the exception of domestics and agricultural workers. Wages were increased by 8 percent, and family and child allowances were doubled. The 8-percent rise was applied also to all other forms of income, such as the Christmas bonus and pensions (see ch. 7, Living Conditions).

The national minimum wage was raised to 10,000 pesos per month, an increase of particular importance for workers in the interior, where income had often been substantially below this figure. In general, because of the allowance increases lower income workers may have enjoyed an income rise of as much as 40 percent.

Employment of Aliens

Resident foreigners have generally the same rights to employment as nationals. They are equally free to engage in commerce or industry. They are also free to practice liberal professions, subject to approval of their credentials by the Central Directive Council, an autonomous government agency.

There are a few exceptions. Foreigners may be employed on aircraft flying the Uruguayan flag only with the approval of the Ministry of National Defense; vessels engaged in coastal traffic must fly the country's flag, and the captain and one-third of the crew must be nationals. At least half of the staffs of foreign banks and banking houses must be Uruguayans. At the white-collar and professional levels all public employees, except teachers in public institutions of higher education, must be citizens. In contracting labor for public works, no more than 10 percent of the blue-collar workers (*obreros*) engaged may be aliens.

LABOR RELATIONS

Employment Contracts

There is no organized body of legislation on labor contracts, and specific labor and related legislation regulating working conditions is so extensive that the area in which labor and management may negotiate is limited. The system in force with respect to contracts derives from provisions of the Commercial Code and the Civil Code and from provisions of isolated laws, such as those providing that certain individual contracts be in writing. The contractual rights of both employer and employee were formerly protected by the Institute of Labor and Related Services of the former Ministry of Industry and Labor. With the introduction of the Constitution of 1967, the responsibility passed to the General Inspectorate of Labor in the newly formed Ministry of Labor and Social Security.

With respect to individual contracts, agreement is consensual, but the large number of supervisory formalities makes this feature of relative unimportance. Supervision of the performance of certain contracts is a responsibility of the Social Welfare Bank. Under terms of a 1968 decree, collective contracts must be deposited with the Ministry of Labor and Social Security within ten days of their signature.

The indefinite contract is customary. If a term of employment has been agreed upon, the worker leaving his job without just cause must pay for the resulting loss. This stipulation does not apply to domestic servants who may terminate work at any time without cause.

The degree of freedom to enter into a contract depends primarily on the type of work performed. The principal obligation of the employer is to pay the wage, and the principal obligation of the worker is to perform his task in the manner prescribed in the contract or, where no such provision is specified, in the manner indicated by the employer, subject to applicable laws and regulations and the provisions of collective union contracts.

If an employee keeps himself available, time spent is considered working time even though no work may be assigned to him. This is also the case when work is interrupted by market conditions or other contingencies for which the worker is not responsible.

Uruguay has subscribed to the ILO convention requiring adoption of measures to stimulate collective bargaining. In the absence of a general law concerning collective contracts, however, it has been necessary to devise solutions for the various questions as they arise. In instances where no special law is applicable, the contract becomes effective with respect to third parties who, in the future, enter into a contract with either of the originating parties. Accordingly, the employer and employee must agree not to enter individual contracts prescribing conditions less favorable to the worker than those stipulated.

Collective bargaining ceased to be an important apparatus with the imposition of the wage-price freeze and the establishment of COPRIN in 1968. Matters with respect to other working conditions and to benefits superior to those stipulated by law remained subject to collective bargaining in 1970, but these tended to be regarded as less important than the wage rate and, as legislation was favorable to workers, extensive, and detailed, resort to bargaining over them was relatively rare.

There are a few specific laws bearing on collective contracts. One stipulates that union agreements covering a majority of both the employers and the employees that have been entered into for the purpose of advancing the closing hour of business shall be generally binding on all establishments in the trade and to commerce in the streets and other public places. Another provides that agreements signed by the majority of the Construction League (Liga de Construcción) or affiliated groups become binding on all employers even though they are not affiliated with that league, provided that a copy of the agreement has been filed with the National Labor Institute. There is also a provision for procedures to follow in adopting collective agreements establishing exceptions to the rules for annual vacations.

Termination of Employment

In individual contracts there is seldom a stipulation with respect to the duration of employment. Where there is a stipulated term, the worker who prematurely vacates his job without just cause must pay an indemnity. This does not apply to domestic personnel, who may leave at any time. On completion of the period, either party is free to terminate the relationship unless there has been a new agreement. The indefinite contract worker can leave an enterprise at any time, and the employer can discharge him by payment of an indemnity or by proving bad conduct.

Rules for compensation for termination of indefinite individual or collective contracts are generally similar. Exceptions to the general rules include harvest workers or those contracted for tasks of limited duration, those who work in their own homes, those paid by the day who have not worked the number of days specified by law, and domestic servants who have worked less than a year for an employer.

The general rule for terminal pay—in the absence of a misdemeanor by the worker—is an indemnity calculated at one month's salary at current prices for each year or part of a year worked. A limit of six month's indemnity is customary. There is, however, no maximum limit for farm and agricultural workers. The dismissed employee who is over the age of forty and has no less than ten years of service is considered pensionable and is entitled to only three months' compensation.

Termination or suspension of employment because of accidents suffered or diseases contracted in connection with the occupations of workers is the responsibility of their employers and must be covered by insurance. The insurance must cover the loss of earnings as well as medical or funeral costs. Sickness benefits are limited. The law prescribes them only for employees in the construction, textile, glass, and certain sections of the transportation industries. Workers in a number of other industries, however, have acquired corresponding rights as a consequence of collective bargaining.

A particular problem with respect to termination of employment concerns those who work for the government. In the late 1960's it was estimated that out of a working force of about 1 million, some 350,000 either were civil servants or worked for state-owned business enterprises, many of which operated at a loss (see ch. 19, Industry). In order to determine with some precision what proportion of the labor force actually was on the public payroll, the National Office of the Civil Service was authorized late in 1969 to conduct a census. Preliminary findings from this undertaking, released early in 1970, revealed a much lower total of some 213,000. Even this number, however, represented an extremely heavy burden on the economy.

One of the purposes of the census had been to determine how many held two or more government jobs in order to require holders of multiple public jobs to reduce their public assignments to one. In mid-1969 it had been estimated that this action alone would reduce the government payroll by at least 5 percent. Early in 1970 legislation was under consideration designed to reduce the number of these public workers by encouraging them to transfer voluntarily to the private sector through tax concessions and a resignation gratuity equal to one year's salary.

It appeared, however, that the job of reducing the rolls would not be easy. During the 1960's the public rolls had been increasing at an estimated rate twice that of the general population growth. Tenure rights acquired through legislation and labor union contracts had made it hard to discharge personnel, even for inefficiency. After a six-month probationary period, employees tended to retain their positions until retirement on pension. In addition, the very size of the public payroll made its reduction politically hazardous. The Constitution prohibits public workers from engaging in partisan political activities in the office or during office hours but does not restrain their freedom to campaign at other times.

Labor Disputes

The Constitution of 1967 prescribed that legislation be enacted promoting the creation of tribunals of conciliation and arbitration. A labor court was in existence at that time, but the tripartite wage and conciliation boards were the principal instruments for settlement of disputes that could not be resolved individually or collectively directly between worker and manager. There was no specific provision for voluntary or mandatory arbitration, but the terms *arbitration*, *mediation*, and *conciliation* had been left legally undefined, and political and labor speakers and writers tended to use these terms indiscriminately.

Because of the elaborate system of guarantees covering employment, most labor disputes are resolved through means that, in one form or another, involve government participation. Initially, this participation took the form of advice or persuasion; since the discontinuance of the collegiate executive system it has turned toward firm action to terminate work stoppages.

Under the law of December of 1968 creating COPRIN, that organization was given provisional authority (still in effect in mid-1970) to police labor disputes, with somewhat different norms applicable to the public and to the private sectors.

In general, no strike or lockout becomes authorized until at least seven days after COPRIN has been advised of the circumstances and the intents of the complaining party. COPRIN may resolve, before or after the beginning of the strike or lockout, that the parties involved define their positions by means of secret ballot. Neither employer nor employee, however, is obliged to participate in the ballot, nor is the resulting vote legally binding. It does not affect the constitutional right to strike and accordingly has only advisory significance.

With regard to public services, whether directly government administered or operated through concessionaires, there are supplementary rules. On receipt of a notice that a strike or lockout is intended, COPRIN may within five days require, subject to administrative and juridical review, that the service be continued on an emergency basis. Except under these circumstances, however, it is understood that the strike is a legitimate suspension of labor contracts and that, after its settlement, the strikers must be permitted to return to work in the absence of other overriding legal considerations.

Strikes tend to be by the employees of an entire economic sector rather than by employees of a single enterprise. Workers continue to be eligible for pay, but the time is counted as part of the annual vacation.

Work stoppages are occasionally of considerable duration but, because of the narrow limits within which labor and management may negotiate, they tend to be protest demonstrations rather than true strikes and are frequent but customarily short. For example, during 1964 the postal workers are out an average of once a month. The general strike is a frequent occurrence. Sometimes widely observed and sometimes largely ineffective, it is usually announced in advance to be of twenty-four or forty-eight hours' duration. There were approximately forty during the 1960's.

Strikes have a pronounced seasonal character. During the winter months, when there are fewer tourists, the availability of foreign exchange declines, and labor restiveness increases.

The Constitution of 1967, like those preceding it during the twentieth century, guarantees trade unions the right to strike subject to enabling laws and regulations enacted in this connection. These are few in number. Beginning in the mid-1950's with the general decline in the economy, unions exercised the right to cease work in search of benefits with an increasing frequency and with an intensity that interfered with the country's ability to realize its full potential in earnings. The incidence increased during the late 1950's and early 1960's and in the year 1966 reached about 700, including partial work stoppages. At no time were there significant numbers of lockouts.

After the referendum of late 1966 in which a majority of the people rejected the collegiate executive, public authorities began to take an increasingly firm position against illegal work stoppages. Strikes during 1967 were as numerous as those in 1966, but as early as January of that year a three-day strike at the National Airport that crippled passenger movement during the height of the tourist season was terminated when military forces occupied the airport and restored services to normal. Strikes continued at a brisk rate during the later months of the year, however, and in February 1968 a strike of some 200 dairy farmers was terminated by military intervention.

In April an estimated 200,000 government workers—although legally prohibited from striking and despite the threat of invocation of legislative provisions calling for severe sanctions, including imprisonment—engaged in a walkout of forty-eight hours over demands for higher pay. On June 13 a state of emergency was declared by the government. This action was answered on June 18 by a widely observed general strike of forty-eight hours. The government, however, had put in abeyance its traditional policy of conversational settlement of labor disputes and committed itself to one of firm resistance to demands for wage increases in order to slow down the inflationary spiral, and on June 26 the wage-price freeze was decreed (see ch. 22, Finance).

The wage-price freeze had been an interim expedient, and in July the government submitted to the legislature the bill to regularize the wage-price control measure that resulted in December in the establishment of COPRIN with authority not only over wages and prices but also over conciliation procedures and strikes. According to its charter, no strike or lockout would be deemed legal if the original problem and the decision to resort to these measures had not been submitted with at least seven days' notice to the COPRIN board.

Labor unrest did not at once abate. As early as July 2, 1968, the National Workers Convention (Convención Nacional de Trabajadores—CNT) had called another general strike to protest the wage-price freeze. There were other strikes during the later months of the year, and the total number for 1968 was substantial, though it did not match that of 1967. Toward the end of the year and in early 1969 the rate of work stoppage slowed, and the economy stabilized sufficiently for the government to terminate the state of emergency in March 1969. In the next two months, however, there were a half dozen twenty-four-hour general strikes. Meatpackers at the big state-owned National Packinghouse (Frígorifico Nacional) in April commenced a work stoppage that was to last four months over replacement of an almost free ration of prime beef (often subsequently sold to restaurants) by a wage increase they considered an inadequate substitute. There were numerous other strikes, student demonstrations, and a variety of other labor disturbances.

At the end of June security laws were reintroduced, giving the government the authority to prohibit union meetings, arrest union leaders, place public services under military control, and suppress public information concerning strikes. The CNT debated the propriety of an all-out challenge to the government over these actions, but after considerable argument the directorate decided against such action, a decision that the CNT president was later to describe as a serious error.

Unrest continued, however, and in early July the union of private bank workers commenced what was to be the most significant work stoppage in at least a decade. At the end of the month the government invoked its emergency authority to mobilize some of the striking elements and, when they refused to return to work, was in a position to declare them punishable by court-martial. Branches of the union were closed, its constitution suspended, and its funds impounded. In August the president successfully challenged a vote of the legislature against this imposition of martial law. The strike, which had seriously disrupted the economy, came to an end by a compromise solution in mid-September, less than an hour before the strikers were to be declared deserters and dismissed.

The vice president and a prominent senator had been acting as mediators in the dispute, but in the final analysis it was the military pressure that had brought about the solution. The army, however, acted with moderation toward the strikers by urging the employers not to use the dispute as an instrument for implementing a long-planned reduction in their personnel.

The end of the bank strike did not mean the end of labor unrest. There was a two-month strike of wool handlers, and a mobilization of the public electrical plant and telephone workers that had been imposed at midyear was not lifted until the end of November. Strikes were less serious, however, and there was a moderate upturn in the economy in late 1969 and early 1970. The 1969 rate of inflation—the lowest in the decade—was lower than the goal that had been set by the government (see ch. 22, Finance). The firm but restrained handling of the banking strike may have been a turning point.

In mid-1970 the state of emergency was still in effect, and a bill had been presented to the legislature providing severe penalties for particpation in organizations engaged in activities detrimental to the social order. The enactment of the legislation provided an additional strike-breaking weapon, but it appeared aimed against the revolutionary Tupamaros (see Glossary) rather than against organized labor.

ORGANIZATION OF LABOR

Origins and Development of the Labor Movement

The forerunners of the trade union movement were the mutual aid societies established in the 1850's in conformity with Spanish tradition. They concerned themselves with care of the sick and disabled and assistance to the workers' survivors. In varying forms descendant organizations remained in existence in the 1960's.

An acceleration of immigration during the 1880's brought with it the first efforts to create true labor organizations and resulted in the first strikes. By 1895 associations of various kinds included those of bricklayers, carpenters, blacksmiths, mechanics, painters, marble cutters, shoemakers, tobacco workers, sailors, seamstresses, vehicle builders, and watchmakers. An anarchist tendency in the early labor movement resulted in a proclivity for independent unions and a shifting of membership from one union to another. Later, in federated groups there has been a tendency toward decentralization with pronounced local autonomy and toward movement of affiliation from one central group to another.

Governments tended to look with disfavor on the young labor movement until the beginning of the first administration of Batlle in 1903. It was decidedly sympathetic, and by 1905 two national federations had come into existence. They were the UGT and the anarchist Uruguayan Regional Workers' Federation, founded in 1902 and considered to be the country's oldest federation. The anarchist philosophy was predominant during this time, and there were many strikes. Direct action was a catchword. Batlle was out of office from 1907 to 1911, and organized labor suffered a pronounced decline.

Labor prospered during the second Batlle administration, which lasted from 1911 to 1915, and celebrated its improved posture with a militancy marked by strikes among bakers, shoemakers, teamsters, and streetcar conductors. For the first time there was some spread of organization into the interior under leadership of the loosely organized Federation of Uruguayan Workers. In 1915 Uruguay became the first Latin American country to establish the eight-hour day.

World War I accelerated the growth of the labor movement, a consequence of its stimulus to industrialization, of labor discontent resulting from price rises, and of an increased willingness of employers to consider the demands of workers. Immediately after the war an important new labor union group, the Maritime Workers Federation, came into being, but in general the labor movement languished during the immediate postwar years and was badly divided along political lines. Estimates vary as to union membership during the 1920's, but the consensus is that its trend was downward.

The first third of the twentieth century was an important one for labor, however, for it was a time of the enactment of labor laws. Batlle had maintained that the employer should pass on a greater share of his gain to his workers and that the young and the old deserved the protection of the state. It was largely his efforts that led to the passage of such measures as the eight-hour-day legislation in 1915, the 1920 legislation calling for twenty-four hours of rest after six days of work, and the 1926 minimum wage legislation for port workers, later extended to other industries.

As late as 1929 union membership was estimated at as low as 25,000, but with the onset of the worldwide depression the ranks began to swell. The first of the modern labor organizations, the predominately Communist and Socialist General Workers' Union

(Unión General de Trabajadores—UGT), in 1942 assembled thirty-one individual unions with an aggregate membership of 40,000. The organization's principal strength was in the maritime, textile, transport, and services occupations.

The UGT found, however, that the country's already extensive social benefits legislation left it with few causes to support. It quickly fell under Communist domination, and one of its first political demands was for recognition of the Soviet Union. In 1959 it announced that it was Moscow oriented.

At the same time, opposite forces were at work. In the early 1950's the General Confederation of Labor came into existence, modeled on the Peronist union system across the Río de la Plata estuary, but at its peak this organization could claim no more than 3,500 members. In 1952, however, anti-Communist forces assumed control of the busdrivers' union and withdrew it from the UGT; subsequently several other groups followed the busdrivers' union into the Federation of Uruguayan Transport Workers.

In the early 1950's democratic workers who were repelled by both Communist and Peronist ideologies drew together in a third central group, the Confederation of Trade Unions of Uruguay (Confederación Sindical del Uruguay—CSU). In 1956 it had become the country's strongest organized labor element, but by 1958 it had fallen behind yet another central organization, the Communist-oriented One Center of Workers (Central Unica de Trabajadores—CUT), which was replacing the faltering UGT in leftist worker leadership.

As early as 1954 the UGT membership had shrunk from 50,000 to 15,000 members. By 1962 it was a defunct organization, replaced by the CUT, which had attracted 50,000 members; it retained, however, some of the old organization's leaders. The CUT itself was to have a short life, at least under that name. A national labor union conference in October of 1966 gave birth to the National Workers Convention (Convention Nacional de Trabajadores—CNT). It contained all the essential elements of the CUT, however, and in 1970 it was decidedly leftist and the dominant element in the organized labor movement.

Union Organizations

Although the Constitution of 1967 stipulates that the law shall promote the organization of trade unions, according them charters and issuing regulations for their recognition as juridical persons (corporate entities), there is no comprehensive body of law and regulations implementing this provision. Those rules in existence provide maximum liberality in establishing new unions and in permitting workers to join them. Government and management are prohibited from interfering in union activities, and workers are protected from discrimination in employment opportunities because of union membership.

Procedures for union recognition are the same as those for any other juridical personality. Recognized unions have the right to appeal the decisions of salary councils, a right of limited effect in 1970 because of the comprehensive wage controls that had been in effect since 1968. A scattering of other regulations concern unions in specific economic sectors.

Union membership is relatively high. There has been, however, no general agreement as to the actual number of union members, mid-1960 reports varying from 150,000 to 350,000 members out of a labor force generally agreed to number slightly over 1 million. Many people—government workers in particular—hold two or more jobs and may belong to two or more unions. In addition, laws and regulations regarding union membership are imprecise, and the CNT, in claiming 400,000 adherents on the occasion of its 1969 congress, included such nonunion elements as worker assemblies from five interior departments, the National Front of Tenants, student federations, and what were described as fraternal organizations. In addition, in the informally structured system of organized labor, many unions bargain—or claim to bargain—for many workers who are not actual members. For example, in early 1970 the 4,000 member Confederation of Government Employees' Organizations was said to bargain for 15,000, and the 5,000 member Uruguayan Federation of Commercial and Industrial Employees also was said to bargain for 15,000.

At the end of 1968 it was estimated by one source that the CNT—the predominant central union organization—had between 200,000 and 250,000 members but spoke for 400,000. Another estimate at about the same time put the number of members as low as 90,000. Undoubtedly, however, the organization grew substantially during the 1960's, partly through the recruitment of new members and partly at the expense of other collective organizations.

At the end of the 1960's, however, the organization may have passed its peak in popular support. In March of 1970 it was reported to have an estimated membership of 200,000. The Bank Employees' Association with 12,000 members, the Federation of Wool Workers with 10,000, the Congress of Textile Workers with 10,000, and the Federation of Meat Packing Workers with 9,000 were the largest affiliated groups.

Nomenclature with respect to organized labor units is not fixed under the law, and national-level CNT units include confederations, federations, and conventional unions organized on a national or regional basis. The organization includes both industrial unions (persons in all kinds of occupations employed in a single sector of industry) and trade unions (persons in a single occupation occupied in various industrial sectors). Unions representing workers in commerce and other services sectors are included, as are government employee as well as private worker organizations. In addition, CNT represents the sugarworkers' union of Artigas Department, the only true rural union. Some farmworkers belong to the Federation of Wool Workers or the Autonomous Workers Association, but these are primarily urban organizations under urban leadership.

Under its president, the approximately forty confederations, federations, and otherwise unaffiliated unions that constitute the CNT were directed by the twenty-seven member National Representative Board, which was elected at the organization's 1969 congress of 600 delegates who were said to represent 400,000 workers. The congress voted to admit four additional labor groups on a tentative basis (enlarging the National Representative Board to thirty-one) and to leave three seats available for three independent organizations that were considering taking up membership. At the time of the 1969 congress, the CNT president and the high command of at least fourteen of the most important member groups were Communists, although the overall Communist element in the organization was believed to be no more than 3 percent.

In 1969 CNT had announced generally radical demands, including termination of the country's relations with the International Monetary Fund (a perennial objective); a moratorium on the foreign debt; nationalization of the private banks, foreign trade, all transportation, and the meat and other basic industries; agrarian reform; establishment of new factories as a means of reducing unemployment; distribution of land to landless farmers; defense of the living standard of the worker; staffing of the Social Welfare Bank with worker delegates and retired persons; and such matters as assured medical care, housing, education, and social security. The demands were virtual restatements of those issued a year earlier.

During the 1950's and early 1960's the moderate CSU was the country's principal non-Communist labor central. In 1956 it began a steady decline. In 1962 it still had an estimated 71,000 members, but by 1967 its membership was down to 10,000. At that time other non-CNT groups included the Uruguayan Trade Union Action, oriented toward the Christian Democratic Party and with roll of about 5,000, and the anarchist-oriented Regional Workers Federation of Uruguay with 2,500.

In March of 1969, however, the CSU had ceased to exist, and a new labor central was formed by a constituent congress made up of about 125 delegates representing the residue of the CSU and other unions unsympathetic to the CNT. It was to become the Uruguayan Confederation of Labor (Confederación Uruguaya de Trabajo), not to be confused with the defunct Communist-dominated One Center of Workers (Central Unica de Trabajadores—CUT) that was the direct predecessor of the CNT.

The constituent congress of the new CUT was broadly representative of labor, but with office employees and construction workers most numerous. A new congress was held and new leaders elected in January of 1970. In March of that year, the membership was estimated at 35,000 with about half belonging to the National Federation of Office Employees and Technicians. Altogether, eight organizations at the national level were participants, with the 6,000-member Federation of Food Industry Workers ranking second.

Among the independent or otherwise associated worker groups, in early 1970 the most important was the National Association of Public Employees, which had an estimated enrollment of 10,000 and claimed to represent 20,000. Next in size was the Federation of Uruguayan Transport Workers with 7,000, a miscellaneous group with stevedores and other port workers predominating, but with the participation of some busdriver unions.

The Federation of Beverage Workers had an estimated 4,000 members; the National Association of Postal Workers (informally linked with the CNT) 3,000; the catchall Federation of Autonomous Unions and Associations of Paysandú 2,000; the Central Organization of Traveling Salesmen 2,000; and the Federation of Government Bank Workers (not to be confused with the CNT-affiliated Bank Employees' Association); the Federation of Naval Workers and Employees of Uruguay, and the Association of Workers of the National Cooperative Dairy Products Producers each between 1,000 and 2,000. A half dozen additional federated union groups had fewer than 1,000 members, as estimated in early 1970.

International Union Affiliations

Through the CNT the bulk of organized labor is affiliated with the WFTU. At a congress held in Prague in 1969, the president of the union of leatherworkers, Enrique Pastorino, was elected WFTU president.

The once important but now defunct CSU was a member of the liberal International Confederation Free Trade Unions and its Latin American affiliate, the Interamerican Organization of Workers. In 1969 the executive secretariat of the newly organized CUT, made up of non-Communist or anti-Communist unions, was authorized to make similar affiliations. In addition, a few unions were associated with the International Federation of Christian Trade Unions.

The State Civil Service Organizations Confederation in 1970 was a member of the Latin American Confederation of Government Workers. The executive committee of this confederation met in

1970 in Montevideo with the participation of representatives of Uruguay, Paraguay, Brazil, Argentina, and Chile. A Peruvian representative, also a member of the executive committee, was unable to attend.

A different kind of international labor affiliation has been that of individual unions and union groups with the American Institute for Free Labor Development (AIFLD), a tripartite United States organization in which government, industry, and labor participate. Between 1962 and 1969 about 5,000 Latin American labor leaders participated in courses running from one to three months on various phase of union organization and practice. The AIFLD affiliate in Montevideo is the Uruguayan Institute for Labor Union Studies.

A charter member of the ILO in 1919, Uruguay by 1969 had adhered to fifty-eight of its conventions, one of the highest adherence rates among the member states. It has also affiliated with several international trade secretariats. Included in these are the International Union of Food and Allied Workers' Associations; the International Metalworkers Associations; the Postal, Telegraph and Telephone International; the Public Services International; and the International Transport Workers' Federation.

Management Associations

Most numerous among the more than forty business associations are the chambers of commerce or industry. The National Chamber of Commerce acts as the voice of wholesalers and retail distributors. It has affiliates in each of the nineteen departments but most of its membership is in the capital city. Two other influential mercantile associations located in Montevideo are the League of Commercial Defense and the Mercantile Chamber of Products of the Nation. The second-named publishes a weekly trade information digest called *Semanario Informativo* (Weekly Informational), which is considered one of the leading trade publications.

Foreign business is represented by a variety of commercial associations. The United States Chamber of Commerce of Uruguay coordinates efforts to promote cultural and commercial exchanges. Under this program and in conjunction with the "Partners of the Alliance" program the state of Minnesota has become the cultural and trade partner of Uruguay. In addition, chambers of commerce of the United Kingdom, Italy, and Brazil maintain organizations supporting their own commercial interests and promote trade with the host country.

In the industrial sector the National Chamber of Industries predominates. Its leadership meets periodically to develop industrial policy positions. It concerns itself particularly with import-export regulations and in 1959 led the battle that resulted in the abolition of the Export-Import Control Board, on which it had been represented.

Among the most important of the other industrial associations is the Consortium of Factory Representatives. Outside of Montevideo an important spokesman for industrial and retail interests is the Federation of Commercial and Industrial Entities of the Interior. The Association of Textile Industries of the Interior is an associate of the National Chamber of Industries but is an autonomous entity acting on behalf of industrialists in the departments. In addition, the Association of Banks, public and private alike, represents the management in negotiations vis-á-vis the politically influential Union of Bank Employees.

The Rural Association, founded in 1871, is essentially a business organization. It concerns itself more with the technology of animal husbandry and agriculture than with politics. Much more politically oriented is the Rural Federation which, like the Rural Association, has a largely aristocratic membership. Conservative, it has become the most politically active rural organization in the country. A third rural organization is the Federal League for Rural Action. Developed in the early 1950's largely as an instrument for the political support of ranchers, it has changed political allegiance in keeping with current political interest.

In 1966 the list of management associations was supplemented by the creation of the Exporters' Union, including representatives of business, financial, and agricultural groups. Among the functions for which it was designed is the exchange of views between public and private entities.

CHAPTER 21

TRADE

In 1970 the country continued its traditional reliance upon wool, meat, and hides for the bulk of its export earnings. Wool usually generates about 40 to 50 percent of export sales, and meat and hides account for another 40 percent. Tourism, especially from Argentina and Brazil, was also an important earner of foreign exchange. Raw materials, capital goods, and fuels and lubricants continued to be the principal import categories. The country's major customers were Great Britain, the United States, the Netherlands, West Germany, Italy, Spain, and the member countries of the Latin American Free Trade Association (LAFTA); these buyers were also the country's main suppliers of imports.

The country's trade policy was shaped by its balance-of-trade deficit, its need for government revenues, and its membership obligations in LAFTA. This policy discouraged nonessential imports; imposed high customs duties, prior deposits, and surcharges; favored national shipping; and pursued the protection of local industries as an aid to industrialization and economic diversification (see ch. 19, Industry). The government had indicated a recognition of the need for eliminating the surcharges and prior deposits as soon as foreign trade conditions permitted it to do so.

In 1970 domestic trade provided about 14 percent of the gross national product (GNP) and employed the same proportion of the labor force (see ch. 4, Population and Labor Force). The principal marketing area was in and around Montevideo, the national capital and the largest urban center. Despite the relatively high purchasing power of the country's comparatively small population, the limited size of the domestic market required the manufacturing sector to seek markets outside the country if it wished to expand (see ch. 17, Character and Structure of the Economy; ch. 19, Industry). The country's transportation network, which was being improved in 1970, allowed easy shipment of agricultural products from the countryside to the capital and the reverse movement of manufactured goods to the other urban centers and to rural areas.

FOREIGN TRADE

The country's total foreign trade in 1970 was expected to be the equivalent of approximately US$370 million, with exports reaching

US$199 million and imports at US$171 million; in 1969 exports had been US$192 million and imports US$190 million. Analysis of the country's foreign trade in 1970 showed that the total value of exports and imports had remained almost unchanged for twenty years. The structure of exports had not changed substantially over the years; the traditional products—wool, meat, and leather—were still predominant and accounted for 80 to 90 percent of the total value of exports.

A change had been apparent, however, in the share of the market held by each of the traditional export products; wool had become relatively less important, whereas the share of livestock products had grown. The pattern of imports had also remained basically unaltered except for a fall in the proportion of imports representing consumer goods; this shift was a result of progress in substituting domestically produced consumer items for imported goods (see ch. 19, Industry).

Composition of Foreign Trade

Exports

Wool and wool products remained the country's major export in 1970, earning the equivalent of an estimated US$79 million. Meat continued in second place, with projected sales of US$77 million. Exports of hides and skins at US$15 million and of other agricultural products at US$13 million brought earnings from agricultural exports to 93 percent of the estimated total value of the country's exports in 1970. The balance was supplied by exports of industrial products, projected at US$12 million, and by miscellaneous exports valued at US$2 million.

The projected increase in total exports in 1970 to US$199 million from US$192 million in 1969 was based on expectations of increased exports of beef and mutton; this rise was principally dependent on the increase in the total output of meat and in the exportable surplus of meat expected to result from continuation of the existing pasture improvement program combined with the impact of increased internal prices of beef on domestic consumption (see ch. 7, Living Conditions; ch. 18, Agriculture; ch. 22, Finance). The expected expansion of exports of meat and meat products also assumed continuing normal conditions in external demand for meat products and further reorganization of the meatpacking industry (see ch. 19, Industry).

Improved sanitation in the meatpacking plants was essential in order to gain reentry into the markets of Great Britain, which had imported an average of 28,000 tons of beef annually from the country but which for sanitary reasons had imposed an embargo, effective June 15, 1969, on the importation of beef from Uruguay.

Exports of cooked meat to the United States had also been placed under an embargo for the same reasons since October 1969. A complementary program for the eradication of hoof-and-mouth disease also needed to be given priority because subsequent entry into the markets of Great Britain and other countries would depend on such eradication. In 1970 hoof-and-mouth disease continued to be a major obstacle for entry into the United States market.

Another significant increase in the earnings of foreign exchange from exports of meat and meat products was expected to occur because of the anticipated addition of meat products more specialized than the chilled and frozen carcasses and canned and jerked meat being produced in 1970 (see ch. 19, Industry). The higher degree of added value that would result from the output of boneless carcass meat, special cuts, and cooked frozen meats would provide productive employment for those workers who were unproductively employed in 1970 in the meatpacking plants (see ch. 20, Labor Relations and Organization).

Improvement in the sanitary conditions of the meatpacking plants appeared in 1970 to be, to a considerable extent, an administrative problem that could be resolved in a relatively short period of time. Other improvements in the operation of the meatpacking plants were a question of management and additional investment, including the replacement of obsolete equipment and the disposition of redundant labor; in 1970 the period of time for carrying out these improvements was estimated at five years. The control of hoof-and-mouth disease was a longer term problem that would require international cooperation with Brazil, Paraguay, and Argentina (see ch. 14, Foreign Relations).

In 1970 exports of wool were expected to remain generally at the levels prevailing in the 1967—70 period. Assuming that prices of wool on the world market continued to increase annually on the order of about 1.5 percent, prospects for the country's earnings from wool exports depended primarily on its wool supply. An increasing portion of the wool clip was expected to be utilized domestically for the manufacture of worsted cloth and other textile products for export (see ch. 19, Industry). The country's wool is of garment quality and therefore had not been much affected by the declines in the late 1960's in the demand for coarse carpet wool (see ch. 18, Agriculture).

The possibilities of expanding exports by the development of agricultural crops did not appear to be substantial in 1970. The country's variable climatic conditions and the shortage of supplementary means of controlling the supply of water, such as irrigation, artificial water preserves, and flood control, resulted in large annual variations in crop yields, which prevented the maintenance of stable returns (see ch. 2, Physical Environment; ch. 18, Agriculture). For this reason, the country had through 1970 been unable to compete on international markets with the large wheat-trading countries. The world market for linseed, one of the country's traditional exports, was in 1970 being undermined by synthetic substitutes.

In 1970 the government estimated that resolution of the country's problems in the production of agricultural crops would involve the investment of considerable funds for control of the supply of water, the change to newer crops such as sorghum, and a switch into high-value crops such as vegetables, fruits, and other specialty crops for export. Such crops would also require investment in processing facilities and the development of outlets in foreign markets. The agricultural crop sector did not, therefore, look promising to the government in 1970 as a field for development of exports in the immediate future.

The promotion of fisheries into a new source of export earnings appeared in 1970 to have considerable potential. Two independent surveys by West German and Soviet fishing vessels operating in the Rio de la Plata area off the coasts of Uruguay and Argentina had indicated a possible annual supply of 5 million tons of fish. One project being considered in 1970 proposed the catch of 30,000 tons of this supply and its conversion into exportable fillets and fishmeal. On the basis of this project, annual returns in export earnings equivalent to US$9 million could be anticipated from an original investment, primarily in foreign exchange, equivalent to US$7.2 million.

There was considerable discussion in and out of the government in 1970 on the possibilities of developing exports of cloth, clothing, shoes, and other leather products; in 1970 these products were being manufactured under high protective tariffs for the domestic market. Production costs were generally high, however, for a number of reasons. Most firms were small and unable to take advantage of the economies of large-scale production; their equipment was in most cases inadequate and unbalanced. There were problems in the control of the quality of production and in the efficiency of management (see ch. 19, Industry). Other factors that might repress the development of manufactured exports were the producers' lack of experience with export sales, absence of contacts in foreign markets, and inability to handle large orders.

These restrictive factors contributed to the country's relative lack of success in developing exports of manufactured goods in the 1960's despite the incentives for the export of such products. These incentives included exemption from a number of taxes, importation of goods needed in the production of exports without the usually required payment of import surcharges, a rebate of up to 35 percent of the value of exports in the form of tax credit certificates, and special export financing privileges (see ch. 22, Finance).

Imports

Through 1970 the country's imports had declined from about 19 percent to about 11 percent of gross national product over a period of fifteen years. The commodity composition of total imports had fluctuated quite markedly; the country's stock of capital goods had become inadequate and obsolete as a result of the more than proportionate decline in the level of imports of capital goods (see ch. 17, Character and Structure of the Economy). The relationship in 1970 of imports of raw materials and capital goods to the general level of economic activity was heavily distorted by the protracted economic stagnation experienced since the late 1950's. Import requirements were expected to increase quite substantially in the 1971—75 period with the projected rise in the rate of investments and the resulting recovery of production and exports.

Raw materials continued in 1969 to dominate import spending, amounting to US$95 million; imports of capital goods were second in value, at US$54 million. Fuels and lubricants, consisting largely of crude petroleum, totaled US$24 million, and imports of consumer goods amounted to US$17 million. The capital goods total represented an increase of US$23 million above the total for this category of imports in 1968; a rise of US$20 million in imports of machinery and US$3 million in kits of automotive parts for domestic assembly accounted for the change.

Direction of Foreign Trade

In 1969 Europe remained the country's major market, absorbing 74 percent of total exports. This situation continued a trend that had become established in the 1965—68 period. The countries of the European Economic Community (EEC) took 35 percent of the total and the European Free Trade Association (EFTA) countries, 31 percent; the balance went to Spain, Greece, and Eastern Europe. Of the remaining 26 percent of total exports, 12.3 percent was shipped to the United States; 11.0 percent, to member countries of LAFTA; 1.7 percent, to Asia; and 1.0 percent, to the rest of the world.

The relative importance of individual countries as markets for Uruguay's exports was as follows: Great Britain first with 18.0 percent; the United States, 12.3 percent; the Netherlands, 7.9 percent; and Italy, Spain, and West Germany, 7.2 percent each. The remaining 39.7 percent of exports was divided among other countries of the world.

In 1969 Europe continued to be the country's major supplier, providing 56 percent of total imports. The EEC countries provided 34 percent and the EFTA member nations, 11 percent; Spain was the source of 5 percent, and 6 percent originated from the countries of Eastern Europe. The remaining 44 percent of total imports included 29 percent supplied by LAFTA member countries, 14 percent by the United States, and the balance of 1 percent by Japan.

Commercial Policy

Import Tariff System

The country's tariff in 1970 consisted of basic duties generally calculated as a percentage of the official customs valuation of imports, plus surtaxes and occasional miscellaneous taxes that were also based on a percentage of the official customs valuation (see ch. 22, Finance). For most products there was a small port handling fee. There were, in addition, foreign exchange surcharges on most imports, ranging from 10 to 300 percent of the cost-insurance-freight (c.i.f.) value of the items, and a consular invoice fee of 12 percent of the c.i.f. value. Duties on a broad extent of imports reached a total of up to 110 percent of the c.i.f. value.

The surcharges were imposed under the authority of Law No. 12,670 of December 17, 1959, which gave the government the power to require prior deposits on imports; to establish surcharges not exceeding 300 percent of the c.i.f. value of goods considered nonessential, of a luxury character, or competitive with national products; and to prohibit the importation of such goods for a period not exceeding six months. Under the provisions of Law No. 12,804 of November 30, 1960, as amended, the government could refund customs duties on imports of machinery and accessories necessary for establishing new industries or expanding existing plants provided they were imported for the manufacture of articles not produced in the country (see ch. 19, Industry). When imported materials were incorporated in goods that were subsequently exported, there was a refund of customs duties.

There were in 1970 six categories of surcharges: 10 percent, 60 percent, 90 percent, 150 percent, 225 percent, and 300 percent. The magnitude of the surcharge varied with the degree to which the product was considered essential. Items exempted from the surcharges included agricultural machinery, industrial machinery, certain construction machinery, medical equipment, pharmaceutical products and raw materials, telephonic and telegraphic materials, and petroleum products.

Certain tariff concessions were granted under the terms of the

General Agreement on Tariffs and Trade (GATT) to imports coming from other GATT contracting parties; the country had become a contracting party of GATT under the authority granted to the government by Law No. 12,019 of November 6, 1953. The country's membership in LAFTA had been approved by Law No. 12,859 of April 28, 1961; as a member of LAFTA, the country granted preferential rates of duty on certain imports from other LAFTA member countries.

Nontariff Import Controls

An import license was required in 1970 for all incoming shipments. The flow of imports was controlled by the imposition of a series of prior deposits, ranging from 150 to 400 percent of the c.i.f. value of the imports. The prior deposits varied with the foreign exchange surcharges applicable. There was one important exception to the system of prior deposits: established importers were allowed to import, free of surcharges and prior deposits or with considerably reduced rates, the same amount of commodities as had been imported by them in certain base years. This arrangement operated on a quarterly basis; authorizations were granted for a period of three months and were limited to the average importations that each importer had made in preestablished base years. For 1970 the base year was 1969.

All imports from LAFTA member countries were subject to reduced prior deposits; special treatment regarding prior deposits was additionally granted to such imports if tariff concessions had been negotiated on them with other LAFTA member countries. Public organizations were exempt from payment of prior deposits.

Export Controls

The exportation of basic traditional products—wool and wool byproducts, flaxseed, linseed oil and linseed flour, sunflower seed and its byproducts, wheat and wheat byproducts, peanuts and peanut byproducts, beef, and dry and salted cowhides and sheepskins —was required, before shipment, to be covered by a contract for the sale of the foreign exchange receipts to authorized banks (see ch. 22, Finance). Varying export retention taxes were in effect in mid-1970 for wool, hides and skins, oilseeds, and meat and meat products (see ch. 18, Agriculture). Export incentives in the form of rebates of export taxes up to a maximum of 35 percent of the free-on-board (f.o.b.) value were authorized for a number of manufactured and semimanufactured goods; each application for rebates was decided on a case-by-case basis (see ch. 19, Industry; ch. 22, Finance).

Trade Agreements

General Agreement on Tariffs and Trade

The country acceded on December 16, 1953, to the General Agreement on Tariffs and Trade (GATT). Through mid-1970 the country had continued for ten years to impose import surcharges that the country had conceded were incompatible with the provisions of GATT. The surcharges had been introduced by a decree dated September 29, 1960; on March 2, 1961, the government had applied to the other GATT contracting parties for a waiver allowing the country to apply the surcharges. The waiver was granted on May 21, 1961, and was originally to expire on July 1, 1963. Subsequent amendments voted by the GATT contracting parties extended the expiration date to August 1, 1971.

The country's representative at GATT presented to the other contracting parties on September 27, 1961, a table of restrictive and discriminatory measures on thirty products that accounted for 97 percent of the country's exports. These measures were in force in nineteen countries that constituted 85 percent of the country's export markets. The table showed 576 individual restrictions on the country's exports.

On November 21, 1961, the country's representative stated that Uruguay would make use of procedures under GATT for consultation with fifteen countries about their restrictions on products exported by Uruguay. In March 1962 the GATT contracting parties appointed a panel of experts to examine these restrictive measures and to consider the possibility that the measures had nullified or impaired benefits accruing to Uruguay under GATT. The panel of experts concluded that the contracting parties should recommend to the governments of seven of the fifteen countries that they immediately consider removal of the measures; on November 16, 1962, the contracting parties adopted the report of the panel of experts and requested the governments of these seven countries to report to the contracting parties on March 1, 1963, on action taken to comply with the recommendations or on any other satisfactory adjustment, such as the provision of suitable concessions acceptable to Uruguay. The contracting parties' decision stated that if by that date any recommendation had not been carried out and no satisfactory adjustment had been effected, Uruguay would be entitled immediately to request authority from the contracting parties to suspend obligations or concessions to these seven countries.

The country's representative requested on June 6, 1963, that the contracting parties authorize a meeting of the panel of experts to consider the reports from the seven countries and to make a recommendation on the degree to which, in the panel's opinion, the seven countries had complied with the contracting parties' decision of

November 16, 1962. The contracting parties approved the Uruguayan government's request. The panel of experts, after reviewing the replies of the seven governments, stated in a report dated October 30, 1963, that it was not empowered to make such a recommendation but only to consider any proposals that Uruguay might wish to make for suspension of its obligations and concessions to these seven countries.

Latin American Free Trade Association

The treaty instituting the Latin American Free Trade Association (LAFTA), commonly known as the Montevideo Treaty, went into effect on June 1, 1961. In 1970, in addition to Uruguay, member countries of LAFTA were Argentina, Bolivia, Brazil, Chile, Colombia, Ecuador, Mexico, Paraguay, Peru, and Venezuela. Under the terms of the treaty as amended, a free trade area was to be brought into full operation among the member countries by December 31, 1980. Chapter VIII of the treaty authorized special measures in favor of member countries at a relatively less advanced stage of economic development. On September 2, 1967, the foreign ministers of the LAFTA member countries passed a resolution declaring that Uruguay was in a situation that permitted it to invoke in its favor the special treatment given in the Montevideo Treaty to relatively less developed countries; other LAFTA member countries were therefore authorized by the resolution to grant special concessions to products of Uruguay. The original authorization was to expire on December 31, 1972, but the LAFTA member countries on December 11, 1969, voted to amend the expiration date to December 31, 1975.

TOURISM

In 1970 tourism was a growing and major enterprise that received governmental support. More than 700,000 tourists, the majority coming from Brazil and Argentina, visited the country in 1970. They spent an average amount in foreign exchange equivalent to US$70 per person, or a total amount in foreign exchange equivalent to between US$45 million and US$50 million, about 22 percent of the country's total earnings for exports of goods and services. Assuming a continuation of the tourist growth rate of 3.1 percent annually for the 1963—69 period, an increase to 770,000 tourists by 1973 could be anticipated; this total would yield estimated foreign exchange earnings of US$58 million. This estimate did not take into account the possibilities of accelerating the growth in the number of tourists through the promotion of tourism and the improvement of facilities.

The climate is ideal during the summer, and there are hundreds of miles of sandy beaches (see ch. 2, Physical Environment). The most popular areas were the beaches between Montevideo and Punta del Este. The government encouraged visitors by limiting visa formalities, promoting a variety of international festivals, and taking steps to ensure an ample supply of beef during the tourist season. The knowledge that steaks are available had been found to play an important role in the vacation plans of the Argentine visitors. Generous tax incentives had greatly benefited the tourist industry and continued to attract private capital (see ch. 22, Finance).

Although the quantity of tourist accommodations was adequate in 1970 for the number of tourists, the quality sometimes left room for improvement. Service in reservation of accommodations, information, restaurants and food preparation, and recreational facilities was at times deficient and reflected a lack of planning, direction, cooperation, and coordination between the responsible government agency and the private industry and within the industry. On March 5, 1970, the Inter-American Development Bank (IDB) lent the country the equivalent of US$1.5 million to assist in financing a three-year program for the renovation of seventy hotels along the Atlantic coast between Montevideo and the border with Brazil and for the possible construction of hotels near the city of Colonia. Funds under this program would be available only to projects involving hotels or motels that could not be classed as luxury establishments when compared with others in the area.

There were in 1970 daily round-trip ferry connections between Colonia and Buenos Aires as well as hydrofoil passenger vessels that operated three times daily, carrying 100 passengers in a fifty-minute crossing. The river transport facilities between the two cities, however, were limited to 4,000 persons per day, although the estimated demand at the peak of the three-month tourist season was 10,000 persons daily.

The planned renovation and construction of hotels were expected to increase the rate of growth in the number of tourists. In 1970 Punta del Este, largely as a result of the expenditure of private capital because of favorable tax incentives, was a booming complex of new restaurants, hotels, nightclubs, apartment buildings, and entertainment centers. During the tourist season its yacht harbor was occupied by hundreds of boats.

DOMESTIC TRADE

Domestic trade in 1970 continued to be focused in Montevideo which, with about half of the country's population, had a higher purchasing power than the rest of the country (see ch. 4, Population and Labor Force). Much of the city's commerce, particularly banking, was in 1970 still concentrated in the older section of the city, characterized by narrow streets and buildings somewhat weakened by old age. In the newer sections of the city, a common arrangement was a collection of many small shops under one roof.

Good-quality fresh fruits and vegetables were available in Montevideo throughout most of the year; they were frequently bought at outdoor markets. These markets were set up daily in different parts of the city and dismantled at night. In addition to the outdoor markets, there were permanent fruit and vegetable stands at various points throughout the city. A number of supermarkets in the city sold a variety of staple food items and a few imported luxury or delicatessen foods.

Hardware, household articles, and cleaners were available generally, but items such as gift wrapping, ribbons, birthday cards, and candles, when they could be purchased, were usually of low quality. There were many little shops specializing in readymade women's wear and accessories, but the prices were uniformly high. A limited amount of good-quality furniture was sold in Montevideo, but it usually had to be custom built and was expensive. Curtain and drapery materials, as well as floor covering, were likewise very costly, and in 1970 there was little of high quality or great variety being offered.

In the field of consumer services, there were beauty parlors and barbershops. Adequate dry cleaning was available, but there were few laundries. Shoe repairs could be obtained quickly and conveniently at reasonable prices. Automobile repairs were expensive, except for bodywork, which was very well executed and moderately priced.

Large wholesale establishments also sold merchandise at retail, sending traveling salesmen from Montevideo to the other urban centers. The smaller wholesaler-retailer in the secondary cities traveled to Montevideo for his purchasing needs. Few of the large firms had branches in other cities. Foreign goods moving into the domestic market did so through the large wholesale importers or through a relatively high number of commission representatives. Credit was extremely scarce in 1970, and most companies were forced to finance their own sales (see ch. 22, Finance). Consumer credit was generally not available unless the retailer had arranged a specific program through the banks; there were no finance compaies to provide loans for consumer credit.

The government had broad powers to regulate the prices of articles of prime necessity under the authority of Law No. 10,940 of September 19, 1947. Prices were controlled directly by fixing maximum, minimum, or variable prices to be charged by the wholesalers, middlemen, or retailers and indirectly by altering customs duties, by purchasing and selling shipments of articles at prices designed to regulate the market, by prohibiting the exportation of scarce articles, by limiting hoarding in warehouses, by creating special price-stabilizing funds, and by granting price subsidies. The law was administered by the National Subsistence and Price Control Council (Consejo Nacional de Subsistencias y Contralor de Precios), an agency of the Ministry of Commerce and Industry. The council maintained official stores throughout the country, in which prime necessities were sold at prices established by the council. The council also controlled the prices at which fruits and vegetables were sold to the public in the street markets (see ch. 7, Living Conditions; ch. 18, Agriculture).

There were in 1970 several special marketing arrangements for agricultural products (see ch. 18, Agriculture). These were operated by rural cooperatives and by associations of farmers. The Farm Confederation of Uruguay (Confederación Granjera del Uruguay), formed in 1968, consisted of twelve agricultural societies established in the departments of Montevideo, Canelones, San José, and Colonia, most of which were truck farmer societies. The Farm Confederation endeavored to find domestic and export markets for the produce of its members; it also represented its member societies in applying to the government for legislation to protect their interests.

The National Federation of Cooperatives (Federación Nacional de Cooperatives) included in 1970 over ninety cooperatives with about 17,000 members. According to its statutes, the national federation was to assist its members in all or some of the operations concerning production, transportation, local sale, and export of commodities produced by the members, as well as in importing products required for the individual or collective operation of the associated cooperatives.

The Poultry Association (Asociación Avícola) was an association of the most important poultry farmers in the southern area of the country. It had successfully exported eggs and frozen chicken since 1963 to Argentina, other South American countries, and Europe.

In 1970 the use of advertising as an aid in domestic trade was well established. The major portion of the advertising was placed through approximately forty advertising agencies recognized by an association of newspaper publishers (see ch. 15, Public Information). Many of these firms also acted as agents for the negotiation of contracts for the purchase and sale of advertising space in newspapers and magazines and advertising time on television broadcasting stations. Newspapers were in 1970 the most effective advertising medium.

Radio was also important. An estimated 98 percent of the homes in the country had at least one set. Among the more than fifty commercial radio stations in the country, competition for advertising was very intense because most of them depended on advertising for their basic revenue. Advertising on television was continuing to grow steadily, but magazine advertising was limited to one weekly general magazine and the weekly news magazine (see ch. 15, Public Information). There were 5,000 sites for outdoor advertising, and numerous walls were used for the indiscriminate placement of advertising posters.

In 1970 the Uruguayan Chamber of Advertisers (Cámara Uruguaya de Anunciantes) was formed in Montevideo. Through the chamber, the leading advertisers of the country planned to utilize modern mass media techniques to promote causes in the public interest and create good will. They intended to establish an audit bureau of circulation and a monitoring service for radio and television. They hoped to raise the artistic, literary, and mechanical standards of the country's advertising, sales promotion, marketing, merchandising, and packing by means of courses, contests, and grants for trips to other countries. At the governmental level, the chamber would strive to protect advertising trade interests against unjustified restrictions and excessive taxation and to foster respect for ethical conduct, truthfulness, and good taste.

ORGANIZATION OF TRADE

By 1970 most medium-sized and large business associations had adopted the form of corporate entities. Other types of business associations were recognized in law, but no relatively large businesses had adopted any of these forms as their legal structure.

Corporate Entities

The principal regulations governing the conduct of a corporate entity were in 1970 those contained in its bylaws; flexibility of operation and control could consequently be achieved through a careful framing of the bylaws. Government control over corporate entities was exercised by attendance at meetings of shareholders, prior approval of the bylaws, approval of annual financial statements for purposes of publication, and verification that clearance statements from the appropriate tax and social security authorities had been obtained before dividends were paid or declared or profits remitted (see ch. 7, Living Conditions; ch. 22, Finance). A corporate entity might be either a domestic corporation or a branch of a foreign company; if the firm was a branch of a foreign company, the headquarters of the foreign company was legally liable for all debts contracted by the local branch and for all acts of the local manager.

Corporations

The capital of a corporation must be expressed in pesos (for value of peso, see Glossary) and divided into shares of equal par value. The authorized capital may not be less than 500,000 pesos. A new corporation may only be legally registered when at least 50 percent of the authorized capital has been subscribed, and the registration becomes effective when at least 20 percent of the amount subscribed is paid. The corporation may commence business during the period of formation, but the directors are personally liable for transactions entered into before registration unless the transactions are subsequently ratified by the properly constituted corporation. There must be a minimum of three founder shareholders, but there are no restrictions as to their nationality or residence, except for radio and television broadcasting companies (see ch. 15, Public Information). The founders may be individuals or corporate entities.

A corporation must be administered by one or more directors elected by the shareholders in a general meeting; the directors need not be shareholders of the corporation, and there are no restrictions as to their nationality or residence. The rights, duties, and responsibilities of the directors of a corporation are restricted to those defined in the bylaws, except that they must present annually to the shareholders a balance sheet and a profit-and-loss statement and that, if the corporation has accumulated losses equivalent to 50 percent of its issued capital stock, they must inform the courts of its position.

Limited Liability Company

A limited liability company is a legal entity distinct from the members forming it; corporations may be participants. The personal liability of each and every participant or quota holder is limited to the capital subscribed by him. The number of participants must be at least two and may not exceed twenty, except that employees, up to a maximum of five, may be admitted as additional participants; there are no restrictions as to nationality or residence. The total capital of the company must be between 5,000 pesos and 1 million pesos and must be divided into quotas of 100 pesos or multiples of 100 pesos. The management of a limited liability company rests with the designated manager or managers, who may or may not be participants in the company but possess all necessary powers to administer and operate it.

Other Types of Business Associations

Other types of business associations include: a general partnership, which consists of two or more partners jointly and severally liable without limit, with each partner having authority to take part in the management; a mixed partnership, which includes both active partners jointly and severally liable without limit and silent partners whose liability is limited to the amount of their capital; and a capital and industry partnership, which has some partners who contribute capital and others who contribute services.

TRANSPORTATION

In 1970 the country's transportation system was being improved to facilitate economic development. The facilities of the principal port of Montevideo, which handled 95 percent of the country's total imports and exports, were being reconstructed and transformed to make it a leading port of the basin of the Río de la Plata. Considerable improvements in the highway system were being made as part of a ten-year highway improvement plan prepared by the government, with the assistance of the International Bank for Reconstruction and Development, or World Bank, and projected to cost the equivalent of US$160 million. General demand for railway services had declined as the interior of the country had increasingly relied on road transportation; the railways had reportedly suffered from overage equipment, shortages of freight cars, and below-standard track.

Highways

The short distances between towns and the low density of population outside of Montevideo make the country well suited to highway transport; highways radiate from Montevideo and connect all important areas (see ch. 2, Physical Environment). Practically any point in the country is within one day's drive of the capital. In 1970 highway traffic was the principal carrier of passengers and freight. Intercity bus service was frequent to most parts of the country and was the most popular means of transport; modern buses, including sleepers, connect Montevideo with Brazil and Argentina. Roads in and around Montevideo were generally good, and there were some excellent hard-surface roads elsewhere.

Most of the country's roads were not paved, however, and high-speed travel, which was common because of the flat and open terrain, was destructive and called for expensive and continued maintenance. Some sections of the main roads were well serviced, but road maintenance was generally below standard, mainly because of the inadequacy of equipment. The more traveled routes, such as the highway between Montevideo and Punta del Este, were well provided with service stations and tow service; this was not true, however, in other parts of the country. Automobile traffic outside of Montevideo was usually very light, and a Sunday drive could therefore be a form of relaxation.

In 1970 work was continuing on the improvement of road transportation, particularly Route 5, the main 320-mile highway running from Montevideo to Rivera. The service area of Route 5 comprised about a quarter of the country and accounted for over a third of livestock and agricultural production (see ch. 18, Agriculture). The improvements to Route 5 being undertaken with the assistance of a loan equivalent to US$18.5 million from the World Bank would provide an all-weather road, assuring year-round accessibility of this important section of the country and reducing transport costs. Under the project, about 300 miles of Route 5 would be improved by widening, paving, raising the grades of certain sections frequently inundated, the replacement of inadequate drainage structures, the widening of eight bridges, and the construction of ten new bridges.

Improvements were also being made in 1970 on Route 26, which extends 321 miles from Rio Branco on the Brazilian border to Paysandú on the Argentine border, passing through Melo and Tacuarembó, and is the major east-west highway. They included work on 145 miles of Route 26 between Tacuarembó and Paysandú and construction of nine bridges and approaches, totaling 22 miles, between Tacuarembó and Melo as part of a highway construction project assisted by an IDB loan equivalent to US$14.8 million signed in July 1969 (see ch. 22, Finance). Year-round use of Route 26, of which 30 percent was totally isolated during one-third of the year because of floods, would be ensured by the improvements to that highway.

The total cost of the highway construction project inaugurated in 1969 was estimated at the equivalent of US$22.4 million; it included the rebuilding of sections of Route 9, which extends 211 miles from Chuy on the Brazilian border to Montevideo. The presidents of Uruguay and Brazil met in Chuy on May 11, 1970, to dedicate the international highway between Route 9 and Brazilian Highway 471 (see ch. 14, Foreign Relations). Major aspects of the 1969 highway construction project affecting Route 9 included the reconstruction, improvement, and paving of an 87-mile stretch of highway between Rocha and Chuy on Route 9; the widening and paving of 22 miles of Route 9 between San Carlos and Pan de Azúcar; and the construction of 19 miles ending at the junction of Routes 9 and 10 at the resort city of Punta del Este.

The country's section of the Pan American Highway includes the 110 miles of Route 1 between Colonia and Montevideo, which is the best road in the country and an important artery of international travel. Route 8 continues the Pan American Highway from Montevideo to the Brazilian border, a distance of about 285 miles, as a paved road passing through Minas, Treinta y Tres, and Melo to Aceguá on the frontier (see ch. 2, Physical Environment). An alternate route to Brazil branches off at Melo and continues on Route 26 to Rio Branco; the mile-long Mauá bridge across the Rio Yaguarón leads to the Brazilian township of Jaguarao.

The question of bridges across the Río Uruguay to link the country with Argentina had been studied in the 1960's by a joint commission created by the governments of the two countries. In 1968 officers of the country's armed forces prepared a report that recommended that a minimum of two bridges across the Río Uruguay be constructed, with first priority assigned to a bridge between Fray Bentos in Uruguay and Puerto Unzué in Argentina. The report pointed out that the proposed Fray Bentos-Puerto Unzué bridge would connect the highway system of Entre Ríos Province in Argentina with that of Uruguay and, through that, with the system of the state of Río Grande do Sul in Brazil; the distance between Argentina and Brazil would be reduced to about 410 miles via this route. The projected bridge would be approximately 2½ miles in length and would require an investment equivalent to about US$15 million. In November 1969 contracts for the preparation of a feasibility study of the proposed Fray Bentos-Puerto Unzué bridge were awarded to a United States firm and an Argentine-Uruguayan company.

The 1968 report on proposed bridges across the Río Uruguay gave second priority to a bridge between Colon in Argentina and Paysandú in Uruguay and commented that this bridge would have a potential for stimulation of economic development equal to that of the Fray Bentos-Puerto Unzué bridge. In the course of an official visit to Argentina in July 1968, the president of Uruguay signed an agreement with the president of Argentina providing for joint action on the construction of the proposed Colon-Paysandú bridge. On March 15, 1970, the two presidents inspected the site of the Colon-Paysandú bridge (see ch. 14, Foreign Relations).

As of December 1967 there were an estimated 120,700 automobiles, 80,100 trucks, and 3,800 buses in the country. The serious shortage of foreign exchange that had existed since the mid-1950's forced the creation of an ability to keep old automobiles in service. A North American observer from an international lending agency noted that models of automobiles built in the 1920's and 1930's were everywhere in evidence in the 1960's, continuing to operate almost as well as when they were new. The problem of obsolescence had been overcome by building domestically the parts and tires that were needed to keep these automobiles on the road. This observer was told that in the rural areas of the country the most popular automobile was the 1928 Ford, which was much sought after when available for sale.

The country's young automotive industry had been assisted by a liberalization of import regulations in 1969, which allowed a substantial increase in the importation of kits of automotive parts for assembly in the country. Through 1969 a total of approximately 8,000 automobiles had been assembled, with the bodies being domestically manufactured; in 1970 there were five vehicle assembly plants, all located in Montevideo (see ch. 19, Industry).

Railways

The country's railroads were in 1970 owned by the government and operated by an autonomous agency, the Administration of State Railroads (Administración de los Ferrocarriles del Estado). There were 1,870 miles of standard-gauge (4 feet 8½ inches) track, 260 locomotives, 200 passenger cars, and 3,500 freight cars. Montevideo was the hub of the railway system, with four main lines radiating from it to penetrate the interior of the country to the Brazilian and Argentine borders, connecting at four points with Brazilian railways. The railroad network supplied direct service to commercially important cities and towns but provided few east-west connections except along the southern coast. Main-line trains were mostly diesel powered.

Inland Waterways and Ports

The country had in 1970 about 700 miles of inland waterways reported to be navigable, of which the Río Uruguay was by far the most important. Oceangoing vessels could travel up this river for 140 miles to Paysandú, and lighter draft ships could proceed 60 miles further to Salto, at which point the river's rapids prevent further passage (see ch. 2, Physical Environment). There were several commercial ports on the Río Uruguay, of which Salto, Paysandú, Fray Bentos, Nueva Palmira, and Carmelo were the most important.

Ports on the estuary of the Río de la Plata and the Atlantic coast included Colonia, Punta del Este, La Paloma, and the country's most important port, Montevideo. A survey taken in 1969 revealed a sharp decline in activity at the port of Montevideo; the number of oceangoing ships handled by the port in that year was 840, about one-third as many as the 2,500 handled thirty-nine years earlier, and the amount of merchandise stored in the port's warehouses had fallen to 28,000 tons from five times that total twenty-eight years earlier.

The National Port Administration (Administración Nacional de Puertos) was in 1970 embarked upon programs designed, first, to reconstruct present harbor and port facilities and, second, to carry out a long-range program to transform the port of Montevideo into a leading port of the basin of the Río de la Plata. Assistance for this purpose had been obtained through a loan equivalent to US$9.4 million from the IDB and a parallel loan from the government of the Netherlands in guilders equivalent to US$3.3 million (see ch. 22, Finance).

There are two free trade zones, one at the port of Colonia and the other at the port of Nueva Palmira, established under Law No. 11,392 of December 13, 1949. These zones permit the installation of plants for processing foreign raw materials when, in the judgment of the government, there is no identical or similar industry in the country. In the free trade zones, any transaction may be effected with respect to goods and raw materials of foreign origin; they may be unloaded or reshipped at any time free of import or export duties and exempt from any existing or future excise tax. Industrial or manufacturing plants that might be installed in a free trade zone would be exempt from taxes for ten years provided that at least 75 percent of the labor employed was domestic; under this same proviso, they would also be relieved of payment of rent on the land they occupy for the same period. A presidential decree of July 17, 1969, liberalized the inflow of goods into the zones; unscheduled cargo carriers were authorized to use the free trade zones, whereas previously only regular shipping lines could do so, and goods were allowed to enter the free trade zones regardless of origin for any destination.

Air Transportation

The government-owned airline, the Uruguayan National Airlines (Primeras Líneas Uruguayas de Navegación Aérea—PLUNA), serves the interior of the country and operates services to Brazil, Paraguay, Bolivia, and Argentina. The number of passengers flown in the late 1960's fluctuated between 35,000 and 60,000 a year, with average flights of 218 miles. The airline acquired one Boeing 727 in 1970. A privately operated airline, the Uruguayan Aeronautic Company (Compania Aeronautica Uruguaya), provides service between Uruguay and Argentina. Foreign airlines provide service to the United States and Europe; several airlines connect Montevideo daily with the most important cities in South America.

COMMUNICATIONS

In 1970 the State Electric Power and Telephones Administration (Administración General de las Usinas Eléctricas y los Teléfonos del Estado) operated the country's telephone system, which was owned by the government (see ch. 19, Industry). The telephone system was heavily overburdened, and new installations were difficult to obtain. There were in 1970 about 195,000 telephones in operation, representing approximately 65 telephones for each 1,000 inhabitants (see ch. 4, Population and Labor Force). International radiotelephone service was also operated by the State Electric Power and Telephones Administration. The domestic telegraph system was owned and operated by the government, and the Administration of State Railroads accepted telegrams for points along its lines. The government operated radio-telegraph systems connecting with New York, London, Paris, Buenos Aires, and other foreign points.

CHAPTER 22

FINANCE

In 1970 inflation remained a problem, although it had been restrained by firm governmental measures in the late 1960's. Recurring annual budgetary deficits consisting of the difference between the expenditures of the entire public sector and total revenues, including domestic and foreign borrowing, had led to accelerating increases in prices. With declines in real earnings from the country's traditional exports of beef and wool, successive governments had been confronted with the dual problem of an inflexible structure for levying taxes and rigid requirements for current expenditures. Sizable expansion of bank credit to both the private and public sectors had been a major reason for the rapid rise in prices. The government that came into office in 1967 exerted firm and coordinated efforts, at sharp variance with customary orientations, to interrupt the inflationary process and to overcome the price instability affecting the country. Significant measures included the creation of the Central Bank (Banco Central), the imposition of restraints on the expansion of bank credit, the 100-percent exchange rate devaluation of November 1967 and the 25-percent exchange rate devaluation of April 1968, and the application of direct wage and price controls in June 1968 (see ch. 20, Labor Relations and Organization). During the July 1968—June 1969 period, the price level rose by only 10 percent.

In 1970 the government was moving toward modification of the tax structure to make revenues less dependent on exports and more responsive to changes in nominal income and to enable it to manage the balance of payments with fewer constraints imposed by the requirements of maintaining revenues. During the 1960—69 period the rates of taxes on exports had varied widely; applied against a relatively constant volume of exports, these taxes had yielded from 6.5 to 19.4 percent of the national government revenues in this ten-year period. This variation in the yield from taxes on exports had been associated with several massive exchange rate devaluations effected in the same span of time. In order to alleviate its chronic fiscal problem, the government had tended to absorb the rise in the domestic currency equivalent of world beef and wool prices that resulted from these devaluations through simultaneous increases in the rates of taxes on exports (see ch. 13, Agriculture).

In 1968 the fiscal operations of the national government yielded a deficit equal to 3.5 percent of expenditures, substantially less than the deficit of 19.6 percent of expenditures in 1967, and the money supply decreased by 10 percent. This result was accomplished with high levels of taxation on exports, a 17-percent decline in the real wages of the civil service, the limitation of direct investment by the national government to less than 1 percent of the gross national product (GNP), and the establishment of absolute ceilings on the expansion of credit by individual banks.

For 1969 the primary goal of the government's financial policy had been to restrict the increase in the cost of living to 20 percent. The government's program had been designed to minimize the upward pressures on prices of increases in costs by limiting the frequency and amount of wage adjustments in the private sector, requiring private businessmen to absorb nominal increases in wages without increasing prices, generally limiting increases in the rates charged by public enterprises to amounts in proportion to the goals set for changes in the price level, and by constructing such increases so as to minimize the secondary effects on prices (see ch. 19, Industry; ch. 20, Labor Relations and Organization). The expansion of the money supply was to be limited by holding the fiscal deficit of the national government to 6.3 percent of expenditures and by continuing the enforcement of absolute ceilings on the granting of credit by private banks. The results obtained in 1969 were generally more favorable than had been anticipated at the beginning of the year—a 14.5-percent increase rather than the 20 percent fixed as the goal.

A large increase in gasoline taxes and marginal adjustments in other tax rates, modification of personal income tax exemptions, and improvements in tax administration effective January 1, 1970, were expected to yield a 24-percent real increase in revenues during the year. An initial installment in early 1970 of the gradual adjustment of the prices charged by certain public enterprises, particularly those in the energy field, for their goods and services, was designed to lead to the establishment of adequate rates of return for these agencies.

The government was also proceeding in 1970 with implementation of the land productivity tax, enacted in 1968 as one of the measures designed to replace the system of export taxes (see ch. 18, Agriculture; ch. 21, Trade). Other noteworthy progress had been made toward the elimination of export taxes. In 1969 export taxes on wool had been cut in half; those on linseed oil had been eliminated entirely. Under legislation passed in November 1969, the previous system of taxing meat exports, under which some fifty categories of meat had been assigned an artificial export value, had been replaced by a tax at a uniform rate on the value of the exported meat as stated in an invoice (see ch. 18, Agriculture; ch. 21, Trade).

Successive balance-of-payments crises had resulted in large accumulations of short-term and medium-term external debt. The country's outstanding external public debt on January 1, 1970, was equivalent to US$261.4 million; this amount was scheduled to be reduced to US$95.7 million by January 1, 1975. This total included publicly issued bonds, loans from private financial institutions, loans from international organizations, loans from governments, suppliers' credits, and miscellaneous forms of external public debt. Through 1969 the total multilateral and bilateral economic assistance received by the country amounted to the equivalent of about US$332 million. On January 1, 1970, its gold and foreign exchange reserves were US$197 million.

Under the Constitution of 1967 each president prepares a five-year budget for his term in office and submits to the General Assembly annual revisions for its approval. The fiscal year is the calendar year. On June 30, 1970, for example, the president was to submit to the General Assembly the accounts for fiscal 1969, the revised budget for fiscal 1970, and the budget for fiscal 1971.

In mid-1970 the only budget data available in absolute figures covered the budget for fiscal 1969, submitted in June 1968 at the height of the inflationary spiral. The number of revisions in the fiscal 1969 budget made by the government through December 1969 had been so great, however, that the original fiscal 1969 budget was only an approximate indication of the amount of revenues and expenditures in that year. In the years before 1969 comparisons of annual totals of revenues and expenditures in current pesos (for value of the peso, see Glossary) had been largely devoid of economic significance because of the rapid pace of inflation until that year. Evaluations of the country's fiscal trends by international lending agencies had therefore usually been in terms of changes from year to year in proportions, ratios, and percentages.

In 1970 the banking system was in the process of change. A central bank had been brought into existence by the Constitution of 1967 but was in 1970 sharing its authority over the monetary structure of the country with the country's largest commercial bank, which still continued to regulate the foreign exchange market and remained the government's fiscal agent. Several other official banks were in operation to serve particular sectors of the economy.

THE BUDGETARY PROCESS

The budget is prepared for each presidential period, spanning five years, with provision for annual adjustments by the General Assembly. Article 214 of the Constitution of 1967 requires the president to prepare the budget for his term of government and submit it to the General Assembly within the first six months of his term which, according to Article 158, begins on the first of March following the presidential election (see ch. 12, The Governmental System). Article 214 requires that the budget which is prepared and adopted contain the current expenditures and investments of the government, the functional wage scales and salaries, estimated revenues, and rules for implementing and interpreting the budget. The fiscal year coincides with the calendar year. Article 214 further requires that the president, within six months after the close of a fiscal year, submit to the General Assembly a rendering of accounts for that year and a computation of the budget for the current fiscal year; the president may propose any changes considered necessary in the total amount of expenditures, investments, salaries, or revenues. He is additionally authorized to create new budget items and to delete or modify budget programs.

The General Assembly is authorized under Article 215 of the Constitution to review the total amount of each budget item and program, the objective of each program, wage scales, the number of officials, and revenues, but it is forbidden to make any changes in the budget that would mean greater expenditures than those proposed by the president. Article 216 permits the establishment by law of a special section in the budget to cover the ordinary permanent expenditures of the government for which periodic revision is not necessary.

Each chamber of the General Assembly is required to act upon the draft budgets or laws governing fiscal accounts within forty-five days of their receipt. if they have not acted within that period, the proposed budgets or fiscal accounting laws are considered rejected. Until a draft budget has been approved, the previous budget continues to be in effect. The General Assembly is prohibited by Article 229 of the Constitution from increasing wages, salaries, retirement allowances, or payments for contracted services within twelve months before the date of the regular elections which, under Article 77, are to be held on the last Sunday in November every five years (see ch. 12, The Governmental System).

The budgets of the autonomous industrial or commercial entities of the government are submitted to the president and, if he approves them, are included in the proposed national budget. If the president disapproves the proposed budgets of the autonomous commercial or industrial entities, the General Assembly is empowered to settle any differences by a two-thirds vote of its full membership; if the General Assembly is unable to reach a decision within forty days, the budgets as amended by the president are considered adopted.

Article 230 of the Constitution provides for a National Office of Planning and Budget (Oficina Nacional de Planeamiento y Presupuesto) immediately under the presidency, which is to be supervised by a commission composed of the ministers concerned with economic development and headed by a director appointed by the president. In 1969 the Planning and Budget Commission (Comisión de Planeamiento y Presupuesto) was established; the commission consisted in 1970 of the ministers of economy and finance; livestock and agriculture; commerce and industry; labor and social security; public works; public health; culture; and transportation, communications and tourism. The commission was presided over by the director of the National Office of Planning and Budget, who had the rank of minister.

The National Office of Planning and Budget prepared annual operation plans that constituted the bases for the annual revisions of the five-year national budget. In 1970, however, coordination between the planning and budget functions was not fully developed; control of the national budget was not in fact under the jurisdiction of the National Office of Planning and Budget. The results of the annual budget reviews based upon operation plans were, therefore, merely recommendations to the president that were transmitted to a body subordinate to the Ministry of Economy and Finance, the office of Comptroller General (Contaduría General), which was responsible for controlling the budget. This office maintained an accounting control of the budget that prevented the administration of the budget by programs. In 1970 the administrative planning system and the national budget were still in the process of being integrated; efforts had begun, however, to coordinate the monetary budget prepared by the Central Bank with the budgets of the public sector for current expenditures and capital investments.

Before 1968 the fiscal transactions of the national government had encompassed those of the ordinary budget and those of three special funds—Export Retentions and Import Surcharges (Detracciones y Recargos), Assigned Taxes (Rentas Afectadas), and the Public Works Fund (Fondo de Obras Públicas). The current budget, which had accounted for about four-fifths of total cash expenditures of the government, had covered the wages and salaries of national government employees, purchases of goods and services, transfers to the rest of the public sector, and servicing of the public debt.

Beginning with the 1968—72 budget, approved by the General Assembly in December 1967, the scope of the budget was extended to include Export Retentions and Import Surcharges and the Public Works Fund; some operations based on receipts from Assigned Taxes were also incorporated into the budget. In 1969 a new fund, the National Housing Fund (Fondo Nacional de Viviendas), was added to the budget. The budget in 1970 therefore consisted of the National Housing Fund, an investment fund, a subsidy fund, and an operating budget that included most of the previous current budget. The investment fund covered primarily the operations previously handled by the Public Works Fund, whereas the subsidy fund brought together the transfers that formerly were made from the current budget and from Export Retentions and Import Surcharges and some of the subsidies paid from Assigned Taxes.

The national government continued in 1970 to be the major fiscal authority, but the decentralized autonomous agencies constituted a substantial portion of the public sector. Before the promulgation of the Constitution of 1967, the executive branch of the national government did not have the necessary authority to control the financial operations of the autonomous agencies. These agencies were, in effect, independent to a considerable extent in fixing the prices to be charged for their goods and services and in planning their annual expenditures, investments, and borrowing.

Through 1968 the real, as compared to the nominal, prices of the goods and services provided by the decentralized autonomous agencies had fallen since 1961. With 1961 as the base year, the index of the real annual average price in 1968 of domestic electricity was 94.4; of industrial electricity, 55.1; of domestic water, 75.0; of diesel oil, 95.7; and of fuel oil, 52.4. For the railroads, again with 1961 as the base year, the index of real rates for passenger fares at the end of 1968 was 39.9; for haulage of produce, 77.9; and for transport of freight, 90.6.

The excess of personnel in the decentralized autonomous agencies and the substantial decrease in the real prices of goods and services provided by these agencies had resulted in an inadequate return on capital investment and, in several cases, deficits on current operations. This situation had been characteristic to varying degrees of the State Electric Power and Telephones Administration; the National Administration for Fuels, Alcohol and Cement; the Administration of State Railroads; the National Port Administration; and the State Sanitary Works Administration (see ch. 7, Living Conditions; ch. 19, Industry; ch. 21, Trade). In the case of the Administration of State Railroads, the situation had been compounded by a stagnation in rail traffic (see ch. 21, Trade). The financing of the investments of these agencies and, in some cases, the subsidization of their current expenditures had burdened the national government with a substantial and growing level of payments.

The deficits of these agencies had been particularly burdensome to the national government in 1967 and 1968; the large deficits in these years were caused by the Administration of State Railroads, the State Electric Power and Telephones Administration, and the National Administration for Fuels, Alcohol and Cement. In 1968 the Administration of State Railroads covered only about 40 percent of its operating costs with its own revenues. At the time of the imposition of direct wage and price controls in June 1968, the national government installed supervisors in the Administration of State Railroads and in the State Electric Power and Telephones Administration; these agencies had not been adhering to the national government's economic policy.

The weak financial position of the autonomous agencies was traceable to a number of causes. Accelerating inflation up to mid-1968 had made increasingly difficult the adjustment of the charges and rates of the agencies to the levels required to keep pace with the rate of inflation. As agencies had been unable to retain and recruit high-quality personnel because of the more attractive salaries and wages offered by the private sector, they suffered a gradual deterioration of administrative efficiency (see ch. 20, Labor Relations and Organization). They had also been adversely affected by insufficient coordination and management of their operations by the national government. During 1968 and 1969 the government made strenuous efforts to improve their operational efficiency and to coordinate and manage them in a rational manner. Some progress had been made in centralization and standardization of the agencies' budgets by introduction of program budgets. The National Administration for Fuels, Alcohol and Cement was engaged in mid-1970 in a process of simplification and modernization with special attention to decentralization and reduction in personnel, in response to a year's study by a United States managerial consulting firm.

TRENDS IN PUBLIC FINANCE

Between 1957 and 1967 the public sector was characterized by serious financial deterioration. The trend was manifested primarily in the large budget deficit of the national government, in some years amounting to more than 30 percent of the total expenditures of the public sector and financed primarily with funds obtained from the official banking system. In 1968 the government made a concentrated effort to limit expenditure and achieve savings and was able to reduce the fiscal deficit to 10.2 percent of total expenditures, the lowest proportion since 1961.

On the basis of the information available in mid-1970, the relation between budgetary expenditures and revenues in 1969 was less favorable than in 1968. The revised 1969 data indicated a deficit amounting to 17.3 percent of total expenditures; the increase in the deficit as a proportion of total expenditures occurred because tax revenues proved to be smaller than had been anticipated.

The 1969 outcome was the continuation of a pattern that had prevailed for eight years. Analysis of the revenues and expenditures of the national government in the 1961—69 period indicates that in most years total annual revenues in real terms were lower than in 1961 whereas total annual expenditures in real terms were significantly higher both in absolute values and as percentages of the GNP. Total annual expenditures in real terms as a proportion of the GNP were 13.0 percent in 1961 and 14.6 percent in 1969, reaching their highest percentage in 1966, when the ratio was 16.1 percent. Total annual revenues in real terms as a proportion of the GNP were 12.3 percent in 1961 and 11.8 percent in 1969; their highest percentage was also in 1966, when the ratio was 12.9 percent.

The country's tax structure in 1970 continued to be based primarily on indirect taxes and taxes on activities related to foreign trade. Through 1969 revenues from direct taxes on income and on net worth had provided a maximum of 15.2 percent of the total tax revenues, whereas taxes on foreign trade and indirect taxes on production, consumption, and transactions had generated 84.8 percent of this total.

During 1968 and 1969 the government introduced important changes in taxes and tried to improve administration and control of tax collection. New legislation on inheritance and real estate transfer taxes, new regulations for inheritance, sales, and service taxes, and legislation changing the tax on income from agriculture and livestock to a tax on the minimum required productivity of agricultural land were affected (see ch. 18, Agriculture).

Tax administration was improved and modernized by employing full-time inspectors and professional experts, improving salary levels, and extending the workday to eight hours (see ch. 20, Labor Relations and Organization). Efforts to simplify the tax system by eliminating insignificant taxes and unifying those of a similar nature were continued in 1969; there were in that year, however, still thirty-six individually identified categories of taxpayers and a large number of individual taxes, many of which failed to produce sufficient revenue to cover the costs of their administration.

Other steps taken to improve tax collection included the concentration of authority in the principal tax collection office, the General Tax Authority (Dirección General Impositiva), an advertising campaign to educate and inform taxpayers, the standardization of the stamp tax and the tax on real estate at a rate of 2 percent, widespread intensive inspection, and the installation of electronic data processing equipment for establishing a registry of taxpayers and auditing tax returns.

The lowering of the minimum levels for imposition of income tax in 1969 led to an increase in the number of taxpayers; in 1968 only 24,760 individuals had filed personal income tax returns. The tax on net worth was increased in 1969 from 1.0 to 1.5 percent.

From 1964 to 1969 gross fixed investment in the public sector averaged annually about 3 percent of the GNP. Around one-third of gross public sector investment was made directly by the national government. The balance was made by the decentralized autonomous agencies, whose investments were financed by transfer payments from the national government. After deducting the estimated depreciation of fixed assets of the public sector in those years, the net amount of public sector investment would presumably have been negligible. The planning of public sector investment had been undertaken unilaterally within the ministries and the decentralized autonomous agencies; the National Office of Planning and Budget created under the Constitution of 1967 to play and carry out public sector investment had been nonoperational, partly because of a lack of authority and personnel and partly because the national government had been unable to allocate sufficient resources to it to permit it to undertake an adequate level of investment.

In 1970 public sector investment was limited to projects in the transportation and agricultural sectors; approximately 45 percent of the investment was financed by disbursements of foreign loans (see ch. 18, Agriculture; ch. 21, Trade). Government bonds denominated in United States dollars were sold to domestic purchasers in order to raise the funds required for the government's contribution in domestic currency to externally financed investment projects.

An international lending agency in 1969 surveyed the investment plans of individual public sector agencies. It found that the agencies planned in the 1971—73 period to invest in road construction and maintenance, the acquisition of commercial aircraft, the expansion and improvement of facilities for the production and distribution of energy, the expansion of facilities for the refining of petroleum, the construction of a new cement plant, housing, and the improvement of municipal sewage and water facilities (see ch. 7, Living Conditions; ch. 19, Industry; ch. 21, Trade).

THE BANKING SYSTEM

The country's banking system in 1970 consisted of the Central Bank (Banco Central) created in March 1967, the government-owned Bank of the Republic (Banco de la República), forty-three commercial banks, and four other official banks. Before the establishment of the Central Bank, the Bank of the Republic had been divided into two departments: the issue department, which performed some of the functions of a central bank, and the banking department which, apart from being the largest commercial bank in the country, regulated the operations of the foreign exchange market and acted as the government's fiscal agent.

The Constitution of 1967 provided in Article 196 for the creation of a central bank; the transitory provisions of the Constitution stipulated that until the new bank's powers were defined by approval of its charter by the General Assembly, it could operate with the powers of the former issue department of the Bank of the Republic. The legislation passed by the General Assembly in August 1967 extended the powers of the Central Bank to include control over the foreign exchange market and supervisory authority over the country's foreign debt.

In addition to the Central Bank and the Bank of the Republic, the official banking sector included the Mortgage Bank of Uruguay (Banco Hipotecário del Uruguay), the National Postal Savings Bank (Caja Nacional de Ahorro Postal), the National Savings and Discount Fund (Fondo Nacional de Ahorros y Descuento), and the Social Welfare Bank (Banco de Previsión Social). The National Savings and Discount Fund was a specialized dependency of the Bank of the Republic. The Constitution of 1967 provided in Article 197 for the creation of the Social Welfare Bank as an autonomous entity, charged with coordinating national social welfare services and organizing social security (see ch. 7, Living Conditions).

These official institutions were not subject to the reserve requirements applicable to private banks; their credit operations and their monetary liabilities were small fractions of those of the entire banking system. The private banking sector included commercial banks and savings banks. Seven foreign banks were operating in the country.

The State Insurance Bank (Banco de Seguros del Estado) had a monopoly of insurance on labor accidents, civil liability for damages to third persons, and agricultural risks. The bank was the principal insurer in the country and, although in certain branches of insurance it competed with free enterprise, the volume of its operations allowed it to determine the conditions of the insurance market. There was in 1970 no express legal prohibition against the placing of insurance risks outside the country; many individuals and corporations consequently contracted insurance coverage abroad where, in general, rates were lower.

The Montevideo Stock Exchange (Bolsa de Valores de Montevideo) was in 1970 the only stock exchange in the country. The total value of all transactions in 1969 was reported at 2.5 billion pesos, or the equivalent of US$10 million at the exchange rate prevailing throughout that year. Other credit institutions operating in the country included investment companies and cooperatives, which were concentrated in the agricultural sector (see ch. 18, Agriculture; ch. 21, Trade).

The Central Bank controlled the operations of the private commercial banks in 1970 by two major means. The first was the determination of the percentage of their deposits that the commercial banks were required to set aside as reserves in the form of deposits at the Central Bank, cash in their vaults, and holdings of government bonds. The commercial banks were authorized to accept deposits both in pesos and in United States dollars; depositors might therefore hold both peso accounts and dollar accounts. Separate reserve requirements were in effect for peso deposits and for dollar deposits. The reserve requirements for peso deposits were further divided into reserve requirements for demand deposits, savings deposits, and time deposits. In mid-1970 the reserve requirements on dollar deposits were 16 percent, on peso demand deposits 40 percent, and on peso times deposits and peso savings deposits 20 percent; these levels had been in effect since November 1967.

In the case of peso deposits, a maximum of 40 percent of the required reserves might be held in the form of government bonds; for dollar deposits, a maximum of 30 percent of the required reserves might be held in the form of government bonds. The usual reserve requirements for the commercial banks applied to their deposits up to an amount equal to eight times their capital and reserves. On deposits that exceeded eight times their capital and reserves but did not exceed ten times their capital and reserves, the reserve requirements were doubled. Deposits in excess of ten times the stipulated amount were subject to a reserve requirement of 100 percent.

Before 1968 the commercial banks had generally held reserves substantially in excess of the amount required to comply with the legal reserve ratios; such excess holdings had been the rule as regards both peso deposits and dollar deposits. Whereas the commercial banks as a whole had been maintaining excess reserves, there were a number of banks with reserve deficiencies. The monetary authorities were empowered to publish the names of banks with reserve deficiencies; this step was believed to be an effective device to assure compliance with the legal requirements. The monetary authorities, however, had been reluctant to use this power for fear of stimulating runs on banks; the banks with reserve deficiencies frequently had been some of the smaller ones, which were in a weak overall financial position. In 1968 the surplus reserves were largely absorbed by the sale of treasury bills to the commercial banks by the monetary authorities and by the monetary authorities' action to require immediate payment by the commercial banks of their outstanding debts to the monetary authorities.

The second means by which the Central Bank controlled the operations of the private commercial banks was the use of absolute ceilings on the peso lending activities of the banks. On July 1, 1968, the commercial banks' peso loan portfolios were frozen at the existing levels, leaving them free to extend new peso credit only to the extent that old loans were repaid. Certain exceptions were made to this general ceiling to facilitate mergers of banking and to provide working capital credit to specific lines of activity, such as wool, cattle, oilseed, wheat, and grape production and slaughterhouse operations (see ch. 18, Agriculture).

Rates of interest on deposits in the commercial banks were in 1970 statutorily limited to 6 percent on time deposits and 14 percent on savings deposits and were forbidden on demand deposits. Most commercial banks had great difficulty in covering their operating costs. In addition to interest on deposits, the commercial banks paid a 6-percent tax on outstanding loans and employed excessive personnel in relation to the low volume of their operations. This personnel surplus stemmed from a banking crisis in 1965, when one-third of the country's banking establishments went into bankruptcy. By arrangement with the government, the surviving institutions were required to absorb personnel from a number of agencies that were forced to close (see ch. 20, Labor Relations and Organization).

The restraints on the lending activity of the commercial banks and the restrictions on interest to depositors had stimulated the operation of a parallel financial market in which lenders discounted the promissory notes of businessmen on terms of about six months and at annual interest rates ranging upward from about 54 percent. The magnitude of the operations of the parallel financial market was unknown, although it was large compared to the lending of the commercial banks. During 1969 several businessmen changed the distribution of their debts by moving from primary reliance on the commercial banks to primary reliance on credit from the parallel market. Peso resources were provided to the parallel market by individuals and firms who would otherwise have placed their currency in peso savings deposits. In response to the various restraints on the operations of the commercial banks, many banks were in 1970 directing clients to parallel market lenders with whom they had established affiliations.

The availability of pesos to the parallel financial market and the competitiveness of this market with the commercial banking system were largely a function of expectations as to the stability of the foreign exchange rate. Since the devaluation of April 1968, there had been little deviation between official and free exchange rates, an equalization of the internal level of prices, relative equilibrium in fiscal operations, and constancy in government policy. The public's willingness to hold pesos had risen to an unusual degree in the period from the April 1968 devaluation through mid-1970.

FLOW OF CAPITAL AND CREDIT

Private Investment

In 1970 the government welcomed private foreign investment. The country had a history of equitable treatment of foreign investment, although in 1970 it had no specific investment law designed to attract private capital. The country's legal system did not discriminate against business because of foreign ownership, nor were there limits placed on foreign participation in local business. No restrictions were present on the entry of foreign capital or the remittance of capital abroad, although strict exchange controls continued in force through mid-1970.

There were no data available in mid-1970 concerning the level of foreign investment in the country. United States investment was concentrated mostly in manufacturing, banking, trading and distribution, meatpacking, cables, insurance, real estate, and a mineral loading dock. The latest available data in mid-1970 indicated that annual sales by affiliates of United States firms engaged in manufacturing amounted to the equivalent of US$59 million.

Foreign Economic Assistance

International Agencies

Through mid-1969 the International Bank for Reconstruction and Development (IBRD; commonly known as World Bank) and its affiliated international organizations had lent the country the equivalent of over US$102 million. The Inter-American Development Bank had been a source of loans totaling the equivalent of slightly over US$61 million. Technical assistance received from the United Nations Development Program amounted to the equivalent of almost US$8 million.

On May 27, 1970, the International Monetary Fund (IMF) approved a standby arrangement that authorized Uruguay to purchase up to the equivalent of US$13.75 million in foreign currencies in exchange for pesos over the twelve-month period beginning with that date. A standby arrangement authorizes a government to make purchases from the IMF in the currencies of other IMF member countries for its own currency up to a maximum amount and for a specified period as negotiated between the IMF and the government for which the standby arrangement is authorized. The standby arrangement of May 2, 1970, was approved upon the basis of a letter dated March 17, 1970, from the government to the IMF delineating the economic program that the government would pursue. The IMF described the program as directed toward maintaining progress made in 1968 and 1969 in reducing the rate of inflation and achieving a further improvement in the balance of payments. The IMF noted that the country's foreign exchange reserves, including the increase in foreign exchange reserves anticipated for 1970, were burdened by heavy foreign debt payments falling due in 1970 and that the standby arrangement would offer a secondary line of reserves to help meet contingencies.

Four previous standby arrangements for the country had been authorized by the IMF. For a period of one year from March 1, 1968, the country had been given the right to purchase from the IMF the currencies of other IMF members in exchange for pesos in an amount equivalent to US$25 million. This authorization was approved on the basis of a letter from the government dated January 17, 1968, with an accompanying memorandum on the government's economic and financial program; the government requested the standby arrangement in view of the large amount of foreign debt that would become due in 1968. The agreement between the government and the IMF on the March 1, 1968, standby arrangement set targets for improvement in the country's foreign exchange reserves and fixed maximum limits for the total expansion of credit by the governmental monetary authorities and for the increase of credit to the public sector. The IMF considered the government's performance under this standby arrangement generally acceptable, and the country purchased foreign currencies equivalent to US$20 million during the one-year period of the arrangement.

Earlier one-year standby arrangements with the IMF went into force in June 1961, in October 1962, and in June 1966. Through January 1968 the country had, under standby arrangements, purchased from the IMF foreign currency totaling the equivalent of US$20 million; of this total, the equivalent of US$15 million had been returned to the IMF before the authorization of the March 1, 1968, standby arrangement.

United States

Total economic assistance from the United States to the country in the period beginning in 1946 and ending in mid-1970 amounted to US$123.6 million, including loans and grants from the United States Agency for International Development (AID) and its predecessor agencies, the sale of agricultural commodities on concessional terms, donations of agricultural products, loans from the Export-Import Bank of the United States, and other United States economic programs. This amount was exclusive of repayments of loans and of interest.

Through mid-1969 the country had purchased from the United States on concessional terms agricultural commodities having a total value equivalent to US$46.3 million; slightly more than half the total value of the agricultural commodities had been paid for in pesos, whereas the balance was payable in United States dollar loans. Of the equivalent in pesos of US$23.8 million used within the country, pesos equal to US$14.9 million were lent to the government for economic development, and the balance of the peso proceeds was lent to private enterprise. The country had also received through mid-1969 donations of agricultural commodities for emergency relief and donations from United States voluntary relief agencies having a value in pesos equivalent to US$5.9 million.

On January 19, 1968, the governments of the United States and Uruguay signed an agreement in Montevideo for the sale of agricultural commodities by the United States to Uruguay. The agreement covered the sale of 200,000 tons of wheat or wheat flour to be supplied during calendar year 1968 and 100,000 tons of corn or grain sorghum to be supplied during the year ending June 30, 1968. Payment for the purchases was to be made in United States dollars. Total value of the commodities, including estimated ocean transportation costs, was calculated at US$19.3 million. The agreement included an undertaking by the government of Uruguay to increase its actual budgetary support of its agricultural agencies and programs, to review its agricultural price policy, and to develop a stable price and incentive program in order to increase agricultural and livestock production (see ch. 18, Agriculture).

On May 7, 1968, the United States and Uruguay signed an agreement for the sale of 50,000 tons of potatoes having a total value, including estimated ocean transportation costs, of US$3.5 million. This agreement was amended on June 28, 1968, to provide for the substitution of 2,000 tons of nonfat dry milk for potatoes of an equivalent value.

The January 19, 1968, agreement had provided that the peso proceeds from the sales of the commodities would be used primarily for aids to agriculture, including feeder roads, storage facilties, agricultural credit, port improvement, and rural education; the agreements signed May 9, 1968, and June 28, 1968, incorporated these provisions. Through 1969 almost 4 billion pesos had been advanced or allocated from the proceeds of the agreements, most of which had been expended on rural development. Major specific uses included the establishment of a fund for the promotion of exports, the construction of rural highways, the establishment and improvement of several veterinary and agricultural research facilities, and the construction of rural schools and fifteen rural hospitals and clinics (see ch. 7, Living Conditions; ch. 8, Education; ch. 18, Agriculture).

Communist Countries

Through 1969 the country had received economic assistance from Communist countries amounting to the equivalent of US$30 million. In 1967 the country received a US$10-million credit from Hungary for the purchase of railroad rolling stock and a factory to produce concrete crossties. In the course of a visit to the Soviet Union by the vice president in February 1969, a commercial treaty and a suppliers' credit arrangement were signed between the two governments (see ch. 14, Foreign Relations). After approval by the General Assembly, the two agreements were promulgated as Law No. 13,746 of September 3, 1969. The suppliers' credit was in the amount of US$20 million for a term of eight years, with interest at the rate of 3½ percent for goods supplied by the Soviet Union to the government and at the rate of 4 percent for goods supplied to private parties; the suppliers' credit arrangement also provided that 30 percent of the exports from Uruguay to the Soviet Union would consist of nontraditional exports. In February 1970 an agreement was signed with Czechoslovakia for a US$5-million suppliers' credit for the import of industrial machinery; the credit was to be available for a period of from eight to ten years, and drawings under the credit would carry a 6-percent interest rate.

MONEY

In 1970 the monetary unit of the country was the peso, divided into 100 centosimos. In mid-1970 the exchange rate of the peso was 250 to 1 United States dollar; this rate had prevailed since April 29, 1968. The devaluation at that time was the tenth reduction in the value of the peso in terms of foreign currencies in a ten-year period; in 1959 the value of the peso had been 3.46 to 1 United States dollar.

The supply of money on January 1, 1969, was 65.4 billion pesos; on January 1, 1959, the money supply had been 1.2 billion pesos. Over a period of ten years, in other words, the supply of money had been multiplied over fifty times.

INFLATION

Ten years of rapidly accelerating inflation reached a maximum annual rate of 183 percent in June 1968; during this period the annual percentage rise in the cost of living had in only one year fallen below 20 percent. In the mid-1960's the process of inflation began to move at a faster pace with annual increases of 43 percent in 1964, 57 percent in 1965, 74 percent in 1966, and 89 percent in 1967. In the four months of July-October 1967 the rate of increase in prices had reached an annual rate of more than 160 percent. During the next few months the government instituted measures to reduce substantially the budget deficit and to bring credit under better control. The general aim of the government was to limit the rise in prices in 1968 to about 50 percent; it was aware that to achieve its price objective financial policies would need to be complemented with an effective policy on incomes but was unable to prepare concrete measures in this field at the time it was framing the rest of its stabilization plan.

The failure to develop an incomes policy meant a continuance of the wage-price spiral. In the early part of 1968 private sector wages were rising faster than in the previous year, as wage adjustments were based on the very high rate of increase in prices recorded in 1967, particularly in the second half of that year (see ch. 20, Labor Relations and Organization). As the first half of 1968 was drawing to a close, the government was confronted by the possible collapse of the stabilization effort as a consequence of a lack of control over wages. In these circumstances the government decided to decree a wage and price freeze effective June 26, 1968. Wage and price controls were accompanied by continued pursuit of a restrictive credit policy in the second half of 1968; both wholesale and consumer prices showed a rise of only about 2 percent in the second semester of 1968, after increases of nearly 64 percent in the first half.

To correct the inequities among the various labor groups that arose from the general freeze of wages adopted in June 1968, some wages in the private sector were adjusted by executive decrees in September and December 1968 (see ch. 20, Labor Relations and Organization). Law No. 13,720 of December 19, 1968, established the Commission on Productivity, Prices and Incomes (Comisión de Productividad, Precios e Ingresos), thereby creating the body that was in the future to be entrusted with wage and price policies (see ch. 19, Industry; ch. 20, Labor Relations and Organization).

SECTION IV. NATIONAL SECURITY

CHAPTER 23

PUBLIC ORDER AND INTERNAL SECURITY

A homogeneous population, extensive social services, a democratic tradition, and the virtual absence of abject poverty tend to eliminate conditions that often breed common crime. In 1970 accurate statistics on the incidence of crime were not available, but figures covering the years from 1958 through 1963 indicated a remarkable degree of uniformity for all reported crime with the exception of homicide, which varied considerably during this period. Common crime was considerably more prevalent in the city and in the department of Montevideo than in the interior departments.

In 1970 the principal government defenses against threats to internal security consisted of the National Police and the Maritime Police, backed up if necessary in time of disorder by the armed forces. Together these organizations had a total strength of about 35,000. Article 168 of the Constitution of 1967 places upon the president the responsibility for the preservation of internal order and external security. During the 1960's there was no apparent external threat to the security of the country, and the occasional disruption of public order resulted mainly from strikes, riots, and demonstrations.

The legal system is based primarily on Roman law. At the apex of the system is the Supreme Court of Justice, created in 1907; it has five justices, who serve five-year terms. Below the Supreme Court of Justice are four appellate courts, forty-seven lawyer courts (juzgados letrados), and over 200 justices of the peace. Constitutional guarantees include the right of habeas corpus; no one may be arrested unless he is caught in a criminal act or there is reasonable ground to believe he has committed a crime, nor may he be imprisoned unless he has been tried and sentenced legally.

The police system dates from 1929. In 1970 the police force numbered approximately 17,000—about equal to the three branches of the armed forces. The National Police are responsible to the minister of interior. In addition to the National Police there is an elite guard and escort organization known as the Metropolitan

Guard and a mounted unit for ceremonies and special police duties called the Republican Guard. A branch known as the Technical Police carries out laboratory work, fingerprinting, photography, and crime detection. In 1966 a small corps of policewomen was created, primarily to act as guides during the tourist season. An additional unit is the Maritime Police. Numbering about 600 in 1970, they carried out antismuggling operations and, in conjunction with the navy, coast guard activities.

The penal code in use in 1970 was first promulgated in 1889 and revised in 1934. Its three books define the methods of punishment, offenses against foreign states or their representatives, and offenses against public order and public morals. The prison system is regulated by the Prison Administration under the Ministry of Culture. There are three prisons, two of them for men. Prisoners are taught handicraft skills and in some cases are required to work on prison farms and on utility projects, such as road construction. Prisoners are paid for work and receive their remuneration at the end of their sentences.

The Communist Party is a legally authorized political organization, which in 1970 numbered about 20,000 and did not appear to constitute an open threat to internal order. A primarily urban organization known as the Tupamaros, believed to be oriented toward the extreme political Left, has committed such crimes as bank robbery, kidnapping, and murder.

THE COURT SYSTEM

The Constitution of 1967 provides that judicial power shall be vested in the Supreme Court of Justice. Below this court are appellate courts, lawyer courts, and justices of the peace. The Supreme Court of Justice is responsible for the administration of the judicial branch of the government, its president being the official spokesman for that branch in any communications with other governmental agencies.

In addition to its original jurisdiction over all violations of the Constitution, it has the power to make judgments regarding conflicts of jurisdiction among the lower courts. It also possesses appellate jurisdiction in some civil matters, including compulsory jurisdiction when a sum greater than 2,000 pesos (for value of the peso, see Glossary) is involved (see ch. 12, The Governmental System).

Immediately below the Supreme Court of Justice are the four appellate courts, three for civil appeals and one for criminal appeals. They have no original jurisdiction. All of them are located in Montevideo. The three civil courts take weekly turns hearing cases, but they are not in session during the annual judicial holidays. Each court has three justices, and in order for it to reach a definitive judgment the vote must be unanimous. The presidency of the appellate courts is rotated annually.

The next courts below the appellate courts are the lawyer courts, of which there are forty-seven. To be a judge of this type of court one must be at least twenty-eight years of age, be either a native-born citizen or have been naturalized for at least four years, and either have been a lawyer for at least four years or have engaged in legal work in the Public Ministry or as a justice of the peace for a minimum of two years. Lawyer court judges who render effective service may remain in office until they reach the age of seventy unless for reasons of conduct they have to be removed. Twenty-six of these judges serve in the city of Montevideo and twenty-one in the departments. The departments of Salto and Paysandú, which have the second and third largest cities, have two lawyer judges each, and the other seventeen departments have one each.

At the lowest level of the court system are the justices of the peace, of whom there are twenty-four in Montevideo and at least one in each of the 224 judicial divisions of the country. Their jurisdiction is limited to minor cases, including financial ones in which the amount involved does not exceed 1,000 pesos. Article 255 of the Constitution of 1967 states that no civil suit may be brought to a court without evidence that a settlement has been attempted before a justice of the peace.

The annual judicial budget includes funds for two lawyers to be assigned as defense counsel for minors and seven lawyers as public defenders in either civil or criminal cases. The basis for these appointments is Article 254 of the Constitution of 1967, which states that the administration of justice shall be gratis for those who are declared to be paupers. Any individual who seeks this benefit must provide pertinent evidence, which is subject to challenge by both the other party and a representative of the national treasury. The treasury is interested because legal documents must be submitted on stamped paper, and in a complicated legal case the cumulative value of these documents may run as high as many thousands of pesos.

Personnel of the judicial branch are divided into two groups—the civil service employees, who are not legally trained, and the career law school graduates. The law school graduates must reside in the area of the court to which they are assigned, except during the regular holidays recognized throughout the country and the annual vacation periods. They must be punctual in the observance of their duties and must be present daily in their offices. Each court must make a semiannual report to the Supreme Court of Justice on the status of its docket, and justices of the peace must report the instances in which they have mediated successfully in civil controversies.

Judges may not practice law nor consult with a client for any purpose unless the case involves their parents or immediate families. Nor may they participate in demonstrations, club meetings, or political activities except to cast votes in regular elections. They may not be elected to departmental political offices or to the General Assembly, but they may accept unpaid appointments in nongovernmental legal committees. They may be removed from office for violation of these rules.

The police have the authority to make arrests for crimes committed in their presence or to arrest a suspect if there is reasonable ground for believing he has committed a felony or misdemeanor. Procedures following the arrest of an individual vary according to whether the crime is a felony or a misdemeanor. Offenses that entail a prison sentence longer than thirty days are felonies and require thorough investigation followed by a trial in an appropriate court. If the punishment for a crime requires only a light jail sentence (thirty days or less) or a fine, or both, it is a misdemeanor and can be settled in the appropriate court of first instance, from which decision there is no appeal.

The first step in the legal process is an investigation called an instruction session, which is carried out for both felonies and misdemeanors. Its purpose is to determine whether a punishable act did, in fact, occur. The judge of instruction, who has initial jurisdiction in all criminal matters, has an additional twenty-four hours in which to file an indictment or release the prisoner. If he finds that sufficient cause exists to remand the prisoner for trial, he may, with the assistance of the police, gather additional evidence and take the testimony of witnesses. During the entire proceedings, from the filing of the indictment to the judgment, the accused is entitled to representation by counsel; if he cannot afford this expense, counsel is provided by the government.

Trials in Uruguay are not public in the sense that there are spectators or oral argument in open court. Depositions of witnesses are taken by the clerk of the court and made a part of the record. The case for the defense is presented in a written brief with the depositions of all its witnesses. When the police investigation has been completed, all testimony recorded, and all evidence introduced, the court studies the data and renders its judgment. In felony cases the judge of instruction will complete the investigation and send the file to the criminal court, which will render judgment.

The two courts of review are the court of appeals and the Supreme Court of Justice. The appellate court reviews matters of fact and judicial judgment, whereas the Supreme Court of Justice concerns itself solely with matters of law and procedure and routinely reviews all criminal judgments. The length of a sentence determines both the place of imprisonment and eligibility for parole. There are places of detention in each of the nineteen departments, but all persons sentenced to terms of more than two years are transferred and serve their terms in the prison in Montevideo.

THE POLICE SYSTEM

The National Police force was established in December 1929, the year after the country gained its independence. In 1970 the police numbered about 17,000, a ratio of about 6 policemen to each 1,000 inhabitants. The police budget for 1969 was 4.5 percent of the national budget. At least 20 percent of the total number of police are assigned to the capital city, which has about half the country's total population. About 40 percent of the police force are assigned to urban areas, and the remainder to rural settlements.

Article 168 of the Constitution of 1967 gives the president, acting through the minister of interior, the responsibility for the preservation of public order. Article 173 authorizes him to appoint a chief of police for each of the departments, whom he may remove at will. These officers must have the same qualifications as senators. The basic responsibility for law enforcement is divided between the National Police and the Maritime Police, the latter being under the supervisory of the Ministry of National Defense.

The National Police

The Ministry of Interior has the responsibility for public safety throughout the country except for the coastal areas and the shores of navigable rivers and lakes. In order to carry out this responsibility, the ministry is organized into four operating agencies, three staff units, and a nationwide communications net. The operating agencies are the Montevideo Police, the Interior Police, the Highway Police, and the National Corps of Firemen. The units are the police General Administration, the Immigration Directorate, and the Employee's Appeal Board.

Police recruitment is handled by each of the departments, and personnel usually remain in a given department throughout their entire careers. Officer candidates must be between seventeen and twenty-three and must have completed the equivalent of high school. Enlisted personnel must be between twenty-one and thirty-five and must have completed the fourth year of primary school. All must be at least five feet six inches in height and must pass a medical examination. The chief of police of Montevideo controls two paramilitary organizations, the Republican Guard and the Metropolitan Guard, as well as the National Corps of Firemen.

The Republican Guard is a mounted unit with a strength of about 450 officers and men usually commanded by an army officer. It is organized into squadrons of about 150 men each. Its personnel are armed with sabers. These, a headquarters and service squadron of about 120 men and two cavalry/cavalry units, are used for guard duty at police headquarters, for parades, for ceremonial occasions, and for riot duty as a backup force for the National Police. A thirty-five-acre farm on the outskirts of Montevideo is used for equitation and training in mounted maneuvers.

The Metropolitan Guard is responsible for collaborating in the maintenance of public order, for taking action alone or with other forces to control disturbances inimical to the national interest, and for maintaining a ready reserve at the disposition of the chief of police. When the organization was first formed, it had a membership of only 60. In 1966 it numbered about 600 officers and men in infantry-type units. Its equipment consists of machineguns, gas weapons, and fire hoses. It was originally intended to be an elite police corps under the ministry of interior, with special requirements such as height, good physical appearance, and special training. Its members were to be assigned as guards at public buildings, such as the presidential offices and the General Assembly buildings, and also to perform special duties as escorts for important foreign visitors. With the increase in their strength they have been assigned duties as guards at banks and large stores. Their commander and deputy commander are army officers.

In 1967 active duty army colonels commanded the police in the departments of Montevideo, Canelones, and Tacuarembó; and retired army colonels, those of Colonia, Cerro Largo, Flores, Río Negro, Treinta y Tres, and Rivera.

The Technical Police

The Technical Police is a branch of the Montevideo Police, in operation since 1945. The staff of about 100 works in three shifts, so that the various sections are on duty twenty-four hours a day. Technical operations include laboratory work, criminal identification, fingerprinting, and photography. In 1970 the patronymic file contained details of 230,000 individuals responsible for a variety of crimes.

The individual filing system is so arranged that it takes only about five minutes to determine whether a person has a police record and, if so, to produce the information needed by the courts. This makes it possible to deal quickly with request for information on previous arrests and also helps speed the release of persons being questioned if they have no police record.

In the planimetric section the technicians prepare sketches used to reconstruct violent incidents and lists of suspects on the basis of identifying data supplied by witnesses. The Technical Police are responsible for investigating clues left by vehicles that cause accidents, and they can determine whether paint traces on clothing belong to a specific type of car. They can also determine whether or not the original serial number on an engine or firearm has been altered. The ballistics section can establish whether a specific projectile was fired from a specific firearm. Details of all the country's criminal offenses that have been reported are kept in the photographic archives of the Technical Police headquarters in Montevideo.

Policewomen

In 1966 a small female police corps was added to the municipal police of Montevideo. The 21 women who were accepted into the organization assist tourists during the tourist season and are assigned regular police duties during the remainder of the year. Of the 200 women who originally applied, 150 were given a physical examination and a test, including typing, dictation, composition, and a demonstration of a knowledge of English, French, and Portuguese. From this group 34 were selected to take courses on police procedure, penal law, personal defense, and knowledge of the city of Montevideo. The 21 who completed the course satisfactorily became special agents of the police on January 1.

The policewomen are between twenty-one and thirty-six years of age and provide information, advice, and assistance to tourists. They are stationed at the Central Railroad Station; the port of Montevideo; the offices of the governmental, private, and Argentine airlines; Carrasco Airport; the interurban bus terminal; the office of the National Organization of Autobuses; and prominent centers in Montevideo. Their professional police duties include the interrogation and guarding of female delinquents and their transportation from police custody to the courts, coroner's office, or elsewhere.

The Quick Action Unit

One of the branches of the Montevideo Police is the Quick Action Unit. This unit has had much success in its operations against the Tupamaros (see Glossary).

The Police Academy

A Police Training Academy was established in Montevideo in 1943, and a decree of 1950 authorized the Office of the Chief of Police, subject to the approval of the minister of interior, to establish and operate a police academy for the training of officers and enlisted personnel of the Police Department, the Fire Department, the Metropolitan Guard, and the Republican Guard. The training is conducted at two schools—one for cadets and officers and the other for enlisted men. Noncommissioned personnel attend classes six hours a day and live at home. Upon graduation enlisted personnel enter the service as agents, and they are paid the salary of that rank during training. They may select the branch of activity in which they prefer to serve and are assigned to this activity if vacancies exist.

Officer cadets are supplied with room, board, uniforms, medical services, and the materials and equipment for the entire program. There are three chiefs of instruction: one each for the officer courses, the Officer Cadet Program, and the School for Enlisted Personnel. The course for agents is for three months, that for non-commissioned officers one year, the cadet program two years, and the in-service qualification courses for promotion of both non-commissioned and commissioned officers, three months.

During 1967 regional courses for the training of policemen in the other eighteen departments were inaugurated. These courses in the departments of Artigas, Salto, and Rivera were more comprehensive than in the other departments because of the difficulty of law enforcement problems along the borders with Brazil and Argentina.

The Maritime Police

The Maritime Police was organized in 1925 under the Ministry of National Defense. In 1934 it was placed directly under the Office of the Naval Chief of Staff, but in 1947, it was removed from that office. At present the command channel extends from the chief executive through the minister of national defense to the director general of the Maritime Police, who usually is the second most senior officer of the navy. Active naval officers are assigned to important command positions and serve for indefinite terms.

The jurisdiction and law enforcement responsibilities of the Maritime Police correspond to those of the National Police. Traditional coast guard functions are performed by both the Maritime Police and the navy. Territorial jurisdiction is restricted to the Atlantic coast, lakes, and inland waterways. Its authorized strength is about 600, which is considered inadequate to execute effectively its mission along the Atlantic coast and the river boundaries with Argentina and Brazil. Close cooperation is maintained with the Bureau of Customs and Immigration, and the Montevideo Police Department.

THE PENAL CODE

The Penal Code of 1889 was revised in 1934 by Law No. 9155.

The 1934 code consists of three books containing 366 articles. Book No. 1 has 131 articles concerned with general principles and the definition of offenses. These are divided according to their gravity into felonies and misdemeanors. Book No. 1 also describes various punishments. These are incarceration in a penitentiary or prison; exile; deprivation of political rights; disqualification from public office; disqualification from a position in the academic, commercial, or industrial fields; suspension of the right to a position in these fields; and fines.

Penitentiary sentences are from two to thirty years, prison sentences are from three months to two years, and exile is from one to ten years. Deprivation of rights is from two to ten years, and suspension of rights is from six months to two years. Fines vary from 50 to 5,000 pesos. Exile requires leaving the territory of the Republic and not returning during the period of the sentence.

Book No. 2 contains 228 articles concerned with crimes against the sovereignty of the state and crimes against foreign states and their chiefs or representatives. These include offenses against the integrity of the national territory, military service in the armed forces of a foreign state at war with Uruguay, passing intelligence information to a foreign power in time of war, sabotage, and crimes against the Constitution. The remaining articles in this book define crimes against individuals and against personal property. Book No. 3 has seven articles concerned with crimes against public order, public morals, and assault against persons.

A code for minors was enacted in 1934 and revised in 1938. This created a juvenile court in Montevideo with jurisdiction over offenders under eighteen. If the environment in which the individual lives is considered harmful to his health and morals, the age limit can be raised to twenty-one. The juvenile court is responsible for the inspection of institutions concerned with child welfare and can pass on the suitability of prospective adoptive parents. It may remove children from their homes and commit them to foster homes or public institutions. Hearings of the juvenile court are not public, but parents and social workers may be present. The court is not one of last resort, and appeals from its decisions may be taken to the appellate courts.

PENAL INSTITUTIONS AND CONDITIONS OF CONFINEMENT

The Ministry of Culture exercises supervision over the three federal prisons and a work colony. Each of the nineteen departments has jails for the temporary detention of criminals, but individuals receiving prison sentences are transported as soon as possible to one of the federal institutions, all of which are in the vicinity of Montevideo. Two of the prisons are for men and the third for women. They are designated Prison No. 1, Prison No. 2, and the Establishment for the Correction and Detention of Women. The other federal institution is the Educational Colony for Work.

Accused men are housed in Prison No. 1 until their sentence is passed. They are examined to determine their state of mental and physical health. After the sentence has been passed, they are usually detained in Prison No. 2 until the end of their sentences. Women prisoners are confined in the Establishment for the Correction and Detention of women. The work colony is designed to aid in the rehabilitation of prisoners for whom agricultural labor is believed to be helpful.

Article 70 of the Uruguayan Penal Code provides that inmates of rural minimum security institutions can be employed in road-building, quarrying, draining and clearing land, and similar improvement projects. The obligation to work is established by law, and work is mandatory for prisoners who have not been tried.

Prison labor is oriented toward the rehabilitation of the individual. Its aims are based on regulations and not on law or administrative practices. A prisoner is trained in a trade or craft according to his aptitudes and physical and mental capabilities. Under this system prison-made goods are sold in the open market either through state-operated stores specializing in such products or through wholesalers and retailers who simply add such goods to their regular stocks.

Marketing, as well as production, becomes a responsibility of the state, and in view of the economics of prison labor, the goods produced must require relatively simple processing if the state is to realize a worthwhile return. This restricts the variety of skills that can be utilized or taught within the penal institutions. Items produced by prison labor do not provide competition to the country's industry.

All working inmates or prisons are paid in accordance with Articles 72 and 73 of the Penal Code. Payments are not made, however, until release of the prisoner, except for small amounts that may be sent to dependents. The remunerations cannot be attached for any reason, and heirs have a legal claim to funds due a prisoner if he dies while incarcerated. If the parent or guardian of a child is serving a prison sentence, the dependent allowance for children that usually stops when a child is fourteen is continued until the child reaches sixteen years of age.

The prison is committed by basic regulations to programs of training in crafts or trades consonant with the mental and physical circumstances of the prisoners and with their postrelease employment opportunities. Newly arrived prisoners are examined by members of the Criminological Institute, created in 1942, and work or training recommendations are made by this agency. Prisoners are compensated for work accidents directly by the Prison Administration, whose regulations provide for the indemnification of sentenced prisoners. This is paid as part of their regular remuneration. The circumstances under which indemnity is granted are in accordance with general Uruguayan laws pertaining to work injuries.

The Educational Colony for Work is located in San José, the capital of San José Department, about thirty miles from Montevideo. It has maximum, medium, and minimum security units in an area of 1,800 acres of arable land. Each of the three units has an independent existence as far as the inmates are concerned, but all three are administered by a single entity. There is a prerelease pavilion for housing prisoners about to complete their term of imprisonment. These individuals may bring their families to live with them until their final discharge. The prisoners themselves are in charge of this facility under the guidance of trained instructors.

The prison buildings are enclosed in a circular area surrounded by two moats. The prerelease pavilion is outside the moat area. The moats are sixty feet wide, and between them is a thirty-foot-wide embankment with a ten-foot wire fence carrying low tension electric current. The buildings include a visiting room, an assembly hall, a theater, and a hospital. Visits to minimum security inmates take place in the open; medium security inmates are separated from visitors by a glass partition, and those in maximum security by reinforced glass partitions with telephones for communication.

Training opportunities include primary education, agricultural training, carpentry, blacksmithing, shoemaking, tailoring, printing, automotive mechanic training, and baking. The sports area includes a football (soccer) field and basketball and volleyball courts.

Statutory provision for a conditional sentence (probation) was made in 1916. Juvenile courts were established in 1939. Since 1960 juvenile delinquency has been on the increase, and juvenile courts have been established in the principal cities. The country has clinics specializing in the mental hygiene and behavior of children and in vocational counseling. There are also juvenile branches of the National Police. The country participates in the United Nations committees on the prevention of crime and the treatment of offenders.

THE INCIDENCE OF CRIME

The most recent statistics on the incidence of crime available in 1970 covered the six-year period 1958 through 1963. These showed about the same frequency from year to year in the incidence of all reported crimes except homicide. Homicide cases varied from 56 recorded in 1958 to 135 in 1962. The six-year average was 107.

Major thefts and burglaries varied from 11,000 in 1958 to almost 17,000 in 1960. Crimes against the person (assault, mayhem) varied from 7,000 in 1958 to 10,000 in both 1959 and 1960. The year 1960 had the highest incidence of all reported serious crimes: homicide, burglary, assault, and theft.

Persons arrested varied from 76,000 in 1958 to 86,700 in 1960. Except for the crime of assault, only a small percentage of the crimes reported were finally cleared by the courts, indicating that the conviction rate for those arrested has been low. The police are required to bring a prisoner before a magistrate within twenty-four hours of his arrest. There are occasions when this is an inadequate length of time to establish a firm prima facie case. The wide latitude accorded the police in making arrests may result in a number of arrests on suspicion. The courts apparently gave little consideration to a confession that has later been repudiated, and they may be influenced by the inadequacy of some detention facilities to exonerate a large number of minor offenders. There are fewer reported crimes in proportion to population and area in the interior departments than in Montevideo. There are also fewer arrests in proportion to reported crimes.

INTERNAL SECURITY

In 1970 the National Police and the branches of the armed forces were capable of maintaining internal security throughout the country. The country's critical economic situation forced the government during the 1960's to freeze the pensions and the wages of government employees; this action produced unrest in certain segments of the population, since incomes could not keep up with the spiraling inflation. Out of a total work force of over a million, some 250,000 people work either for national or departmental government agencies or for the government-owned autonomous agencies, of which there are more than twenty. In addition, 250,000 Uruguayans were receiving social security pensions in 1970 (see ch. 4, Population and Labor Force; ch. 22, Finance).

Increased unrest resulted in 700 strikes in 1966 and the same number in 1967. In 1968 the president declared a state of emergency to prevent further disorder. He lifted security measures in March 1969 but reinstituted them four months later. This caused further opposition to the government even by members of the General Assembly since these individuals believed the institution of security measures to be an arbitrary act on the part of the president, which violated the constitutional rights of the Senate and the Chamber of Representatives.

In 1970 the Communist Party did not appear to represent a threat to public order or to the internal security of the nation. Communists occupied a large percentage of the highest offices in the fourteen most important labor unions, but they represented only about 3 percent of the total membership. Since 1963 public order has been disturbed occasionally by the Tupamaros, who have operated primarily in the city of Montevideo.

The Communist Party

The Communist Party of Uruguay developed as the result of a division in the Socialist Party. In 1919 one sector of that party wished to become affiliated with the Communist International, whereas another sector opposed any such participation. In 1920 the Eighth Congress of the Socialist Party was held in Montevideo. The majority of participating members voted to join the Communist International, and in 1922 the Uruguayan Communist Party was accepted for membership at the International Communist Congress in Moscow (see ch. 3, Historical Setting; ch. 13, Political Dynamics).

In 1969 the strength of the party was estimated to be about 20,000, and in the 1966 national elections the party was the dominant element in the FIdeL front, which registered 5.7 percent of the total vote. The country's liberal political atmosphere has been favorable to the overt operation of the Communist Party, which has been influential in the labor movement and among university students. In 1969 and 1970, however, relations between the Communist Party and the government were strained because of the almost continuous agitation on the part of the Communist-dominated National Workers Convention (Convención Nacional de Trabajadores—CNT) and the University Students' Federation of Uruguay (Federación de Estudiantes Universitarios del Uruguay—FEUU). The governmental response resulted in the reimposing of a limited state of siege, the impressing of striking workers into military service, and the closure of the Communist Party's newspaper *El Popular* for a 10-day period.

The party has three overt sources of funds: monthly dues paid by the members, which are graduated on the basis of income; a percentage of the incomes of members who hold elective governmental positions; and voluntary contributions from members and friends. The national congress is the supreme authority; it elects the Central Committee, which conducts the affairs of the party until the next congress is held. The Central Committee elects a first secretary, an executive committee, and a secretariat. A Control Commission is responsible for party discipline and the auditing and disbursing of funds and, in general, checks on the various activities of party members. In each of the country's nineteen departments the part has a departmental conference (the highest authority), a departmental committee, a general assembly of members, and a base group that is directly in touch with the people.

Shortly after the party was established the Communist Youth Group was created, and this organization held its first congress in 1923. In 1955 this group and the student section of the party joined to form the Union of Communist Youth (Unión de la Juventud Comunista—UJC). The UJC holds a congress every three years. In 1969 there were fourteen sections of the UJC in Montevideo and one in each of the other eighteen departments. It is the largest youth organization in the country, since children may join at age six and the upper age limit is twenty-five. In 1969 the membership was estimated to be 5,000. The UJC works closely with the FEUU.

The Communist Party controls the largest labor organization, the CNT, and its efforts to penetrate student organizations have enjoyed considerable success. The University of the Republic in Montevideo is controlled by the leftist-oriented FEUU.

The party has also attempted to penetrate the theater, the motion picture industry, literary societies, chess and photography clubs, the press, radio, television, and religious organizations. Since 1958 the party has been prominent in a coalition of a number of leftist organizations known as the Leftist Liberty Front (Frente Izquierda de Libertad—FIdeL) (see ch. 13, Political Dynamics).

The Tupamaros

The Tupamaros took their name from either one or both of two Inca chieftains. The first was the Inca ruler Tupac Amaru, who harassed the Spaniards and maintained his court in the mountains near Cuzco, Peru. He was captured, however, and executed by the Spaniards in 1571. His lineal descendant José Gabriel Condorcanqui, born in Bolivia in 1742, preferred to be known as Tupac Amaru like his famous ancestor. He too led an uprising against the Spaniards in 1780 when they would do nothing about alleviating the tragic living conditions of the Indians.

At first the Tupamaros were considered by many to be modern-day Robin Hoods. They raided food distribution centers, stole food-laden trucks, and distributed the produce in slum areas of suburban Montevideo. They uncovered illegal operations of banks and other businesses by stealing account books and revealing their contents to the public. But then they began to use powerful bombs to damage banks and business offices and resort to bank robbery, kidnapping, and murder.

One of the first known lawless acts of the Tupamaros took place in 1963, when members of their organization stole a large quantity of firearms from a rifle club in the interior of the country. By early

1970, as the National Police force had been expanded and equipped and trained to deal with guerrillas, the Tupamaros were operating somewhat more cautiously. The full extent of their activities was difficult to ascertain, however, as press censorship provisions included limitations on the reporting of guerrilla activities and the prohibition of direct reference to the Tupamaros. The arrests of editors and the closing of newspapers that have covered their activities have had strong repercussions in congressional circles.

It was asserted in March 1970 that many of the Tupamaro leaders had been imprisoned. Nevertheless, what police described as the biggest robbery in Uruguayan history, the theft of a tobacco company safe containing gold valued at about US$250,000, was carried out on April 6, 1970, and the Tupamaros symbol, a five-pointed star surrounding the letter *T*, was scrawled on walls at the site of the robbery. On May 29, 1970, they conducted an armed raid on the Naval Training Station in Montevideo and escaped with a large number of arms and large quantity of ammunition. The Tupamaros are also known as the National Liberation Movement (Movimiento de Liberación Nacional—MLN). Although their political affiliation has not been made clear, they are extreme leftist oriented. In August 1970 Raúl Sendic Antonaccio, a lawyer of Serbo-Sicilian descent and reportedly the leader of the Tupamaros, and a number of other Tupamaro leaders, were captured.

Their capture came about during a massive effort by the police and military forces to locate the kidnappers of a United States Agency for International Development public safety adviser and a Brazilian diplomat. These two were kidnapped on July 31, and the former was murdered on August 10. Another foreigner, a United States citizen under contract to the Ministry of Livestock and Agriculture, was kidnapped by the Tupamaros on August 7. The Tupamaros demanded the release of all their imprisoned fellow members in return for the release of their hostages—a demand to which the government refused to accede.

CHAPTER 24

THE ARMED FORCES

In 1970 the armed forces were being maintained at minimum strengths necessary for the successful accomplishment of their missions. Operating within the confines of constitutional law under civil authority, they were particularly concerned with the problem of urban guerrillas and worked with the National Police to suppress these lawless elements.

After José Batlle y Ordóñez overcame the last of the insurgent *caudillos* (political strong men), Aparicio Saravia, in 1904, he laid the basis for a system in which political maneuvering on the part of the military was effectively precluded. Approval by the General Assembly was required for the promotion of military officers, who were subjected to close scrutiny by civilian superiors in the executive and legislative branches. Between 1904 and 1970, with the exception of the mid-1930's, the country was administered by civilian governments.

The total strength of the three branches of the armed forces in 1970 was about 17,000, approximately equal to the number of National Police and Maritime Police. The army numbered about 12,000 and was by far the largest branch. There was no threat of external aggression, and together these forces had the capability of maintaining internal security. The position of the armed forces was clearly defined in the Constitution of 1967, which made the president the commander in chief of all armed forces and gave him the authority to regulate the retirement and pensions of military personnel. The General Assembly was given the right to declare war and to designate every year the number of armed forces deemed necessary.

The army, navy, and air force are subordinate to the Ministry of National Defense, but this distinction is primarily for administrative rather than for command purposes. The Ministry of National Defense controls the Maritime Police, whose responsibility includes the maintenance of public order in the river and coastal areas.

In 1970 enlisted service in the armed forces was voluntary. Legislation for compulsory military service had been submitted to the General Assembly in 1916, 1928, and 1939, but in each case the bills were not approved. In 1940, however, a bill passed by the General Assembly (Law No. 9943) required all male citizens between the ages of eighteen and sixty-five to participate in military training for a certain number of hours each week and those between ten and eighteen to take premilitary instruction.

The members of the officer corps are commissioned from the service academies. The armed forces do not constitute a significant drain on the country's manpower since they represent only 0.6 percent of the population and 2 percent of the total labor force. Total defense expenditures from 1961 through 1969 averaged 8.1 percent of total government expenditures and did not represent an adverse impact on the standard of living. In terms of the country's gross national product (GNP), defense expenditures average 1.4 percent.

The highest military court is the Supreme Military Tribunal, but crimes committed by military personnel are under the jurisdiction of the Supreme Court of Justice. Punishments vary from reprimand, demotion, or relief of assignment to penitentiary sentences of up to thirty years.

In 1970 fringe benefits for military personnel included hospitalization and medical and dental treatment for commissioned and noncommissioned personnel and their dependents and adequate pensions based on the highest grade acquired after a relatively small number of years of active-duty service. The government did not award decorations to military personnel.

All three branches of the armed forces have operated in the civic action field. The army has constructed buildings, bridges, and airfields; assisted in flood relief operations; donated blood to hospitals; and built additional classrooms for overcrowded schools. The air force has conducted air evacuation flights and search and rescue missions and in emergencies, has transported medical personnel and supplies. The navy conducts surface and air search and rescue operations at sea.

ORGANIZATION

The Ministry of National Defense

The responsibilities of the Ministry of National Defense were defined in Article 5 of the Decree of March 1, 1967. Among the twenty assigned responsibilities, those of major importance are defense against external aggression; preservation of internal security and public order; the maintenance of the national defense policy; organization and administration of all units of the armed forces; recruitment of members of the armed forces; and study of the science of war.

The ministry is also responsible for the administration of military training, justice, health, communications, and construction, and it supervises the military retirement and pension service. It may also, after approval by the General Assembly, permit the entrance of foreign troops into the national territory and the departure of national troops to foreign areas. The ministry also cooperates with other governmental agencies in cases of national emergencies.

In 1970 the chain of command extended from the president of the Republic through the minister of national defense to the commanders of the army, navy, and air force. There was no joint staff organization.

The Army

The first soldiers to arrive in the country came from Spain. The horses that came with the cavalry units multiplied in great numbers and provided the mounts for the gauchos who followed José Gervasio Artigas during the wars for independence. The first constitution (1830) established the precept that it was the responsibility of the legislative branch of government to issue regulations concerning the militia, to fix their number, and to designate the times they shall be called to service. The 1967 Constitution has the same statute.

In 1853 the first governmental measures were introduced for the creation of a national guard. These acts provided that each town would have a military unit incorporating the several branches of the army and that the personnel would consist of citizens from eighteen to thirty years of age, who would drill on nonworkdays during the fall months of the year (February, March, and April). The national guard remained in existence for several years, but its importance was supplanted by the regular army that was formed and provided a few thousand men who participated with the armed forces of Brazil and Argentina in the war against Paraguay (see ch. 3, Historical Setting).

Army officers were commissioned from the ranks until 1885, when the Military Academy was established. This academy also provided officers for the naval service until the naval academy was opened in 1916, and in 1913 the Military Academy began to conduct a military aviation course that was discontinued when the Air Force Academy was established in 1950.

The commander in chief of the army is assisted by a chief of staff and a general staff. For operational and internal security purposes the country is divided into four military regions, with army units stationed in each. The army has nine horse and mechanized cavalry squadrons, six infantry battalions, six field artillery battalions, and six engineer battalions.

Mechanized units are equipped with both light and medium tanks. Artillery materiel and tanks are procured from foreign sources. The army maintains an extensive training program. In addition to the

Military Academy, which has a four-year course for cadets, the School of Arms and Services trains junior officers in the technicalities of the various branches; the Command and Staff School teaches army staff officers; and the Military Institute of Superior Studies instructs senior military personnel. The Military Institute of Superior Studies is the highest Uruguayan military institution and, although it is administered by the army, its students include field grade officers of the three branches of the armed forces.

The Navy

The total strength of the navy and the naval air arm in 1970 was approximately 450 officers and 2,000 enlisted men. In addition to its regular duties, the navy commanded the coast guard, provided officers for the merchant marine, and supervised the services that maintained buoys and lighthouses.

The commander in chief of the navy was assisted by a chief of staff, who supervised the Naval War College, the naval attachés, and a general staff of five divisions, but the commanders of a number of important naval functions reported directly to the commander in chief. Among these were directors general of personnel, and finance and materiel; the commanding officers of the Naval Training Center and of Naval Aviation; and the commanders of the two fleet operating units.

In 1970 the operating units included an escort division with two destroyer escorts and a patrol division with several patrol craft. The naval air arm had about 35 qualified naval pilots and 200 enlisted men. There were some fourteen aircraft, most of the liaison type. The navy conducted a training program for its reserves—volunteers who received a few hours of training each day.

The Naval Academy provides a five-year course; its graduates are commissioned in the navy, the coast guard, or the merchant marine. The average number of graduates varies between twenty-five and thirty-five. Most of those entering the navy serve in the line, although a few are selected for the Naval Engineering Corps. The senior naval officers school is the Naval War College. Most of the students are naval commanders and lieutenant commanders, although a few lieutenants are selected. Each class usually has a field grade officer of the army and the air force. Enlisted men are trained in the School of Naval Specialties located in the Naval Training Center in the Montevideo port area.

Senior naval officers are assigned as director of the merchant marine, chief of the Maritime Police, and prefects of the ports of Montevideo, Colonia, Carmelo, and Maldonado.

The Air Force

Military aviation was begun in 1913 as the Military Aeronautics Branch of the army. In 1950 the Air Force Academy was established, and the aviation instruction that had been conducted at the Military Academy was discontinued. In 1953, after the promulgation of Law No. 12,070, the air force, which had been an integral part of the army, became a separate organization.

In 1970 the strength of the air force was 1,700, and it was equipped with about sixty aircraft. The commanding general of the air force had direct control of the three operating groups. Under the commanding general was the chief of staff, who controlled foreign liaison and the four staff sections of personnel, intelligence, operations, and supply. Reporting directly to the commanding general were the air force comptroller and the inspectors for aviation security, schools, and armament.

The operating groups were the Tactical Command, the Training Command, and the Materiel Command. The principal units of the Tactical Command were Air Brigade 1 and Air Brigade 2. Air Brigade 1 was stationed at Carrasco airfield, outside of Montevideo, and consisted of two transport groups, one fighter group, and one search and rescue group. Air Brigade 2 was stationed at the airfield at Durazno, the capital of Durazno Department, and had a tactical reconnaissance group. It also conducted advanced flying instruction.

The mission of the Training Command is to formulate and direct programs designed to increase the efficiency of all units of the air force school system. Its functions include the recruiting and training of air force personnel, the formulation of air force educational policy, the promotion of professional technical proficiency, and the formulation of joint plans and exercises with other branches of the armed forces. The educational institutions under the Training Command include the Air Force Academy, the Command and General Staff School, the Technical School, and the Parachutist School. The Air Force Academy is located at Pando, twenty miles northeast of the capital. A student completing the four-year course is commissioned as a sublieutenant (*alférez*) in the air force. Graduates during the years 1965 through 1967 numbered eleven, twenty-eight, and fifteen, respectively.

The Command and Staff School conducts general staff courses and prepares officers for the duty of higher rank. It is located at Carrasco airfield. Courses include general staff duties, intelligence, operations, logistics, communications and electronics, strategy, air-to-ground cooperation, constitutional law, and atomic energy. Between forty and fifty officers attend the regular courses. The Technical School instructs officers and trains air force recruits. The

Parachutist School provides instruction to officers and enlisted personnel. The Materiel Command consists of a Maintenance and Supply Brigade, a Communications and Electronics Brigade, and an Airdrome Administration division.

The aircraft are mostly of United States manufacture. They include jet fighters, jet trainers, and propeller-operated transport and training aircraft.

MANPOWER AND ECONOMIC CONSIDERATIONS

According to the Constitution of 1967, the General Assembly is responsible for designating annually the number of personnel required for the armed forces, and this number may be increased only by a majority of votes of the full membership of both the Senate and the Chamber of Representatives. The General Assembly also approves the annual budget for the national defense establishment.

Young men are attracted to military service through benefits that include early retirement with adequate pensions, and the armed forces operate schools for enlisted personnel that provide skills useful in future civilian occupations. It has not been difficult to keep enlisted men's vacancies filled. Noncommissioned officers, all of whom are career soldiers, sailors, or airmen, are chosen from the recruits toward the end of their initial period of active service. The small size of the armed forces allows selection of physically qualified applicants and, as the country has a high rate of literacy, the recruits generally have had a basic education.

Military instruction for students in primary, secondary, and industrial schools is given in levels dependent on the age and physical development of the individuals. Courses are available for those aged thirteen to fifteen to prepare them for field exercises, and more advanced training is given to those aged sixteen to eighteen. In order to prepare them for service in the armed forces, persons between the ages of eighteen and thirty are given courses in physical education, discipline, and maneuvers on various bases operated by the Ministry of National Defense.

In 1970 enlisted personnel for the three branches of the armed forces came from volunteers between the ages of eighteen and forty-five, who contracted for one or two years of active service. An estimated 120,000 reserves are available from among those who have retired from active duty and those who have received annual training under the law for compulsory military instruction. The country has no paramilitary force of any significance, but in cases of emergency the services of the Maritime Police, Metropolitan Guard, Republican Guard, and Firemans Corps can be utilized.

The cost of national defense has not had a significant impact on the country's economy, and military appropriations have remained fairly constant since 1965. The purchasing power has been adversely affected, however, by the rising costs of living because of inflation and periodic devaluations of the currency.

The size of the defense forces—as approved by the General Assembly—has averaged 2 percent of the total labor force and 0.6 percent of the total population, thus not constituting a drain on the country's available manpower.

In 1970 the cost of maintaining the military establishment did not adversely affect the living standards of the population, and there was no need for austerity because of national defense. During the nine-year period from 1961 through 1969 governmental expenditures for national defense averaged 8.1 percent of total governmental expenditures, with a low of 6 percent in 1962 and a high of 12.2 percent in 1967. Defense expenditures varied from 1.1 to 1.9 percent of the gross national product, the average being 1.4 percent. The United States Military Assistance Program grants from 1962 through 1969 represented a total of US$17.3 million.

MILITARY JUSTICE

Article 253 of the 1967 Constitution states that military jurisdiction over offenses committed by military personnel is restricted to those committed during a state of warfare and that crimes committed by military personnel in peacetime, regardless of the place in which they are committed, shall be subject to the jurisdiction of the civil courts. In 1970 the Code of Military Justice was a combination of three codes: the Military Penal Code, the Organization of Military Courts, and the Code for Military Penal Procedures.

The Supreme Court of Justice is the highest level at which military cases are heard. When this court sits to resolve a military crime and determine the sentence, two military officers of either general or field grade are added. These officers are appointed by executive authority with approval of the Senate; if the Senate is in recess, designation is made by the Permanent Commission of the General Assembly.

The Code of Military Justice has adopted a system of criminal jurisdiction. Military crimes committed by members of the armed forces are subject to military penal jurisdiction. Common crimes committed by military personnel are subject to civil jurisdiction. Military crimes wherein civilians are the principals or accessories in conjunction with military personnel are subject to military jurisdiction. In cases of civilian and military crimes, if the offenders are both military and civilian, the latter are remanded to civilian justice and the former to military justice.

The Supreme Military Tribunal is the highest military court and is composed of five members: three from the army, one from the navy, and a lawyer who may be either military or civilian. All military members must be at least field grade officers. If the accused is a member of the navy or air force, one of the army incumbents is eliminated by drawing lots and replaced by an officer of the navy or air force. The members of the tribunal are appointed by executive authority with the consent of the Senate or the Permanent Commission of the General Assembly. They serve for four years and may be reelected.

Beneath the Supreme Military Tribunal are two military judges of first instance and three military examining judges, the former appointed by the executive authority and the latter by the Supreme Military Tribunal. The military examining judges prepare indictments for military crimes and present them for prosecution. The military judges of first instance hear and pass sentence on those cases forwarded to them by the military examining judges after the indictment has been concluded. They also act as appellate judges and serve for four-year terms. Summary court judges are the officers so designated by the commanders of army and air force bases and naval ships. Their function is to gather essential data concerning a crime and to present them upon the arrival of the military examining judge.

Within the system of military justice, retired military personnel may serve as members of the Supreme Court of Justice or the Supreme Military Tribunal or as military judges of first instance and military examining judges.

According to Article 131 of the Military Penal Code of 1941, penal action in military cases is always public and is performed by military prosecutors. There is a judicial organization known as the Public Ministry that is the legal representative of the federal government. As far as military justice is concerned, it is encumbent upon the Public Ministry to initiate penal actions stemming from military crimes committed within the territory of the Republic and to cooperate with the military authorities in investigations and other actions necessary for the arraignment of the guilty person or persons.

MEDICAL SERVICES

The Medical Service of the Armed Forces has as its basic mission the protection of the health and the treatment of the illnesses of members of the armed forces and others entitled to these services by regulations. In general, those entitled to medical services include all military personnel, both active duty and retired; dependents of military personnel; pensioned dependents of military personnel; officers and enlisted men of foreign armed forces serving in the country on official or diplomatic missions, and civilian employees of the Ministry of National Defense. In order to fulfill the requirements of its mission, the Directorate of the Medical Service of the Armed Forces depends upon the medical and dental facilities of the three branches of the armed forces.

In 1964 a law was passed designed to improve medical facilities for the armed services. This authorized the Ministry of National Defense to withold 1 percent of the monthly pay of all officers, including police officers under the Ministry of Interior, both active duty and retired, and civilian employees of the Ministry of National Defense. About 0.5 percent is withheld from the monthly pay of noncommissioned officers and enlisted men, both on active duty and retired (including police personnel under the Ministry of Interior), and of cadets attending the service academies. These funds are given to the medical services for the purchase of medicines and laboratory equipment and the construction of new hospital facilities and other improvements.

LOGISTICS

The Ministry of National Defense does not maintain a centralized system for the acquisition and distribution of all items necessary for the armed forces, but it does have a single agency that provides items of personal equipment and subsistence. Each branch of the service obtains petroleum products in quantities sufficient for its own needs. Ammunition and those items of ordnance equipment that can be produced in the country are contracted for by the individual services, and such other items as naval vessels, aircraft, and artillery materiel are procured from foreign sources.

Requisitions proceed from the tactical unit to the unit's base and from there to the respective branch arsenal. The arsenal then purchases the item directly on the open market. In the case of items difficult to obtain, if the cost is considerable, requests to purchase from foreign sources must receive the approval of the branch commander in chief.

UNIFORMS, INSIGNIA, AWARDS, AND DECORATIONS

All three branches of the service have summer, winter, dress, and full dress uniforms, although the full-dress ones are generally reserved for special ceremonies. The army winter uniform is made of green gabardine and the summer uniform of beige tropical worsted. For dress a white blouse is worn in summer. Army rank insignia are indicated on the shoulder boards, which have different colored piping to indicate the various branches of the army. The shoulder board of a sublieutenant has a round gold-colored sunburst about one-half inch in diameter; a second lieutenant, two sunbursts—one smaller than the other; a first lieutenant, two sunbursts of the larger size; a captain, three; a major, one sunburst surmounted by a gold-colored crown; a lieutenant colonel, two sunbursts and a crown; a colonel, a gold-colored five-pointed star surmounted by a replica of the national emblem; and a brigadier general (the highest army rank), two gold-colored stars, the national emblem, and a line of gold leaves on both sides of the insignia. The piping along the sides of the shoulder boards is scarlet for general officers and artillery, moss green for infantry, dark red for cavalry, black for engineers and signal corps, yellow orange for ordnance, violet for medical and veterinary, and brown for quartermaster and transportation corps.

Navy and air force uniforms are similar in style and color to those of the United States Navy and United States Air Force. The blouse for the navy winter uniform is double brested, and that of the summer uniform is single breasted. Rank insignia for both services is indicated by gold bands on the sleeves of the winter uniform and similar bands on shoulder boards of summer uniforms. The top band on the navy uniform has a circle, whereas that of the air force has a diamond. Special insignia are worn on the right breast of the uniform blouse by officers who are aides to President Jorge Pacheco Areco, the minister of national defense, and the deputy minister of national defense. These consist of gold-colored metal bars in the center of which is a silver-colored sun for the aide to the president, and the insignia for the aides to the ministers have four and three silver-colored five-pointed stars, respectively.

The ranks of officers and noncommissioned officers correspond generally to those of the United States Armed Forces, except that the junior officer is a sublieutenant, who ranks below a second lieutenant. The senior rank is that of brigadier general or rear admiral; there are three in the air force, four in the navy, and fourteen in the army.

In 1970 there were no military decorations awarded by the government or the branches of the armed forces. The three branches of the armed forces do, however, award special emblems for excellence in graduation standing at the service academies and at service schools.

CIVIC ACTION

Each year all three branches of the armed forces have continued their role in the field of civic action. In 1968 the army participated in twenty-two of these projects, which included maintenance and improvement of roads, construction of an airport at Rivera, preparation of building sites for government buildings, construction of emergency dams, repair of broken telephone lines, building of additional classrooms for overcrowded schools, and construction of bridges and children's playgrounds. Army units have also provided vehicles for transportation on special occasions, and they are constantly being called upon for blood donations for hospitals.

The air force conducts various activities that contribute to the development and well-being of the country. This is usually accomplished through the transportation of cargo and passengers, not only to the principal population centers, but also to isolated communities and otherwise inaccessible areas. It also evacuates individuals from disaster areas and transports medical personnel and supplies to those areas. Other activities include aerial photography, construction of runways, and search and rescue operations. During calendar year 1969 the air force transported over 6,000 passengers and more than 35,000 pounds of cargo and medical supplies. This included over 200 evacuation flights and 2 search and rescue missions. The air force also participates in other functions of public interest, such as band concerts, sporting events, and repair of schools and public buildings. In June 1970 the air force transported food and medical supplies to the earthquake-striken area of Peru.

The navy provides surface and air search and rescue operations at sea, conducts oceanographic studies, and maintains the lighthouse service. It also provides transportation for personnel and cargo in emergencies and inspects inland waterways and the coastal area in order to ensure the maintenance of proper health standards. The navy operates a 28,000-ton fuel oil tanker that hauls crude oil from distant ports to the national refinery. The naval repair facility provides drydock, repair, and overhaul operations within its capabilities to merchant and fishing fleets. The navy's machine shops perform work for schools, hospitals, and private industry. In addition to the lighthouse service, the navy operates navigational aids along the inland waterways. The River Patrol Squadron provides support and disaster relief to island dwellers on the Río Uruguay.

CONDITIONS OF SERVICE

Morale is good in the military services and, in spite of the fact that the pay is low, there are certain benefits that tend to compensate. Pensions, although not exorbitant, offer a relatively high degree of security, since for military personnel they include parents, wives, grown daughters, and sons until the sons reach the age of twenty-one. If an individual dies while on active duty, there are certain circumstances—depending on the type of duty performed—wherein the heirs could receive a pension based upon the deceased's next higher grade.

Officers may retire on partial pay after twenty years of service; if they complete thirty years, they receive full pay. For noncommissioned officers these terms are fifteen and twenty years. Thus an individual may receive economic security while still young enough to begin a second career. Additional allowances are provided for hazardous duty, such as flying, handling explosives, or assignment to areas where there has been a disease epidemic.

Military personnel and their entire families are entitled to medical care, including hospitalization and outpatient treatment. For these services all ranks contribute a small percent of their monthly salaries. Family allowances are extended to those with sons being educated in official institutions until the sons reach the age of twenty-one, rental allowances are provided, and funeral expenses are paid. Houses in the vicinity of military installations may be rented to military personnel at low rates, and special banking arrangements can be made for the construction of houses anywhere in the country. The officer promotion system is stimulated by the enforced retirement every two years of the two senior general or flag officers in each service.

BIBLIOGRAPHY

Section I. Social

RECOMMENDED SOURCES

Alba, Victor. *The Latin Americans.* New York: Praeger, 1969.

Alisky, Marvin. *Uruguay: A Contemporary Survey.* New York: Praeger, 1969.

Beals, R. "Social Stratification in Latin America." Pages 342—361 in Dwight B. Heath and Richard N. Adams (eds.), *Contemporary Cultures and Societies of Latin America.* New York: Random House, 1965.

Bollo, Sarah. *Literatura Uruguaya, 1807—1965,* I and II. Montevideo: Ediciones Orfeo, 1965.

Bullrich, Francisco. *New Directions in Latin American Architecture.* New York: George Braziller, 1969.

Butland, Gilbert J. *Latin America: A Regional Geography.* (2d ed.) New York: Wiley, 1966.

Castedo, Leopoldo. *A History of Latin American Art and Architecture from Pre-Columbian Times to the Present.* (Trans., Phyllis Freeman.) New York: Praeger, 1969.

Centro Latino Americano de Demografia. *Boletín Demográfico,* I, No. 1, January 1968.

Cohen, J. M. (ed.) *Latin American Writing Today.* Baltimore: Penguin Books, 1967.

Crawford, William Rex. *A Century of Latin American Thought.* Cambridge: Harvard University Press, 1961.

Davis, Harold E. *Latin American Social Thought.* Washington: University Press, 1961.

Ferguson, J. Halcro. *The River Plate Republics.* New York: Time, 1968.

Fitzgibbon, Russell H. "The Political Impact on Religious Development in Uruguay," *Church History,* XXII, No. 1, March 1953, 21—32.

_____. *Uruguay: Portrait of a Democracy.* New Brunswick: Rutgers University Press, 1954.

Franco, Jean. "The Spanish American Novel." Pages 764—771 in Claudio Véliz (ed.), *Latin America and the Caribbean: A Handbook.* New York: Praeger, 1968.

Ganón, Isaac. *Estructura Social del Uruguay*. Montevideo: Editorial As, 1966.

Gillin, John. "Ethos Components in Modern Latin American Culture." Pages 503—517 in Dwight B. Heath and Richard N. Adams (eds.), *Contemporary Societies and Cultures of Latin America*. New York: Random House, 1965.

Haddox, John H. "Carlos Vaz Ferreira: Uruguayan Philosopher," *Journal of Inter-American Studies*, VIII, No. 4, October 1966, 595—600.

Herring, Hubert. *A History of Latin America*. (3rd ed., rev.) New York: Knopf, 1968.

Ibargoxen Islas, Saúl. "Six Uruguayan Poets." Pages 105—116 in *Young Poetry of the Americas*, I. (Cultural Themes Series.) Washington: Pan American Union, n.d.

Inter-American Development Bank. Social Progress Trust Fund. *Second Annual Report, 1962*. Washington: 1963.

———. *Third Annual Report, 1963*. Washington: 1964.

———. *Fourth Annual Report, 1964*. Washington: 1965.

———. *Fifth Annual Report, 1965*. Washington: 1966.

———. *Socio-Economic Progress in Latin America*. (Sixth Annual Report, 1966.) Washington: 1967.

———. *Socio-Economic Progress in Latin America*. (Seventh Annual Report, 1967.) Washington: 1968.

———. *Socio-Economic Progress in Latin America*. (Eighth Annual Report, 1968.) Washington: 1969.

———. *Socio-Economic Progress in Latin America*. (Ninth Annual Report, 1969.) Washington: 1970.

Johnson, John J. *Political Change in Latin America: The Emergence of the Middle Sectors*. Palo Alto: Stanford University Press, 1958.

Lambert, Jacques. *Latin America: Social Structures and Political Institutions*. (Trans., Helen Katel.) Berkeley: University of California Press, 1967.

Lipset, Seymour M., and Solari, Aldo. *Elites in Latin America*. New York: Oxford University Press, 1967.

Mecham, J. Lloyd. *The Church and State in Latin America*. Chapel Hill: University of North Carolina Press, 1966.

Pan American Health Organization. *Annual Report of the Director: 1968*. (Official Document No. 95.) Washington: 1969.

Pendle, George. *Uruguay*. (3d ed.) London: Oxford University Press, 1963.

Pereda Valdes, Ildefonso. "El campo Uruguayo a traves de tres grandes novelistas: Acevedo Díaz, Javier de Viana y Carlos Reyles," *Journal of Inter-American Studies*, VIII, No. 4, October 1966, 535—540.

Rama, Carlos M. *La Religion en el Uruguay*. Montevideo: Ediciones "Nuestro Tiempo," 1964.

______. *Sociología del Uruguay*. Buenos Aires: Editorial Universitaria de Buenos Aires, 1965.

Ramirez, Manuel D. "Florencio Sanchez and His Social Consciousness of the River Plate Region," *Journal of Inter-American Studies*, VII, No. 4, October 1966, 585—594.

Read, William R.; Monterroso, Victor M.; and Johnson, Harmon A. *Latin American Church Growth*. Grand Rapids: Eerdmans, 1969.

Robertson, William Spence. *History of the Latin American Nations*. (Rev. ed.) New York: Appleton, 1925.

Robinson, Harry. *Latin America: A Geographical Survey*. (American ed.) New York: Praeger, 1967.

Santos, John F. "Personal Values." Pages 3—11 in Samuel Shapiro (ed.), *Integration of Man and Society in Latin America*. Notre Dame: University of Notre Dame Press, 1967.

Solari, Aldo. *El Desarrollo Social del Uruguay en la Postguerra: Ensayo*. Montevideo: Editorial Alfa, 1968.

Sormani, Guiseppe (ed.). *The World and Its Peoples: Venezuela, Colombia, Ecuador, Guiana, Uruguay*. New York: Greystone Press, 1966.

Torres-Ríoseco, Arturo. *Antología de la Literatura Hispano Americana*. (2d ed.) New York: Appleton-Century-Crofts, 1941.

United Nations Education, Scientific and Cultural Organization. *World Survey of Education*, IV, Higher Education. New York: 1966.

U.S. Interdepartmental Committee on Nutrition for National Defense. *Republic of Uruguay Nutrition Survey, March—April 1962*. Washington: Office of the Assistant Secretary of Defense, May 1963.

Zea, Leopoldo. *The Latin American Mind*. (Trans., James H. Abbott and Lowell Dunham.) Norman: University of Oklahoma Press, 1963.

Zum Felde, Alberto. *Evolución Historica del Uruguay: Esquema de su Sociologia*. (3d ed.) Montevideo: Maximo Garcia, 1945.

OTHER SOURCES USED

Annuario Pontificio per L'Anno 1968. Città del Vaticano: Tipografia Poliglotta Vaticana, 1968.

Arratia, Alejandro, and Hamilton, Carlos (eds.). *Diez Cuentos Hispanoamericanos*. New York: Oxford University Press, 1958.

"Aspects of the Uruguayan Crisis," *Review of the River Plate*, CLII, No. 3644, July 12, 1967, 19—21.

Beller, Jacob. *Jews in Latin America*. New York: Jonathan David, Publishers, 1969.

Bernstein, Harry. *Making an Inter-American Mind*. Gainesville: University of Florida Press, 1961.

Bon Espassandin, Mario. *Cantegriles*. Montevideo: Editorial Tupac Amaru, 1963.

Bonino, José. "Catholics and Protestants in Latin America," *Frontier*, II, No. 8, Summer 1965, 129–132.

Brannon, Russell H. *The Agricultural Development of Uruguay*. New York: Praeger, 1968.

Bray, Donald W. "Uruguay." Chapter XVI in Ben G. Burnett and Kenneth F. Johnson (eds.), *Political Forces in Latin America: Dimensions of the Quest for Stability*. Belmont: Wadsworth, 1968.

Canfield, D. Lincoln. *East Meets West: South of the Border*. Carbondale: Southern Illinois University Press, 1968.

———. "Trends in American Castilian," *Hispania*, L, No. 4, December 1967, 912–918.

Cardoso, Fernando Henrique. "The Entrepreneurial Elite in Latin America," *America Latina*, X, No. 4, October–December 1967, 22–47.

Castedo, Leopoldo. "Latin American Painting and Sculpture." Pages 795–801 in Claudio Véliz (ed.), *Latin America and the Caribbean: A Handbook*. New York: Praeger, 1968.

Catholic Inter-American Cooperation Program. *Integration of Man and Society in Latin America*. Notre Dame: University of Notre Dame Press, 1968.

Catholic University of America. Conference on the Migration of Peoples to Latin America, April 27–28, 1956. *The Migration of Peoples to Latin America*. (ed., Margaret Bates.) Washington: 1957.

Centro de Cooperación Cientifica de la UNESCO para America Latina en Colaboración con la OEA. *Directorio de Instituciónes Científicas y Científicos del Uruguay*. Montevideo: 1965.

Coates, Mary Weld. "The Spanish Language in Uruguay," *Hispania*, XLI, No. 2, May 1958, 206–208.

Cohen, J. M. "Spanish American Poetry." Pages 772–778 in Claudio Véliz (ed.), *Latin America and the Caribbean: A Handbook*. New York: Praeger, 1968.

"Communist Influences in Uruguay Analyzed," *Este y Oeste* (East and West), Caracas, May–June 1969. [Translated by U.S. Department of Commerce. Office of Technical Services, Joint Publications Research Service (Washington). JPRS: 48,379, *Translations on Latin America* No. 200, July 9, 1969.]

Considine, John J. *New Horizons in Latin America*. New York: Dodd, Mead, 1958.

Considine, John J. (ed.) *Social Revolution in the New Latin America: A Catholic Appraisal*. Notre Dame: Fides Publishers, 1965.

Correa de Azevedo, Luis Heitor. "Latin America Music." Pages 814–819 in Claudio Véliz (ed.), *Latin America and the Caribbean: A Handbook*. New York: Praeger, 1968.

Dauster, Frank. "The Latin American Theater." Pages 789-794 in Claudio Véliz (ed.), *Latin America and the Caribbean: A Handbook*. New York: Praeger, 1968.

Davis, Harold E. *History of Latin America*. New York: Ronald Press, 1968.

Davis, Jack Emory. "The Spanish of Argentina and Uruguay: An Annotated Bibliography for 1940—1965," *Orbis*, XV, No. 1, June 1966, 160—189; and XV, No. 2, December 1966, 442—488.

Davis, Kingley. *World Urbanization 1950—1970*, I: Basic Data for Cities, Countries, and Regions. (Population Monograph Series No. 4.) Berkeley: University of California Press, 1969.

de Armas, Andreas. "The Gaucho's Long Shadow Falls Over Uruguay," *Americas*, XI, No. 4, April 1959, 5—11.

de Carvalho Neto, Paulo. "The Candomble, a Dramatic Dance From Afro-Uruguayan Folklore," *Ethnomusicology*, VI, No. 3, September 1962, 164—174.

Demographic Yearbook, 1967. New York: United Nations, 1968.

de Sherbinin, Betty. *The River Plate Republics*. New York: Coward-McCann, 1945.

Faraone, Roque. *El Uruguay en que Vivimos, 1900—1965*. Montevideo: Aica, 1965.

Fernández Artucio, Hugo. *The Nazi Underground in South America*. New York: Farrar and Rinehart, 1942.

Figueira, Gastón. "Interpretación del Uruguay," *Journal of Inter-American Studies*, IX, No. 4, October 1967, 483—487.

Fitzgibbon, Russell H. "Argentina and Uruguay: A Tale of Two Attitudes," *Pacific Spectator*, VIII, No. 1, Winter 1954, 6—20.

______. "Uruguay: A Model for Freedom and Reform in Latin America." Chapter X in Frederick B. Pike (ed.), *Freedom and Reform in Latin America*. Notre Dame: University of Notre Dame Press, 1959.

Foster, George M. *Culture and Conquest: America's Spanish Heritage*. (Viking Fund Publications in Anthropology, No. 27.) Chicago: Quadrangle Books, 1960.

Galeano, Eduardo. "Uruguay: Promise and Betrayal." Pages 454—466 in James Petras and Maurice Zeitlin (eds.), *Latin America: Reform or Revolution?* (Political Perspectives Series.) Greenwich: Fawcett Publications, 1968.

Ganón, Isaac. "Estratificación social de Montevideo," *America Latina*, IV, No. 4, November 1961, 303—330.

Gillin, John P. "Changing Cultural Values of the Latin American Lower Classes." Pages 1—18 in Cole Blasier (ed.), *Constructive Change in Latin America*. Pittsburgh: University of Pittsburgh Press, 1968.

______. "Middle Segments and Their Values." Pages 23—41 in Robert D. Tomasek (ed.), *Latin American Politics: Studies of the Contemporary Scene*. Garden City: Doubleday, 1966.

Goshko, John M. "Bishops Taking More Liberal Positions," *Washington Post*, March 11, 1968, A—1.

______. "Latin Bishops Chart Future," *Washington Post*, September 7, 1968, B—5.

Goshko, John M., and MacKaye, William R. "Pope Fails to Resolve Issues Dividing Latin Church." *Washington Post*, August 27, 1968, D—1.

Gunther, John. *Inside South America*. New York: Harper and Row, 1967.

Hanke, Lewis. *South America*, II. (Modern Latin America: Continent in Ferment Series.) Princeton: Van Nostrand, 1967.

Harris, Marvin. *Patterns of Race in the Americas*. New York: Walker, 1964.

Hensey, Fritz. "Livramento/Rivera: The Linguistic Side of International Relations," *Journal of Inter-American Studies*, VIII, No. 4, October 1966, 520—535.

Hillekamps, Carl H. *Religion, Kirche, und Staat in Lateinamerika*. Munich: Kösel-Velag, 1966.

Houtart, François, and Pin, Emile. *The Church and the Latin American Revolution*. (Trans., Gilbert Barth.) New York: Sheed and Ward, 1965.

Hudson, W. H. *The Purple Land*. (2d ed.) New York: Three Sirens Press, 1904.

Hutchinson, Bertram. "Social Mobility Rates in Buenos Aires, Montevideo, and Sao Paulo: A Preliminary Comparison," *América Latina*, V, No. 4, October—December 1962, 3—20.

Institute for Comparative Study of Political Systems. *Uruguay: Election Factbook*. Washington: 1966.

The International Atlas. Chicago: Rand McNally, 1969.

Iutaka, Sugiyama. "Estratificación Social y Oportunidades Educacionales Entres Metrópolis Latinoamericanas: Buenos Aires, Montevideo y São Paulo," *América Latina*, V, No. 4, October—December 1962, 53—77.

______. "Mobilidade Social e Oportunidades Educacionais em Buenos Aires e Montevidéu: Uma Análise Comparativa (I)," *América Latina*, VI, No. 2, April—June 1963, 21—39.

Johnson, John J. *Continuity and Change in Latin America*. Palo Alto: Stanford University Press, 1964.

Kantor, Harry. *Patterns of Politics and Political Systems in Latin America*. Chicago: Rand McNally, 1969.

Lange, Francisco Curt. "Los estudios musicales de la America Latina publicados ultimamente." Pages 528—546 in Lewis Hande (ed.), *Handbook of Latin American Studies*. Cambridge· Harvard University Press, 1938.

Lewis, Oscar. "The Culture of Poverty." Pages 149—175 in John J. TePaske and Sydney N. Fisher (eds.), *Explosive Forces in Latin America*. Columbus: Ohio State University, 1964.

Litvinoff, Barnet. *A Peculiar People*. New York: Weybright and Talley, 1969.
Mallet, Alfredo. "Diversification or Standardization: Trends in Latin American Social Security," *International Labour Review*, CI, No. 1, January 1970, 49—83.
Martinez Arona, Galo R. *Función de la Iglesia en la Cultura Nacional*. Montevideo: Ediciones Ap. O. C. E., 1966.
Mecham, J. Lloyd. "The Church in Colonial Spanish America." Pages 200—240 in A. Curtis Wilgus (ed.), *Colonial Hispanic America*. New York: Russell and Russell, 1963.
Milne, Jean. *Fiesta Time in Latin America*. Los Angeles: Ward Ritchie, 1965.
Naciones Unidos. Comision Economica para America Latina. *Educación, Recursos Humanos y Desarrollo en América Latina*. New York: 1968.
1970 Catholic Almanac. (Ed., Felician A. Foy.) Paterson: St. Anthony's Guild, 1970.
Oddone, Juan Antonioa. *La Formación del Uruguay Moderno: La Inmigración y el Desarrollo Económica Social*. Buenos Aires: Editorial Universitaria de Buenos Aires, 1966.
Organización de Estados Americanos. *Datos Básicos de Población en América Latina*. Washington: 1970.
Organization for Economic Development in 53 Countries. *Statistics of the Occupation and Educational Structure of the Labor Force in 53 Countries*. Paris: 1969.
Oxman, Ramón. "Aspectos estructurales básicos de la sociedad Uruguay," *Boletín Uruguayo de Sociologia*, VII, Nos. 13 and 14, December 1968, 16—39.
Pan American Health Organization. *Health Conditions in the Americas, 1963—1964*. Washington: World Health Organization, 1966.
______. *Reported Cases of Notifiable Diseases in the Americas, 1965*. (Scientific Publications No. 149.) Washington: 1967.
Pan American Union. *Constitution of the Republic of Uruguay, 1967*. Washington: 1967.
______. *A Statement of the Laws of Uruguay in Matters Affecting Business*. Washington: 1963.
______. *Uruguay*. (American Republics Series, No. 20.) Washington: 1962 (reprint, 1968).
Pecaut, Daniel. "The Urban Working Class." Pages 674—681 in Claudio Véliz (ed.), *Latin America and the Caribbean: A Handbook*. New York: Praeger, 1968.
Pendle, George. *A History of Latin America*. (Rev. ed.) Baltimore: Penguin Books, 1967.
______. *Paraguay and Uruguay*. London: Black, 1959.
Pereda Valdes, Ildefonso. *El Negro en el Uruguay: Pasado y Presente*, XXV. Montevideo: Revista del Institúto Histórico y Geográfico del Uruguay, 1965.

Peter, Robert. "One Day in the Life of an Uruguayan," *National Review*, XV, No. 12, September 24, 1963, 222.

Picón-Salas, Mariano. *A Cultural History of Spanish America from Conquest to Independence*. (Trans., Irving A. Leonard.) Berkeley: University of California Press, 1962.

Pike, Frederick B. (ed.) *The Conflict Between Church and State in Latin America*. New York: Knopf, 1964.

Poblete Barth, Renato. "The Roman Catholic Church." Pages 730—735 in Claudio Véliz (ed.), *Latin America and the Caribbean: A Handbook*. New York: Praeger, 1968.

Population Reference Bureau. *Desarrollo Urbano en América Latína*. (Programas Internacionales de Población Series.) Bogotá: October 1969.

Price, Waterhouse and Company. *Information Guide for Doing Business in Uruguay*. N.pl.: 1968.

———. *Information Guide for Doing Business in Uruguay*. N.pl.: 1969.

Promper, Werner. *Priesternot in Lateinamerika*. Löwen: Lateinamerika Kolleg der Katholischen Universität, 1965.

Prudencio, Damboriena. *El Protestantismo en America Latina*, II. Bogotá: Oficina Inter-nacional de Investigaciones Sociales de FERES, 1963.

Rama, Carlos M. "The Passing of the Afro-Uruguayans from Caste Society into Class Society." Pages 28—50 in Magnus Morner (ed.), *Race and Class in Latin America*. New York: Columbia University Press, 1970.

"Report on Uruguay," *Latin American Report*, V, No. 12, December—January 1966, 5—27.

República Oriental del Uruguay. *Uruguay*. Montevideo: Talleres Graficos de "Impresora Uruguaya," 1961.

República Oriental del Uruguay. Direccion de Migracion. *Memoria: Correspondiente al Año 1968*. Montevideo: Imprenta Nacional, 1969.

República Oriental del Uruguay. Ministerio de Ganadería y Agricultura. *Censo General Agropecuario, 1966*. Montevideo: 1968.

República Oriental del Uruguay. Ministerio de Ganadería y Agricultura. Deparamento de Sociologia Rural. *Las Sociedades Campesinas del Area Rioplatense: Su Formación Histórica; Sus Caracteres Estructurales; Sus Vínculos Con La Economiá Urbana*, by Daniel D. Vidart. (Publication No. 4) Montevideo: Deparamento de Sociologia Rural, 1960.

Roberts, C. Paul (ed.). *Statistical Abstract of Latin America, 1969*. (12th ed.) Los Angeles: University of California at Los Angeles, December 1969.

Rycroft, W. Stanley. *Religion and Faith in Latin America*. Philadelphia: Westminster Press, 1958.

Sanders, Thomas G. "The Church in Latin America," *Foreign Affairs*, XLVIII, No. 2, January 1970, 285—300.
Scott, John. *How Much Progress? A Report to the Editors of Time*. New York: Time, 1963.
Silvert, Kalman H. *The Conflict Society: Reaction and Revolution in Latin America*. New Orleans: Hauser Press, 1961.
Smith, T. Lynn. *The Process of Rural Development in Latin America*. Gainesville: University of Florida Press, 1964.
Solari, Aldo. "El Envecemiento de la población en el Uruguay y sus consecuencias," *América Latina*, IV, No. 1, February 1961, 55—65.
The South American Handbook, 1970. (ed., Andrew Marshall.) Chicago: Rand McNally, 1970.
Taylor, Philip B., Jr. *Government and the Politics of Uruguay*. (Tulane Studies in Political Science, VII.) New Orleans: Tulane University Press, 1960.
———. "Uruguay's Dysfunctional Political System." Pages 514—542 in Robert D. Tomasek (ed.), *Latin American Politics: Studies of the Contemporary Scene*. Garden City: Doubleday, 1966.
Terry, Edward Davis (ed.). *Artists and Writers in the Evolution of Latin America*. University: University of Alabama Press, 1969.
Unión Panamericana. *America en Cifras 1967; Situación Cultural: Educación y Ostros Aspectos Culturales*. Washington: 1969.
———. *America en Cifras 1967: Situación Física: Territorio y Clima*. Washington: 1967.
———. *América en Cifras, 1967; Situación Social: Hogar Habitación, Mejoramiento Urbano, Previsión, Social, Asistancia Medica y de Salud, y Trabajo*. Washington: 1969.
———. *Compositores de América*, XIII. Washington: 1967.
———. *La Formacion del Professorado de la Escuelas Normales Latinoamericanas*. Washington: 1964.
———. *Los Libros de Texte de las Escuelas Primarias de América*. Washington: 1964.
United Nations Educational, Scientific and Cultural Organization. *World Survey of Education*, II: Primary Education. New York: 1958.
———. *World Survey of Education*, III: Secondary Education. New York: 1961.
U.S. Agency for International Development. *Population Program Assistance*. Washington: 1969.
U.S. Agency for International Development. Bureau for Latin America. Office of Development Programs. *Summary Economic and Social Indicators: 18 Latin American Countries, 1960—1969*. Washington: June 1970 (mimeo.).

_____. *Summary Economic and Social Indicators, 18 Latin American Countries, 1961—1968*. Washington: June 1969 (mimeo.).

U.S. Department of Labor. *Labor Conditions in Uruguay, 1964*. (Labor Digest No. 88.) Washington: 1964.

U.S. Department of State. *State Department Background Notes: Uruguay*. Washington: 1968.

U.S. Department of State. Foreign Area Research Documentation Center. External Research Staff. *Urban Classes and Acculturation in Latin America*, by Emilio Willems. (Foreign Affairs Research Series No. 7191.) Madison: University of Wisconsin, March 1968 (mimeo.).

Ureña, Pedro Henriquez. *A Concise History of Latin American Culture*. New York: Praeger, 1966.

Vekemans, Roger, and Segundo, J. L. "Essay of a Socio-Economic Typology of the Latin American Countries." Pages 67—94 in Egbert de Vries and José Medina Echavarría (eds.), *Social Aspects of Economic Development in America*, I. (Papers submitted to the Expert Working Group on Social Aspects of Economic Development in Latin America, meeting, December 12—21, 1960.) Touri: United Nations Educational, Scientific and Cultural Organization, 1963.

Wagley, Charles. *The Latin American Tradition*. New York: Columbia University Press, 1968.

Whitaker, Arthur P. "Nationalism and Religion in Argentina and Uruguay." Pages 73—90 in William V. D'Antonio and Frederick B. Pike (eds.), *Religion, Revolution and Reform: New Forces for Change in Latin America*. New York: Praeger, 1964.

Wilgus, A. Curtis. *The Development of Hispanic America*. New York: Farrar and Rinehart, 1941.

Williams, Mary Wilhelmine; Bartlett, Ruhl J.; and Miller, Russell E. *The People and Politics of Latin America* (4th Ed.) Boston: Ginn, 1958.

Wolfe, Marshall. "Rural Settlement Patterns and Social Change in Latin America," *Latin American Research Review*, I, No. 2, Spring 1966, 5—64.

Wood, James R., and Weinstein, Euguene A. "Industrialization, Values and Occupational Evaluation in Uruguay," *American Journal of Sociology*, LXXII, No. 1, July 1966, 47—57.

World Christian Handbook, 1968. (Eds., H. Wakelin Coxill and Kenneth Grubb.) Nashville: Abingdon Press, 1967.

World Health Organization. *Second Report of the World Health Situation, 1957—1960*. (Official Records of World Health Organization No. 122.) Geneva: 1963.

Worldmark Encyclopedia of the Nations, III: Americas. (3d ed.) New York: Harper and Row, 1967.

Yearbook of Labour Statistics, 1969. International Labour Office. Geneva: International Labour Office, n.d.

Various issues of the following periodicals were also used in the preparation of this section: *Baltimore Sun*, May 1968—May 1970; *Carta de Montevideo* February—August 1970; *Christian Science Monitor*, January 1967—August 1970; *Latin American Airmail* [London], March 1968—August 1970; *La Manaña* [Montevideo], January—August 1970; *Marcha* [Montevideo], April—May 1970; *New York Times*, May 1969—August 1970; *Plateo* [Montevideo] April—May 1970; *Times of the Americas* [Washington], April 1969—July 1970; and *Washington Post*, January 1968—August 1970.

Section II. Political

RECOMMENDED SOURCES

Alisky, Marvin. *Uruguay: A Contemporary Survey*. New York: Praeger, 1969.

Bray, Donald W. "Uruguay." Chapter XVI in Ben G. Burnett and Kenneth F. Johnson (eds.), *Political Forces in Latin America: Dimensions of the Quest for Stability*. Belmont: Wadsworth, 1968.

Connel-Smith, Gordon. "The Political Problems of Latin American Integration." Pages 395—402 in Claudio Véliz (ed.), *Latin America and the Caribbean: A Handbook*. New York: Praeger, 1968.

Craig, Alexander. "Uruguay: Back to One-Man Rule," *World Today*, XXIII, No. 2, February 1967, 43—46.

Dreier, John C. *The Organization of American States and the Hemisphere Crisis*. New York: Harper and Row, 1962.

Editor and Publisher International Year Book, 1970. New York: Editor and Publisher, 1970.

Figueira, Gastón. "Interpretación del Uruguay," *Journal of Inter-American Studies*, IX, No. 4, October 1967, 483—487.

Fitzgibbon, Russell H. "Uruguay: A Model for Freedom and Reform in Latin America." Chapter X in Frederick B. Pike (ed.), *Freedom and Reform in Latin America*. Notre Dame: University of Notre Dame Press, 1959.

———. *Uruguay: Portrait of a Democracy*. New Brunswick: Rutgers University Press, 1954.

Foreign Broadcast Information Service. *Broadcasting Stations of the World*. Part I: Amplitude Modulation Broadcasting Stations According to Country and City. Washington: GPO, 1969.

Foreign Broadcast Information Service. *Broadcasting Stations of the World*, Part IV: Television Stations. Washington: GPO, 1969.

Galeano, Eduardo. "Uruguay: Promise and Betrayal." Pages 454—466 in James Petras and Maurice Zeitlin (eds.), *Latin America: Reform or Revolution?* (Political Perspectives Series.) Greenwich: Fawcett Publications, 1968.

Ganón, Isaac. *Estructura Social del Uruguay*. Montevideo: Editorial As, 1966.

Gunther, John. *Inside South America*. New York: Harper and Row, 1967.

Hall, John O. *Public Administration in Uruguay*. Montevideo: Institute of Inter-American Affairs, 1954.

Herring, Hubert. *A History of Latin America*. (3d ed., rev.) New York: Knopf, 1968.

Institute for the Comparative Study of Political Systems. *Uruguay: Election Factbook*. Washington: 1966.

Johnson, John J. *Political Change in Latin America: The Emergence of the Middle Sectors*. Palo Alto: Stanford University Press, 1958.

Lindhal, Goran G. "Uruguay: Government by Institutions." Chapter 19 in Martin C. Needler (ed.), *Political Systems of Latin America*. Princeton: Van Nostrand, 1964.

______. *Uruguay's New Path: A Study of Politics During the First Colegiado, 1919—33*. (Institute of Ibero-American Studies Series.) Stockholm: Bröderna Lagerström, 1962.

Lipset, Seymour M., and Solari, Aldo. *Elites in Latin America*. New York: Oxford University Press, 1967.

Martínez-Montero, Homer. "Law and the River," *Americas*, No. 2, February 1966, 1—4.

Mecham, J. Lloyd. *The United States and Inter-American Security: 1889—1960*. Austin: University of Texas Press, 1961.

Mercier Vega, Luis. *Roads to Power in Latin America*. (Trans., Robert Rowland.) New York: Praeger, 1969.

Pan American Union. *Constitution of the Republic of Uruguay, 1967*. Washington: 1967.

Pendle, George. *Uruguay*. (3d ed.) London: Oxford University Press, 1963.

Political Handbook and Atlas of the World, 1970. (Eds., Richard P. Stebbins and Alba Amoia). New York: Simon and Schuster, 1970.

Publishers' World 68/69. New York: R. R. Bowker, 1968.

República Oriental del Uruguay. Presidencia de la República. Oficina de Planeamiento y Presupuesto. *Una Estrategia para el Desarrollo*. Montevideo: June 1970.

Silvert, Kalman H. *The Conflict Society: Reaction and Revolution in Latin America*. New Orleans: Hauser Press, 1961.

Taylor, Philip B., Jr. *Government and the Politics of Uruguay*. (Tulane Studies in Political Science, VII.) New Orleans: Tulane University Press, 1960.

______. "Uruguay's Dysfunctional Political System." Pages 514—542 in Robert D. Tomasek (ed.), *Latin American Politics: Studies of the Contemporary Scene*. Garden City: Doubleday, 1966.

Unión Panamericana. *America en Cifras 1967; Situación Cultural: Educacion y Otros Aspectos Culturales*. Washington: 1967.

United Nations Educational, Scientific and Cultural Organization. *World Communications—Press, Radio, Television, Film*. (4th ed.) New York: 1966.

Uruguayan Institute of International Law. *Uruguay and the United Nations*. (National Studies on International Organization Series.) New York: Manhattan Publishing, 1958.
Wainhouse, David W., et al. *International Peace Observation*. Baltimore: Johns Hopkins University Press, 1966.
World Radio-TV Handbook 1970. (Ed., J. M. Frost). (24th ed.) Soliljevej: H. P. J. Meakin, 1970

OTHER SOURCES USED

"Argentina More Susceptible: River Plate No Barrier to Terrorists," *Times of the Americas*, February 18, 1970, 7.
"Assalts no Uruguai," *O Estado de São Paulo*, April 7, 1970, 12.
Beller, Jacob. *Jews in Latin America*. New York: Jonathan David Publishers, 1969.
Busey, James L. *Latin America: Political Institutions and Processes*. New York: Random House, 1964.
Calvert, Peter. *Latin America: Internal Conflict and International Peace*. (Making of the Twentieth Century Series.) London: Macmillan, 1969.
Claude, Inis L., Jr. "The OAS, the UN, and the United States." Pages 3 21 in Joseph S. Nye, Jr. (ed.), *International Regionalism: Readings*. Boston: Little, Brown, 1968.
Davis, Harold E. *History of Latin America*. New York: Ronald Press, 1968.
Economist Intelligence Unit. *Quarterly Economic Review: Uruguay, Paraguay*. London: 1970.
Ferguson, J. Halcro. *The River Plate Republics*. New York: Time, 1968.
Fernández Artucio, Hugo. *The Nazi Underground in South America*. New York: Farrar and Rinehart, 1942.
Fitzgibbon, Russell H. "Argentina and Uruguay: A Tale of Two Attitudes," *Pacific Spectator*, VIII, No. 1, Winter 1954, 6—20.
Gallatin International Business Service. *Uruguay*. N.pl.: Copley International Corporation, 1966.
Gibson, Carlos. "American Regionalism and the United Nations," *Annals of the American Academy of Political and Social Science*, CCCLX, July 1965, 120—127.
Goshko, John M. "Uruguay President is Keeping the Lid on Unrest," *Washington Post*, December 6, 1969, A—21.
José, James R. "An Inter-American Peace Force Within the Framework of the Organization of American States: Advantages, Impediments and Implications." (Unpublished doctoral dissertation, American University, School of International Service, 1968.)
Kantor, Harry. *Patterns of Politics and Political Systems in Latin America*. Chicago: Rand McNally, 1969.

Mecham, J. Lloyd. *A Survey of United States-Latin American Relations*. Boston: Houghton Mifflin, 1965.

Mercier Vega, Luis. *Guerrillas in Latin America: The Technique of the Counter-State*. New York: Praeger, 1969.

Organización de los Estados Americanos. Consejo Permanente. *Informe de la Comisión de Asuntos Juridico—Politicos sobre una Resolución Condenatoria de los Actos de Terrorismo, el Secuestro de Personas y la Extorsion Conexa con este Delito*. (OEA Documentos Oficiales, Ser. G., CP/Doc. 19/70.) Washington: May 13, 1970.

O'Shaugnessy, Hugh. "Uruguayans Say Police Torturing," *Washington Post*, June 22, 1970, A—19.

Pan American Union. *Uruguay*. (American Republics Series, No. 20.) Washington: 1962 (reprint, 1968).

Parkinson, Fred. "Latin American Foreign Policies." Pages 414—424 in Claudio Véliz (ed.), *Latin America and the Caribbean: A Handbook*. New York: Praeger, 1968.

Pendle, George. "Uruguay." Pages 127—136 in Claudio Véliz (ed.), *Latin America and the Caribbean: A Handbook*. New York: Praeger, 1968.

Pereda Valdes, Ildefonso. "El campo Uruguayo a traves de tres grandes novelistas: Acevedo Díaz, Javier de Viana y Carlos Reyles," *Journal of Inter-American Studies*, VIII, No. 4, October 1966, 535—540.

———. *El Negro en el Uruguay, Pasado y Presento*, XXV. Montevideo: Revista del Institúto Histórico y Geográfico del Uruguay, 1965.

Rama, Carlos M. *Sociología del Uruguay*. Buenos Aires: Editorial Universitaria de Buenos Aires, 1965.

Redding, David. "Uruguay: An Advanced Case of the English Sickness?" Washington: July 28, 1966 (Federal Reserve System published manuscript).

República Oriental del Uruguay. Ministerio de Relaciones Exteriores. *Nomina de Misiones Diplomaticas y Oficinas Consulares del Uruguay*. (Publicacion Oficial No. 2.) Montevideo: Editorial "Libertad Republicana," 1970.

Schmitter, Philippe C. "New Strategies for the Comparative Analysis of Latin American Politics," *Latin American Research Review*, IV, No. 2, Summer 1969, 83—110.

Sormani, Giuseppe (ed.). *The World and Its Peoples: Venezuela, Colombia, Ecuador, Giana, Uruguay*. New York: Greystone Press, 1966.

Stateman's Year Book, 1969—1970. New York: St. Martin's Press, 1969.

Tomassini, Luciano. "Towards a Latin American Nationalism," *World Today*, XXV, No. 12, December 1969, 544—556.

"Tupamaros Restrained: Less Terrorism as Economy Stabilizes," *Times of the Americas*, February 11, 1970, 7.
Unión Panamericana. *America en Cifras 1967; Situación Física: Territorio y Clima*. Washington: 1967.
U.S. Agency for International Development. Office of Program and Policy Coordination. Statistics and Reports Division. *U.S. Overseas Loans and Grants and Assistance from International Organizations: Obligations and Loan Authorizations, July 1, 1945—June 30, 1968*. (Special Report Prepared for the House Foreign Affairs Committee.) Washington: May 29, 1969.
"The Uruguayan Scene: Still at It," *Review of the River Plate*, CXLII, No. 3675, May 22, 1968, 747—749.
Worldmark Encyclopedia of the Nations, III: Americas. (3d ed.) New York: Harper and Row, 1967.
Zimmerman, Irene. *A Guide to Current Latin American Periodicals —Humanitarian and Social Sciences*. Gainesville: Kallman, 1961.
Various issues of the following periodicals were also used in the preparation of this section: *Bank of London and South America Review* [London], May 1969—June 1970; *Carta de Montevideo*, February—August 1970; *Christian Science Monitor*, January 1967—August 1970; *Embassy of Uruguay News* [Washington], January 1967—January 1969; *O Estado de São Paulo*, April—May 1970; *Latin America Airmail* [London], March 1968—August 1970; *La Manaña* [Montevideo], January—August 1970; *Marcha* [Montevideo], March—July 1970; *New York Times*, May 1969—August 1970; *Times of the Americas* [Washington], April 1969—July 1970; and *Washington Post*, January 1968—August 1970.

Section III. Economic

RECOMMENDED SOURCES

Alexander, Robert. *Organized Labor in Latin America.* New York: Free Press, 1965.

Alisky, Marvin. *Uruguay: A Contemporary Survey.* New York: Praeger, 1969.

Brannon, Russell H. *The Agricultural Development of Uruguay.* New York: Praeger, 1968.

Cassinelli Muñoz, Horacio. *A Statement of the Laws of Uruguay in Matters Affecting Business.* (4th ed., rev.) (National Law Series No. 342—E—5636.) Washington: Pan American Union, 1963.

Economist Intelligence Unit. *Quarterly Economic Review: Uruguay, Paraguay.* London: 1970.

Inter-American Committee for Agricultural Development. *Inventory of Information Basic to the Planning of Agricultural Development of Latin America: Uruguay.* (No. 325—3—E—7145.) Washington: Pan American Union, 1964.

Inter-American Committee on the Alliance for Progress. *Domestic Efforts and the Needs for External Financing for the Development of Uruguay.* (CIAP/399.) Washington: Pan American Union, 1970.

Inter-American Development Bank. Social Progress Trust Fund. *Socio-Economic Progress in Latin America.* (Ninth Annual Report, 1969.) Washington: 1970.

Price, Waterhouse and Company. *Information Guide for Doing Business in Uruguay.* N.pl.: 1968.

______. *Information Guide for Doing Business in Uruguay.* N.pl.: 1969.

United Nations. Department of Economic and Social Affairs. Statistical Office of the United Nations. *The Growth of World Industry,* I. (1967 ed.) New York: 1969.

U.S. Agency for International Development. *U.S. Foreign Aid and the Alliance for Progress: Proposed Fiscal Year 1971 Program.* Washington: March 1970.

U.S. Agency for International Development. Bureau for Latin America. Office of Development Programs. *Summary Economic and Social Indicators: 18 Latin American Countries, 1960—1969.* Washington: June 1970 (mimeo.).

———. *Summary Economic and Social Indicators: 18 Latin American Countries, 1961—1968*. Washington: June 1969 (mimeo.).

U.S. Agency for International Development. Bureau for Program and Policy Coordination. Office of Statistics and Reports. *Latin America: Economic Growth Trends*. Washington: December 1969.

———. *U.S. Overseas Loans and Grants and Assistance from International Organizations*. Washington: April 1970.

U.S. Department of Agriculture. *1969 Annual Report on Public Law 480*. Washington: June 1970.

U.S. Department of Agriculture. Economic Research Service. Foreign Development and Trade Division. International Monetary and Trade Research Branch. *Foreign Gold and Exchange Reserves*. (FGER—8.) Washington: May 1970.

U.S. Department of Agriculture. Economic Research Service. Foreign Regional Analysis Division. *A Survey of Agriculture in Uruguay*. (ERS—Foreign Series No. 254.) Washington: GPO, 1970.

OTHER SOURCES USED

Cale, Edward G. *Latin American Free Trade Association: Progress, Problems, Prospects*. Washington: GPO, 1969.

Contracting Parties to the General Agreement on Tariffs and Trade. *Basic Instruments and Selected Documents*, Eleventh Supplement: Decisions, Reports, etc., of the Twentieth Session. Geneva: March 1963.

———. *International Trade, 1968*. Geneva: 1969.

Frick Davie, Carlos. *Cual Reforma Agraria: Reformas Progresistas y Regresivas*. Montevideo: Barreiro y Ramos, S. A., 1964.

Gunther, John. *Inside South America*. New York: Harper and Row, 1967.

Inter-American Development Bank. *Ten Years of Work in Latin America*. Washington: 1970.

———. *Tenth Annual Report, 1969*. Washington: 1970.

International Bank for Reconstruction and Development. International Development Association. *Annual Report, 1969*. Washington: 1970.

Kantor, Harry. *Patterns of Politics and Political Systems in Latin America*. Chicago: Rand McNally, 1969.

Organization of American States. General Secretariat. Department of Economic Affairs. *Latin America's Foreign Trade: Problems and Policies*. Washington: 1967.

Pan American Union. *Constitution of the Republic of Uruguay, 1967*. Washington: 1967.

———. *A Statement of the Laws of Uruguay in Matters Affecting Business*. Washington: 1963.

——. *Uruguay*. (American Republics Series No. 20.) Washington: 1962 (reprint, 1968).

Pendle, George. *Uruguay*. (3d ed.) London: Oxford University Press, 1963.

República Oriental del Uruguay. Ministerio de Ganadería y Agricultura. Dirección de Economía Agraria. Departamento de Estadística. Division Censos y Encuestas. *Censo General Agropecuario, 1966*. Montevideo: 1968.

República Oriental del Uruguay. Ministerio de Ganadería y Agricultura. Ofician de Programacion y Politica Agropecuario. *Credito Agropecuario en el Uruguay*. Montevideo: 1966.

——. *Estudio Economico y Social de la Agricultura en el Uruguay*, I and II. Montevideo: Impresora Rex, S. A., 1967.

U.S. Department of Labor. *Labor Conditions in Uruguay, 1964*. (Labor Digest No. 88.) Washington: 1964.

U.S. Department of State. *State Department Background Notes: Uruguay*. Washington: 1968.

World Bank Group. *El Grupo del Banco Mundial en las Americas*. Washington: February 1970.

World Peace Through Law Center. *Law and the Judicial System of Nations*. Washington: 1968.

Worldmark Encyclopedia of the Nations, III: Americas. (3d ed.) New York: Harper and Row, 1967.

Various issues of the following periodicals were also used in the preparation of this section: *Bank of London and South America Review*, London, May 1969—June 1970; *Carta de Montevideo*, February—August 1970; *Christian Science Monitor*, January 1967—August 1970; *Embassy of Uruguay News* [Washington], January 1967—January 1969; *O Estado de São Paulo*, April—May 1970; *Latin America Airmail* [London], March 1968—August 1970; *La Mañaña* [Montevideo], January August 1970; *New York Times*, May 1969—August 1970; *Times of the Americas* [Washington], April 1969—July 1970; and *Washington Post*, January 1968 August 1970.

Section IV. National Security

RECOMMENDED SOURCES

Alisky, Marvin. *Uruguay: A Contemporary Survey*. New York: Praeger, 1969.

Burnett, Ben G., and Johnson, Kenneth F. *Political Forces in Latin America: Dimensions of the Quest for Stability*. Belmont: Wadsworth, 1968.

Carballa, Juan B. *Codigo Penal de la República Oriental del Uruguay*. Montevideo: Centro Estudiantes de Derecho, 1968.

Clagett, Helen L. *Administration of Justice in Latin America*. New York: Oceana Publications, 1952.

Cossini, Miguel A. *Military Justice of the Republic of Uruguay*. Montevideo: Imprenta Militar, 1965 (mimeo.).

Folle, Juan Carlos Gomez. *Criminalid Femenina en el Uruguay, 1940—1950*. Montevideo: Direccion General de Institutos Penales, 1951.

Hierro, Atanasildo. *History of the Uruguayan Army*. Montevideo: 1968. [Translated by U.S. Department of Commerce. Office of Technical Services, Joint Publications Research Service (Washington). JPRS: 47,081, *Translations on Latin America*, No. 200, 1968.]

Taylor, Philip B., Jr. *Government and the Politics of Uruguay*. (Tulane Studies in Political Science, VII.) New Orleans: Tulane University Press, 1960.

Teeters, Negley K. *World Penal Systems*. Florida: Temple University Press, 1944.

United Nations. Department of Economic and Social Affairs. *Prison Labor*. New York: 1955.

U.S. Department of State. Bureau of Intelligence and Research. *World Strength of the Communist Party Organizations*. Washington: GPO, 1969.

Wood, David. *Armed Forces in Central and South America*. (Adelphia Paper No. 34.) London: Institute for Strategic Studies, April 1967.

OTHER SOURCES USED

Cramer, James. *The World's Police*. London: Cassell, 1964.

Economist Intelligence Unit. *Quarterly Economic Review: Uruguay, Paraguay*. London: 1969.

Ferguson, J. Halcro. *The River Plate Republics*. New York: Time, 1968.

Fitzgibbon, Russell H. *Uruguay: Portrait of a Democracy*. New Brunswick: Rutgers University Press, 1954.

Lipset, Seymour M., and Solari, Aldo. *Elites in Latin America*. New York: Oxford University Press, 1967.

Stateman's Year Book, 1967. New York: St. Martin's Press, 1967.

Unión Panamericana. Comite Juridico Interamericano. *El Ministerio Publico en los Paises Americanos*. Washington: 1967.

United Nations. *International Review of Criminal Policy*. New York: 1961.

———. *New Forms of Juvenile Delinquency*. London: 1960.

United Nations. Department of Social Affairs. *Probation and Related Measures*. New York: 1951.

U.S. Agency for International Development. *Summary Economic and Social Indicators: 18 Latin American Countries, 1961–1968*. Washington: June 1969 (mimeo.).

U.S. Arms Control and Disarmament Agency. Economics Bureau. *World Military Expenditures, 1969*. Washington: 1969.

World Peace Through Law Center. *Law and the Judicial System of Nations*. Washington: 1968.

Various issues of *La Manaña* [Montevideo], January–August 1970, were also used in the preparation of this section.

GLOSSARY

agua potable—Drinking water.

AIFLD—American Institute for Free Labor Development. Has headquarters in Washington, D.C.

bachillerato—Certificate awarded for completion of two-year college preparatory cycle of general secondary school.

Batllistas—Followers of José Batlle y Ordóñez or adherents of his political philosophy.

cantegrile—Shantytown on the outskirts of Montevideo and some interior towns.

caudillismo—A political concept involving the exercise of authority by a *caudillo* or political strong man.

caudillo—Political strong man.

CELAM—Consejo Episcopal Latino Americano (Latin American Bishops' Conference).

CNT—Convención Nacional de Trabajadores (National Workers Convention). Country's largest confederation of labor unions; leftist-oriented.

colegiado—"Collegiate executive" or, in Uruguay, a national council proposed by Batlle y Ordóñez as a substitute for the presidency with a view to preventing one-man dictatorships. The Constitution of 1919 provided for a *colegiado* designated as Consejo Nacional de Administración (National Council of Administration) but retained the office of president—with limited powers. The Constitution of 1934 abolished the *colegiado*. The Constitution of 1952 abolished the presidency and reestablished the *colegiado* as the Consejo Nacional de Govierno (National Council of Government). The Constitution of 1967 reestablished the presidency and abolished the *colegiado*.

Colorado Party—The more liberal and urban-oriented of the two major parties.

Contentious-Administrative Tribunal—Tribunal of five judges appointed by the Supreme Court of Justice. Hears pleas for the nullification of governmental administrative acts that may be contrary to law.

COPRIN—Comisión de Productividad, Precios e Ingresos (Commission on Productivity, Prices and Incomes).

criollos—Descendants of Europeans who settled in the New World during the colonial period.

cuchilla—A range of hills.

CUT—(1) Central Unica de Trabajadores (One Center of Workers), now defunct radical organization; (2) Confederación Uruguaya de Trabajo (Uruguayan Confederation of Labor), moderate organization formed in 1969.

Electoral Court (Corte Electoral)—Court of nine members that supervises national, departmental, and municipal elections. Five members are appointed by the General Assembly, and the other four are elected (two from each party) by the General Assembly from the two political parties receiving the most votes in a national election.

estancia—Large ranch or country estate. Plural is *estancias.*

Estatuto del Funcionario—Civil Service Regulations established according to Article 59 of the 1967 Constitution.

facultades—Departments within the University of the Republic. Singular is *facultad.*

FEUU—Federación de Estudiantes Universitarios del Uruguay (University Students' Federation of Uruguay).

Frente Izquierda de Libertad—FIdeL (Leftist Liberty Front). A coalition of leftist groups organized in 1958 under the leadership of the Uruguayan Communist Party.

gaucho—Cowboy.

General Assembly—Joint session of Uruguayan Senate (thirty-one members) and Chamber of Representatives (ninety-nine members).

IAVA—Instituto Académico Vázquez Acevedo (Vázquez Acevedo Academic Institute). Largest public secondary school providing two-year college-preparatory course.

ICEM—International Committee for European Migration.

intendente—Governor of a department elected by the people for a five-year term. Supervises (with departmental board) the functioning of a departmental government.

IPA—Instituto de Profesores Artigas (Artigas Institute for Professors). National school for the training of secondary school teachers.

IPPF—International Planned Parenthood Federation.

Junta Departamental—Board of thirty-one individuals elected by the people of each department that supervises the government of the department. Department of Montevideo has sixty-five members on its board.

juzgados letrados—Lawyer courts of a single judge each. They are appointed by the Supreme Court of Justice and have original jurisdiction in civil and commercial cases not specifically reserved for other courts.

LAFTA—The Latin American Free Trade Association was created through the Treaty of Montevideo, which went into effect June 1, 1961. Its purpose is to achieve a free trade area among the signatories that in 1970 included Mexico and all of the South American states except Guyana.

lemas—Major party labels under which various factions (*sub-lemas*) are grouped for electoral purposes.

liceos—General secondary schools.

machismo—The ideal of masculinity.

mestizo—Person of mixed European and American Indian ancestry.

National Council of Government—Nine-man popularly elected council that governed Uruguay from 1952 to 1967. Six members elected from political party with greatest number of votes and three from second party.

National (Blanco) Party—The more conservative and rural-oriented of the two major parties.

OAS—The Organization of American States, created in 1948, is a regional organization of general competence, comprising most of the Western Hemisphere nations.

PDC—Partido Democrático Cristiano (Christian Democratic Party).

peso—Monetary unit. Value per US$1: 1948—54, 1.50; 1955, 1.71; 1956, 1.90; 1957, 2.16; 1958—59, 3.46; 1960, 11.03; 1961—62, 10.98; 1963, 16.40; 1964, 18.70; 1965, 59.90; 1966, 76.20; 1967, 200.00; and 1968—70, 250.00.

profesor—Title of either university or secondary teacher in Uruguay.

rancherio—A rural slum settlement.

sub-lemas—Labels adopted by the various factions of the major parties in order to make proportional representation operative within the parties.

Tribunal of Accounts—Seven-member tribunal appointed by the General Assembly. Principal responsibility is monitoring expenditure of public funds.

Tupamaros—Designated the Movimiento de Liberación Nacional (MLN—National Liberation Movement). An organization characterized by revolutionary motives and unconventional guerrilla tactics that appeared in the early 1960's. The name is derived from that of the Inca rebel, Tupac Amaru.

universitario—University student.

UTU—Universidad del Trabajo del Uruguay (Uruguayan Labor University). A central organization providing administration for the public technical and vocational secondary schools.

WFTU—World Federation of Trade Unions. Moscow controlled.

zafra—Sugarcane harvest season.

INDEX

PUBLISHED AREA HANDBOOKS

550—65	Afghanistan
550—44	Algeria
550—59	Angola
550—73	Argentina
550—20	Brazil
550—61	Burma
550—83	Burundi
550—50	Cambodia
550—26	Colombia
550—60	Communist China
550—91	Congo (Brazzaville)
550—67	Congo (Kinshasa)
550—90	Costa Rica
550—22	Cyprus
550—54	Dominican Republic
550—52	Ecuador
550—29	Germany
550—78	Guatemala
550—82	Guyana
550—21	India
550—39	Indonesia
550—31	Iraq
550—68	Iran
550—25	Israel
550—30	Japan
550—34	Jordan
550—56	Kenya
550—41	Republic of Korea
550—58	Laos
550—24	Lebanon
550—38	Liberia
550—85	Libya
550—45	Malaysia
550—76	Mongolia
550—49	Morocco
550—64	Mozambique
550—88	Nicaragua
550—81	North Korea
550—57	North Vietnam
550—48	Pakistan
550—72	The Philippines
550—84	Rwanda
550—51	Saudi Arabia
550—70	Senegal
550—86	Somalia
550—55	South Vietnam
550—27	Sudan
550—47	Syria
550—62	Tanzania
550—53	Thailand
550—89	Tunisia
550—80	Turkey
550—74	Uganda
550—43	United Arab Republic
550—71	Venezuela
550—75	Zambia
550—92	Peripheral States of the Arabian Peninsula
550—93	South Africa, Republic of
550—94	Oceania
550—95	Soviet Union
550—96	Ceylon

☆ U.S. GOVERNMENT PRINTING OFFICE: 1971 O436-797 (PO 15)